Asset and Risk Management

Asset and Risk Management

Risk Oriented Finance

Louis Esch, Robert Kieffer and Thierry Lopez

C. Berbé, P. Damel, M. Debay, J.-F. Hannosset

John Wiley & Sons, Ltd

Published by   John Wiley & Sons Ltd, The Atrium, Southern Gate, Chichester,
                      West Sussex PO19 8SQ, England

                      Telephone (+44) 1243 779777

Email (for orders and customer service enquiries): cs-books@wiley.co.uk
Visit our Home Page on www.wileyeurope.com or www.wiley.com

Other Wiley Editorial Offices

John Wiley & Sons Inc., 111 River Street, Hoboken, NJ 07030, USA

Jossey-Bass, 989 Market Street, San Francisco, CA 94103-1741, USA

Wiley-VCH Verlag GmbH, Boschstr. 12, D-69469 Weinheim, Germany

John Wiley & Sons Australia Ltd, 33 Park Road, Milton, Queensland 4064, Australia

John Wiley & Sons (Asia) Pte Ltd, 2 Clementi Loop #02-01, Jin Xing Distripark, Singapore 129809

John Wiley & Sons Canada Ltd, 22 Worcester Road, Etobicoke, Ontario, Canada M9W 1L1

Wiley also publishes its books in a variety of electronic formats. Some content that appears
in print may not be available in electronic books.

Library of Congress Cataloging-in-Publication Data

Esch, Louis.
   Asset and risk management : risk oriented finance / Louis Esch, Robert Kieffer, and Thierry
Lopez.
      p. cm.
   Includes bibliographical references and index.
   ISBN 0-471-49144-6 (cloth : alk. paper)
   1. Investment analysis. 2. Asset-liability management. 3. Risk management. I. Kieffer,
Robert. II. Lopez, Thierry. III. Title.
   HG4529.E83 2005
   332.63′2042—dc22
                                                                        2004018708

British Library Cataloguing in Publication Data

A catalogue record for this book is available from the British Library

ISBN 0-471-49144-6

Typeset in 10/12pt Times by Laserwords Private Limited, Chennai, India
Printed and bound in Great Britain by Antony Rowe Ltd, Chippenham, Wiltshire
This book is printed on acid-free paper responsibly manufactured from sustainable forestry
in which at least two trees are planted for each one used for paper production.

Contents

Collaborators

Christian Berbé, Civil engineer from Université libre de Bruxelles and ABAF financial analyst. Previously a director at PricewaterhouseCoopers Consulting in Luxembourg, he is a financial risk management specialist currently working as a wealth manager with Bearbull (Degroof Group).

Pascal Damel, Doctor of management science from the University of Nancy, is conference master for management science at the IUT of Metz, an independent risk management consultant and ALM.

Michel Debay, Civil engineer and physicist of the University of Liège and master of finance and insurance at the High Business School in Liège (HEC), currently heads the Data Warehouse Unit at SA Kredietbank in Luxembourg.

Jean-François Hannosset, Actuary of the Catholic University of Louvain, currently manages the insurance department at Banque Degroof Luxembourg SA, and is director of courses at the Luxembourg Institute of Banking Training.

Foreword

by Philippe Jorion

Risk management has truly undergone a revolution in the last decade. It was just over 10 years ago, in July 1993, that the Group of 30 (G-30) officially promulgated best practices for the management of derivatives.[1] Even though the G-30 issued its report in response to the string of derivatives disasters of the early 1990s, these best practices apply to all financial instruments, not only derivatives.

This was the first time the term 'Value-at-Risk' (*VaR*) was publicly and widely mentioned. By now, *VaR* has become the standard benchmark for measuring financial risk. All major banks dutifully report their *VaR* in quarterly or annual financial reports.

Modern risk measurement methods are not new, however. They go back to the concept of portfolio risk developed by Harry Markowitz in 1952. Markowitz noted that investors should be interested in total portfolio risk and that 'diversification is both observed and sensible'. He provided tools for portfolio selection. The new aspect of the *VaR* revolution is the application of consistent methods to measure market risk across the whole institution or portfolio, across products and business lines. These methods are now being extended to credit risk, operational risk, and to the final frontier of enterprise-wide risk.

Still, risk measurement is too often limited to a passive approach, which is to measure or to control. Modern risk-measurement techniques are much more useful than that. They can be used to *manage* the portfolio. Consider a portfolio manager with a myriad of securities to select from. The manager should have strong opinions on most securities. Opinions, or expected returns on individual securities, aggregate linearly into the portfolio expected return. So, assessing the effect of adding or subtracting securities on the portfolio expected return is intuitive. Risk, however, does not aggregate in a linear fashion. It depends on the number of securities, on individual volatilities and on all correlations. Risk-measurement methods provide tools such as marginal *VaR*, component *VaR*, and incremental *VaR*, that help the portfolio manager to decide on the best trade-off between risk and return. Take a situation where a manager considers adding two securities to the portfolio. Both have the same expected return. The first, however, has negative marginal *VaR*; the second has positive marginal *VaR*. In other words, the addition of the first security will reduce the

---

[1] The G-30 is a private, nonprofit association, founded in 1978 and consisting of senior representatives of the private and public sectors and academia. Its main purpose is to affect the policy debate on international economic and financial issues. The G-30 regularly publishes papers. See www.group30.org.

portfolio risk; the second will increase the portfolio risk. Clearly, adding the first security is the better choice. It will increase the portfolio expected return and decrease its risk. Without these tools, it is hard to imagine how to manage the portfolio. As an aside, it is often easier to convince top management of investing in risk-measurement systems when it can be demonstrated they can add value through better portfolio management.

Similar choices appear at the level of the entire institution. How does a bank decide on its capital structure, that is, on the amount of equity it should hold to support its activities? Too much equity will reduce its return on equity. Too little equity will increase the likelihood of bankruptcy. The answer lies in risk-measurement methods: The amount of equity should provide a buffer adequate against all enterprise-wide risks at a high confidence level. Once risks are measured, they can be decomposed and weighted against their expected profits. Risks that do not generate high enough payoffs can be sold off or hedged. In the past, such trade-offs were evaluated in an ad-hoc fashion.

This book provides tools for going from risk measurement to portfolio or asset management. I applaud the authors for showing how to integrate *VaR*-based measures in the portfolio optimisation process, in the spirit of Markowitz's portfolio selection problem. Once risks are measured, they can be managed better.

Philippe Jorion
University of California at Irvine

Acknowledgements

We want to acknowledge the help received in the writing of this book. In particular, we would like to thank Michael May, managing director, Bank of Bermuda Luxembourg S.A. and Christel Glaude, Group Risk Management at KBL Group European Private Bankers.

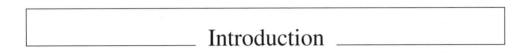

Introduction

The rapid expansion of international finance is a prerequisite for growth of world trade in both goods and services. The risks associated with international investment should make us think of the desirability of creating a wider and more stable basis for our international financial system.

It appears that the stability of the whole financial system is conditioned by the capacity of those actively involved in economics, and especially in finance, to manage all types of risk more effectively. It is not just a matter of ensuring that the risks are properly diversified, but a matter of mastering each of them separately.

The aim of this publication is to deal with the issue at its root. In fact, preservation of our standard of living depends on the durability of the banking and insurance systems, because we confide our savings in the system and because we transfer our risks to the institutions that mutualise those savings. If the managers that we have trusted to return our savings to us cannot handle them, then the mutual funds to which we have transferred our risks will not be able to act properly in our place.

AREAS COVERED

Our publication therefore aims to study three essential components of *modern finance*, namely *risk management, asset management* and *asset and liability management*, together with the *links that bind them together*. To do this, we have divided the book into five parts:

1. The context, the regulations and the market.
2. Asset management.
3. Risk management.
4. The complementary aspects of risk management and asset management.
5. The strategic aspect of risk management – that is, asset and liability management.

Part I is called *The Massive Changes in the World of Finance*.

- *Chapter 1* sets out the *regulatory context* (precautionary surveillance, the Basle Committee, harmonised accounting standards) in which financial institutions are developing today.

- *Chapter 2* shows the ways in which the *risk management* function has *developed* in financial institutions, in the context of a tense insurance market and a prolonged financial crisis together with a crisis of confidence. This function is becoming more and more important right across the financial sector, and its area of skill is increasing (in addition to the traditional credit and market risks, there is now a need to consider not only the threefold risk of operations, BCP and insurance, but the liquidity risk, the legal risk inherent in financial transactions, and others). The chapter explains how this area of work provides the decision-makers with a contribution that is largely strategic in nature.

Part II is dedicated to the theories that underlie asset management, and deals with the *evaluation of financial assets.*

- *Chapter 3* concentrates on *equities*. The basics (that is, return and risk, market efficiency etc.) are of course explained before the principle of diversification linked to portfolio management is touched on; the models produced by Markowitz, Sharpe and Elton, Gruber and Padberg (EGP) are all presented in detail. The theory of utility and optimal portfolio selection is also covered, as are market models. Next comes the financial asset equilibrium model, which analyses the capital asset pricing model (CAPM) and arbitrage pricing theory (APT), performance evaluation, and equity portfolio management strategies. Finally, the chapter examines share development (deterministic and stochastic models).
- *Chapter 4* deals with *bonds*. After describing their characteristics and developments, it touches on the question of their inherent financial risks. The issues of deterministic interest rate structure, passive and active bond portfolio management strategies, and stochastic bond development models (arbitrage models with one state variable, Vasicek model, Cox, Ingersoll and Ross model and stochastic duration), are all addressed in separate sections.
- *Chapter 5* is dedicated to *options*. After describing their characteristics and areas of use, we look at their value and the various models for evaluating them (the binomial model, Black and Scholes model and others). The last section in this chapter introduces the simple and more complex strategies for options.

Part III deals with the central theory of *risk management*, the general theory of *Value at Risk* or *VaR*.

- *Chapter 6* is a general presentation of *VaR theory* (starting from the concept of risk per equity, the *VaR* for a single equity is studied before being extrapolated to cover an entire portfolio according to whether or not the typology of the evaluation models is linear), and also introduces extensions for the use of that theory (components of *VaR* and incremental *VaR*).
- *Chapter 7* deals with the *techniques for estimating VaR*. It analyses the estimated variance-covariance matrix method, the Monte Carlo simulation and the historical simulation in succession, together with an extension (extreme values). The advantages and disadvantages of each of these methods are compared.
- *Chapter 8*, together with the attached CD-ROM, sets out the stages necessary for *setting up a VaR methodology* (putting together a database, calculations for treasury and bond portfolios, normality hypothesis study).

Part IV is the point at which *asset management* and *risk management* meet.

- *Chapter 9* introduces the *portfolio risk management* method, which relates to private management. It deals with the application of risk-management methods (value of one basis point, *VaR* etc.) to portfolios managed in the classic way.
- *Chapter 10* proposes an *optimisation of a global portfolio using VaR*. More specifically, we deal with methods of optimising asset portfolios that verify the hypotheses of normal law, which is, under certain circumstances, the case with equities. In particular, we adapt the Sharpe and EGP simple index methods to the *VaR*, in order to find the extent to which *VaR* improves the optimisation process.
- *Chapter 11* deals with *institutional management*. Here we will see the significance of applying the APT method to investment funds in terms of behavioural analysis.

Part V is the point at which *risk management* and *asset and liability management* (ALM) meet.

- *Chapter 12* introduces *techniques for measuring structural balance sheet risks*. It sets out the tools for analysing risks in asset and liability management together with simulations, the use of *VaR* in ALM, repricing schedules, and replicating portfolios.

WHO IS THIS BOOK FOR?

This book is aimed at two sections of the public.

The work is aimed at *professionals working in the market* (private or business fund managers or pension managers, market operators and business managers), *risk managers* and *asset and liability managers*, *auditors* and people working generally in the field of risk management.

This book also provides a very useful teaching tool suitable for use by both *undergraduates* and *postgraduates*, who have chosen to include a *financial* element in their studies. There are many numbered illustrations and a CD-ROM for practical application.

Part I
The Massive Changes in the World of Finance

Introduction

The financial world of today has three main aspects:

- An insurance market that is tense, mainly because of the events of 11 September 2001 and the claims that followed them.
- Pressure of regulations, which are compelling the banks to quantify and reduce the risks hitherto not considered particular to banks (that is, operational risks).
- A prolonged financial crisis together with a crisis of confidence, which is pressurising the financial institutions to manage their costs ever more carefully.

Against this background, the risk management function is becoming more and more important in the finance sector as a whole, increasing the scope of its skills and giving the decision-makers a contribution that is mostly strategic in nature. The most notable result of this is that the perception of cost is currently geared towards the creation of value, while as recently as five years ago, shareholders' perceptions were too heavily weighted in the direction of the 'cost of doing business'.

It is these subjects that we propose to develop in the first two chapters.

1

The Regulatory Context

1.1 PRECAUTIONARY SURVEILLANCE

One of the aims of precautionary surveillance is to increase the quality of risk management in financial institutions. Generally speaking:

- Institutions whose market activity is significant in terms of contribution to results or expenditure of equity fund cover need to set up a risk management function that is independent of the 'front office' and 'back office' functions.
- When the establishment in question is a consolidating business, it must be a decision-making centre. The risk management function will then be responsible for suggesting a group-wide policy for the monitoring of risks. The management committee then takes the risk management policy decisions for the group as a whole.
- To do this, the establishment must have adequate financial and infrastructural resources for managing the risk. The risk management function must have systems for assessing positions and measuring risks, as well as adequate limit systems and human resources.

The aim of precautionary surveillance is to:

- Promote a well-thought-out and prudent business policy.
- Protect the financial stability of the businesses overseen and of the financial sector as a whole.
- Ensure that the organisation and the internal control systems are of suitable quality.
- Strengthen the quality of risk management.

1.2 THE BASLE COMMITTEE

We do not propose to enter into methodological details on the adequacy[1] of equity capital in relation to credit, market and operational risks.

On the other hand, we intend to spend some time examining the underlying philosophy of the work of the Basle Committee[2] on banking controls, paying particular attention to the qualitative dynamic (see 1.2.2 below) on the matter of operational risks.

1.2.1 General information

The Basle Committee on Banking Supervision is a committee of banking supervisory authorities, which was established by the central bank governors of the Group of Ten countries in 1975. It consists of senior representatives of bank supervisory authorities and central banks from Belgium,

---

[1] Interested readers should read P. Jorion, *Financial Risk Manager Handbook (Second Edition)*, John Wiley & Sons, Inc. 2003, and in particular its section on regulation and compliance.

[2] Interested readers should consult http://www.bis.org/index.htm.

Canada, France, Germany, Italy, Japan, Luxembourg, the Netherlands, Sweden, Switzerland, the United Kingdom and the United States. It usually meets at the Bank for International Settlements in Basle, where its permanent Secretariat is located.[3]

1.2.1.1   The current situation

The aim of the capital adequacy ratio is to ensure that the establishment has sufficient equity capital in relation to credit and market risks. The ratio compares the eligible equity capital with overall equity capital requirements (on a consolidated basis where necessary) and must total or exceed 100 % (or 8 % if the denominator is multiplied by 12.5). Two methods, one standard and the other based on the internal models, allow the requirements in question to be calculated.

In addition, the aim of overseeing and supervising major risks is to ensure that the credit risk is suitably diversified within the banking portfolios (on a consolidated basis where necessary).

1.2.1.2   The point of the 'New Accord'[4]

The Basle Committee on Banking Supervision has decided to undertake a second round of consultation on more detailed capital adequacy framework proposals that, once finalised, will replace the 1988 Accord, as amended.

The new framework is intended to align capital adequacy assessment more closely with the key elements of banking risks and to provide incentives for banks to enhance their risk measurement and management capabilities.

The Committee's ongoing work has affirmed the importance of the three pillars of the new framework:

1. Minimum capital requirements.
2. Supervisory review process.
3. Market discipline.

A. First aspect: minimum capital requirements

The primary changes to the minimum capital requirements set out in the 1988 Accord are in the approach to credit risk and in the inclusion of explicit capital requirements for operational risk. A range of risk-sensitive options for addressing both types of risk is elaborated. For credit risk, this range begins with the standardised approach and extends to the "foundation" and "advanced" internal ratings-based (IRB) approaches. A similar structure is envisaged for operational risk. These evolutionary approaches will motivate banks to continuously improve their risk management and measurement capabilities so as to avail themselves of the more risk-sensitive methodologies and thus more accurate capital requirements.

B. Second aspect: supervisory review process

The Committee has decided to treat interest rate risk in the banking book under Pillar 2 (supervisory review process). Given the variety of underlying assumptions needed, the Committee

---

[3] The Bank for International Settlements, Basle Committee on Banking Supervision, *Vue d'ensemble du Nouvel accord de Bâle sur les fonds propres*, Basle, January 2001, p. 1.

[4] Interested readers should also consult: The Bank for International Settlements, Basle Committee on Banking Control, *The New Basle Capital Accord*, January 2001; and The Bank for International Settlements, Basle Committee on Banking Control, *The New Basle Capital Accord: An Explanatory Note*, January 2001.

believes that a better and more risk-sensitive treatment can be achieved through the supervisory review process rather than through minimum capital requirements. Under the second pillar of the New Accord, supervisors should ensure that each bank has sound internal processes in place to assess the adequacy of its capital based on a thorough evaluation of its risks. The new framework stresses the importance of bank's management developing an internal capital assessment process and setting targets for capital that are commensurate with the bank's particular risk profile and control environment.

C. Third aspect: Market discipline

The Committee regards the bolstering of market discipline through enhanced disclosure as a fundamental part of the New Accord.[5] The Committee believes the disclosure requirements and recommendations set out in the second consultative package will allow market partici-pants to assess key pieces of information on the scope of application of the revised Accord, capital, risk exposures, assessment and management processes, and capital adequacy of banks. The risk-sensitive approaches developed by the Committee rely extensively on banks' internal methodologies giving banks more discretion in calculating their capital requirements. Separate disclosure requirements are put forth as prerequisites for supervisory recognition of internal methodologies for credit risk, credit risk mitigation techniques and asset securitisation. In the future, disclosure prerequisites will also attach to advanced approaches to operational risk. In the view of the Committee, effective disclosure is essential to ensure that market participants can better understand banks' risk profiles and the adequacy of their capital positions.

1.2.2 Basle II and the philosophy of operational risk[6]

In February 2003, the Basle Committee published a new version of the document *Sound Practices for the Management and Supervision of Operational Risk*. It contains a set of principles that make up a structure for managing and supervising operational risks for banks and their regulators.

In fact, risks other than the credit and market risks can become more substantial as the deregulation and globalisation of financial services and the increased sophistication of financial technology increase the complexity of the banks' activities and therefore that of their risk profile.

By way of example, the following can be cited:

- The increased use of automated technology, which if not suitably controlled, can trans-form the risk of an error during manual data capture into a system breakdown risk.
- The effects of e-business.
- The effects of mergers and acquisitions on system integration.
- The emergence of banks that offer large-scale services and the technical nature of the high-performance back-up mechanisms to be put in place.

---

[5] See also Point 1.3, which deals with accounting standards.

[6] This section is essentially a summary of the following publication: The Bank for International Settlements, Basle Com-mittee on Banking Control, *Sound Practices for the Management and Supervision of Operational Risk*, Basle, February 2003. In addition, interested readers can also consult: Cruz M. G., *Modelling, Measuring and Hedging Operational Risk*, John Wiley & Sons, Ltd, 2003; Hoffman D. G., *Managing Operational Risk: 20 Firm-Wide Best Practice Strategies*, John Wiley & Sons, Inc., 2002; and Marshall C., *Measuring and Managing Operational Risks in Financial Institutions*, John Wiley & Sons, Inc., 2001.

- The use of collateral,[7] credit derivatives, netting and conversion into securities, with the aim of reducing certain risks but the likelihood of creating other kinds of risk (for example, the legal risk – on this matter, see Point 2.2.1.4 in the section on 'Positioning the legal risk').
- Increased recourse to outsourcing and participation in clearing systems.

1.2.2.1 A precise definition?

Operational risk, therefore, generally and according to the Basle Committee specifically, is defined as 'the risk of loss resulting from inadequate or failed internal processes, people and systems or from external events'. This is a very wide definition, which includes legal risk but excludes strategic and reputational risk.

The Committee emphasises that the precise approach chosen by a bank in the management of its operational risks depends on many different factors (size, level of sophistication, nature and complexity of operations, etc.). Nevertheless, it provides a more precise definition by adding that despite these differences, clear strategies supervised by the board of directors and management committee, a solid 'operational risk' and 'internal control' culture (including among other things clearly defined responsibilities and demarcation of tasks), internal reporting, and plans for continuity[8] following a highly damaging event, are all elements of paramount importance in an effective operational risk management structure for banks, regardless of their size and environment.

Although the definition of operational risk varies *de facto* between financial institutions, it is still a certainty that some types of event, as listed by the Committee, have the potential to create substantial losses:

- Internal fraud (for example, insider trading of an employee's own account).
- External fraud (such as forgery).
- Workplace safety.
- All matters linked to customer relations (for example, money laundering).
- Physical damage to buildings (terrorism, vandalism etc.).
- Telecommunication problems and system failures.
- Process management (input errors, unsatisfactory legal documentation etc.).

1.2.2.2 Sound practices

The sound practices proposed by the Committee are based on four major themes (and are subdivided into 10 principles):

- Development of an appropriate risk management environment.
- Identification, assessment, monitoring, control and mitigation in a risk management context.
- The role of supervisors.
- The role of disclosure.

---

[7] On this subject, see 2.1.1.4.
[8] On this subject, see 2.1.1.3.

Developing an appropriate risk management environment

Operational risk management is first and foremost an organisational issue. The greater the relative importance of ethical behaviour at all levels within an institution, the more the risk management is optimised.

The first principle is as follows. The board of directors should be aware of the major aspects of the bank's operational risks as a distinct risk category that should be managed, and it should approve and periodically review the bank's operational risk management framework. The framework should provide a firm-wide definition of operational risk and lay down the principles of how operational risk is to be identified, assessed, monitored, and controlled/mitigated.

In addition (second principle), the board of directors should ensure that the bank's operational risk management framework is subject to effective and comprehensive internal audit[9] by operationally independent, appropriately trained and competent staff. The internal audit function should not be directly responsible for operational risk management.

This independence may be compromised if the audit function is directly involved in the operational risk management process. In practice, the Committee recognises that the audit function at some banks (particularly smaller banks) may have initial responsibility for developing an operational risk management programme. Where this is the case, banks should see that responsibility for day-to-day operational risk management is transferred elsewhere in a timely manner.

In the third principle senior management should have responsibility for implementing the operational risk management framework approved by the board of directors. The framework should be consistently implemented throughout the whole banking organisation, and all levels of staff should understand their responsibilities with respect to operational risk management. Senior management should also have responsibility for developing policies, processes and procedures for managing operational risk in all of the bank's material products, activities, processes and systems.

Risk management: Identification, assessment, monitoring and mitigation/control

The fourth principle states that banks should identify and assess the operational risk inherent in all material products, activities, processes and systems. Banks should also ensure that before new products, activities, processes and systems are introduced or undertaken, the operational risk inherent in them is subject to adequate assessment procedures.

Amongst the possible tools used by banks for identifying and assessing operational risk are:

- *Self- or risk-assessment.* A bank assesses its operations and activities against a menu of potential operational risk vulnerabilities. This process is internally driven and often incorporates checklists and/or workshops to identify the strengths and weaknesses of the operational risk environment. Scorecards, for example, provide a means of translating qualitative assessments into quantitative metrics that give a relative ranking of different types of operational risk exposures. Some scores may relate to risks unique to a specific business line while others may rank risks that cut across business lines. Scores may address inherent risks, as well as the controls to mitigate them. In addition, scorecards may be used by banks to allocate economic capital to business lines in relation to performance in managing and controlling various aspects of operational risk.

---

[9] See 2.2.1.3.

- *Risk mapping.* In this process, various business units, organisational functions or process flows are mapped by risk type. This exercise can reveal areas of weakness and help prioritise subsequent management action.
- *Risk indicators.* Risk indicators are statistics and/or metrics, often financial, which can provide insight into a bank's risk position. These indicators tend to be reviewed on a periodic basis (such as monthly or quarterly) to alert banks to changes that may be indicative of risk concerns. Such indicators may include the number of failed trades, staff turnover rates and the frequency and/or severity of errors and omissions.
- *Measurement.* Some firms have begun to quantify their exposure to operational risk using a variety of approaches. For example, data on a bank's historical loss experience could provide meaningful information for assessing the bank's exposure to operational risk.

In its fifth principle, the Committee asserts that banks should implement a process to regularly monitor operational risk profiles and material exposures to losses. There should be regular reporting of pertinent information to senior management and the board of directors that supports the proactive management of operational risk.

In addition (sixth principle), banks should have policies, processes and procedures to control and/or mitigate material operational risks. Banks should periodically review their risk limitation and control strategies and should adjust their operational risk profile accordingly using appropriate strategies, in light of their overall risk appetite and profile.

The seventh principle states that banks should have in place contingency and business continuity plans to ensure their ability to operate on an ongoing basis and limit losses in the event of severe business disruption.

Role of supervisors

In the eighth principle banking supervisors should require that all banks, regardless of size, have an effective framework in place to identify, assess, monitor and control/mitigate material operational risks as part of an overall approach to risk management.

In the ninth principle supervisors should conduct, directly or indirectly, regular independent evaluation of a bank's policies, procedures and practices related to operational risks. Supervisors should ensure that there are appropriate mechanisms in place which allow them to remain apprised of developments at banks.

Examples of what an independent evaluation of operational risk by supervisors should review include the following:

- The effectiveness of the bank's risk management process and overall control environment with respect to operational risk;
- The bank's methods for monitoring and reporting its operational risk profile, including data on operational losses and other indicators of potential operational risk;
- The bank's procedures for the timely and effective resolution of operational risk events and vulnerabilities;
- The bank's process of internal controls, reviews and audit to ensure the integrity of the overall operational risk management process;
- The effectiveness of the bank's operational risk mitigation efforts, such as the use of insurance;
- The quality and comprehensiveness of the bank's disaster recovery and business continuity plans; and

- The bank's process for assessing overall capital adequacy for operational risk in relation to its risk profile and, if appropriate, its internal capital targets.

Role of disclosure

Banks should make sufficient public disclosure to allow market participants to assess their approach to operational risk management.

1.3   ACCOUNTING STANDARDS

The financial crisis that started in some Asian countries in 1998 and subsequently spread to other locations in the world revealed a need for reliable and transparent financial reporting, so that investors and regulators could take decisions with a full knowledge of the facts.

1.3.1   Standard-setting organisations[10]

Generally speaking, three main standard-setting organisations are recognised in the field of accounting:

- The IASB (International Accounting Standards Board), dealt with below in 1.3.2.
- The IFAC (International Federation of Accountants).
- The FASB (Financial Accounting Standards Board).

The International Federation of Accountants, or IFAC,[11] is an organisation based in New York that combines a number of professional accounting organisations from various countries. Although the IASB concentrates on accounting standards, the aim of the IFAC is to promote the accounting profession and harmonise professional standards on a worldwide scale.

In the United States, the standard-setting organisation is the Financial Accounting Standards Board or FASB.[12] Although it is part of the IASB, the FASB has its own standards. Part of the FASB's mandate is, however, to work together with the IASB in establishing worldwide standards, a process that is likely to take some time yet.

1.3.2   The IASB[13]

In 1998 the ministers of finance and governors of the central banks from the G7 nations decided that private enterprises in their countries should comply with standards, principles and good practice codes decided at international level. They then called on all the countries involved in the global capital markets to comply with these standards, principles and practices.

Many countries have now committed themselves, including most notably the European Union, where the Commission is making giant strides towards creating an obligation for all quoted companies, to publish their consolidated financial reports in compliance with IAS standards.

The IASB or International Standards Accounting Board is a private, independent standard-setting body based in London. In the public interest, the IASB has developed

---

[10] http://www.cga-canada.org/fr/magazine/nov-dec02/Cyberguide_f.htm.
[11] Interested readers should consult http://www.ifac.org.
[12] Interested readers should consult http://www.fasb.org.
[13] Interested readers should consult http://www.iasc.org.uk/cmt/0001.asp.

a set of standardised accounting rules that are of high quality and easily understandable (known as the IAS Standards). Financial statements must comply with these rules in order to ensure suitable transparency and information value for their readers.

Particular reference is made to Standard IAS 39 relating to financial instruments, which is an expression of the IASB's wish to enter the essence of balance-sheet items in terms of *fair value*. In particular, it demands that portfolios derived from cover mechanisms set up in the context of asset and liability management be entered into the accounts at market value (see Chapter 12), regardless of the accounting methods used in the entries that they cover.

In the field of financial risk management, it should be realised that in addition to the impact on asset and liability management, these standards, once adopted, will doubtless affect the volatility of the results published by the financial institutions as well as affecting equity capital fluctuations.

2
Changes in Financial Risk Management

2.1 DEFINITIONS

Within a financial institution, the purpose of the risk management function is twofold.

1. It studies all the quantifiable and non-quantifiable factors (see 2.1.1 below) that in relation to each individual person or legal entity pose a threat to the return generated by rational use of assets and therefore to the assets themselves.
2. It provides the following solutions aimed at combating these factors.
   — **Strategic.** The onus is on the institution to propose a general policy for monitoring and combating risks, ensure sensible consolidation of risks at group management level where necessary, organise the reports sent to the management committee, participate actively in the asset and liability management committee (see Chapter 12) and so on.
   — **Tactical.** This level of responsibility covers economic and operational assessments when a new activity is planned, checks to ensure that credit has been spread safely across various sectors, the simulation of risk coverage for exchange interest rate risk and their impact on the financial margin, and so on.
   — **Operational.** These are essentially first-level checks that include monitoring of internal limits, compliance with investment and stop loss criteria, traders' limits, etc.

2.1.1 Typology of risks

The risks linked to financial operations are classically divided into two major categories:

1. *Ex ante* non-quantifiable risks.
2. *Ex ante* quantifiable risks.

2.1.1.1 Standard typology

It is impossible to overemphasise the importance of proactive management in the avoidance of non-quantifiable risks within financial institutions, because:

1. Although these risks cannot be measured, they are, however, identifiable, manageable and avoidable.
2. The financial consequences that they may produce are measurable, but *a posteriori* only.

The many non-quantifiable risks include:

1. The *legal risk* (see 2.2.1.4), which is likely to lead to losses for a company that carries on financial deals with a third-party institution not authorised to carry out deals of that type.

2. The *media risk*, when an event undermines confidence in or the image of a given institution.
3. The *operational risk* (see 2.1.1.2 below), although recent events have tended to make this risk more quantifiable in nature.

The quantifiable risks include:

1. The market risk, which is defined as the impact that changes in market value variables may have on the position adopted by the institution. This risk is subdivided into:
   — interest rate risk;
   — FX risk;
   — price variation risk;
   — liquidity risk (see 2.1.1.4)
2. The credit risk that arises when an opposite party is unable or unwilling to fulfil his contractual obligations:
   — relative to the on-balance sheet (direct);
   — relative to the off-balance sheet (indirect);
   — relating to delivery (settlement risk).

2.1.1.2   Operational risk[1]

According to the Basle Committee, operational risk is defined as the risk of direct or indirect loss resulting from inadequate or failed internal processes, people and systems or from external events.

In the first approach, it is difficult to classify risks of this type as ones that could be quantified *a priori*, but there is a major change that makes the risk quantifiable *a priori*. In fact, the problems of corporate governance, cases of much-publicised internal checks that brought about the downfall of certain highly acclaimed institutions, the combination of regulatory pressure and market pressure have led the financial community to see what it has been agreed to call *operational risk management* in a completely different light.

Of course operational risk management is not a new practice, its ultimate aim being to manage the added volatility of the results as produced by the operational risk. The banks have always attached great importance to attempts at preventing fraud, maintaining integrity of internal controls, reducing errors and ensuring that tasks are appropriately segregated.

Until recently, however, the banks counted almost exclusively on internal control mechanisms within operational entities, together with the internal audit,[2] to manage their operational risks.

This type of management, however, is now outdated. We have moved on from operational risk management fragmented into business lines to transfunctional integrity; the attitude is no longer reactive but proactive. We are looking towards the future instead of back to the past, and have turned from 'cost avoidance' to 'creation of value'.

---

[1] See also Point 1.2.2.
[2] Interested readers should consult the Bank for International Settlements, Basle Committee for Banking Controls, *Internal Audit in Banks and the Supervisor's Relationship with Auditors*, Basle, August 2001.

The operational risk management of today also includes:

- Identifying and measuring operational risks.
- Analysing potential losses and their causes, as well as ways of reducing and preventing losses.
- Analysing risk transfer possibilities.
- Allocating capital specifically to operational risk.

It is specifically this aspect of measurement and quantification that has brought about the transition from *ex post* to *ex ante*. In fact, methodological advances in this field have been rapid and far-reaching, and consist essentially of two types of approach.

- The qualitative approach. This is a process by which management identifies the risks and controls in place in order to manage them, essentially by means of discussions and workshops. As a result, the measurement of frequency and impact is mostly subjective, but it also has the advantage of being prospective in nature, and thus allows risks that cannot be easily quantified to be understood.
- The quantitative approach. A specific example, although not the only one, is the *loss distribution approach*, which is based on a database of past incidents treated statistically using a Value at Risk method. The principal strength of this method is that it allows the concept of correlation between risk categories to be integrated, but its prospective outlook is limited because it accepts the hypothesis of stationarity as true.

Halfway between these two approaches is the *scorecards* method, based on risk indicators. In this approach, the institution determines an initial regulatory capital level for operational risk, at global level and/or in each trade line. Next, it modifies this total as time passes, on the basis of so-called scorecards that attempt to take account of the underlying risk profile and the risk control environment within the various trade lines. This method has several advantages:

- It allows a specific risk profile to be determined for each organisation.
- The effect on behaviour is very strong, as managers in each individual entity can act on the risk indicators.
- It allows the best practices to be identified and communicated within the organisation.

It is, however, difficult to calibrate the scorecards and allocate specific economic funds.

A refined quantification of operational risk thus allows:

- Its cost (expected losses) to be made clear.
- Significant exposures (unexpected losses) to be identified.
- A framework to be produced for profit-and-cost analysis (and excessive controls to be avoided).

In addition, systematic analysis of the sources and causes of operational losses leads to:

- Improvements in processes and quality.
- Optimal distribution of best practices.

A calculation of the losses attributable to operational risk therefore provides a framework that allows the controls to be linked to performance measurement and shareholder value.

That having been said, this approach to the mastery of operational risk must also allow insurance programmes to be rationalised (concept of risk transfer), in particular by integrating the business continuity plan or BCP into it.

2.1.1.3 The triptych: Operational risk – risk transfer – BCP

See Figure 2.1.

A. The origin, definition and objective of Business Continuity Planning

A BCP is an organised set of provisions aimed at ensuring the survival of an organisation that has suffered a catastrophic event.

The concept of BCP originated in the emergency computer recovery plans, which have now been extended to cover the human and material resources essential for ensuring continuity of a business's activities. Because of this extension, activities that lead to the constitution of a BCP relate principally to everyone involved in a business and require coordination by all the departments concerned.

In general, the BCP consists of a number of interdependent plans that cover three distinct fields.

- The preventive plan: the full range of technical and organisational provisions applied on a permanent basis with the aim of ensuring that unforeseen events do not render critical functions and systems inoperative.
- The emergency plan: the full range of provisions, prepared and organised in advance, required to be applied when an incident occurs in order to ensure continuity of critical systems and functions or to reduce the period of their non-availability.
- The recovery plan: the full range of provisions, prepared and organised in advance, aimed at reducing the period of application of the emergency plan and re-establishing full service functionality as soon as possible.

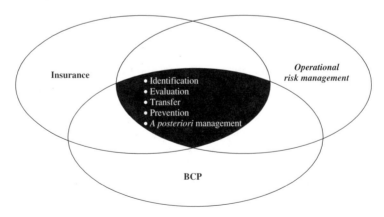

Figure 2.1 Triptych

B. The insurance context

After the events of 11 September 2001, the thought processes and methods relating to the compilation of a BCP were refined. Businesses were forced to realise that the issue of continuity needed to be overseen in its entirety (prevention, insurance, recovery plan and/or crisis management).

The tensions prevailing in the insurance market today have only increased this awareness; reduction in capacity is pushing business towards a policy of self-insurance and, in consequence, towards the setting up of new processes believed to favour a more rapid recovery after the occurrence of a major incident.

Several major actors in the market are currently reflecting on the role that they should play in this context, and some guidelines have already been laid down.

The insurance and reinsurance companies thus have an essential communication role to play. They have a wealth of information that is unrivalled and clearly cannot be rivalled, on 'prejudicial' events and their causes, development, pattern and management. Sharing of insured persons' experiences is a rich source of information for learning about processes, methods and errors so that clients may benefit from them. Another source is training.

The wealth of information available to them also allows insurers and reinsurers to provide well-informed advice based on a pragmatic approach to the problems encountered.

In this context, the integration of BCP into the risk management function, provided that insurance management is also integrated, will bring the benefits of shared information and allow better assessment of the practical opportunities for implementation

Similarly, the undisputed links between certain insurance policies and the BCP also argue for integration, together with operational risk management, which must play an active role in the various analyses relating to the continuity plan.

C. The connection between insurance and the BCP

In order to illustrate our theme, here we examine three types of policy.

- The 'all risks' policy, which guarantees the interests of the person taking out the insurance in all fixed and movable assets owned or used by that person. The policy may include an extension of the 'extra expenses' cover. Such expenses correspond to the charges that the institution has to bear in order to function 'normally' following an incident (for example: hire of premises or equipment, additional working hours etc.). In this case, the insurance compensates for the full range of measures taken in the event of a BCP.
- The 'Business Interruption' policy, which guarantees the institution against loss of income, interest and additional charges and business expenses arising from interruption of its activity in its premises following the occurrence of an insured event. The objective, in fine, is to compensate losses that affect results following the occurrence of an incident covered by another guarantee (direct damage to property owned by the institution, for example). In this case also, the links are clear: the agreements concluded will compensate for the inevitable operating losses between the occurrence of the event and the resumption of activities as made possible more quickly by the BCP.
- The 'crisis management' policy, which guarantees payment of consultants' costs incurred by the institution in an effort to deal with its crisis situation, that is, to draw up plans of action and procedures to manage the crisis and ensure the communication and legal resources needed to contain it and minimise its initial effects. If an event

that satisfies the BCP implementation criteria occurs, this insurance policy will provide additional assistance in the effort to reduce the consequences of the crisis. In addition, this type of agreement usually sets out a series of events likely to lead to a 'crisis situation' (death of a key figure, government inquiry or investigation, violent incidents in the work place etc.). Bringing such a policy into parallel can thus provide an interesting tool for optimising developments in the BCP.

D. *The connection between operational risk and the BCP*

The starting hypothesis generally accepted for compiling a BCP takes account of the consequences, not the causes, of a catastrophic event. The causes, however, cannot be fully ignored and also need to be analysed to make the continuity plan as efficient as possible.

As operational risk is defined as the risk of direct or indirect loss resulting from inadequate or failed internal processes, people and systems or from external events, there is a strong tendency for the measures provided for by the BCP to be designed following the occurrence of an operational risk.

E. *Specific expressions of the synergy*

The specific expression of the synergy described above can be:

- Use of the BCP in the context of negotiations between the institution and the insurers. The premium payable and cover afforded under certain insurance policies (all risks and Business Interruption) may be directly influenced by the content of the institution's BCP. Coordination of the said BCP within the risk management function thus favours orientation of the provisions in the direction 'desired' by the insurers and allows the strategies put in place to be optimised.
- Once set up, the plan must be refined as and when the operational risks are identified and evaluated, thus giving it added value.
- Insurance policies can play a major financial role in the application of the steps taken to minimise the effects of the crisis, and in the same order of ideas.
- The possibility of providing 'captive cover' to deal with the expenses incurred in the application of the steps provided for in the BCP may also be of interest from the financial viewpoint.

2.1.1.4 *Liquidity risk:[3] the case of a banking institution*

This type of risk arises when an institution is unable to cover itself in good time or at a price that it considers reasonable.

A distinction is drawn between ongoing liquidity management, which is the role of the banking treasury, and liquidity crisis management.

The Basle Committee asserts that these two aspects must be covered by the banking institutions' asset and liability management committees.

A crisis of liquidity can be reproduced in a simulation, using methods such as the maximum cash outflow, which allows the survival period to be determined.

---

[3] Interested readers should consult the Bank for International Settlements, Basle Committee for Banking Controls, *Sound Practices for Managing Liquidity in Banking Organisations*, Basle, February 2000.

A. *Maximum Cash Outflow and Survival Period*

The first stage consists of identifying the liquidity lines:

1. Is the institution a net borrower or net lender in the financial markets, and does it have a strategic liquidity portfolio?
2. Can the bond and treasury bill portfolios be liquidated through repos and/or resales?
3. Can the 'credit' portfolios of the synthetic asset swap type be liquidated by the same means? And, last but not least:
4. What would be the potential level of assistance that may be expected from the reference shareholder or from other companies in the same group?

An extreme liquidity crisis situation can then be simulated, on the premise that the institution cannot borrow on the markets and does not rely on assistance from its reference shareholder or other companies within the group.

A number of working hypotheses can be taken as examples. On the crisis day (D) let us suppose that:

- The institution has had no access to borrowing on the interbank market for five working days.
- Both private and institutional clients have immediately withdrawn all their cash deposits within the legal framework:
  — All current accounts are repaid on $D + 1$.
  — All deposits with 24 and 48 hours' notice are repaid on $D + 1$ and $D + 2$ respectively.
  — All savings accounts are repaid on $D + 1$.
- The institution has to meet all its contractual obligations in terms of cash outflows:
  — The institution repays all the borrowings contracted out by it and maturing between D and $D + 5$.
  — The institution meets all the loans contracted out by it with start dates between D and $D + 5$.
- The only course of action that the institution can take to obtain further liquidity is to sell its assets.
  — It is assumed, for example, that the treasury bill portfolio can be liquidated one-quarter through repos on $D + 1$ and three-quarters by sales on $D + 2$.
  — It is assumed, for example, that the debenture and floating-rate note portfolios can be liquidated via repo or resale 85 % on $D + 1$, if the currency (GB£) allows, and by sale on $D + 2$.
  — It is assumed, for example, that the synthetic asset swap portfolio can be liquidated 30 % on $D + 3$, 30 % on $D + 4$ and the balance on $D + 5$ taking account of the ratings.

The cash in and cash out movements are then simulated for each of the days being reviewed. As a result, the cash balance for each day will be positive or negative. The survival period is that for which the institution shows a positive cash balance. See Figure 2.2.

In the following example it will be noted that in view of the hypothetical catastrophic situation adopted, the institution is nevertheless capable of facing a serious liquidity crisis for three consecutive dealing days without resorting to external borrowing.

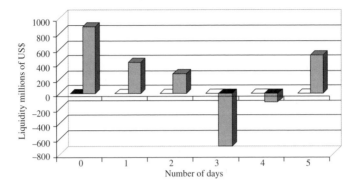

Figure 2.2   Survival period

It should, however, be noted that recourse to repos in particular will be much more effective if the financial institution optimises its collateral management. We now intend to address this point.

B. Collateral management[4]

Collateral management is one of the three techniques most commonly used in financial markets in order to manage credit risks, and most notably counterparty risk. The main reason for the success of collateral management is that the transaction-related costs are limited (because the collateral agreement contracts are heavily standardised). The three fields in which collateral management is encountered are:

1. The repos market.
2. The OTC derivatives market (especially if the institution has no rating).
3. Payment and settlement systems.

The assets used as collateral are:

- Cash (which will be avoided as it inflates the balance sheet, to say nothing of the operational risks associated with transfers and the risk of depositor bankruptcy).
- Government bonds (although the stocks are becoming weaker).
- The effects of major indices (because these are liquid, as their capitalisation classifies them as such indices).
- Bonds issued by the private sector (although particular attention will be paid to rating here).

Generally speaking, the counterparty receiving the collateral is clearly less exposed in terms of counterparty risk. There is, however, a credit risk on the collateral itself: the issuer risk (inherent in the bill) and the liquidity risk (associated with the bill). The risks linked to the collateral must be 'monitored', as both the product price variation

---

[4] Interested readers should consult the Bank for International Settlements, BIS Quarterly Review, *Collateral in Wholesale Financial Markets*, Basle, September 2001, pp. 57–64. Also: Bank for International Settlements, Committee on the Global Financial System, *Collateral in Wholesale Financial Markets: Recent Trends, Risk Management and Market Dynamics*, Basle, March 2001.

that necessitates the collateral and the collateral price variation have an effect on the coverage of the potential loss on the counterparty and the collateral that the counterparty will have provided.

Collateral management is further complicated by the difficulty in estimating the correlation between collateral price fluctuations and the 'collateralised' derivative. A negative correlation will significantly increase the credit risk, as when the value of the collateral falls, the credit risk increases.

The question of adjustment is of first importance. Too much sophistication could lead to the risk of hesitation by the trader over whether to enter into 'collateralised' deals. Conversely, too little sophistication risks a shift from counterparty risk to issuer and liquidity risk, and what is the good of that?

Collateral management improves the efficiency of the financial markets; it makes access to the market easier. If it is used, more participants will make the competition keener; prices will be reduced and liquidity will increase. Cases of adverse effects have, however, been noted, especially in times of stress.

The future of collateral management is rosy: the keener the competition in the finance markets, the tighter the prices and the greater the need for those involved to run additional risks.

2.1.2   Risk management methodology

While quantifiable risks, especially market risks, can of course be measured, a good understanding of the risk in question will depend on the accuracy, frequency and interpretation of such measurement.

2.1.2.1   Value of one basis point (VBP)

The VBP quantifies the sensitivity of a portfolio to a parallel and unilateral upward or downward movement of the interest rate curve for a resolution of one one-hundredth per cent (or a basis point). See Figure 2.3.

This simple method quantifies the sensitivity of an asset or portfolio of assets to interest rates, in units of national currency; but it must be noted that the probability of a parallel fluctuation in the curve is low, and that the method does not take account of any curvature or indeed any alteration in the gradient of the curve.

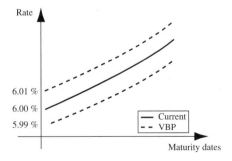

Figure 2.3   VBP

Finally, it should be noted that the measurement is immediate and the probability of occurrence is not grasped.

2.1.2.2 Scenarios and stress testing

Scenarios and stress testing allow the rates to be altered at more than one point in the curve, upwards for one or more maturity dates and downwards for one or more maturity dates at the same time. See Figure 2.4.

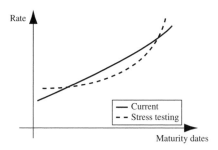

Figure 2.4   Stress testing

This method is used for simulating and constructing catastrophe scenarios (a forecast of what, it is assumed, will never happen). More refined than the VBP, this method is more difficult to implement but the time and probability aspects are not involved.

2.1.2.3 Value at risk (VaR)

Regardless of the forecasting technique adopted, the *VaR* is a number that represents the maximum estimated loss for a portfolio that may be multi-currency and multi-product (expressed in units of national currency) due to market risks for a specific time horizon (such as the next 24 hours), with a given probability of occurrence (for example, five chances in 100 that the actual loss will exceed the *VaR*). See Figure 2.5.

In the case of the *VaR*, as Figure 2.5 shows, we determine the movement of the curve that with a certain chance of occurrence (for example, 95%) for a given time horizon (for example, the next 24 hours) will produce the least favourable fluctuation in value for the portfolio in question, this fluctuation being of course estimated. In other words, the

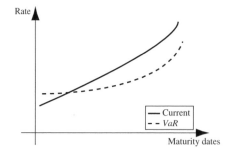

Figure 2.5   *VaR*

Table 2.1   VBP, stress testing and *VaR*

	VBP	Stress testing	*VaR*
Indication	'Uniform' sensitivity	'Multi-way' sensitivity	Maximum estimated loss
Time	Immediate	Immediate	Time horizon
Probability	No	No	Yes
Advantages	Simple	More realistic curve movement	Standard and complete
Disadvantages	Not greatly refined	Probability of scenario occurring?	Methodological choice and hypotheses

actual loss observed must not exceed the *VaR* in more than 5 % of cases (in our example); otherwise, the *VaR* will be a poor estimation of the maximum loss.

This method, which we explore in detail in Chapter 6, is complementary in comparison with VBP and stress testing. In other words, none of these methods should be judged sufficient in itself, but the full range of methods should produce a sufficiently strong and reliable risk matrix.

As can be seen from the comparison in Table 2.1, the *VaR* represents *a priori* the most comprehensive method for measuring market risk. However, methodological choices must be made and well-thought-out hypotheses must be applied in order to produce a realistic *VaR* value easily. If this is done, *VaR* can then be considered as the standard market for assessing risks inherent in market operations.

2.2   CHANGES IN FINANCIAL RISK MANAGEMENT

2.2.1   Towards an integrated risk management

As Figure 2.6 shows, the risk management function is multidisciplinary, the common denominator being the risk vector. From this, an 'octopus' pattern is evident; there is only one step, but...

2.2.1.1   Scope of competence

The risk management function must operate within a clearly defined scope of competence, which will often be affected by the *core business* of the institution in question.

Although it is generally agreed that the job of monitoring the market risk falls to risk management, for example, what happens to the risk of reputation, the legal risk (see 2.2.1.4), and the strategic risk? And let us not forget the operational risk: although the Basle Committee (see Chapter 1) explicitly excludes it from the field of skills of internal audit and includes it in the field of skills of risk management, it must be noted that a significant number of institutions have not yet taken that step.

Naturally, this leads to another problem. The controlling aspect of a risk management function is difficult to define, as one is very often limited to certain back-office control checks and there is also a tendency to confuse the type of tasks assigned to internal audit with those proper to risk management.

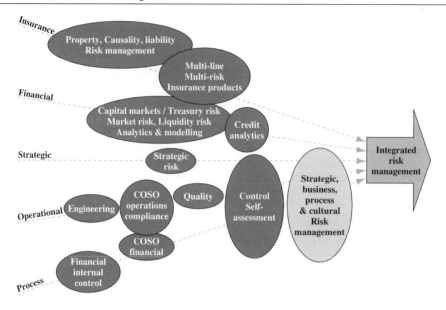

Figure 2.6   Integrated Risk Management
Source: Deloitte & Touche

2.2.1.2   Back office vs. risk management

With regard to the back office vs. risk management debate, it is well worth remembering that depending on the views of the regulator, the back office generally deals with the administration of operations and as such must, like every other function in the institution, carry out a number of control checks.

There are two types of back office control check:

- The daily control checks carried out by staff, for example each employee's monitoring of their suspense account.
- The ongoing continuous checks, such as monitoring of the accuracy and comprehensiveness of data communicated by persons responsible for business and operational functions in order to oversee the operations administratively.

However, when mentioning checks to be made by risk management, one refers to exception process checks in accordance with the bank's risk management policy, for example:

- Monitoring any limit breaches (limits, stop losses etc.).
- Monitoring (reconciliation of) any differences between positions (or results) taken (calculated) within various entities (front, back, accounting etc.).

2.2.1.3   Internal audit vs. risk management

The role of audit in a financial group is based on four main aspects:

- Producing a coherent plan for the audit activities within the group.

- Ensuring that the whole of the auditable activities, including the group's subsidiaries and holding company within the responsibilities of the parent company, are covered through the conduct or review of audits.
- Applying a uniform audit method across all group entities.
- On the basis of a homogeneous style of reporting, providing the directors of the parent company and of the subsidiaries maximum visibility on the quality of their internal control systems.

Although risk management by its very nature is also involved with the efficiency of the internal control system, it must be remembered that this function is a tool designed to help the management of the institution in its decision making. Risk management is therefore part of the auditable domain of the institution.

We saw the various responsibilities of risk management in Section 2.1.

2.2.1.4 Position of legal risk

In practice, every banking transaction is covered by a contract (spoken or written) that contains a certain degree of legal risk. This risk is more pronounced in transactions involving complex securities such as derivative products or security lending.

From the regulator's point of view, legal risk is the risk of contracts not being legally enforceable. Legal risk must be limited and managed through policies developed by the institution, and a procedure must be put in place for guaranteeing that the parties' agreements will be honoured.

Before entering into transactions related to derivatives, the bank must ensure that its counterparties have the legal authority to enter into these deals themselves. In addition, the bank must verify that the conditions of any contract governing its activities in relation to the counterpart are legally sound.

The legal risk linked to stock-market deals can in essence be subdivided into four types of subrisk.

1. *Product risk,* which arises from the nature of the deal without taking into account the counterparty involved; for example, failure to evaluate the legal risk when new products are introduced or existing products are changed.
2. *Counterparty risk.* Here the main risk is that the counterparty does not have the legal capacity to embark on the deal in question. For example, the counterparty may not have the capacity to trade in derivative products or the regulatory authority for specific transactions, or indeed may not even have the authority to conclude a repo contract.
3. *Transaction risk.* This is certainly the most significant part of the legal risk and covers actions undertaken in the conclusion of operations (namely, transaction and documentation). When the deal is negotiated and entered into, problems may arise in connection with regulatory or general legal requirements. For example: closing a spoken agreement without listing the risks involved beforehand, compiling legal documentation or contracts without involving the legal department, negotiating derivative product deals without involving the legal department or without the legal department reviewing the signed ISDA Schedules, signing Master Agreements with foreign counterparties without obtaining an outside legal opinion as to the validity of default, and finally documentary errors such as inappropriate signatures, failure to sign the document or

failure to set up procedures aimed at ensuring that all contractual documentation sent to counterparties is returned to the institution duly signed.

4. *Process risk.* In the event of litigation in connection with a deal or any other consequence thereof, it will be necessary to undertake certain action to ensure that the financial consequences are minimised (protection of proof, coordination of litigation etc.). Unfortunately, this aspect is all too often missing: records and proof of transaction are often insufficient (failure to record telephone conversations, destruction of emails etc.).

These four categories of risk are correlated. Fundamentally, the legal risk can arise at any stage in the deal (pre-contractual operations, negotiation, conclusion and post-contractual procedures).

In this context of risk, the position of the legal risk connected with the financial deals within the risk management function presents certain advantages:

- Assessment of the way in which the legal risk will be managed and reduced.
- The function has a central position that gives an overall view of all the bank's activities.
- Increased efficiency in the implementation of legal risk management procedures in financial transactions, and involvement in all analytical aspects of the legal risk on the capital market.

2.2.1.5 Integration

It is worrying to note the abundance of energy being channelled into the so-called problem of the 'fully integrated computerised risk-management system'. One and the same system for market risks, credit risks and operational risks? Not possible!

The interesting problem with which we are confronted here is that of integrating systems for monitoring different types of risk. We have to ask ourselves questions on the real added value of getting everything communicated without including the unmentionable – the poorly secured accessories such as spreadsheets and other non-secured relational databases.

Before getting involved with systems and expensive balance sheets relating to the importance of developing 'black boxes' we think it wiser to ask a few questions on the cultural integration of risk management within a business.

The regulator has clearly understood that the real risk management debate in the next 10 years will be on a qualitative, not a quantitative, level. Before moving onto the quantitative models proposed by Basle II, should we not first of all pay attention to a series of qualitative criteria by organising ourselves around them? Surely the figures produced by advanced operational risk methods are of a behavioural nature in that they show us the 'score to beat'. To sum up, is it better to be well organised with professional human resources who are aware of the risk culture, or to pride ourselves on being the owners of the Rolls Royce of the Value at Risk calculation vehicles?

When one remembers that Moody's[5] is attaching ever-increasing importance to the evaluation of operational risk as a criterion for awarding its ratings, and the impact of these ratings on finance costs, is it not worth the trouble of achieving *compliance* from

---

[5] Moody's, *Moody's Analytical framework for Operational Risk Management of Banks*, Moody's, January 2003.

the qualitative viewpoint (notwithstanding the savings made on capital through bringing the equity fund into line)?

A risk management function should ideally:

- Report directly to executive management.
- Be independent of the front and back office functions.
- Be located at a sufficiently senior hierarchical level to guarantee real independence, having the authority and credibility it needs to fulfil its function, both internally (especially vis-à-vis the front and back offices) and externally (vis-à-vis the regulator, external audit and the financial community in general).
- Be a member of the asset and liability management committee.
- Where necessary, oversee all the decentralised risk-management entities in the subsidiaries.
- Have as its main task the proposal of an institution-wide policy for monitoring risks and ensuring that the decisions taken by the competent bodies are properly applied, relying on the methodologies, tools and systems that it is responsible for managing.
- Have a clearly defined scope of competence, which must not be limited to market and credit risks but extend to operational risks (including insurance and BCP), the concentration risk and the risks linked to asset management activity in particular.
- Play a threefold role in the field of risks: advice, prevention and control.

But at what price?

2.2.2 The 'cost' of risk management

A number of businesses believed that they could make substantial savings by spending a bare minimum on the risk management function. It is this serious lack of foresight, however, that has led to collapse and bankruptcy in many respectable institutions. The commonest faults are:

1. One person wearing two 'hats' for the front and back office, a situation that is, to say the least, conducive to fraud.
2. Non-existence of a risk management function.
3. Inability of management or persons delegated by management to understand the activities of the market and the products used therein.
4. Lack of regular and detailed reporting.
5. Lack of awareness of employees at all levels, of quantifiable and/or non-quantifiable risks likely to be generated, albeit unwittingly, by those employees.
6. Incompatibility of volumes and products processed both with the business and with back-office and accounting procedures.

At present, market and regulatory pressure is such that it is unthinkable for a respectable financial institution not to have a risk management function. Instead of complaining about its cost, however, it is better to make it into a direct and indirect profit centre for the institution, and concentrate on its added value.

We have seen that a well-thought-out risk management limits:

- Excessive control (large-scale savings, prevention of doubling-up).

- Indirect costs (every risk avoided is a potential loss avoided and therefore money gained).
- Direct costs (the capital needed to be exposed to the threefold surface of market, credit and operational risk is reduced).

The promotion of a real risk culture increases the stability and quality of profits, and therefore improves the competitive quality of the institution and ensures that it will last.

2.3   A NEW RISK-RETURN WORLD

2.3.1   Towards a minimisation of risk for an anticipated return

Assessing the risk from the investor's point of view produces a paradox:

- On one hand, taking the risk is the only way of making the money. In other terms, the investor is looking for the risk premium that corresponds to his degree of aversion to risk.
- On the other hand, however, although accepting the 'risk premium' represents profit first and foremost, it also unfortunately represents potential loss.

We believe that we are now moving from an era in which investors continually looked to maximise return for a given level of risk (or without thinking about risk at all), into a new era in which the investor, for an anticipated level of return, will not rest until the attendant risk has been minimised.

We believe that this attitude will prevail for two different reasons:

1. Institutions that offer financial services, especially banks, know the levels of return that their shareholders demand. For these levels of return, their attitude will be that they must find the route that allows them to achieve their objective by taking the smallest possible risk.
2. The individual persons and legal entities that make up the clientele of these institutions, faced with an economic future that is less certain, will look for a level of return that at least allows them to preserve their buying and investing power. This level is therefore known, and they will naturally choose the financial solution that presents the lowest level of risk for that level.

2.3.2   Theoretical formalisation

As will be explained in detail in Section 3.1.1[6] in the section on equities, the return R is a random factor for which the probability distribution is described partly by two parameters: a location index, the expected value of which is termed $E(R)$, and a dispersion index, the variance which is noted var(R). The first quantity corresponds to the expected return.

---

[6] Readers are referred to this section and to Appendix 2 for the elements of probability theory needed to understand the considerations that follow.

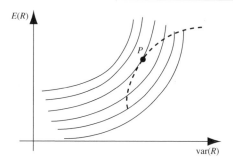

Figure 2.7   Selecting a portfolio

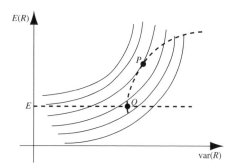

Figure 2.8   Selecting a portfolio

The square root of the second, $\sigma(R) = \sqrt{\text{var}(R)}$, is the standard deviation, which is a measurement of risk.

A portfolio, like any isolated security, will therefore be represented by a *mean-variance couple*. This couple depends on the expected return level and variance on return for the various assets in the portfolio, but also on the correlations between those assets. A portfolio will be 'ideal' for an investor (that is, *efficient*), if, for a given expected return, it has a minimal variance or if, for a fixed variance, it has a maximum expected return. All the portfolios thus defined make up what is termed the *efficient frontier*, which can be represented graphically in the Figure 2.7.

In addition, in the same plane the indifference curves represent the portfolios with an equivalent mean-variance combination in the investor's eyes (that is, they have for him the same level of utility[7]). The selection is therefore made theoretically by choosing the portfolio P from the efficiency frontier located on the indifference curve located furthest away (that is, with the highest level of utility), as shown in Figure 2.7.

In a situation in which an investor no longer acts on the basis of a classic utility structure, but instead wishes for a given return E and then tries to minimise the variance, the indifference curves will be cut off at the ordinate E and the portfolio selected will be Q, which clearly presents a lower expected return than that of P but also carries a lower risk that P. See Figure 2.8.

---

[7] Readers are referred to Section 3.2.7.

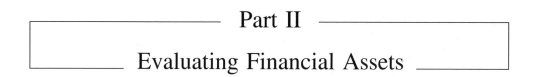

Part II

Evaluating Financial Assets

Introduction

Two fundamental elements

Evaluation of financial assets should take account of two fundamental aspects – chance and time.

The random aspect

It is obvious that the changes in value of a financial asset cannot be predicted in a deterministic manner purely by looking at what happened in the past. It is quite clear that for equities, whose rates fluctuate according to the law of supply and demand, these rates are themselves dictated by the perception that market participants have of the value of the business in question. The same applies to products that are sometimes defined as 'risk-free', such as bonds; here, for example, there is the risk of bankruptcy, the risk of possible change and the risk posed by changes in interest rates.

For this reason, financial assets can only be evaluated in a random context and the models that we will be putting together cannot work without the tool of probability (see Appendix 2 for the essential rules).

The temporal aspect

Some financial asset valuation models are termed *monoperiodic*, such as Markowitz's portfolio theory. These models examine the 'photograph' of a situation at a given moment and use historical observations to analyse that situation.

On the other hand, there may be a wish to take account of development over time, with the possible decision for any moment according to the information available at that moment. The random variables mentioned in the previous paragraph then turn into stochastic processes and the associated theories become much more complex.

For this reason, the following chapters (3, 4 and 5) will feature both *valuation models* (from the *static* viewpoint) and *development models* (from the *dynamic* viewpoint). In addition, for the valuation of options only, the development models for the underlying asset are essential because of the intrinsic link between this product and the time variable.

The dynamic models can be further divided into *discrete models* (where development is observed at a number of points spaced out over time) and *continuous models* (where the time variable takes its values within a continuous range such as an interval). The mathematical tools used for this second model are considerably more complex.

Two basic principles

The evaluation (or development) models, like all models, are based on a certain number of hypotheses. Some of these are purely technical and have the aim of guaranteeing the meaning of the mathematical expressions that represent them; they vary considerably according to the model used (static or dynamic, discrete or continuous) and may take the form of integrability conditions, restrictions on probability laws, stochastic processes, and so on.

Other hypotheses are dictated by economic reality and the behaviour of investors,[1] and we will be covering the two economic principles generally accepted in financial models here.

---

[1] We will be touching on this last aspect in Section 3.2.6

The perfect market

Often, a hypothesis that is so simplistic as to be unrealistic – that of the perfect market – will be put forward. Despite its reductive nature, it defines a context in which financial assets can be modelled and many studies have been conducted with the aim of weakening the various elements in this hypothesis.

The perfect market[2] is a market governed by the law of supply and demand, on which:

- Information is available in equal measure to all investors.
- There are no transactional or issue costs associated with the financial assets.
- There is no tax deduction on the income produced by the financial assets (where increases in value or dividends are involved, for example).
- Short sales are authorised without restriction.

Absence of arbitrage opportunity

An arbitrage opportunity is a portfolio defined in a context in which:

- No financial movement occurs within the portfolio during the period in question.
- The risk-free interest rate does not alter during the period in question and is valid for any maturity date (a flat, constant rate curve).

This is a portfolio with an initial value (value at the point of constitution) that is negative but presents a certain positive value at a subsequent time. More specifically, if the value of the portfolio at the moment t is termed V_t, we are looking at a portfolio for which: $V_0 < 0$ and $V_T \geq 0$ or $V_0 \leq 0$ and $V_T > 0$.

Generally speaking, the *absence of arbitrage opportunity* hypothesis is constructed in the financial modelling process. In fact, if it is possible to construct such portfolios, there will be considerable interest in putting together a large number of them. However, the numerous market operations (purchases/sales) that this process would require would lead, through the effect of supply and demand, to alterations to the prices of the various portfolio components until the profits obtained through the position of arbitrage would all be lost.

Under this hypothesis, it can therefore be said that for a portfolio of value V put together at moment 0, if $V_T = 0$, no financial movement occurs in that portfolio between 0 and T and the interest rate does not vary during that period and is valid for any maturity date (flat, constant rate curve), then $V_t = 0$ for any $t \in [0; T]$.

This hypothesis of absence of arbitrage can be expressed as follows: in the context mentioned above, a portfolio which has been put together so as not to contain any random element will always present a return equal to the risk-free rate of interest.

The concept of 'valuation model'

A valuation model for a financial asset is a relation that expresses quite generally the price p (or the return) for the asset according to a number of explanatory variables[3]

---

[2] See for example Miller and Modigliani, Dividend policy, growth and the valuation of shares, *Journal of Business*, 1961.
[3] In these circumstances it is basically the risk of the security that is covered by the study; these explanatory variables are known as *risk factors*.

$X_1, X_2, \ldots, X_n$ that represent the element(s) of the market likely to affect the price: $p = f(X_1, X_2, \ldots, X_n) + \varepsilon$.

The residual ε corresponds to the difference between reality (the effective price p) and the valuation model (the function f).

Where the price valuation model is a *linear model* (as for equities), the risk factors combine together to give, through the Central Limit Theorem, a distribution for the variable p that is normal (at least in the first approximation), and is therefore defined by the two mean-variance parameters only.

On the other hand, for some types of assets such as options, the valuation model ceases to be linear. The previous reasoning is no longer valid and neither are its conclusions.

We should state that alongside the risk factors that we will be mentioning, the explanatory elements of the market risk can also include:

- The imperfect nature of valuation models.
- The imperfect knowledge of the rules and limitations particular to the institution.
- The impossibility of anticipating changes to legal regulations.

We should also point out that alongside this market risk, the investor will be confronted with other types of risk that correspond to the occurrence of exceptional events such as wars, oil crises etc. This group of risks cannot of course be evaluated using techniques designed for the risk market. The technique presented here will not therefore be including these 'event-based' risks. However, this does not mean that the careful risk manager should not include 'catastrophe scenarios', in order to take account of the exceptional risks, alongside the methods designed to deal with the market risks.

In this section we will be covering a number of general principles relative to valuation models, and mentioning one or another specific model[4] that will be analysed in further detail in this second part.

Linear models

We will look first at the simple case in which the function f of the valuation model is linear, or more specifically, the case in which the price variation $\Delta p = p_t - p_0$ is a first-degree function of the variations $\Delta X_1, \ldots, \Delta X_n$ of the various explanatory variables and of that ($\Delta \varepsilon$) of the residue:

$$\Delta p = a_0 + a_1 \Delta X_1 + \ldots + a_n \Delta X_n + \Delta \varepsilon.$$

An example of the linear valuation model is the Sharpe simple index model used for equities (see Section 3.2.4). This model suggests that the variation[5] in price of an equity is a first-degree function of the variation in a general index of the market (of course, the coefficients of this first-degree function vary from one security to another: $\Delta p = \alpha + \beta \Delta I + \Delta \varepsilon$.

In practice, the coefficients α and β are evaluated using a regression technique.[6]

---

[4] Brearley R. A. and Myers S. C., *Principles of Corporate Finance*, McGraw-Hill, 1991.
Broquet C., Cobbaut R., Gillet R. and Vandenberg A., *Gestion de Portefeuille*, De Boeck, 1997.
Copeland T. E. and Weston J. F., *Financial Theory and Corporate Policy*, Addison-Wesley, 1988.
Devolder P., *Finance Stochastique*, Éditions de l'ULB, 1993.
Roger P., *L'Évalation Des Actifs Financiers*, De Boeck, 1996.
[5] This is a relative variation in price, namely a return. The same applies to the index.
[6] Appendix 3 contains the statistical base elements needed to understand this concept.

Nonlinear models independent of time

A more complex case is that in which the function f of the relation $p = f(X_1, X_2, \ldots, X_n) + \varepsilon$ is not linear.

When time is not taken into consideration, Δp is evaluated using a Taylor development, as follows:

$$\Delta p = \sum_{k=1}^{n} f'_{X_k}(X_1, \ldots, X_n)\Delta X_k + \frac{1}{2!} \sum_{k=1}^{n} \sum_{l=1}^{n} f''_{X_k X_l}(X_1, \ldots, X_n)\Delta X_k \Delta X_l + \ldots + \Delta \varepsilon$$

For as long as the ΔX_k variations in the explanatory variables are low, the terms of the second order and above can be disregarded and it is possible to write:

$$\Delta p \approx \sum_{k=1}^{n} f'_{X_k}(X_1, \ldots, X_n)\Delta X_k + \Delta \varepsilon$$

This brings us back to a linear model, which will then be processed as in the previous paragraph.

For example, for bonds, when the price of the security is expressed according to the interest rate, we are looking at a nonlinear model. If one is content to approximate using only the *duration* parameter (see Section 4.2.2), a linear approximation will be used. If, however one wishes to introduce the concept of *convexity* (see Section 4.2.3), the Taylor development used shall take account of the second-degree term.

Nonlinear models dependent on time

For some types of asset, duration is of fundamental importance and time is one of the arguments of the function f.

This is the case, for example, with conditional assets; here, the life span of the contract is an essential element. In this case, there is a need to construct specific models that take account of this additional ingredient. We no longer have a *stationary random model*, such as Sharpe's example, but a model that combines the random and temporal elements; this is known as a *stochastic process*.

An example of this type of model is the *Black–Scholes model* for equity options (see Section 5.3.2), where the price p is a function of various variables (price of underlying asset, realisation price, maturity, volatility of underlying asset, risk-free interest rate). In this model, the price of the underlying asset is itself modelled by a stochastic process (standard Brownian motion).

3

Equities

3.1 THE BASICS

An *equity* is a financial asset that corresponds to part of the ownership of a company, its value being indicative of the health of the company in question. It may be the subject of a sale and purchase, either by private agreement or on an organised market. The law of supply and demand on this market determines the price of the equity. The equity can also give rise to the periodic payment of dividends.

3.1.1 Return and risk

3.1.1.1 Return on an equity

Let us consider an equity over a period of time $[t-1;t]$ the duration of which may be one day, one week, one month or one year. The value of this equity at the end of the period, and the dividend paid during the said period, are random variables[1] referred to respectively as C_t and D_t.

The return on the equity during the period in question is defined as:

$$R_t = \frac{C_t - C_{t-1} + D_t}{C_{t-1}}$$

We are therefore looking at a value without dimension, which can easily be broken down into the total of two terms:

$$R_t = \frac{C_t - C_{t-1}}{C_{t-1}} + \frac{D_t}{C_{t-1}}$$

- The first of these is the *increase in value*, which is fictitious in that the holder of the equity does not profit from it unless the equity is sold at the moment t.
- The second is the *rate of return*, which is real as it represents an income.

If one wishes to take account of the rate of inflation when defining the return parameter, the nominal return $R_t^{(n)}$ (excluding inflation), the real return $R_t^{(r)}$ (with inflation) and the rate of inflation τ are all introduced. They are linked by the relation $1 + R_t^{(n)} = (1 + R_t^{(r)}) \cdot (1 + \tau)$.

The real return can then be easily calculated:

$$R_t^{(r)} = \frac{1 + R_t^{(n)}}{1 + \tau} - 1$$

---

[1] Appendix 2 contains the basic elements of probability theory needed to understand these concepts.

Example

An equity is quoted at 1000 at the end of May and 1050 at the end of June; it paid a dividend of 80 on 12 June. Its (monthly) return for this period is therefore:

$$R_{june} = \frac{1050 - 1000 + 80}{1000} = 0.13 = 13\,\%$$

This consists of an increase in value of 5 % and a rate of return of 8 %.

We are looking here at the nominal return. If the annual rate of inflation for that year is 5 %, the real return will be:

$$R_{june}^{(r)} = \frac{1.13}{(1.05)^{1/12}} - 1 = 0.1254 = 12.54\,\%$$

For certain operations carried out during the return calculation period, such as division or merging of equities, free issue or increase in capital, the principle of definition of return is retained, but care is taken to include comparable values only in the formula. Therefore, when an equity is split into X new equities, the return will be determined by:

$$R_t = \frac{X \cdot C_t - C_{t-1} + D_t}{C_{t-1}} \quad \text{or} \quad \frac{X \cdot C_t - C_{t-1} + X \cdot D_t}{C_{t-1}}$$

This will depend on whether the dividends are paid before or after the date of the split.

If a return is estimated on the basis of several returns relating to the same duration but for different periods (for example, 'average' monthly return estimated on the basis of 12 monthly returns for the year in question), then mathematical common sense dictates that the following logic should be applied:

$$1 + R_{1\,year} = (1 + R_1) \cdot (1 + R_2) \cdot \ldots \cdot (1 + R_{12})$$

Therefore:

$$R_{1\,month} = \sqrt[12]{(1 + R_1) \cdot \ldots \cdot (1 + R_{12})} - 1$$

The expression $(1 + R_{1\,month})$ is the *geometric mean* of the corresponding expressions for the different months. We therefore arrive at, and generally use in practice, the *arithmetic mean*.

$$R_{1\,month} = \frac{R_1 + \ldots + R_{12}}{12}$$

This last relation is not in fact correct, as is shown by the example of a security quoted at 1000, 1100 and 1000 at moments 0, 1 and 2, respectively. The average return on this security is obviously zero. The returns on the two subperiods total 10 % and −9.09 %, respectively, which gives the following values for the average return: 0 % for the geometric mean and 0.45 % for the arithmetical mean.

Generally speaking, the arithmetic mean always overestimates the return, all the more so if fluctuations in partial returns are significant. We are, however, more inclined to use the arithmetic mean because of its simplicity[2] and because this type of mean is generally used for statistical estimations,[3] and it would be difficult to work with variances and covariances (see below) estimated in any other way.

Note

We also use another calculation formula when no dividend is paid – that of the *logarithmic return*.

$$R_t^* = \ln\left(\frac{C_t}{C_{t-1}}\right).$$

This formula differs only slightly from the formula shown above, as it can be developed using the Taylor formula as follows, if the second-degree and higher terms, which are almost always negligible, are not taken into consideration:

$$R_t^* = \ln\left(1 + \frac{C_t - C_{t-1}}{C_{t-1}}\right)$$

$$= \ln(1 + R_t)$$

$$\approx R_t$$

The advantage of R_t^* compared to R_t is that:

- Only R_t^* can take values as small as one wishes: if $C_{t-1} > 0$, we have:

$$\lim_{C_t \to 0+} \ln\left(\frac{C_t}{C_{t-1}}\right) = -\infty$$

which is compatible with statistical assumption about return, though $\dfrac{C_t - C_{t-1}}{C_{t-1}} \geq -1$

- R_t^* allows the variation to be calculated simply over several consecutive periods:

$$\ln\left(\frac{C_t}{C_{t-2}}\right) = \ln\left(\frac{C_t}{C_{t-1}} \cdot \frac{C_{t-1}}{C_{t-2}}\right) = \ln\left(\frac{C_t}{C_{t-1}}\right) + \ln\left(\frac{C_{t-1}}{C_{t-2}}\right)$$

which is not possible with R_t. We will, however, be using R_t in our subsequent reasoning.

Example

Let us calculate in Table 3.1 the quantities R_t and R_t^* for a few values of C_t.
   The differences observed are small, and in addition, we have:

$$\ln\left(\frac{11\,100}{12\,750}\right) = 0.0039 + 0.0271 - 0.0794 - 0.0907 = -0.1391$$

---

[2] An argument that no longer makes sense with the advent of the computer age.
[3] See, for example, the portfolio return shown below.

Table 3.1   Classic and logarithmic returns

C_t	R_t	R_t^*
12 750		
12 800	0.0039	0.0039
13 150	0.0273	0.0271
12 150	−0.0760	−0.0794
11 100	−0.0864	−0.0907

3.1.1.2   Return on a portfolio

Let us consider a portfolio consisting of a number N of equities, and note n_j, C_{jt} and R_{jt}, respectively the number of equities (j), the price for those equities at the end of period t and the dividend paid on the equity during that period.

The total value V_t of the portfolio at the moment t, and the total value D_t of the dividends paid during period t, are therefore given by:

$$V_t = \sum_{j=1}^{N} n_j C_{jt}$$

$$D_t = \sum_{j=1}^{N} n_j D_{jt}$$

The *return of the portfolio* will therefore be given by:

$$R_{P,t} = \frac{V_t - V_{t-1} + D_t}{V_{t-1}}$$

$$= \frac{\sum_{j=1}^{N} n_j C_{jt} - \sum_{j=1}^{N} n_j C_{j,t-1} + \sum_{j=1}^{N} n_j D_{jt}}{\sum_{k=1}^{N} n_k C_{k,t-1}}$$

$$= \frac{\sum_{j=1}^{N} n_j (C_{jt} - C_{j,t-1} + D_{jt})}{\sum_{k=1}^{N} n_k C_{k,t-1}}$$

$$= \sum_{j=1}^{N} \frac{n_j C_{j,t-1}}{\sum_{k=1}^{N} n_k C_{k,t-1}} R_{jt}$$

The quantity $X_j = \dfrac{n_j C_{j,t-1}}{\sum_{k=1}^{N} n_k C_{k,t-1}}$ represents the portion of the equity (j) invested in the portfolio at the moment $t-1$, expressed in terms of equity market capitalisation, and one thus arrives at $\Sigma X_j = 1$. With this notation, the return on the portfolio takes the following form:

$$R_{P,t} = \sum_{j=1}^{N} X_j R_{jt}$$

Note

The relations set out above assume, of course, that the number of each of the securities in the portfolio remains unchanged during the period in question. Even if this condition is satisfied, the proportions X_j will be dependent on t through the prices. If therefore one wishes to consider a portfolio that has identical proportions at two given different moments, the n_j must be altered in consequence. This is very difficult to imagine in practice, because of transaction costs and other factors, and we will not take account of it in future. Instead, our reasoning shall be followed as though the proportions remained unchanged.

As for an isolated security, when one considers a return estimated on the basis of several returns relating to the same duration but from different periods, one uses the arithmetical mean instead of the geometric mean, which gives:

$$R_{P,1 \text{ month}} = \frac{1}{12} \sum_{t=1}^{12} R_{P,t}$$

$$= \frac{1}{12} \sum_{t=1}^{12} \sum_{j=1}^{N} X_j R_{jt}$$

$$= \sum_{j=1}^{N} X_j \left(\frac{1}{12} \sum_{t=1}^{12} R_{jt} \right)$$

Therefore, according to what was stated above:[4]

$$R_{P,1 \text{ month}} = \sum_{j=1}^{N} X_j R_{j,1 \text{ month}}.$$

3.1.1.3 Market return

From a theoretical point of view, the market can be considered as a portfolio consisting of all the securities in circulation. The market return is therefore defined as: $R_{M,t} = \sum_{j=1}^{N} X_j R_{jt}$ where X_j represents the ratio of global equity market capitalisation of the security (j) and that of all securities.

These figures are often difficult to process, and in practice, the concept is usually replaced by the concept of a *stock exchange index* that represents the market in question:
$$R_{I,t} = \frac{I_t - I_{t-1}}{I_{t-1}}.$$

---

[4] Note that this relationship could not have existed if the arithmetical mean was not used.

A statistical index is a parameter that allows a magnitude X between the basic period t and the calculation period s to be described as: $I_t(s) = \dfrac{X(s)}{X(t)}$.

When X is composite, as for the value of a stock exchange market, several methods of evaluation can be envisaged. It is enough to say that:

- Some relate to prices and others to returns.
- Some use arithmetic means for prices, others use equity market capitalisation.
- Some take account of dividends paid, others do not.
- Others relate to all quoted securities, others are sectorial in nature.

The best known stock exchanges indexes are the Dow Jones (USA), the S&P 500 (USA), the Nikkei (Japan) and the Eurostoxx 50 (Europe).

3.1.1.4 *Expected return and ergodic estimator*

As we indicated above, the return of an equity is a random variable, the distribution of which is usually not fully known. The essential element of this probability law is of course its expectation:[5] the *expected return* $E_j = E(R_j)$.

This is an *ex ante* mean, which as such is inaccessible. For this reason, it is estimated on the basis of available historical observations, calculated for the last T periods. Such an *ex post* estimator, which relates to historical data, is termed *ergodic*. The estimator for the expected return on the security (j) is therefore:

$$\overline{R}_j = \frac{1}{T} \sum_{t=1}^{T} R_{jt}$$

In the same way, for a portfolio, the expected return equals:

$E_P = E(R_P) = \sum_{j=1}^{N} X_j E_j = X'E$, introducing the X and E vectors for the proportions and expected returns on N securities:

$$X = \begin{pmatrix} X_1 \\ X_2 \\ \vdots \\ X_N \end{pmatrix} \qquad E = \begin{pmatrix} E_1 \\ E_2 \\ \vdots \\ E_N \end{pmatrix}$$

The associated ergodic estimator is thus given by:

$$\overline{R}_P = \frac{1}{T} \sum_{t=1}^{T} R_{Pt} = \sum_{j=1}^{N} X_j \overline{R}_j.$$

In the following theoretical developments, we will use the probability terms (expectation) although it is acknowledged that for practical calculations, the statistical terms (ergodic estimator) should be used.

---

[5] From here on, we will use the index t not for the random return variable relative to period t, but for referencing a historical observation (the realised value of the random variable).

3.1.1.5   Risk of one equity

The performance of an equity cannot be measured on the basis of its expected return only. Account should also be taken of the magnitude of fluctuations of this return around its mean value, as this magnitude is a measurement of the *risk* associated with the security in question. The magnitude of variations in a variable around its average is measured using dispersion indices. Those that are adopted here are the variance σ_j^2 and the standard deviation σ_j of the return:

$$\sigma_j^2 = \text{var}(R_j) = E[(R_j - E_j)^2] = E(R_j^2) - E_j^2$$

In practice, this is evaluated using its ergodic estimator:

$$s_j^2 = \frac{1}{T} \sum_{t=1}^{T} (R_{jt} - \overline{R}_j)^2 = \frac{1}{T} \sum_{t=1}^{T} R_{jt}^2 - \overline{R}_j^2$$

Note

Two typical values are currently known for the return on an equity: its (expected) return and its risk. With regard to the distribution of this random variable, if it is possible to accept a *normal distribution*, then no other parameter will be needed as the law of probability is characterised by its average and its standard deviation.

The reason for the omnipresence of this distribution is the *central limit theorem* (CLT), which requires the variable in question to be the sum of a very large number of 'small' independent effects.

This is probably the reason why (number of transactions) it is being noted empirically that returns relating to long periods (a month or a year) are often normally distributed, while this is not necessarily the case for daily returns, for example. In these cases, we generally observe distributions with fatter tails[6] than those under the normal law. We will examine this phenomenon further in Part III, as value at risk is particularly interested in these distribution tails.

However, we will consider in this part that the distribution of the return is characterised by the 'expected return-risk' couple, which is sufficient for the Markowitz portfolio theory.[7] In other cases (dynamic models), it will be supposed in addition that this is normal.

Other dispersion indices could be used for measuring risk, as mean deviation $E(|R_j - E_j|)$ or semi-variance, which is defined as the variance but takes account only of those return values that are less than the expected return. It is nevertheless the variance (and its equivalent, the standard deviation) that is almost always used, because of its probability-related and statistical properties, as will be seen in the definition of portfolio risk.

3.1.1.6   Covariance and correlation

The risk of a portfolio depends of course on the risk of the securities of which it is composed, but also on the links present between the various securities, through the effect

---

[6] This is referred to as *leptokurtic* distribution.
[7] Markowitz H., Portfolio selection, *Journal of Finance*, Vol. 7, No. 1, 1952, pp. 419–33.

of diversification. The linear dependence between the return of the security (i) and its security (j) is measured by the covariance:

$$\sigma_{ij} = \operatorname{cov}(R_i, R_j) = E\lfloor(R_i - E_i)(R_j - E_j)\rfloor = E(R_i R_j) - E_i E_j$$

This is evaluated by the ergodic estimator

$$s_{ij} = \frac{1}{T}\sum_{t=1}^{T}(R_{it} - \overline{R}_i)(R_{jt} - \overline{R}_j) = \frac{1}{T}\sum_{t=1}^{T}(R_{it}R_{jt}) - \overline{R}_i\overline{R}_j$$

The interpretation of the covariance sign is well known, but its order of magnitude is difficult to express. To avoid this problem, we use the correlation coefficient

$$\rho_{ij} = \operatorname{corr}(R_i, R_j) = \frac{\sigma_{ij}}{\sigma_i \cdot \sigma_j}$$

For this coefficient, the ergodic estimator is of course given by

$$r_{ij} = \frac{s_{ij}}{s_i \cdot s_j}$$

Remember that this last parameter is a pure number located between -1 and 1, of which the sign indicates the way of dependency between the two variables and the values close to ± 1 correspond to near-perfect linear relations between the variables.

3.1.1.7 Portfolio risk

If one remembers that $R_{P,t} = \sum_{j=1}^{N} X_j R_{jt}$, and given that the formula for the variance of a linear combination of random variables, the variance of the return on the portfolio takes the following form:

$$\sigma_P^2 = \operatorname{var}(R_P) = \sum_{i=1}^{N}\sum_{j=1}^{N} X_i X_j \sigma_{ij} = X^t V X$$

Here: $\sigma_{ii} = \sigma_i^2$ and one has determined

$$X = \begin{pmatrix} X_1 \\ X_2 \\ \vdots \\ X_N \end{pmatrix} \qquad V = \begin{pmatrix} \sigma_1^2 & \sigma_{12} & \cdots & \sigma_{1N} \\ \sigma_{21} & \sigma_2^2 & \cdots & \sigma_{2N} \\ \vdots & \vdots & \ddots & \vdots \\ \sigma_{N1} & \sigma_{N2} & \cdots & \sigma_N^2 \end{pmatrix}$$

If one wishes to show the correlation coefficients, the above formula becómes:

$$\sigma_P^2 = \sum_{i=1}^{N}\sum_{j=1}^{N} X_i X_j \sigma_i \sigma_j \rho_{ij}$$

Example

The risk of a portfolio consisting of two equities in respective proportions, 30% and 70%, and such that $\sigma_1^2 = 0.03$, $\sigma_2^2 = 0.02$, $\sigma_{12} = 0.01$, is calculated regardless by:

$$\sigma_P^2 = 0.3^2 \cdot 0.03 + 0.7^2 \cdot 0.02 + 2 \cdot 0.3 \cdot 0.7 \cdot 0.01 = 0.0167, \text{ or by:}$$

$$\sigma_P^2 = \begin{pmatrix} 0.3 & 0.7 \end{pmatrix} \begin{pmatrix} 0.03 & 0.01 \\ 0.01 & 0.02 \end{pmatrix} \begin{pmatrix} 0.3 \\ 0.7 \end{pmatrix} = 0.0167.$$

It is interesting to compare the portfolio risk with the individual security risk.

The 'expected return-risk' approach to the portfolio therefore requires a knowledge of the expected returns and individual variances as well as all the covariances two by two. Remember that the multi-normal distribution is characterised by these elements, but that Markowitz's portfolio theory does not require this law of probability.

3.1.1.8 Security risk within a portfolio

The portfolio risk can also be written as:

$$\sigma_P^2 = \sum_{i=1}^{N} \sum_{j=1}^{N} X_i X_j \sigma_{ij} = \sum_{i=1}^{N} X_i \left(\sum_{j=1}^{N} X_j \sigma_{ij} \right)$$

The *total risk* for the security (i) within the portfolio therefore depends on σ_i^2 but also on the covariances with other securities in the portfolio. It can be developed as follows:

$$\sum_{j=1}^{N} X_j \sigma_{ij} = \sum_{j=1}^{N} X_j \, \text{cov}(R_i, R_j)$$

$$= \text{cov}\left(R_i, \sum_{j=1}^{N} X_j R_j \right)$$

$$= \text{cov}(R_i, R_P)$$

$$= \sigma_{iP}$$

The relative importance of the total risk for the security (i) in the portfolio risk is therefore measured by:

$$\frac{\sigma_{iP}}{\sigma_P^2} = \frac{\displaystyle\sum_{j=1}^{N} X_j \sigma_{ij}}{\sigma_P^2}.$$

These *relative risks* are such as:

$$\sum_{i=1}^{N} X_i \frac{\sigma_{iP}}{\sigma_P^2} = 1.$$

Example

Using the data in the previous example, the total risks for the two securities within the portfolio are given as:

$$\begin{cases} \sigma_{1P} = 0.3 \cdot 0.03 + 0.7 \cdot 0.01 = 0.016 \\ \sigma_{2P} = 0.3 \cdot 0.01 + 0.7 \cdot 0.02 = 0.017 \end{cases}$$

The corresponding relative risks therefore total 0.958 and 1.018 respectively. Note that what we actually have is: $0.3 \cdot 0.958 + 0.7 \cdot 1.018 = 1$.

The concept of the relative risk applied to the market as a whole or to a particular portfolio leads us to the concept of *systematic risk*:

$$\beta_i = \frac{\sigma_{iM}}{\sigma_M^2}$$

It therefore represents the relative importance of the total security risk (i) in the market risk, that is, the volatility of R_i in relation to R_M, as the quotient in question is the slope of the regression line in which the return on the security (i) is explained by the return of the market (see Figure 3.1):

$$R_i = \alpha_i + \beta_i R_M$$

It can be accepted, in conclusion, that the risk of a particular security should never be envisaged in isolation from the rest of the portfolio in which it is included.

3.1.2 Market efficiency

Here follows a brief summary of the concept of market efficiency,[8] which is a necessary hypothesis (or one that must be at least verified approximately) for the validity of the various models of financial analysis and is closely linked to the concept of the 'perfect market'.

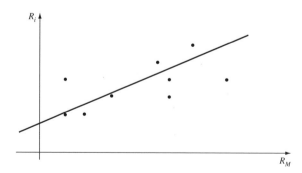

Figure 3.1 Systematic risk

---

[8] A fuller treatment of this subject is found in Gillet P., *L'Efficience Des Marchés Financiers*, Economica, 1999.

3.1.2.1   General principles

It was Eugene Fama[9] who explicitly introduced the concept of 'efficiency'. The definition that he gave to the concept was as follows: 'A financial market is said to be *efficient* if, and only if, all the available information on each financial asset quoted on the market is immediately included in the price of that asset'.

Indeed, he goes so far as to say that there is no overvaluation or undervaluation of securities, and also that no asset can produce a return greater than that which corresponds to its own characteristics.

This hypothesis therefore guarantees equality of treatment of various investors: no category of investor has any informational advantage. The information available on this type of market therefore allows optimum allocation of resources.

The economic justification for this concept is that the various investors, in competition and possessing the same information, will, through their involvement and because of the law of supply and demand, make the price of a security coincide with its intrinsic value.

We are of course looking at a hypothesis that divides the supporters of *fundamental analysis* from the supporters of *technical analysis*. The former accept the hypothesis and indeed make it the entire basis for their reasoning; they assume that returns on securities are unpredictable variables and propose portfolio management techniques that involve minimising the risks linked to these variables.[10] The latter propose methods[11] that involve predicting courses on the basis of historically observed movements.

From a more mathematical point of view, market efficiency consists of assuming that the prices will follow a *random walk*, that is, that the sequence $C_t - C_{t-1}$ $(t = 1, 2, \ldots)$ consists of random variables that are independent and identically distributed. In these circumstances, such a variation can only be predicted on the basis of available observations.

The economic conditions that define an efficient market are:

- The economic agents involved on the market behave rationally; they use the available information coherently and aim to maximise the expected utility of their wealth.
- The information is available simultaneously to all investors and the reaction of the investors to the information is instantaneous.
- The information is available free of charge.
- There are no transaction costs or taxes on the market.
- The market in question is completely liquid.

It is obvious that these conditions can never be all strictly satisfied in a real market. This therefore raises the question of knowing whether the differences are significant and whether they will have the effect of invalidating the efficiency hypothesis. This question is addressed in the following paragraphs, and the analysis is carried out at three levels according to the accessibility of information. The least that can be said is that the conclusions of the searches carried out in order to test efficiency are inconclusive and should not be used as a basis for forming clear and definitive ideas.

---

[9] Fama E. F., Behaviour of Stock Market Prices, *Journal of Business*, Vol. 38, 1965, pp. 34–105. Fama E. F., Random Walks in Stock Market Prices, *Financial Analysis Journal*, 1965. Fama E. F., Efficient Capital Markets: A Review of Theory and Empirical Work, *Journal of Finance*, Vol. 25, 1970.

[10] This approach is adopted in this work.

[11] Refer for example to Bechu T. and Bertrand E., *L'Analyse Technique*, Economica, 1998.

3.1.2.2 Weak form

The *weak form* of the efficiency hypothesis postulates that it is not possible to gain a particular advantage from the range of historical observations; the rates therefore purely and simply include the previous rate values.

The tests applied in order to verify this hypothesis relate to the possibility of predicting rates on the basis of their history. Here are a few analyses carried out:

- The autocorrelation test. Is there a correlation (positive or negative) between the successive return on security values that allows forecasts to be made?
- The run test. Is the distribution of the sequence lengths for positive returns and negative returns normal?
- Statistical tests for random walk.
- Simulation tests for technical analysis methods. Do the speculation techniques give better results than passive management?

Generally speaking, most of these tests lead to acceptance of the weak efficiency hypothesis, even though the most demanding tests from the statistical viewpoint sometimes invalidate it.

3.1.2.3 Semi-strong form

The semi-strong form of the efficiency hypothesis postulates that it is not possible to gain a particular advantage from information made public in relation to securities; the rates therefore change instantly and correctly when an event such as an increase in capital, division of securities, change of dividend policy, balance sheet publication or take-over bid is announced publicly.

The tests carried out to verify this hypothesis therefore relate to the effects of the events announced. They consist successively of:

- Determining the theoretical return on a security $R_{it} = \alpha_i + \beta_i R_{Mt}$ on the basis of historical observations relating to a period that does not include such events.
- When such an event occurs, comparing the difference between the theoretical return and the real return.
- Measuring the reaction time in order for the values to be altered again.

3.1.2.4 Strong form

The strong form of the efficiency hypothesis postulates that it is not possible to gain a particular advantage from nonpublic information relating to securities; the rates therefore change instantly and correctly when an event that is not public, that is, an insider event, occurs.

The tests carried out to verify this hypothesis therefore relate to the existence of privileged information. They follow a method similar to that used for the semi-strong form, but in specific circumstances:

- In recognised cases of misdemeanour by an initiated person.

- In cases of intensive trading on a market without the public being informed.
- In cases of intensive trading on the part of initiated persons.
- In cases of portfolios managed by professionals likely to have specific information before the general public has it, as in collective investment organisations.

3.1.2.5 Observed case of systematic inefficiency

Although the above analyses suggest that the efficiency hypothesis can be globally accepted, cases of systematic inefficiency have been discovered. In these cases, the following have sometimes been observed:

- Higher than average profitability at the end of the week, month or year.
- Higher profitability for low equity market capitalisation businesses than for high capitalisation companies.

Alongside these differences, *pockets of inefficiency* allowing arbitrage may present themselves. Their origin may be:

- *Speculative bubbles*, in which the rate of a security differs significantly and for a long time from its intrinsic value before eventually coming back to its intrinsic value, without movements of the market economic variables as an explanation for the difference.
- Irrational behaviour by certain investors.

These various elements, although removed from the efficiency hypothesis, do not, however, bring it into question. In addition, the profit to investors wishing to benefit from them will frequently be lost in transaction costs.

3.1.2.6 Conclusion

We quote P. Gillet in conclusion of this analysis.

Financial market efficiency appears to be all of the following: an intellectual abstraction, a myth and an objective.

The intellectual abstraction. Revealed by researchers, the theory of financial market efficiency calls into question a number of practices currently used by the financial market professionals, such as technical analysis. (...) It suggests a passive management, while technical analysis points towards an active management. (...) In addition, it is one of the basic principles of modern financial theory. (...).

The myth. All the hypotheses necessary for accepting the theory of efficiency are accepted by the theory's supporters. In addition to the classic hypotheses on circulation of information or absence of transaction costs, which have been addressed, other underlying hypotheses have as yet been little explored, especially those linked to the behaviour of investments and to liquidity. (...).

An objective. The market authorities are aware that the characteristics of efficiency make the market healthy and more credible, and therefore attract investors and businesses. To make a market more efficient is to reduce the risk of the speculation bubble. (...). The aim of the authorities is therefore to improve the efficiency of the financial markets (...).

3.1.3 Equity valuation models

The principle of equivalence, the basis of financial mathematics, allows the expression that the intrinsic value V_0 of an equity at the moment 0 is equal to the discounted values of the future financial flows that the security will trigger. Put more simply, if one assumes that the dividends (future financial flows) are paid for periods 1, 2 etc. and have a respective total of D_1, D_2 etc., and if the discount rate k is included, we will obtain the relation:

$$V_0 = \sum_{t=1}^{\infty} D_t (1+k)^{-t}$$

Note 1

The direct use of this relation can be sensitive. In fact:

- The value of all future dividends is not generally known.
- This formula assumes a constant discount rate (ad infinitum).
- It does not allow account to be taken of specific operations such as division or regrouping of equities, free issues or increases in capital.

The formula does, however, provide a number of services and later we will introduce a simplified formula that can be obtained from it.

Note 2

This formula, which links V_0 and k, can be used in two ways:

- If V_0 is known (intrinsic value on an efficient market), the value of k can be deduced from it and will then represent the expected return rate for the security in question.
- If k is given, the formula provides an assessment of the security's value, which can then be compared to the real rate C_0, thus allowing overevaluation or underestimation of the security to be determined.

3.1.3.1 The Gordon–Shapiro formula

This relation[12] is based on the following hypotheses:

- The growth of the firm is self-financing.
- The rate of return r of the investments, and the rate of distribution d of the profits, are constant from one period to the next.

---

[12] See Gordon M. and Shapiro E., Capital equipment analysis: the required rate profit, *Management Science*, Vol. 3, October 1956.

Under these hypotheses, if B_t is fixed as the profit for each action sold during the period t and E_t is the accounting value per equity at the moment t (capital divided by number of equities), we have:

$$\begin{cases} \dfrac{D_t}{B_t} = d \\ B_t = r \cdot E_{t-1} \end{cases}$$

And therefore:

$$B_{t+1} = B_t + r \cdot (B_t - D_t)$$
$$= B_t[1 + r(1 - d)]$$

The profits therefore increase at a constant rate $g = r(1 - d)$, which is the rate of profitability of the investments less the proportion distributed. The dividends also increase at this constant rate and it is possible to write $D_{t+1} = g.D_t$, hence: $D_t = D_1(1 + g)^{t-1}$. The present value can therefore be worked out as follows:

$$V_0 = \sum_{t=1}^{\infty} D_1(1 + g)^{t-1}(1 + k)^{-t}$$

$$= \frac{D_1}{1 + k} \sum_{t=0}^{\infty} \left(\frac{1 + g}{1 + k} \right)^t$$

$$= \frac{\dfrac{D_1}{1 + k}}{1 - \dfrac{1 + g}{1 + k}}$$

This is provided the discount rate k is greater than the rate of growth g. This leads to the Gordon–Shapiro formula:

$$V_0 = \frac{D_1}{k - g} = \frac{d B_1}{k - g} = \frac{d r E_0}{k - g}$$

Example

The capital of a company consists of 50 000 equities, for a total value of 10 000 000. The investment profitability rate is 15 %, the profit distribution rate 40 %, and the discount rate 12 %.
The profit per equity will be:

$$B = 0.15 \cdot \frac{10\,000\,000}{50\,000} = 30$$

The dividend per equity will therefore be $D = 0.4 \times 30 = 12$. In addition, the rate of growth is given as follows: $g = 0.15 \times (1 - 0.4) = 0.09$.

The Gordon–Shapiro formula therefore leads to:

$$V_0 = \frac{12}{0.12 - 0.09} = \frac{12}{0.03} = 400$$

The market value of this company is therefore $50\,000 \times 400 = 20\,000\,000$, while its accounting value is a mere $10\,000\,000$.

The Gordon–Shapiro formula produces the equation $k = g + \dfrac{D_1}{V_0}$, which shows that the return k can be broken down into the dividend growth rate and the rate of payment per security.

3.1.3.2 The price-earning ratio

One of the most commonly used evaluation indicators is the *PER*. It equals the ratio of the equity rate to the expected net profit for each equity:

$$PER_0 = \frac{C_0}{B_1}$$

Its interpretation is quite clear: when purchasing an equity, one pays $PER_0 \times €1$ for a profit of $€1$. Its inverse (profit over price) is often considered as a measurement of returns on securities, and securities whose *PER* is below the market average are considered to be undervalued and therefore of interest.

This indicator can be interpreted using the Gordon–Shapiro formula, if the hypotheses relative to the formula are satisfied. In fact, by replacing the rate with the V_0 value given for this formula:

$$C_0 = \frac{D_1}{k - g} = \frac{d B_1}{k - r(1 - d)}$$

we arrive directly at:

$$PER_0 = \frac{d}{k - r(1 - d)}$$

This allows the following expression to be obtained for the rate of return k:

$$k = r(1 - d) + \frac{d}{PER_0}$$

$$= r(1 - d) + \frac{1}{PER_0} - \frac{1 - d}{PER_0}$$

As $PER_0 = C_0 / r E_0$, we find that:

$$k = \frac{1}{PER_0} + \frac{r(1 - d)(C_0 - E_0)}{C_0}$$

Example

If one takes the same figures as in the previous paragraph:

$$r = 15\,\%$$

$$d = 40\,\%$$

$$E_0 = \frac{10\,000\,000}{50\,000} = 200$$

and the effectively observed price is 360, we arrive at: $PER_0 = \dfrac{360}{30} = 12$.

This allows the rate of output[13] to be determined as follows:

$$k = \frac{1}{12} + \frac{0.15 \cdot (1 - 0.4) \cdot (360 - 200)}{360}$$

$$= 0.0833 + 0.04$$

$$= 12.33\,\%$$

3.2 PORTFOLIO DIVERSIFICATION AND MANAGEMENT

3.2.1 Principles of diversification

Putting together an optimum equity portfolio involves an answer to the following two questions, given that a list of N equities is available on the market,

- Which of these equities should I choose?
- In what quantity (number or proportion)?

The aim is to look for the portfolio that provides the greatest return. This approach would logically lead to holding a portfolio consisting of just one security, that with the greatest expected return. Unfortunately, it misses out the risk aspect completely and can lead to a catastrophe scenario if the price for the adopted security falls.

The correlations between the returns on the various available securities can, on the other hand, help compensate for the fluctuations in the various portfolio components. This, in sharp contrast to the approach described above, can help reduce the portfolio risk without reducing its expected return too much.

It is this phenomenon that we will be analysing here and use at a later stage to put together an optimum portfolio.

3.2.1.1 The two-equity portfolio

According to what was stated above, the expected return and variance for a two-equity portfolio represented in proportions[14] X_1 and X_2 are given as follows:

$$\begin{cases} E_P = X_1 E_1 + X_2 E_2 \\ \sigma_P^2 = X_1^2 \sigma_1^2 + X_2^2 \sigma_2^2 + 2 X_1 X_2 \sigma_1 \sigma_2 \rho \end{cases}$$

---

[13] Of course, if the rate had been equal to the intrinsic value $V_0 = 400$, we arrive at $k = 12\,\%$.

[14] It is implicitly supposed in this paragraph that the proportions are between 0 and 1, that is to say, there are no short sales.

In order to show clearly the effect of diversification (the impact of correlation on risk), let us first consider the case in which the two securities have the same expected return ($E_1 = E_2 = E$) and the same risk ($\sigma_1 = \sigma_2 = \sigma$). Since $X_1 + X_2 = 1$, the equations will become:

$$\begin{cases} E_P = E \\ \sigma_P^2 = (X_1^2 + X_2^2 + 2X_1X_2\rho)\sigma^2 \end{cases}$$

The expected return on the portfolio is equal to that on the securities, but the risk is lower because the maximum value that it can take corresponds to $\rho = 1$ for which $\sigma_P = \sigma$ and when $\rho < 1, \sigma_P < \sigma$. Note that in the case of a perfect negative correlation ($\rho = -1$), the risk can be written as $\sigma_P^2 = (X_1 - X_2)^2\sigma^2$.

This cancels itself out if one chooses $X_1 = X_2 = 1/2$; in this case, the expected return is retained but the risk is completely cancelled.

Let us now envisage the more general case in which the expected return and the risk is of whatever quantity. An equity is characterised by a couple (E_i, σ_i) for $i = 1$ or 2 and can therefore be represented as a point in space (E, σ); of course the same applied for the portfolio, which corresponds to the point (E_P, σ_P). Depending on the values given to X_1 (and therefore to X_2), the representative point for the portfolio will describe a curve in (E, σ) plane. Let us now study in brief the shape of the curve with respect to the values for the correlation coefficient ρ.

When $\rho = 1$, the portfolio variance[15] becomes $\sigma_P^2 = (X_1\sigma_1 + X_2\sigma_2)^2$.

By eliminating X_1 and X_2 from the three equations

$$\begin{cases} E_P = X_1E_1 + X_2E_2 \\ \sigma_P = X_1\sigma_1 + X_2\sigma_2 \\ X_1 + X_2 = 1 \end{cases}$$

we arrive at the relation

$$\sigma_P = \frac{E_P - E_2}{E_1 - E_2}\sigma_1 + \frac{E_1 - E_P}{E_1 - E_2}\sigma_2$$

This expresses σ_P as a function of E_P, a first-degree function, and the full range of portfolios is therefore the sector of the straight line that links the representative points for the two securities (see Figure 3.2).

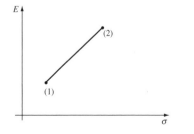
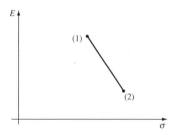

Figure 3.2   Two-equity portfolio ($\rho = 1$ case)

---

[15] Strictly speaking, one should say 'the portfolio return variance'.

Faced with the situation shown on the left, the investor will choose a portfolio located on the sector according to his attitude to the matter of risk: portfolio (1) will give a low expected return but present little risk, while portfolio (2) is the precise opposite. Faced with a situation shown on the right-hand graph, there is no room for doubting that portfolio (2) is better than portfolio (1) in terms of both expected return and risk incurred.

When $\rho = -1$, the variance in the portfolio will be: $\sigma_P^2 = (X_1\sigma_1 - X_2\sigma_2)^2$.

In other words, $\sigma_P = |X_1\sigma_1 - X_2\sigma_2|$. Applying the same reasoning as above leads to the following conclusion: the portfolios that can be constructed make up two sectors of a straight line from points (1) and (2), meet together at a point on the vertical axis ($\sigma = 0$), and have equal slopes, excepted the sign (see Figure 3.3).

Of these portfolios, of course, only those located in the upper sector will be of interest; those in the lower sector will be less attractive from the point of view of both risk and expected return.

In the general case, $-1 < \rho < 1$, and it can be shown that all the portfolios that can be put together form a curved arc that links points (1) and (2) located between the extreme case graphs for $\rho = \pm 1$, as shown in Figure 3.4.

If one expresses σ_P^2 as a function of E_P, as was done in the $\rho = 1$ case, a second-degree function is obtained. The curve obtained in the (E, σ) plane will therefore be a hyperbolic branch.

The term *efficient portfolio* is applied to a portfolio that is included among those that can be put together with two equities and cannot be improved from the double viewpoint of risk and expected return.

Graphically, we are looking at portfolios located above contact point A^{16} of the vertical tangent to the portfolio curve. In fact, between A and (2), it is not possible to improve

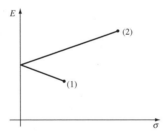

Figure 3.3   Two-equity portfolio ($\rho = -1$ case)

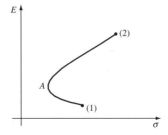

Figure 3.4   Two-equity portfolio (general case)

---

[16] This contact point corresponds to the minimum risk portfolio.

E_P without increasing the risk or to decrease σ_P without reducing the expected return. In addition, any portfolio located on the arc that links A and (1) will be less good than the portfolios located to its left.

3.2.1.2 Portfolio with more than two equities

A portfolio consisting of three equities[17] can be considered as a mixture of one of the securities and a portfolio consisting of the two others. For example, a portfolio with the composition $X_1 = 0.5$, $X_2 = 0.2$ and $X_3 = 0.3$ can also be considered to consist of security (1) and a portfolio that itself consists of securities (2) and (3) at rates of 40 % and 60 % respectively. Therefore, for the fixed covariances σ_{12}, σ_{13} and σ_{23}, the full range of portfolios that can be constructed using this process corresponds to a continuous range of curves as shown in Figure 3.5.

All the portfolios that can be put together using three or more securities therefore form an area within the plane (E, σ).

The concept of 'efficient portfolio' is defined in the same way as for two securities. The full range of efficient portfolios is therefore the part of the boundary of this area limited by security (1) and the contact point of the vertical tangent to the area, corresponding to the minimum risk portfolio. This arc curve is known as the *efficient frontier*.

The last part of this Section 3.2 is given over to the various techniques used to determine the efficient frontier, according to various restrictions and hypotheses.

An investor's choice of a portfolio on the efficient frontier will be made according to his attitude to risk. If he adopts the most cautious approach, he will choose the portfolio located at the extreme left point of the efficient frontier (the least risky portfolio, very diversified), while a taste for risk will move him towards the portfolios located on the right part of the efficient frontier (acceptance of increased risk with hope of higher return, generally obtained in portfolios made up of a very few profitable but highly volatile securities).[18]

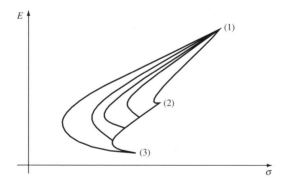

Figure 3.5   Three-equity portfolio

---

[17] The passage from two to three shares is a general one: the results obtained are valid for N securities. The attached CD-ROM shows some more realistic examples of the various models in the Excel sheets contained in the 'Ch 3' directory.
[18] This question is examined further in Section 3.2.6.

3.2.2   Diversification and portfolio size

We have just seen that diversification has the effect of reducing the risk posed by a portfolio through the presence of various securities that are not perfectly correlated. Let us now examine the limits of this diversification; up to what point, for a given correlation structure, can diversification reduce the risk?

3.2.2.1   Mathematical formulation

To simplify the analysis, let us consider a portfolio of N securities in equal proportions:

$$X_j = \frac{1}{N} \qquad j = 1, \ldots, N$$

The portfolio risk can therefore be developed as:

$$\sigma_P^2 = \sum_{i=1}^{N} \sum_{j=1}^{N} X_i X_j \sigma_{ij}$$

$$= \frac{1}{N^2} \left\{ \sum_{i=1}^{N} \sigma_i^2 + \sum_{i=1}^{N} \sum_{\substack{j=1 \\ j \neq i}}^{N} \sigma_{ij} \right\}$$

This double sum contains $N(N-1)$ terms, and it is therefore natural to define the average variance and the average covariance as:

$$\overline{\mathrm{var}} = \frac{1}{N} \sum_{i=1}^{N} \sigma_i^2$$

$$\overline{\mathrm{cov}} = \frac{1}{N(N-1)} \sum_{i=1}^{N} \sum_{\substack{j=1 \\ j \neq i}}^{N} \sigma_{ij}$$

As soon as N reaches a sufficient magnitude, these two quantities will almost cease to depend on N. They will then allow the portfolio variance to be written as follows:

$$\sigma_P^2 = \frac{1}{N} \overline{\mathrm{var}} + \frac{N-1}{N} \overline{\mathrm{cov}}$$

3.2.2.2   Asymptotic behaviour

When N becomes very large, the first term will decrease back towards 0 while the second, now quite stable, converges towards $\overline{\mathrm{cov}}$. The portfolio risk, despite being very diversified, never falls below this last value, which corresponds to:

$$\overline{\mathrm{cov}} = \lim_{N \to \infty} \left[\frac{1}{N} \overline{\mathrm{var}} + \frac{N-1}{N} \overline{\mathrm{cov}} \right] = \lim_{N \to \infty} \sigma_P^2 = \sigma_M^2$$

In other words, it corresponds to the market risk.

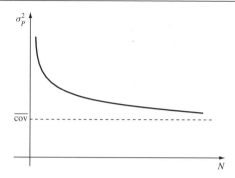

Figure 3.6   Diversification and portfolio size

The behaviour of the portfolio variance can be represented according to the number of securities by the graph shown in Figure 3.6.

The effects of diversification are initially very rapid (the first term loses 80% of its value if the number of securities increases from 1 to 5) but stabilise quickly somewhere near the $\overline{\text{cov}}$ value.

3.2.3   Markowitz model and critical line algorithm

3.2.3.1   First formulation

The efficient frontier is the 'North-West' part of the curve, consisting of portfolios defined by this principle: for each fixed value r of E_P, the proportions for which σ_P^2 is minimal X_j $(j = 1, \ldots, N)$ are determined. The efficient frontier is this defined by giving r all the possible values.

Mathematically, the problem is therefore presented as a search for the minimum with respect to $X_1, \ldots, X_N$ of the function:

$$\sigma_P^2 = \sum_{i=1}^{N} \sum_{j=1}^{N} X_i X_j \sigma_{ij}$$

under the double restriction:

$$\begin{cases} \sum_{j=1}^{N} X_j E_j = r \\ \sum_{j=1}^{N} X_j = 1 \end{cases}$$

The Lagrangian function[19] for the problem can thus be written as:

$$L(X_1, \ldots, X_N; m_1, m_2) = \sum_{i=1}^{N} \sum_{j=1}^{N} X_i X_j \sigma_{ij} + m_1 \cdot \left(\sum_{j=1}^{N} X_j E_j - r \right) + m_2 \cdot \left(\sum_{j=1}^{N} X_j - 1 \right)$$

---

[19] Please refer to Appendix 1 for the theory of extrema.

Taking partial derivatives with respect to the variables $X_1, \ldots, X_n$ and to the Lagrange multipliers m_1 and m_2 leads to the system of $N + 2$ equations with $N + 2$ unknowns:

$$\begin{cases} L'_{X_j}(X_1, \ldots, X_N; m_1, m_2) = 2 \sum_{i=1}^{N} X_i \sigma_{ij} + m_1 E_j + m_2 = 0 \qquad (j = 1, \ldots, N) \\ L'_{m_1}(X_1, \ldots, X_N; m_1, m_2) = \sum_{i=1}^{N} X_i E_i - r = 0 \\ L'_{m_2}(X_1, \ldots, X_N; m_1, m_2) = \sum_{i=1}^{N} X_i - 1 = 0 \end{cases}$$

This can be written in a matrix form:

$$\begin{pmatrix} 2\sigma_1^2 & 2\sigma_{12} & \cdots & 2\sigma_{1N} & E_1 & 1 \\ 2\sigma_{21} & 2\sigma_2^2 & \cdots & 2\sigma_{2N} & E_2 & 1 \\ \vdots & \vdots & \ddots & \vdots & \vdots & \vdots \\ 2\sigma_{N1} & 2\sigma_{N2} & \cdots & 2\sigma_N^2 & E_N & 1 \\ E_1 & E_2 & \cdots & E_N & \cdot & \cdot \\ 1 & 1 & \cdots & 1 & \cdot & \cdot \end{pmatrix} \begin{pmatrix} X_1 \\ X_2 \\ \vdots \\ X_N \\ m_1 \\ m_2 \end{pmatrix} = \begin{pmatrix} \cdot \\ \cdot \\ \vdots \\ \cdot \\ r \\ 1 \end{pmatrix}$$

By referring to the matrix of coefficients,[20] the vector of unknowns[21] and the vector of second members as M, X^* and G respectively, we give the system the form $MX^* = G$. The resolution of this system passes through the inverse matrix of M: $X^* = M^{-1}G$.

Note 1

In reality, this vector only supplies one stationary point of the Lagrangian function; it can be shown (although we will not do this here) that it constitutes the solution to the problem of minimisation that is concerning us.

Note 2

This relation must be applied to the different possible values for r to find the frontier, of which only the efficient ('North-West') part will be retained. The interesting aspect of this result is that if r is actually inside the vector G, it does not appear in the matrix M, which then has to be inverted only once.[22]

Example

We now determine the efficient frontier that can be constructed with three securities with the following characteristics:

$$\begin{array}{lll} E_1 = 0.05 & E_2 = 0.08 & E_3 = 0.10 \\ \sigma_1 = 0.10 & \sigma_2 = 0.12 & \sigma_3 = 0.15 \\ \rho_{12} = 0.3 & \rho_{13} = 0.1 & \rho_{23} = 0.4 \end{array}$$

---

[20] In its order N zone of the upper left corner, this contains the $2V$ matrix in which V is the variance–covariance matrix.

[21] The vector of unknowns does not contain the proportions only; it also involves the Lagrange multipliers (which will not be of use to us later). For this reason we will use the notation X^* instead of X (which is reserved for the vector of proportions). This remark applies to all the various models developed subsequently.

[22] The attached CD-ROM contains a series of more realistic examples of the various models in an Excel™ file known as Ch 3.

The variance–covariance matrix is given by:

$$V = \begin{pmatrix} 0.0100 & 0.0036 & 0.0015 \\ 0.0036 & 0.0144 & 0.0072 \\ 0.0015 & 0.0072 & 0.0225 \end{pmatrix}$$

The matrix M is therefore equal to:

$$M = \begin{pmatrix} 0.0200 & 0.0072 & 0.0030 & 0.05 & 1 \\ 0.0072 & 0.0288 & 0.0144 & 0.08 & 1 \\ 0.0030 & 0.0144 & 0.0450 & 0.10 & 1 \\ 0.05 & 0.08 & 0.010 & . & . \\ 1 & 1 & 1 & . & . \end{pmatrix}$$

This matrix inverts to:

$$M^{-1} = \begin{pmatrix} 31.16 & -24.10 & -7.06 & 0.57 \\ -24.10 & 40.86 & -16.76 & 0.24 \\ -7.06 & -16.76 & 23.82 & 0.19 \\ 0.57 & 0.24 & 0.19 & -0.01 \end{pmatrix}$$

By applying this matrix to the vector $G = \begin{pmatrix} \vdots \\ r \\ 1 \end{pmatrix}$, for different values of r, we find a range of vectors X^*, the first three components of which supply the composition of the portfolios (see Table 3.2).

These proportions allow σ_P to be calculated[23] for the various portfolios (Table 3.3).

It is therefore possible, from this information, to construct the representative curve for these portfolios (Figure 3.7).

Table 3.2 Composition of portfolios

r	X_1	X_2	X_3
0.00	2.1293	−0.3233	−0.8060
0.01	1.8956	−0.2391	−0.6565
0.02	1.6620	−0.1549	−0.5071
0.03	1.4283	−0.0707	−0.3576
0.04	1.1946	0.0135	−0.2801
0.05	0.9609	0.0933	−0.0586
0.06	0.7272	0.1820	0.0908
0.07	0.4935	0.2662	0.2403
0.08	0.2598	0.3504	0.3898
0.09	0.0262	0.4346	0.5392
0.10	−0.2075	0.5188	0.6887
0.11	−0.4412	0.6030	0.8382
0.12	−0.6749	0.6872	0.9877
0.13	−0.9086	0.7714	1.1371
0.14	−1.1423	0.8556	1.2866
0.15	−1.3759	0.9398	1.4361

[23] The expected return is of course known.

Table 3.3 Calculation of σ_P

E_P	σ_P
0.00	0.2348
0.01	0.2043
0.02	0.1746
0.03	0.1465
0.04	0.1207
0.05	0.0994
0.06	0.0857
0.07	0.0835
0.08	0.0937
0.09	0.1130
0.10	0.1376
0.11	0.1651
0.12	0.1943
0.13	0.2245
0.14	0.2554
0.15	0.2868

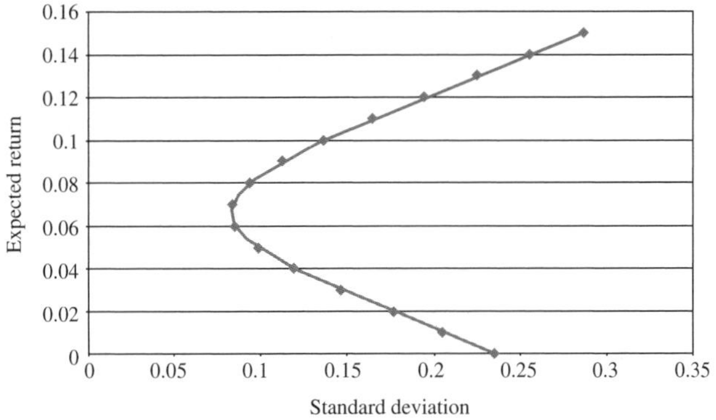

Figure 3.7 Efficient frontier

The efficient part of this frontier is therefore the 'North-West' part, the lower limit of which corresponds to the minimum risk portfolio. For this portfolio, we have values of $E_P = 0.0667$ and $\sigma_P = 0.0828$.

The method just presented does not require the proportions to be positive. Moreover, a look at the preceding diagram will show that negative values (and values over 1) are sometimes obtained, as the 'classic' portfolios ($0 \leq X_j \leq 1$ for any j) correspond only to expected return values between 0.06 and 0.09.

A negative value for a proportion corresponds to a *short sale*. This type of transaction, which is very hazardous, is not always authorised, especially in the management of invest-ment funds. Symmetrically, a proportion of over 1 indicates the purchase of a security for an amount greater than the total invested.

In addition, many portfolios contain regulatory or internal restrictions stating that certain types of security cannot be represented for a total over a fixed percentage. In this case, the problem must be resolved by putting together portfolios in which proportions of the type $B_j^- \leq X_j \leq B_j^+$ for $j = 1, \ldots, N$ are subject to regulations. We will examine this problem at a later stage.

3.2.3.2 Reformulating the problem

We now continue to examine the problem without any regulations on inequality of proportions. We have simply altered the approach slightly; it will supply the same solution but can be generalised more easily into the various models subsequently envisaged.

If instead of representing the portfolios graphically by showing σ_P as the x-axis and E_p as the y-axis (as in Figure 3.7), E_P is now shown as the x-axis and σ_P^2 as the y-axis, the efficient frontier graph now appears as shown in Figure 3.8.

A straight line in this graph has the equation $\sigma^2 = a + \lambda E$ in which a represents the intercept and λ the slope of the straight line. We are looking specifically at a straight line at a tangent to the efficient frontier. If the slope of this straight line is zero ($\lambda = 0$), the contact point of the tangent shows the least risky portfolio in the efficient frontier. Conversely, the more λ increases, the further the contact point moves away from the efficient frontier towards the risky portfolios. The λ parameter may vary from 0 to $+\infty$ and is therefore representative of the portfolio risk corresponding to the contact point of the tangent with this λ value for a slope.

For a fixed λ value, the tangent to the efficient frontier with slope λ is, of all the straight lines with that slope and with at least one point in common with the efficient frontier, that which is located farthest to the right, that is, the one with the smallest coordinate at the origin $a = \sigma^2 - \lambda E$.

The problem is therefore reformulated as follows: for the various values of λ between 0 and ∞, minimise with respect to the proportions $X_1, \ldots, X_N$ the expression:

$$\sigma_P^2 - \lambda E_P = \sum_{i=1}^{N} \sum_{j=1}^{N} X_i X_j \sigma_{ij} - \lambda \sum_{j=1}^{N} X_j E_j$$

under the restriction $\sum_{j=1}^{N} X_j = 1$.

Once the solution, which will depend on λ, has been found, it will be sufficient to make this last parameter vary between 0 and $+\infty$ to arrive at the efficient frontier.

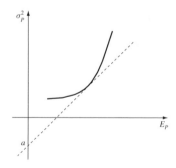

Figure 3.8   Reformulation of problem

The Lagrangian function for the problem can be written as:

$$L(X_1, \ldots, X_N; m) = \sum_{i=1}^{N} \sum_{j=1}^{N} X_i X_j \sigma_{ij} - \lambda \sum_{j=1}^{N} X_j E_j + m \cdot \left(\sum_{j=1}^{N} X_j - 1 \right)$$

A reasoning similar to that used in the first formulation allows the following matrix expression to be deduced from the partial derivatives:

$$MX^* = \lambda E^* + F$$

Here, it has been noted that[24]

$$
M = \begin{pmatrix}
2\sigma_1^2 & 2\sigma_{12} & \cdots & 2\sigma_{1N} & 1 \\
2\sigma_{21} & 2\sigma_2^2 & \cdots & 2\sigma_{2N} & 1 \\
\vdots & \vdots & \ddots & \vdots & \vdots \\
2\sigma_{N1} & 2\sigma_{N2} & \cdots & 2\sigma_N^2 & 1 \\
1 & 1 & \cdots & 1 & .
\end{pmatrix}
\quad
X^* = \begin{pmatrix} X_1 \\ X_2 \\ \vdots \\ X_N \\ m \end{pmatrix}
\quad
E^* = \begin{pmatrix} E_1 \\ E_2 \\ \vdots \\ E_N \\ . \end{pmatrix}
\quad
F = \begin{pmatrix} . \\ . \\ \vdots \\ . \\ 1 \end{pmatrix}
$$

The solution to this system of equations is therefore supplied by: $X^* = \lambda(M^{-1}E^*) + (M^{-1}F)$.

As for the first formulation, the matrix M is independent of the parameter λ, which must be variable; it only needs to be inverted once.

Example

Let us take the same data as those used in the first formulation, namely:

$$
\begin{array}{lll}
E_1 = 0.05 & E_2 = 0.08 & E_3 = 0.10 \\
\sigma_1 = 0.10 & \sigma_2 = 0.12 & \sigma_3 = 0.15 \\
\rho_{12} = 0.3 & \rho_{13} = 0.1 & \rho_{23} = 0.4
\end{array}
$$

The same variance–covariance matrix V as above will be used, and the matrix M can be expressed as:

$$
M = \begin{pmatrix}
0.0200 & 0.0072 & 0.0030 & 1 \\
0.0072 & 0.0288 & 0.0144 & 1 \\
0.0030 & 0.0144 & 0.0450 & 1 \\
1 & 1 & 1 & .
\end{pmatrix}
$$

This matrix inverts to:

$$
M^{-1} = \begin{pmatrix}
31.16 & -24.10 & -7.06 & 0.57 \\
-24.10 & 40.86 & -16.76 & 0.24 \\
-7.06 & -16.76 & 23.82 & 0.19 \\
0.57 & 0.24 & 0.19 & -0.01
\end{pmatrix}
$$

[24] In the same way as the function carried out for X^*, we are using the E^* notation here as E is reserved for the N-dimensional vector for the expected returns.

Table 3.4 Solutions for different values of λ

λ	X_1	X_2	X_3	E_P	σ_P
2.0	−1.5810	1.0137	1.5672	0.0588	0.3146
1.9	−1.4734	0.9750	1.4984	0.1542	0.3000
1.8	−1.3657	0.9362	1.4296	0.1496	0.2854
1.7	−1.2581	0.8974	1.3607	0.1450	0.2709
1.6	−1.1505	0.8586	1.2919	0.1404	0.2565
1.5	−1.0429	0.8198	1.2231	0.1357	0.2422
1.4	−0.9353	0.7810	1.1542	0.1311	0.2280
1.3	−0.8276	0.7423	1.0854	0.1265	0.2139
1.2	−0.7200	0.7035	1.0165	0.1219	0.2000
1.1	−0.6124	0.6647	0.9477	0.1173	0.1863
1.0	−0.5048	0.6259	0.8789	0.1127	0.1729
0.9	−0.3972	0.5871	0.8100	0.1081	0.1597
0.8	−0.2895	0.5484	0.7412	0.1035	0.1470
0.7	−0.1819	0.5096	0.6723	0.0989	0.1347
0.6	−0.0743	0.4708	0.6035	0.0943	0.1231
0.5	0.0333	0.4320	0.5437	0.0897	0.1123
0.4	0.1409	0.3932	0.4658	0.0851	0.1027
0.3	0.2486	0.3544	0.3970	0.0805	0.0945
0.2	0.3562	0.3157	0.3282	0.0759	0.0882
0.1	0.4638	0.2769	0.2593	0.0713	0.0842
0.0	0.5714	0.2381	0.1905	0.0667	0.0828

As the vectors E^* and F are given by $E^* = \begin{pmatrix} 0.05 \\ 0.08 \\ 0.10 \\ \cdot \end{pmatrix}$ $F = \begin{pmatrix} \cdot \\ \cdot \\ \cdot \\ 1 \end{pmatrix}$, the solutions
to the problem for the different values of λ are shown in Table 3.4.

The efficient frontier graph then takes the form shown in Figure 3.9.

The advantage of this new formulation is twofold. On one hand, it only shows the truly efficient portfolios instead of the boundary for the range of portfolios that can be put together, from which the upper part has to be selected. On the other hand, it readily

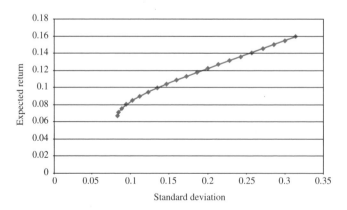

Figure 3.9 Efficient frontier for the reformulated problem

lends itself to generalisation in the event of problems with inequality restrictions, as well as to the simple index models with non-risk titles.

3.2.3.3 Constrained Markowitz model

The problem to be solved is formulated here as follows: for the different values of λ between 0 and $+\infty$, minimise with respect to the proportions $X_1, \ldots, X_N$ the expression

$$\sigma_P^2 - \lambda E_P = \sum_{i=1}^{N} \sum_{j=1}^{N} X_i X_j \sigma_{ij} - \lambda \sum_{j=1}^{N} X_j E_j$$

with the restrictions:

$$\begin{cases} \sum_{j=1}^{N} X_j = 1 \\ B_j^- \leq X_j \leq B_j^+ \quad j = 1, \ldots, N \end{cases}$$

We will first of all introduce the concept of a security's 'status'. The security (j) is defined as 'down' (resp. 'up') if its proportion is equal to the 'lower' (resp. 'upper') bound imposed on it: $X_j = B_j^-$ (resp. $X_j = B_j^+$). For an efficient portfolio (that is, one that minimises the Lagrangian function), the partial derivative of the Lagrangian function with respect to X_j is not zero in an optimum situation; it is strictly positive (resp. strictly negative) as can be seen in Figure 3.10.

In the system of equations produced by the partial derivatives of the Lagrangian function, the equations relating to the 'down' (resp. 'up') securities should therefore be replaced here by $X_j = B_j^-$ (resp. $X_j = B_j^+$).

The other securities are defined as 'in', and are such that $B_j^- < X_j < B_j^+$, and in an optimum situation, the partial derivative of the Lagrangian function with respect to X_j is zero. The equations relating to these securities should not be altered.

The adaptation to the system of equations produced by the partial derivatives of the Lagrangian function $MX^* = \lambda E^* + F$, will therefore consist of not altering the components that correspond to the 'in' securities, and if the security (j) is 'down' or

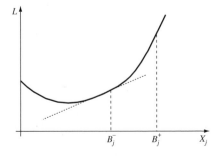
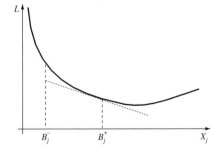

Figure 3.10 'Up' security and 'down' security

'up', of altering the jth line of M and the jth component of E^* and F, as follows:

$$
M = \begin{pmatrix}
2\sigma_1^2 & \cdots & 2\sigma_{1j} & \cdots & 2\sigma_{1N} & 1 \\
\vdots & \ddots & \vdots & & \vdots & \vdots \\
0 & \cdots & 1 & \cdots & 0 & 0 \\
\vdots & & \vdots & & \vdots & \vdots \\
2\sigma_{N1} & \cdots & 2\sigma_{Nj} & \cdots & 2\sigma_N^2 & 1 \\
1 & \cdots & 1 & \cdots & 1 & 0
\end{pmatrix}
\quad
E^* = \begin{pmatrix}
E_1 \\
\vdots \\
0 \\
\vdots \\
E_N \\
0
\end{pmatrix}
\quad
F = \begin{pmatrix}
0 \\
\vdots \\
B_j^{\pm} \\
\vdots \\
0 \\
1
\end{pmatrix}
$$

With this alteration, in fact, the jth equation becomes $X_j = B_j^{\pm}$. In addition, when considering the jth line of the equality $M^{-1}M = I$, it is evident that M^{-1} has the same j^{th} line as M and the jth component of the solution $X^* = \lambda(M^{-1}E^*) + (M^{-1}F)$. This is also written as $X_j = B_j^{\pm}$.

If (j) has an 'in' status, this j^{th} component can of course be written as $X_j = \lambda u_j + v_j$, a quantity that is strictly included between B_j^- and B_j^+.

The method proceeds through a series of stages and we will note M_0, E_0^* and F_0, the matrix elements as defined in the 'unconstrained' case. The index develops from one stage to the next.

The method begins with the major values for λ $(+\infty$ ideally). As we are looking to minimise $\sigma_P^2 - \lambda E_P$, E_P needs to be as high as possible, and this is consistent with a major value for the risk parameter λ. The first portfolio will therefore consist of the securities that offer the highest expected returns, in equal proportions to the upper bounds B_j^+, until (with securities in proportions equal to B_j^-) the sum of the proportions equals 1.[25] This portfolio is known as the first *corner portfolio*.

At least one security will therefore be 'up'; one will be 'in', and the others will be 'down'. The matrix M and the vectors E^* and F are altered as shown above. This brings us to M_1, E_1^* and F_1, and we calculate: $X^* = \lambda\,(M_1^{-1}E_1^*) + (M_1^{-1}F_1)$.

The parameter λ is thus decreased until one of the securities changes its status.[26] This first change will occur for a value of λ equal to $\lambda_c^{(1)}$, known as the first critical λ. To determine this critical value, and the security that will change its status, each of the various securities for which a potentially critical λ_j is defined will be examined.

A 'down' or 'up' security (j) will change its status if the equation corresponding to it becomes $L'_{X_j} = 0$, that is:

$$
2\sum_{k=1}^{N} X_k \sigma_{jk} - \lambda_j E_j + m = 0
$$

This is none other than the jth component of the equation $M_0 X^* = \lambda E_0^* + F_0$, in which the different X_k and m are given by the values obtained by $X^* = \lambda\,(M_1^{-1}E_1^*) + (M_1^{-1}F_1)$.

---

[25] If the inequality restrictions are simply $0 \le X_j \le 1$ $\forall j$ (absence of short sales), the first portfolio will consist only of the security with the highest expected return.

[26] For the restrictions $0 \le X_j \le 1$ $\forall j$, the first corner portfolio consists of a single 'up' security, all the others being 'down'. The first change of status will be a transition to 'in' of the security that was 'up' and of one of the securities that were 'down'. In this case, on one hand the matrix elements M_1, E_1^* and F_1 are obtained by making the alteration required for the 'down' securities but for the one that it is known will pass to 'in' status, and on the other hand there is no equation for determining the potential critical λ for this security.

For an 'in' security (j), it is known that $X_j = \lambda_j u_j + v_j$ and it will change its status if it becomes a 'down' ($u_j > 0$ as λ decreases) or 'up' security ($u_j < 0$), in which case we have $B_j^{\pm} = \lambda_j u_j + v_j$. This is none other than the jth component of the relation $X^* = \lambda(M_1^{-1} E_1^*) + (M_1^{-1} F_1)$, in which the left member is replaced by the lower or upper bound depending on the case.

We therefore obtain N equations for N values of potentially critical λ_j. The highest of these is the first critical λ_j or $\lambda_c^{(1)}$. The proportions of the various securities have not changed between $\lambda = +\infty$ and $\lambda = \lambda_c^{(1)}$. The corresponding portfolio is therefore always the first corner portfolio.

The security corresponding to this critical λ therefore changes its status, thus allowing M_2, E_2^* and F_2 to be constructed and the second critical λ, $\lambda_c^{(2)}$, to be determined together with all the portfolios that correspond to the values of λ between $\lambda_c^{(1)}$ and $\lambda_c^{(2)}$. The portfolio corresponding to $\lambda_c^{(2)}$ is of course the second corner portfolio.

The process is then repeated until all the potentially critical λ values are negative, in which case the last critical λ is equal to 0. The last and least risky corner portfolio, located at the extreme left point of the efficient frontier, corresponds to this value.

The corner portfolios are of course situated on the efficient frontier. Between two consecutive corner portfolios, the status of the securities does not change; only the proportions change. These proportions are calculated, between $\lambda_c^{(k-1)}$ and $\lambda_c^{(k)}$, using the relation $X^* = \lambda(M_k^{-1} E_k^*) + (M_k^{-1} F_k)$.

The various sections of curve thus constructed are connected continuously and with same derivative[27] and make up the efficient frontier.

Example

Let us take the same data as were processed before:

$$E_1 = 0.05 \quad E_2 = 0.08 \quad E_3 = 0.10$$
$$\sigma_1 = 0.10 \quad \sigma_2 = 0.12 \quad \sigma_3 = 0.15$$
$$\rho_{12} = 0.3 \quad \rho_{13} = 0.1 \quad \rho_{23} = 0.4$$

Let us impose the requirement of absence of short sales: $0 \leq X_j \leq 1$ ($j = 1, 2, 3$).
We have the following basic matrix elements:

$$M_0 = \begin{pmatrix} 0.0200 & 0.0072 & 0.0030 & 1 \\ 0.0072 & 0.0288 & 0.0144 & 1 \\ 0.0030 & 0.0144 & 0.0450 & 1 \\ 1 & 1 & 1 & . \end{pmatrix} \quad E_0^* = \begin{pmatrix} 0.05 \\ 0.08 \\ 0.10 \\ . \end{pmatrix} \quad F_0 = \begin{pmatrix} . \\ . \\ . \\ 1 \end{pmatrix}$$

The first corner portfolio consists only of security (3), the one with the highest expected return. As securities (1) and (2) are 'down', we construct:

$$M_1 = \begin{pmatrix} 1 & . & . & . \\ . & 1 & . & . \\ 0.0030 & 0.0144 & 0.0450 & 1 \\ 1 & 1 & 1 & . \end{pmatrix} \quad E_1^* = \begin{pmatrix} . \\ . \\ 0.10 \\ . \end{pmatrix} \quad F_1 = \begin{pmatrix} . \\ . \\ . \\ 1 \end{pmatrix}$$

---

[27] That is, with the same tangent.

We have:

$$M_1^{-1} = \begin{pmatrix} 1 & \cdot & \cdot & \cdot \\ \cdot & 1 & \cdot & \cdot \\ -1 & -1 & \cdot & 1 \\ 0.0420 & 0.0306 & 1 & -0.0450 \end{pmatrix}$$

and therefore

$$X^* = \lambda(M_1^{-1}E_1^*) + (M_1^{-1}F_1) = \lambda \begin{pmatrix} \cdot \\ \cdot \\ \cdot \\ 0.1 \end{pmatrix} + \begin{pmatrix} \cdot \\ \cdot \\ 1 \\ -0.045 \end{pmatrix}$$

The first two components of $M_0 X^* = \lambda E_0^*$ and F_0, with the vector X^* obtained above, give:

$$0.003 + (0.1 \, \lambda_1 - 0.045) = 0.05 \, \lambda \, \lambda_1$$
$$0.0144 + (0.1 \, \lambda_2 - 0.045) = 0.08 \, \lambda_2$$

This will give the two potential critical λ values: $\lambda_1 = 0.84$ and $\lambda_2 = 1.53$. The first critical λ is therefore $\lambda_c^{(1)} = 1.53$ and security (2) becomes 'in' together with (3), while (1) remains 'down'.

We can therefore construct:

$$M_2 = \begin{pmatrix} 1 & \cdot & \cdot & \cdot \\ 0.0072 & 0.0288 & 0.0144 & 1 \\ 0.0030 & 0.0144 & 0.0450 & 1 \\ 1 & 1 & 1 & \cdot \end{pmatrix} \qquad E_2^* = \begin{pmatrix} \cdot \\ 0.08 \\ 0.10 \\ \cdot \end{pmatrix} \qquad F_2 = \begin{pmatrix} \cdot \\ \cdot \\ \cdot \\ 1 \end{pmatrix}$$

This successively gives:

$$M_2^{-1} = \begin{pmatrix} 1 & \cdot & \cdot & \cdot \\ -0.7733 & 22.22 & -22.22 & 0.68 \\ -0.2267 & -22.22 & 22.22 & 0.32 \\ 0.0183 & 0.68 & 0.32 & -0.0242 \end{pmatrix}$$

$$X^* = \lambda(M_2^{-1}E_2^*) + (M_2^{-1}F_2) = \lambda \begin{pmatrix} \cdot \\ -0.4444 \\ 0.4444 \\ 0.0864 \end{pmatrix} + \begin{pmatrix} \cdot \\ 0.68 \\ 0.32 \\ -0.0242 \end{pmatrix}$$

The first component of $M_0 X^* = \lambda E_0^* + F_0$, with vector X^* obtained above, gives: $0.0072 \cdot (-0.4444\lambda_1 + 0.68) + 0.0030 \cdot (0.4444\lambda_1 + 0.32) + (0.0864\lambda_1 - 0.0242) = 0.05\lambda_1$. This produces a potential critical λ of $\lambda_1 = 0.5312$.

The second and third components of the relation $X^* = \lambda(M_2^{-1}E_2^*) + (M_2^{-1}F_2)$, in which the left member is replaced by the suitable bound, produce

$$\begin{cases} -0.4444 \, \lambda_2 + 0.68 = 1 \\ 0.4444 \, \lambda_3 + 0.32 = 0 \end{cases}$$

In consequence, $\lambda_2 = \lambda_3 = -0.7201$. The second critical λ is therefore $\lambda_c^{(2)} = 0.5312$ and the three securities acquire an 'in' status.

The matrix elements M_3, E_3^* and F_3 are therefore the same as those in the base and the problem can be approached without restriction. We therefore have:

$$M_3^{-1} = \begin{pmatrix} 31.16 & -24.10 & -7.06 & 0.57 \\ -24.10 & 40.86 & -16.76 & 0.24 \\ -7.06 & -16.76 & 23.82 & 0.19 \\ 0.57 & 0.24 & 0.19 & -0.01 \end{pmatrix}$$

and therefore

$$X^* = \lambda(M_3^{-1} E_3^*) + (M_3^{-1} F_3) = \lambda \begin{pmatrix} -1.0762 \\ 0.3878 \\ 0.6884 \\ 0.0667 \end{pmatrix} + \begin{pmatrix} 0.5714 \\ 0.2381 \\ 0.1905 \\ -0.0137 \end{pmatrix}$$

With suitable bounds, the first three components of this give: $-1.0762\, \lambda_1$ etc.

We therefore arrive at $\lambda_1 = -0.3983$, $\lambda_2 = -0.6140$ and $\lambda_3 = -0.2767$. The last critical λ is therefore $\lambda_c^{(3)} = 0$ and the three securities retain their 'in' status until the end of the process.[28] The various portfolios on the efficient frontier, as well as the expected return and the risk, are shown in Table 3.5.

Of course, between $\lambda = 0.5312$ and $\lambda = 0$, the proportions obtained here are the same as those obtained in the 'unrestricted' model as all the securities are 'in'. The efficient frontier graph therefore takes the form shown in Figure 3.11.

Table 3.5 Solution for constrained Markowitz model

λ	X_1	X_2	X_3	E_P	σ_P
1.53	0	0	1	0.1000	0.1500
1.5	0	0.0133	0.9867	0.0997	0.1486
1.4	0	0.0578	0.9422	0.0988	0.1442
1.3	0	0.1022	0.8978	0.0980	0.1400
1.2	0	0.1467	0.8533	0.0971	0.1360
1.1	0	0.1911	0.8089	0.0962	0.1322
1.0	0	0.2356	0.7644	0.0953	0.1286
0.9	0	0.2800	0.7200	0.0944	0.1253
0.8	0	0.3244	0.6756	0.0935	0.1222
0.7	0	0.3689	0.6311	0.0926	0.1195
0.6	0	0.4133	0.5867	0.0917	0.1170
0.5312	0	0.4439	0.5561	0.0911	0.1155
0.5	0.0333	0.4320	0.5347	0.0897	0.1123
0.4	0.1409	0.3932	0.4658	0.0851	0.1027
0.3	0.2486	0.3544	0.3970	0.0805	0.0945
0.2	0.3562	0.3157	0.3282	0.0759	0.0882
0.1	0.4638	0.2769	0.2853	0.0713	0.0842
0.0	0.5714	0.2381	0.1905	0.0687	0.0828

---

[28] It is quite logical to have significant diversification in the least risk-efficient portfolio.

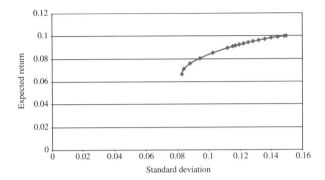

Figure 3.11 Efficient frontier for the constrained Markowitz model

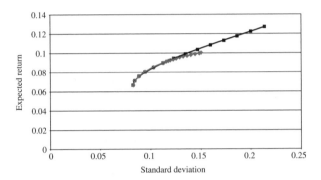

Figure 3.12 Comparison of unconstrained and constrained efficient frontiers

Figure 3.12 superimposes the two efficient frontiers (constrained and unconstrained). The zones corresponding to the short sales, and those in which all the securities are 'in', can be clearly seen.

3.2.3.4 Critical line algorithm

H. Markowitz has proposed an algorithmic method for resolving the problem with the restrictions $X_j \geq 0$ $(j = 1, \ldots, N)$. It is known as the *critical line algorithm*.

This algorithm starts with the first corner portfolio, which of course consists of the single security with the highest expected return. It then passes through the successive corner portfolios by testing, at each stage, the changes in the function to be minimised when:

- A new security is introduced into the portfolio.
- A security is taken out of the portfolio.
- A security in the portfolio is replaced by one that was not previously present.

The development of the algorithm is outside the scope of this work and is instead covered in specialist literature.[29] Here, we will simply show the route taken by a three-security problem

---

[29] For example Markowitz, H., *Mean Variance Analysis in Portfolio Choice and Capital Markets*, Basil Blackwell, 1987.

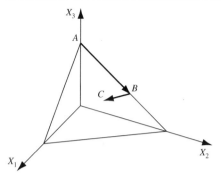

Figure 3.13 Critical line

such as the one illustrated in this section. The restrictions $\begin{cases} \sum_{j=1}^{3} X_j = 1 \\ 0 \leq X_j \leq 1 \qquad j = 1, 2, 3 \end{cases}$
define, in a three-dimensional space, a triangle with points referenced $(1, 0, 0)$ $(0, 1, 0)$ and
$(0, 0, 1)$ as shown in Figure 3.13. The critical line is represented in bold and points AB and
C correspond to the corner portfolios obtained for $\lambda = \lambda_c^{(1)}$, $\lambda_c^{(2)}$ and $\lambda_c^{(3)}$ respectively.

In this algorithm, only the corner portfolios are determined. Those that are located
between two consecutive corner portfolios are estimated as linear combinations of the
corner portfolios.

3.2.4 Sharpe's simple index model

3.2.4.1 Principles

Determining the efficient frontier within the Markowitz model is not an easy process. In
addition, the amount of data required is substantial as the variance–covariance matrix
is needed. For this reason, W. Sharpe[30] has proposed a simplified version of Markowitz's
model based on the following two hypotheses.

1. The returns of the various securities are expressed as first-degree functions of the return
   of a market-representative index: $R_{jt} = a_j + b_j R_{It} + \varepsilon_{jt}$ $\qquad j = 1, \ldots, N$. It is also
   assumed that the residuals verify the classical hypotheses of linear regression,[31] which
   are, among others, that the residuals have zero expectation and are not correlated to
   the explanatory variable R_{It}.
2. The residuals for the regressions relative to the various securities are not correlated:
   $\mathrm{cov}\,(\varepsilon_{it}, \varepsilon_{jt}) = 0$ for all different i and j.

By applying the convention of omitting the index t, the return on a portfolio will therefore
be written, in this case, as

$$R_P = \sum_{j=1}^{N} X_j R_j$$

---

[30] Sharpe W., A simplified model for portfolio analysis, *Management Science*, Vol. 9, No. 1, 1963, pp. 277–93.
[31] See Appendix 3 on this subject.

$$= \sum_{j=1}^{N} X_j(a_j + b_j R_I + \varepsilon_j)$$

$$= \sum_{j=1}^{N} X_j a_j + \left(\sum_{j=1}^{N} X_j b_j\right) R_I + \sum_{j=1}^{N} X_j \varepsilon_j$$

$$= \sum_{j=1}^{N} X_j a_j + Y R_I + \sum_{j=1}^{N} X_j \varepsilon_j$$

where we have inserted $Y = \Sigma X j b j$.

The expected return and portfolio variance can, on the basis of the hypotheses in the model, be written

$$E_P = \sum_{j=1}^{N} X_j a_j + Y E_I$$

$$\sigma_P^2 = \sum_{j=1}^{N} X_j^2 \sigma_{\varepsilon_j}^2 + Y^2 \sigma_I^2$$

Note 1

The variance of the portfolio can be written as a matrix using a quadratic form:

$$\sigma_P^2 = (X_1 \quad \cdots \quad X_N \quad Y) \begin{pmatrix} \sigma_{\varepsilon_1}^2 & & & \cdot \\ & \ddots & & \\ & & \sigma_{\varepsilon_N}^2 & \\ \cdot & & & \sigma_I^2 \end{pmatrix} \begin{pmatrix} X_1 \\ \vdots \\ X_N \\ Y \end{pmatrix}$$

Because of the structure of this matrix, the simple index model is also known as a *diagonal model*.

However, contrary to the impression the term may give, the simplification is not excessive. It is not assumed that the returns from the various securities will not be correlated, as

$$\sigma_{ij} = \text{cov}(a_i + b_i R_I + \varepsilon_i, a_j + b_j R_I + \varepsilon_j)$$

$$= b_i b_j \sigma_I^2$$

Note 2

In practice, the a_j and b_j coefficients for the various regressions are estimated using the least squares method: $\hat{a}_j$ and $\hat{b}_j$. The residuals are estimated using the relation

$$\hat{\varepsilon}_{jt} = R_{jt} - (\hat{a}_j + \hat{b}_j R_{It})$$

On the basis of these estimations, the residual variances will be determined using their ergodic estimator.

3.2.4.2 Simple index model

We therefore have to resolve the following problem: for the different values of λ between 0 and $+\infty$, minimise the following expression with respect to the proportions $X_1, \ldots, X_N$ and the variable Y:

$$\sigma_P^2 - \lambda E_P = \sum_{j=1}^{N} X_j^2 \sigma_{\varepsilon_j}^2 + Y^2 \sigma_I^2 - \lambda \cdot \left(\sum_{j=1}^{N} X_j a_j + Y E_I \right)$$

with the restrictions

$$\begin{cases} \displaystyle\sum_{j=1}^{N} X_j b_j = Y \\ \displaystyle\sum_{j=1}^{N} X_j = 1 \end{cases}$$

The Lagrangian function for the problem is written as:

$$L(X_1, \ldots, X_N, Y; m_1, m_2)$$
$$= \sum_{j=1}^{N} X_j^2 \sigma_{\varepsilon_j}^2 + Y^2 \sigma_I^2 - \lambda \cdot \left(\sum_{j=1}^{N} X_j a_j + Y E_I \right)$$
$$+ m_1 \cdot \left(\sum_{j=1}^{N} X_j b_j - Y \right) + m_2 \cdot \left(\sum_{j=1}^{N} X_j - 1 \right)$$

Calculation of the partial derivatives of this lagrangian function leads to the equality $MX^* = \lambda E^* + F$, where we have:

$$M = \begin{pmatrix} 2\sigma_{\varepsilon_1}^2 & & \cdot & \cdot & b_1 & 1 \\ & \ddots & & \vdots & \vdots & \vdots \\ \cdot & & 2\sigma_{\varepsilon_N}^2 & \cdot & b_N & 1 \\ \cdot & \cdots & \cdot & 2\sigma_I^2 & -1 & \cdot \\ b_1 & \cdots & b_N & -1 & \cdot & \cdot \\ 1 & \cdots & 1 & \cdot & \cdot & \cdot \end{pmatrix} \qquad X^* = \begin{pmatrix} X_1 \\ \vdots \\ X_N \\ Y \\ m_1 \\ m_2 \end{pmatrix}$$

$$E^* = \begin{pmatrix} a_1 \\ \vdots \\ a_N \\ E_I \\ \cdot \\ \cdot \end{pmatrix} \qquad F = \begin{pmatrix} \cdot \\ \vdots \\ \cdot \\ \cdot \\ \cdot \\ 1 \end{pmatrix}$$

The solution for this system is written as: $X^* = \lambda(M^{-1}E^*) + (M^{-1}F)$.

Example

Let us take the same data as those used in the first formulation, namely:[32]

$$
\begin{array}{lll}
E_1 = 0.05 & E_2 = 0.08 & E_3 = 0.10 \\
\sigma_1 = 0.10 & \sigma_2 = 0.12 & \sigma_3 = 0.15 \\
\rho_{12} = 0.3 & \rho_{13} = 0.1 & \rho_{23} = 0.4
\end{array}
$$

Let us then suppose that the regression relations and the estimated residual variances are given by:

$$
\begin{array}{ll}
R_1 = 0.014 + 0.60R_I & (\sigma_{\varepsilon_1}^2 = 0.0060) \\
R_2 = -0.020 + 1.08R_I & (\sigma_{\varepsilon_2}^2 = 0.0040) \\
R_3 = 0.200 + 1.32R_I & (\sigma_{\varepsilon_3}^2 = 0.0012)
\end{array}
$$

Let us also suppose that the expected return and index variance represent respectively $E_I = 0.04$ and $\sigma_I^2 = 0.0045$.

These data allow us to write:

$$
M = \begin{pmatrix}
0.0120 & . & . & . & 0.60 & 1 \\
. & 0.0080 & . & . & 1.08 & 1 \\
. & . & 0.0024 & . & 1.32 & 1 \\
. & . & . & 0.0090 & -1 & . \\
0.60 & 1.08 & 1.32 & -1 & . & . \\
1 & 1 & 1 & . & . & .
\end{pmatrix}
$$

$$
E^* = \begin{pmatrix} 0.014 \\ -0.020 \\ 0.200 \\ 0.040 \\ . \\ . \end{pmatrix}
\qquad
F = \begin{pmatrix} . \\ . \\ . \\ . \\ . \\ 1 \end{pmatrix}
$$

We can therefore calculate:

$$
M^{-1}E^* = \begin{pmatrix} -7.46 \\ -18.32 \\ 25.79 \\ 9.77 \\ 0.05 \\ 0.07 \end{pmatrix}
\qquad
M^{-1}F = \begin{pmatrix} 0.513 \\ 0.295 \\ 0.192 \\ 0.880 \\ 0.008 \\ -0.011 \end{pmatrix}
$$

The portfolios for the different values of λ are shown in Table 3.6. The efficient frontier is represented in Figure 3.14.

We should point out that although the efficient frontier has the same appearance as in Markowitz's model, there is no need to compare the proportions here as the regression equations that have been relied upon are arbitrary and do not arise from an effective analysis of the relation between the returns on securities and the returns on the index.

---

[32] These values are clearly not necessary to determine the proportions using Sharpe's model (in addition, one reason for this was to avoid the need to calculate the variance–covariance matrix). We will use them here only to calculate the efficient frontier.

Table 3.6   Solution for Sharpe's simple index model

λ	X_1	X_2	X_3	E_P	σP
0.100	−0.2332	−1.5375	2.7706	0.1424	0.3829
0.095	−0.1958	−1.4458	2.6417	0.1387	0.3647
0.090	−0.1585	−1.3542	2.5127	0.1350	0.3465
0.085	−0.1212	−1.2626	2.3838	0.1313	0.3284
0.080	−0.0839	−1.1710	2.2548	0.1276	0.3104
0.075	−0.0465	−1.0793	2.1259	0.1239	0.2924
0.070	−0.0092	−0.9877	1.9969	0.1202	0.2746
0.065	0.0281	−0.8961	1.8680	0.1165	0.2568
0.060	0.0654	−0.8045	1.7390	0.1128	0.2392
0.055	0.1028	−0.7129	1.6101	0.1091	0.2218
0.050	0.1401	−0.6212	1.4812	0.1054	0.2046
0.045	0.1774	−0.5296	1.3522	0.1017	0.1877
0.040	0.2147	−0.4380	1.2233	0.0980	0.1711
0.035	0.2521	−0.3464	1.0943	0.0943	0.1551
0.030	0.2894	−0.2547	0.9654	0.0906	0.1397
0.025	0.3267	−0.1631	0.8364	0.0869	0.1252
0.020	0.3640	−0.0715	0.7075	0.0832	0.1119
0.015	0.4014	0.0201	0.5785	0.0795	0.1003
0.010	0.4387	0.1118	0.4496	0.0758	0.0912
0.005	0.4760	0.2034	0.3206	0.0721	0.0853
0.000	0.5133	0.2950	0.1917	0.0684	0.0832

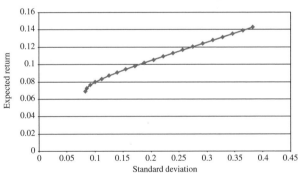

Figure 3.14   Efficient frontier for Sharpe's simple index model

Note 1

The saving in data required, compared to Markowitz's model, is considerable: in the last model the expected returns, variances and covariances (two by two) corresponds to $N + N + \dfrac{N(N-1)}{2} = \dfrac{N(N+3)}{2}$, while in the simple index model we need only the regression coefficients and residual variances as well as the expected return and the variance in the index, namely: $2N + N + 2 = 3N + 2$.

For example, on a market on which there is a choice between 100 securities, the number of items of information required is 5150 in the first case and just 302 in the second.

Note 2

If, in addition to the restrictions envisaged above, the inequality restrictions $B_j^- \leq X_j \leq B_j^+$ $j = 1, \ldots, N$ are imposed, the simple model index can still be used by applying the same principles as for Markowitz's model (alteration of matrix elements according to the 'down', 'in' and 'up' status of the various securities, calculation of critical λ and corner portfolios).

3.2.4.3 Multi-index model

One criticism that can be made of the simple index model is that the behaviour of every security is made according to just one index. Probably a more consistent way of proceeding is to divide all the market securities into sectors and express the return on each security in the same sector as a first-degree function of the return on a sectorial index.

The general method for writing this model is heavy and complex. We will be showing it in relation to two sectors, the first corresponding to securities $j = 1, \ldots, N_1$ and the second to $j = N_1 + 1, \ldots, N_1 + N_2 = N$. The sectorial indices will be noted as I_1 and I_2 respectively.

The regression equations take the form:

$$\begin{cases} R_{jt} = a_j + b_j R_{I_1 t} + \varepsilon_{jt} & j = 1, \ldots, N_1 \\ R_{jt} = a_j + b_j R_{I_2 t} + \varepsilon_{jt} & j = N_1 + 1, \ldots, N_1 + N_2 = N \end{cases}$$

The return on the portfolio, and its expected return and variance, are shown as

$$R_P = \sum_{j=1}^{N} X_j R_j$$

$$= \sum_{j=1}^{N} X_j a_j + Y_1 R_{I_1} + Y_2 R_{I_2} + \sum_{j=1}^{N} X_j \varepsilon_j$$

$$E_P = \sum_{j=1}^{N} X_j a_j + Y_1 E_{I_1} + Y_2 E_{I_2}$$

$$\sigma_P^2 = \sum_{j=1}^{N} X_j^2 \sigma_{\varepsilon_j}^2 + Y_1^2 \sigma_{I_1}^2 + Y_2^2 \sigma_{I_2}^2 + 2 Y_1 Y_2 \sigma_{I_1 I_2}$$

$$= (X_1 \quad \cdots \quad X_N \quad Y_1 \quad Y_2) \begin{pmatrix} \sigma_{\varepsilon_1}^2 & & & & \cdot \\ & \ddots & & & \\ & & \sigma_{\varepsilon_N}^2 & & \\ & & & \sigma_{I_1}^2 & \sigma_{I_1 I_2} \\ \cdot & & & \sigma_{I_2 I_1} & \sigma_{I_2}^2 \end{pmatrix} \begin{pmatrix} X_1 \\ \vdots \\ X_N \\ Y_1 \\ Y_2 \end{pmatrix}$$

Here, we have introduced the parameters

$$\begin{cases} Y_1 = \sum_{j=1}^{N_1} X_j b_j \\ Y_2 = \sum_{j=N_1+1}^{N} X_j b_j \end{cases}$$

The usual reasoning leads once again to the relation: $MX^* = \lambda E^* + F$. This resolves into $X^* = \lambda(M^{-1}E^*) + (M^{-1}F)$, with the notations:

$$M = \begin{pmatrix}
2\sigma^2_{\varepsilon_1} & & & & & & & & & b_1 & . & 1 \\
& \ddots & & & & & & & & \vdots & \vdots & \vdots \\
& & 2\sigma^2_{\varepsilon_{N_1}} & & & & & & . & b_{N_1} & . & 1 \\
& & & 2\sigma^2_{\varepsilon_{N_1+1}} & & & & & . & b_{N_1+1} & 1 \\
& & & & \ddots & & & & \vdots & \vdots & \vdots & \vdots \\
& & & & & 2\sigma^2_{\varepsilon_N} & . & . & . & b_N & 1 \\
. & \cdots & . & . & \cdots & . & 2\sigma^2_{I_1} & 2\sigma_{I_1 I_2} & -1 & . & . \\
. & \cdots & . & . & \cdots & . & 2\sigma_{I_2 I_1} & 2\sigma^2_{I_2} & . & -1 & . \\
b_1 & \cdots & b_{N_1} & . & \cdots & . & -1 & . & . & . & . \\
. & \cdots & . & b_{N_1+1} & \cdots & b_N & . & -1 & . & . & . \\
1 & \cdots & 1 & 1 & \cdots & 1 & . & . & . & . & .
\end{pmatrix}$$

$$X^* = \begin{pmatrix} X_1 \\ \vdots \\ X_N \\ Y_1 \\ Y_2 \\ m_1 \\ m_2 \\ m_3 \end{pmatrix} \qquad E^* = \begin{pmatrix} a_1 \\ \vdots \\ a_N \\ E_{I_1} \\ E_{I_2} \\ . \\ . \\ . \end{pmatrix} \qquad F = \begin{pmatrix} . \\ \vdots \\ . \\ . \\ . \\ . \\ . \\ 1 \end{pmatrix}$$

It should be noted that compared to the simple index model, the two-index model requires only three additional items of information: expected return, variance and covariance for the second index.

3.2.5   Model with risk-free security

3.2.5.1   Modelling and resolution

Let us now examine the case in which the portfolio consists of a certain number N of equities (of returns $R_1, \ldots, R_N$) in proportions $X_1, \ldots, X_N$ and a risk-free security with a return of R_F that is in proportion X_{N+1} with $X_1 + \ldots + X_N + X_{N+1} = 1$.

This risk-free security is seen as a hypothesis formulated as follows. The investor has the possibility of investing or loaning ($X_{N+1} > 0$) or of borrowing ($X_{N+1} < 0$) funds at the same rate R_F.

Alongside the returns on equities, which are the random variables that we looked at in previous paragraphs (with their expected returns E_j and their variance–covariance matrix V), the return on the risk-free security is a degenerated random variable:

$$\begin{cases} E_{N+1} = R_F \\ \sigma^2_{N+1} = 0 \\ \sigma_{j,N+1} = 0 \quad (j = 1, \ldots, N) \end{cases}$$

Note

We will now study the effect of the presence of a risk-free security in the portfolio on the basis of Markowitz's model without inequality restriction. We can easily adapt the presentation to cover Sharpe's model, or take account of the inequality restrictions. The result in relation to the shape of the efficiency curve (see below) is valid in all cases and only one presentation is necessary.

The return on the portfolio is written as $R_P = X_1 R_1 + \ldots + X_N R_N + X_{N+1} R_F$. This allows the expected return and variance to be calculated:

$$\begin{cases} E_P = \sum_{j=1}^{N} X_j E_j + X_{N+1} R_F \\ \sigma_P^2 = \sum_{i=1}^{N} \sum_{j=1}^{N} X_i X_j \sigma_{ij} \end{cases}$$

We must therefore solve the problem, for the different values of λ between 0 and $+\infty$, of minimisation with respect to the proportions $X_1, \ldots, X_N$ and X_{N+1} of the expression $\sigma_P^2 - \lambda E_P$, under the restriction:

$$\sum_{j=1}^{N} X_j + X_{N+1} = 1$$

The Lagrangian function for this problem can be written as

$$L(X_1, \ldots, X_N, X_{N+1}; m) = \sum_{i=1}^{N} \sum_{j=1}^{N} X_i X_j \sigma_{ij} - \lambda \cdot \left(\sum_{j=1}^{N} X_j E_j + X_{N+1} R_F \right)$$
$$+ m \cdot \left(\sum_{j=1}^{N} X_j + X_{N+1} - 1 \right)$$

Calculation of its partial derivatives leads to the system of equations $MX^* = \lambda E^* + F$, where we have:

$$M = \begin{pmatrix} 2\sigma_1^2 & 2\sigma_{12} & \cdots & 2\sigma_{1N} & . & 1 \\ 2\sigma_{21} & 2\sigma_2^2 & \cdots & 2\sigma_{2N} & . & 1 \\ \vdots & \vdots & \ddots & \vdots & \vdots & \vdots \\ 2\sigma_{N1} & 2\sigma_{N2} & \cdots & 2\sigma_N^2 & . & 1 \\ . & . & \cdots & . & . & 1 \\ 1 & 1 & \cdots & 1 & 1 & . \end{pmatrix} \qquad X^* = \begin{pmatrix} X_1 \\ X_2 \\ \vdots \\ X_N \\ X_{N+1} \\ m \end{pmatrix}$$

$$E^* = \begin{pmatrix} E_1 \\ E_2 \\ \vdots \\ E_N \\ R_F \\ . \end{pmatrix} \qquad F = \begin{pmatrix} . \\ . \\ . \\ . \\ . \\ 1 \end{pmatrix}$$

The solution for this system is of course written as: $X^* = \lambda(M^{-1}E^*) + (M^{-1}F)$.

Example

Let us take the same data as those used in the first formulation, namely:

$$
\begin{array}{lll}
E_1 = 0.05 & E_2 = 0.08 & E_3 = 0.10 \\
\sigma_1 = 0.10 & \sigma_2 = 0.12 & \sigma_3 = 0.15 \\
\rho_{12} = 0.3 & \rho_{13} = 0.1 & \rho_{23} = 0.4
\end{array}
$$

Let us suppose that the risk-free interest rate is $R_F = 0.03$.
We therefore have:

$$
M = \begin{pmatrix}
0.0200 & 0.0072 & 0.0030 & . & 1 \\
0.0072 & 0.0288 & 0.0144 & . & 1 \\
0.0030 & 0.0144 & 0.0450 & . & 1 \\
. & . & . & . & 1 \\
1 & 1 & 1 & 1 & .
\end{pmatrix}
\quad
E^* = \begin{pmatrix}
0.05 \\ 0.08 \\ 0.10 \\ 0.03 \\ .
\end{pmatrix}
\quad
F = \begin{pmatrix}
. \\ . \\ . \\ . \\ 1
\end{pmatrix}
$$

and therefore:

$$
M^{-1}E^* = \begin{pmatrix}
0.452 \\ 1.024 \\ 1.198 \\ -2.674 \\ 0.030
\end{pmatrix}
\quad
M^{-1}F = \begin{pmatrix}
. \\ . \\ . \\ 1 \\ .
\end{pmatrix}
$$

This leads to the portfolios shown in Table 3.7.

Table 3.7 Solution for model with risk-free security

λ	X_1	X_2	X_3	$X(R_F)$	E_P	σP
2.0	0.9031	2.0488	2.3953	−4.3472	0.3182	0.5368
1.9	0.8580	1.9464	2.2755	−4.0799	0.3038	0.5100
1.8	0.8128	1.8439	2.1558	−3.8125	0.2894	0.4831
1.7	0.7677	1.7415	2.0360	−3.5451	0.2749	0.4563
1.6	0.7225	1.6390	1.9162	−3.2778	0.2605	0.4295
1.5	0.6774	1.5366	1.7965	−3.0104	0.2461	0.4026
1.4	0.6322	1.4342	1.6767	−2.7431	0.2317	0.3758
1.3	0.5870	1.3317	1.5569	−2.4757	0.2173	0.3489
1.2	0.5419	1.2293	1.4372	−2.2083	0.2029	0.3221
1.1	0.4967	1.1268	1.3174	−1.9410	0.1885	0.2952
1.0	0.4516	1.0244	1.1976	−1.6736	0.1741	0.2684
0.9	0.4064	0.9220	1.0779	−1.4063	0.1597	0.2416
0.8	0.3613	0.8195	0.9581	−1.1389	0.1453	0.2147
0.7	0.3161	0.7171	0.8384	−0.8715	0.1309	0.1879
0.6	0.2709	0.6146	0.7186	−0.6042	0.1165	0.1610
0.5	0.2258	0.5122	0.5988	−0.3368	0.1020	0.1342
0.4	0.1806	0.4098	0.4791	−0.0694	0.0876	0.1074
0.3	0.1355	0.3073	0.3593	0.1979	0.0732	0.0805
0.2	0.0903	0.2049	0.2395	0.4653	0.0588	0.0537
0.1	0.0452	0.1024	0.1198	0.7326	0.0444	0.0268
0.0	0.0000	0.0000	0.0000	1.0000	0.0300	0.0000

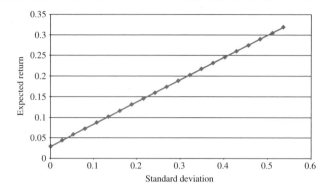

Figure 3.15   Efficient frontier for model with risk-free security

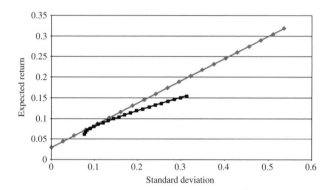

Figure 3.16   Comparison of efficient frontiers with and without risk-free security

The efficient frontier is shown in Figure 3.15.

If the efficient frontier obtained above and the frontier obtained using Markowitz's model (without risk-free security) are superimposed, Figure 3.16 is obtained.

3.2.5.2   Efficient frontier

The graphic phenomenon that appears in the previous example is general. In fact, a portfolio consisting of N securities and the risk-free security can be considered to consist of the risk-free security in the proportion $X = X_{N+1}$ and a portfolio of equities with a proportion of $1 - X$, and the return R (of parameters E and σ). The return of the risk-free security has a zero variance and is not correlated with the equity portfolio. The parameters for the portfolio are given by

$$\begin{cases} E_P = X R_F + (1 - X)E \\ \sigma_P^2 = (1 - X)^2 \sigma^2 \end{cases}$$

which gives, after X has been eliminated:

$$E_P = R_F \pm \sigma_P \left(\frac{E - R_F}{\sigma} \right)$$

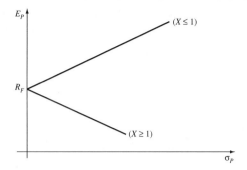

Figure 3.17   Portfolios with risk-free security

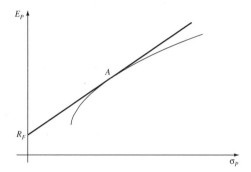

Figure 3.18   Efficient frontier with risk-free security present

following that $X \leq 1$ or $X \geq 1$. The equations for these straight lines show that the portfolios in question are located on two semi-straight lines with the same slope, with the opposite sign (see Figure 3.17).

The lower semi-straight line $(X \geq 1)$ corresponds to a situation in which the portfolio of equities is sold at a short price in order to invest more in the risk-free security. From now on, we will be interested in the upper part.

If the efficient frontier consisting only of equities is known, the optimum semi-straight line, which maximises E_P for a given σ_P, is the line located the highest, that is, the tangent on the efficient frontier of the equities (see Figure 3.18).

The portfolios located between the vertical axis and the contact point A are characterised by $0 \leq X \leq 1$, and those beyond A are such that $X \leq 0$ (borrowing at rate R_F to invest further in contact portfolio A).

3.2.6   The Elton, Gruber and Padberg method of portfolio management

The Elton, Gruber and Padberg or EGP method[33] was developed[34] to supply a quick and coherent solution to the problem of optimising portfolios. Instead of determining

---

[33] Or more precisely, methods; in fact, various models have been developed around a general idea according to the hypotheses laid down.

[34] Elton E., Gruber M. and Padberg M., Simple criteria for optimal portfolio selection, *Journal of Finance*, Vol. XI, No. 5, 1976, pp. 1341–57.

the efficient frontier as in Markowitz's or Sharpe's models, this new technique simply determines the portfolio that corresponds to the contact point of the tangent with the efficient frontier, produced by the point $(0, R_F)$.

3.2.6.1 Hypotheses

The method now being examined assumes that:

• The mean–variance approach is relevant, which will allow a certain number of results from Markowitz's theory to be used.
• There is a risk-free asset with a return indicated as R_F.

Alongside these general hypotheses, Elton, Gruber and Padberg have developed resolution algorithms in two specific cases:

• Constant correlations. In this first model, it is assumed that the correlation coefficients for the returns on the various securities are all equal: $\rho_{ij} = \rho \ \forall i, j$.
• Sharpe's simple index model can be used.

The first of these two simplifications is quite harsh and as such not greatly realistic, and we will instead concentrate on the second case. Remember that it is based on the following two conditions.

1. The returns on the various securities are expressed as first-degree functions of the return on a market-representative index: $R_{jt} = a_j + b_j R_{It} = \varepsilon_{jt}. \ j = 1, \ldots, N$.
   It is also assumed that the residuals verify the classic hypotheses of linear regression, including the hypothesis that the residuals have zero-expected return and are not correlated with the explanatory variable R_{it}.
2. The residuals of the regressions relative to the various securities are not correlated: cov $(\varepsilon_{it}, \varepsilon_{jt}) = 0$ for all the different i and j values.

3.2.6.2 Resolution of case in which short sales are authorised

First of all, we will carry out a detailed analysis of a case in which the proportions are not subject to inequality restrictions. Here, the reasoning is more straightforward[35] than in cases where short sales are prohibited. Nevertheless, as will be seen (but without demonstration), applying the algorithm is scarcely any more complex in the second case.

If one considers a portfolio P consisting solely of equities in proportions $X_1, X_2, \ldots, X_N$, the full range of portfolios consisting partly of P and partly of risk-free securities

---

Elton E., Gruber M. and Padberg M., Optimal portfolios from simple ranking devices, *Journal of Portfolio Management*, Vol. 4, No. 3, 1978, pp. 15–19.

Elton E., Gruber M. and Padberg M., Simple criteria for optimal portfolio selection; tracing out the efficient frontier, *Journal of Finance*, Vol. XIII No. 1, 1978, pp. 296–302.

Elton E., Gruber M. and Padberg M., Simple criteria for optimal portfolio selection with upper bounds, *Operation Research*, 1978.

Readers are also advised to read Elton E. and Gruber M., *Modern Portfolio Theory and Investment Analysis*, John Wiley & Sons, Inc, 1991.

[35] In addition, it starts in the same way as the demonstration of the CAPM equation (see §3.3.1).

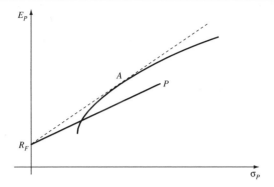

Figure 3.19 EGP method

R_F shall make up the straight line linking the points $(0, R_F)$ and (σ_P, E_P) as illustrated in Figure 3.19.

The slope of the straight line in question is given by $\Psi_P = \dfrac{E_P - R_F}{\sigma_P}$, which may be interpreted as a risk premium, as will be seen in Section 3.3.1.

According to the reasoning set out in the previous paragraph, the ideal portfolio P corresponds to the contact point A of the tangent to the efficient frontier coming from the point $(0, R_F)$ for which the slope is the maximum. We are therefore looking for proportions that maximise the slope Ψ_P or, which amounts to the same thing, maximise Ψ_P^2. Such as:

$$\begin{cases} E_P - R_F = \displaystyle\sum_{j=1}^{N} X_j E_j - \left(\sum_{j=1}^{N} X_j\right) R_F = \sum_{j=1}^{N} X_j(E_j - R_F) \\[4mm] \sigma_P^2 = \displaystyle\sum_{i=1}^{N}\sum_{j=1}^{N} X_i X_j \sigma_{ij} \end{cases}$$

the derivative of:

$$\Psi_P^2 = \frac{(E_P - R_F)^2}{\sigma_P^2} = \frac{\left(\displaystyle\sum_{j=1}^{N} X_j(E_j - R_F)\right)^2}{\displaystyle\sum_{i=1}^{N}\sum_{j=1}^{N} X_i X_j \sigma_{ij}}$$

with respect to X_k is given by:

$$(\Psi_P^2)_{X_k}' = \frac{2\left(\displaystyle\sum_{j=1}^{N} X_j(E_j - R_F)\right)(E_k - R_F)\cdot\sigma_P^2 - \left(\displaystyle\sum_{j=1}^{N} X_j(E_j - R_F)\right)^2 \cdot 2\displaystyle\sum_{j=1}^{N} X_j \sigma_{kj}}{\sigma_P^4}$$

$$= \frac{2(E_P - R_F)(E_k - R_F)\sigma_P^2 - 2(E_P - R_F)^2 \displaystyle\sum_{j=1}^{N} X_j \sigma_{kj}}{\sigma_P^4}$$

$$= \frac{2(E_P - R_F)}{\sigma_P^2} \cdot \left((E_k - R_F) - \gamma \cdot \sum_{j=1}^{N} X_j \sigma_{kj} \right)$$

In which we have provisionally $\gamma = (E_p - R_F)/\sigma_P^2$.

This derivative will be zero if:

$$E_k - R_F = \gamma \cdot \sum_{j=1}^{N} X_j \sigma_{kj}$$

By introducing $Z_j = \gamma \cdot X_j$ ($j = 1, \ldots, N$), the system to be resolved with respect to $Z_1, \ldots, Z_N$ is therefore

$$E_k - R_F = \sum_{j=1}^{N} Z_j \sigma_{kj} \qquad k = 1, \ldots, N$$

Before proceeding with the resolution, note that finding the Z_k quantities allows the X_k quantities to be found, as

$$X_k = \frac{Z_k}{\gamma} = \frac{Z_k}{\gamma \cdot \displaystyle\sum_{j=1}^{N} X_j} = \frac{Z_k}{\displaystyle\sum_{j=1}^{N} Z_j}$$

The hypotheses from Sharpe's model allow the following to be written:

$$\sigma_{kj} = \text{cov}(a_k + b_k R_I + \varepsilon_k, a_j + b_j R_I + \varepsilon_j)$$
$$= b_k b_j \sigma_I^2 + \begin{cases} \sigma_{\varepsilon_k}^2 & \text{si } j = k \\ 0 & \text{si } j \neq k \end{cases}$$

The kth equation in the system can then be written:

$$E_k - R_F = b_k \left(\sum_{j=1}^{N} Z_j b_j \right) \sigma_I^2 + Z_k \sigma_{\varepsilon_k}^2$$

or also, by resolving with respect to Z_k:

$$Z_k = \frac{1}{\sigma_{\varepsilon_k}^2} \left\{ (E_k - R_F) - b_k \left(\sum_{j=1}^{N} Z_j b_j \right) \sigma_I^2 \right\}$$
$$= \frac{b_k}{\sigma_{\varepsilon_k}^2} \left\{ \theta_k - \left(\sum_{j=1}^{N} Z_j b_j \right) \sigma_I^2 \right\}$$

where we have:

$$\theta_k = \frac{E_k - R_F}{b_k}$$

All that now remains is to determine the sum between the brackets. On the basis of the last result, we find:

$$\sum_{k=1}^{N} Z_k b_k = \sum_{k=1}^{N} \frac{b_k^2}{\sigma_{\varepsilon k}^2} \left\{ \theta_k - \left(\sum_{j=1}^{N} Z_j b_j \right) \sigma_I^2 \right\}$$

$$= \sum_{k=1}^{N} \frac{b_k^2}{\sigma_{\varepsilon k}^2} \theta_k - \left(\sum_{k=1}^{N} \frac{b_k^2}{\sigma_{\varepsilon k}^2} \right) \left(\sum_{j=1}^{N} Z_j b_j \right) \sigma_I^2$$

the resolution of which gives

$$\sum_{j=1}^{N} Z_j b_j = \frac{\displaystyle\sum_{k=1}^{N} \frac{b_k^2}{\sigma_{\varepsilon k}^2} \theta_k}{1 + \left(\displaystyle\sum_{k=1}^{N} \frac{b_k^2}{\sigma_{\varepsilon k}^2} \right) \sigma_I^2}$$

By introducing the new notation

$$\phi = \left(\sum_{j=1}^{N} Z_j b_j \right) \cdot \sigma_I^2 = \frac{\displaystyle\sum_{k=1}^{N} \frac{b_k^2}{\sigma_{\varepsilon k}^2} \theta_k}{1 + \left(\displaystyle\sum_{k=1}^{N} \frac{b_k^2}{\sigma_{\varepsilon k}^2} \right) \sigma_I^2} \cdot \sigma_I^2$$

and by substituting the sum just calculated within the expression of Z_k, we find

$$Z_k = \frac{b_k}{\sigma_{\varepsilon k}^2} (\theta_k - \phi) \quad k = 1, \ldots, N$$

Example

Let us take the same data as those used in the simple index model (only essential data mentioned here).

$$E_1 = 0.05 \qquad E_2 = 0.08 \qquad E_3 = 0.10$$

with the regression relations and the estimated residual variances:

$$R_1 = 0.014 + 0.60 R_I \qquad (\sigma_{\varepsilon 1}^2 = 0.0060)$$
$$R_2 = -0.020 + 1.08 R_I \qquad (\sigma_{\varepsilon 2}^2 = 0.0040)$$
$$R_3 = 0.200 + 1.32 R_I \qquad (\sigma_{\varepsilon 3}^2 = 0.0012)$$

Assume that the variance of the index is equal to $\sigma_I^2 = 0.0045$. Finally, assume also that as for the model with the risk-free security, this last value is $R_F = 0.03$. These data allow calculation of:

$$\theta_1 = 0.0333 \qquad \theta_2 = 0.0463 \qquad \theta_3 = 0.0530.$$

Therefore, $\phi = 0.0457$. The Z_k values are deduced:

$$Z_1 = -1.2327 \qquad Z_2 = 0.1717 \qquad Z_3 = 8.1068$$

The proportions of the optimum portfolio are therefore deduced:

$$X_1 = -0.1750 \qquad X_2 = 0.0244 \qquad X_3 = 1.1506$$

3.2.6.3 Resolution of case in which short sales are prohibited

Let us now examine cases in which restrictions are introduced. These are less general than those envisaged in Markowitz's model, and are written simply as $0 \le X_j \le 1 (j = 1, \ldots, N)$.

The method, which we are showing here without supporting calculations, is very similar to that used for cases in which short sales are authorised. As above, the following are calculated:

$$\theta_k = \frac{E_k - R_F}{b_k} \qquad k = 1, \ldots, N$$

The securities are then sorted in decreasing order of θ_k and this order is preserved until the end of the algorithm. Instead of having just one parameter ϕ, one parameter is calculated for each security:

$$\phi_k = \frac{\displaystyle\sum_{j=1}^{k} \frac{b_j^2}{\sigma_{\varepsilon_j}^2} \theta_j}{1 + \left(\displaystyle\sum_{j=1}^{k} \frac{b_j^2}{\sigma_{\varepsilon_j}^2}\right) \sigma_I^2} \cdot \sigma_I^2 \qquad k = 1, \ldots, N$$

It can be shown that the sequence of ϕ_k numbers first increases, then passes through a maximum and finally ends with a decreasing phase. The value K of the k index corresponding to the maximum ϕ_k, is noted. The ϕ_K number is named the 'cut-off rate' and it can be shown that the calculation of the Z_k values for the same relation as before (replacing ϕ by ϕ_K) produces positive values for $k = 1, \ldots, K$ and negative values for $k = K + 1, \ldots, N$. Only the first K securities are included in the portfolio. The calculations to be made are therefore:

$$Z_k = \frac{b_k}{\sigma_{\varepsilon_k}^2}(\theta_k - \phi_K) \qquad k = 1, \ldots, K$$

This, for the proportions of integrated K securities, gives:

$$X_k = \frac{Z_k}{\displaystyle\sum_{j=1}^{K} Z_j} \qquad k = 1, \ldots, K$$

Example

Let us take the same data as above. Of course, we still have:

$$\theta_1 = 0.0333 \qquad \theta_2 = 0.0463 \qquad \theta_3 = 0.0530$$

This allows the securities to be classified in the order (3), (2), (1). We will provisionally renumber the securities in this new order, thus producing:

$$\phi_1 = 0.04599 \qquad \phi_2 = 0.04604 \qquad \phi_3 = 0.04566$$

This shows that $K = 2$ and the cut-off rate is $\phi_2 = 0.04604$. The Z_k values will therefore be deduced:

$$Z_1 = 7.6929 \qquad Z_2 = 0.0701$$

The proportions of the optimum portfolio are therefore deduced:

$$X_1 = 0.9910 \qquad X_2 = 0.0090$$

If one then reverts to the initial order, the securities to be included in the portfolio shall therefore be securities (2) and (3) with the following relative proportions:

$$X_2 = 0.0090 \qquad X_3 = 0.9910$$

3.2.7 Utility theory and optimal portfolio selection

Once the efficient frontier has been determined, the question that faces the investor is that of choosing from all the efficient portfolios the one that best suits him. The portfolio chosen will differ from one investor to another, and the choice made will depend on his attitude and behaviour towards the risk. The efficient frontier, in fact, contains as many prudent portfolios (low expected return and risk, located at the left end of the curve) as more risky portfolios (higher expected return and risk, located towards the right end).

3.2.7.1 Utility function

The concept of *utility function* can be introduced generally[36] to represent from an individual person's viewpoint the utility and interest that he finds in a project, investment, strategy etc., the elements in question presenting a certain level of risk. The numerical values of this risk function are of little importance, as it is essentially used to compare projects, investments, strategies etc. Here, we will present the theory of utility in the context of its application to a return (which, remember, is random) of, for example, a portfolio of equities.

Because of the presence of the risk, it is evident that we cannot be content with taking $E(R)$ as utility of return $U(R)$. This was clearly shown by D. Bernoulli in 1732 through the 'St Petersburg paradox'. The question is: How much would you be prepared to stake to participate in the next game? I toss a coin a number of times and I give you two \$ if tails comes up on the first throw, four \$ if tails comes up for the first time on the second throw, eight \$ if tails appears for the first time on the third throw, and so on. I will therefore give you 2^n \$ if tails comes up for the first time on the nth throw. Most people would lay down a small sum (at least two \$), but would be reluctant to invest more because of the increased risk in the game. A player who put down 20 \$ would have a

---

[36] An excellent presentation on the general concepts of behaviour in the face of risk (not necessarily financial) and the concept of 'utility' is found in Eeckhoudt L. and Gollier C., *Risk*, Harvester Wheatsheaf, 1995.

probability of losing of $1/2 + 1/4 + 1/8 + 1/16 = 15/16 = 0.9375$, and would therefore only win on 6.25 stakes out of every 100. The average gain in the game, however, is

$$\sum_{n=1}^{\infty} 2^n \left(\frac{1}{2}\right)^n = 1 + 1 + 1 + \ldots = \infty$$

It is the aversion to the risk that justifies the decision of the player. The aim of the utility function is to represent this attitude.

In utility theory, one compares projects, investments, strategies etc. (in our case, returns) through a relation of *preference* (R_1 is preferable to $R_2 : R_1 > R_2$) and a relation of *indifference* (indifference between R_1 and $R_2 : R_1 \sim R_2$). The behaviour of the investor can be expressed if these two relations obey the following axioms:

- *(Comparability)*: The investor can always compare two returns. $\forall R_1, R_2$. We always have $R_1 > R_2, R_2 < R_1$, or $R_1 \sim R_2$.
- *(Reflexivity)*: $\forall R \ \ R \sim R$.
- *(Transitivity)*: $\forall R_1, R_2, R_3$, if $R_1 > R_2$ and $R_2 > R_3$, then $R_1 > R_3$.
- *(Continuity)*: $\forall R_1, R_2, R_3$, if $R_1 > R_2 > R_3$, there is a single $X \in [0; 1]$ such as $[X.R_1 + (1 - X).R_3] \sim R_2$.
- *(Independence)*: $\forall R_1, R_2, R_3$ and $\forall X \in [0; 1]$, if $R_1 > R_2$, then $[X.R_1 + (1 - X).R_3] > [X.R_2 + (1 - X).R_3]$.

Von Neumann and Morgenstern[37] have demonstrated a *theorem of expected utility*, which states that if the preferences of an investor obey the axioms set out above, there is a function U so that $\forall R_1, R_2, R_1 > R_2 \Leftrightarrow E[U(R_1)] > E[U(R_2)]$.

This utility function is clearly a growing function. We have noted that its numerical values are not essential as it is only used to make comparisons of returns. The theorem of expected utility allows this concept to be defined more accurately: if an investor's preferences are modelled by the utility function U, there will be the same system of preferences based on the function $aU + b$ with $a > 0$. In fact, if $R_1 > R_2$ is expressed as $E[U(R_1)] > E[U(R_2)]$, we have:

$$E[U^*(R_1)] = E[aU(R_1) + b]$$
$$= aE[U(R_1)] + b$$
$$> aE[U(R_2)] + b$$
$$= E[aU(R_2) + b]$$
$$= E[U^*(R_2)]$$

The utility function is an element that is intrinsically associated with each investor (and is also likely to evolve with time and depending on circumstances). It is not easy or indeed even very useful to know this function. If one wishes to estimate it approximately, one has to define a list of possible values $R_1 < R_2 < \ldots < R_n$ for the return, and then for $i = 2, \ldots, n - 1$, ask the investor what is the probability of it being indifferent to obtain

---

[37] Von Neumann J. and Morgenstern O., *Theory of Games and Economic Behaviour*, Princeton University Press, 1947.

a definite return R_i or play in a lottery that gives returns of R_1 and R_n with the respective probabilities $(1 - p_i)$ and p_i. If one chooses arbitrarily $U(R_1) = 0$ and $U(R_n) = 100$, then $U(R_i) = 100 \, p_i (i = 2, \ldots, n - 1)$.

3.2.7.2   Attitude towards risk

For most investors, an increase in return of 0.5 % would be of greater interest if the current return is 2 % than if it is 5 %. This type of attitude is called *risk aversion*. The opposite attitude is known as *taste for risk*, and the middle line is termed *risk neutrality*. How do these behaviour patterns show in relation to utility function?

Let us examine the case of aversion. Generally, if one wishes to state that the utility of return $U(R)$ must increase with R and give less weight to the same variations in return when the level of return is high, we will have: $R_1 < R_2 \Rightarrow U(R_1 + \Delta R) - U(R_1) > U(R_2 + \Delta R) - U(R_2)$.

This shows the decreasing nature of the *marginal utility*. In this case, the derivative of the utility function is a decreasing function and the second derivative is therefore negative; the utility function is concave.

The results obtained from these considerations are summarised in Table 3.8, and a representation of the utility function in the various cases is shown in Figure 3.20.

Let us now define this concept more precisely. We consider an investor who has a choice between a certain return totalling R on one hand and a lottery that gives him a random return that may have two values $(R - r)$ and $(R + r)$, each with a probability of 1/2. If he shows an aversion to risk, the utility of the certain return will exceed the expected utility of the return on the lottery:

$$U(R) > \tfrac{1}{2}[U(R - r) + U(R + r)]$$

This is shown in graphic form in Figure 3.21.

Table 3.8   Attitude to risk

	Marginal utility	U''	U
Risk aversion	Decreasing	< 0	Concave
Risk neutrality	Increasing	$= 0$	Linear
Taste for risk	Increasing	> 0	Convex

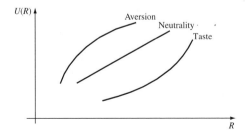

Figure 3.20   Utility function

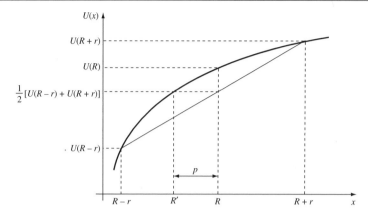

Figure 3.21   Aversion to risk

This figure shows R', the certain return, for which the utility is equal to the expected return on the lottery. The difference $p = R - R'$ represents the price that the investor is willing to pay to avoid having to participate in the lottery; this is known as the *risk premium*.

Taylor expansions for $U(R + r)$, $U(R - r)$ and $U(R') = U(R - p)$ readily lead to the relation:

$$p = -\frac{U''(R)}{U'(R)} \cdot \frac{r^2}{2}$$

The first factor in this expression is the *absolute risk aversion coefficient*:

$$\alpha(R) = -\frac{U''(R)}{U'(R)}$$

The two most frequently used examples of the utility function corresponding to the risk aversion are the exponential function and the quadratic function.

If $U(R) = a.e^{bR}$, with a and $b < 0$, we will have $\alpha(R) = -b$.

If $U(R) = aR^2 + bR + c$, with $a < 0$ and $b < 0$, we of course have to limit ourselves to values for R that do not exceed $-b/2a$ in order for the utility function to remain an increasing function. The absolute risk aversion coefficient is then given by:

$$\alpha(R) = \frac{1}{-\dfrac{b}{2a} - R}$$

When this last form can be accepted for the utility function, we have another justification for defining the distribution of returns by the two parameters of mean and variance alone, without adding a normality hypothesis (see Section 3.1.1). In this case, in fact, the expected utility of a return on a portfolio (the quantity that the investor wishes to optimise) is given as:

$$E[U(R_P)] = E[aR_P^2 + bR_P + c]$$
$$= aE(R_P^2) + bE(R_P) + c$$
$$= a(\sigma_P^2 + E_P^2) + bE_P + c$$

This quantity then depends on the first two moments only.

3.2.7.3 Selection of optimal portfolio

Let us now consider an investor who shows an aversion for risk and has to choose a portfolio from those on the efficient frontier.

We begin by constructing *indifference curves* in relation to its utility function, that is, the curves that correspond to the couples (expectation, standard deviation) for which the expected utility of return equals a given value (see Figure 3.22). These indifference curves are of close-fitting convex form, the utility increasing as the curve moves upwards and to the left.

By superimposing the indifference curves and the efficient frontier, it is easy to determine the portfolio P that corresponds to the maximum expected utility, as shown in Figure 3.23.

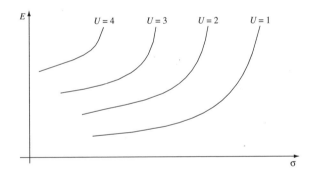

Figure 3.22   Indifference curves

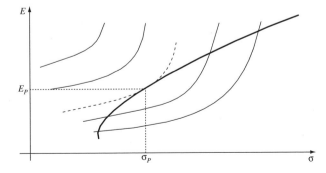

Figure 3.23   Selection of optimal portfolio

3.2.7.4 Other viewpoints

Alongside the efficient portfolio based on the investor preference system, shown through the utility function, other objectives or restrictions can be taken into consideration.

Let us examine, for example, the case of *deficit constraint*. As well as optimising the couple (E, σ), that is, determining the efficient frontier, and before selecting the portfolio (through the utility function), the return on the portfolio here must not be less than a fixed threshold[38] u except with a very low probability p, say: $\Pr[R_P \leq u] \leq p$.

If the hypothesis of normality of return is accepted, we have:

$$\Pr\left[\frac{R_P - E_P}{\sigma_P} \leq \frac{u - E_P}{\sigma_P}\right] \leq p$$

that is:

$$\frac{u - E_P}{\sigma_P} \leq z_p$$

Here, z_p is the p-quantile of the standard normal distribution ($z_p < 0$ as p is less than 1/2). The condition can thus be written as $E_P \geq u - z_p.\sigma_P$.

The portfolios that obey the deficit constraint are located above the straight line for the equation $E_P = u = z_p.\sigma_P$ (see Figure 3.24).

The portion of the efficient frontier delimited by this straight line of constraint is the range of portfolios from which the investor will make his selection.

If p is fixed, an increase of u (higher required return) will cause the straight line of constraint to move upwards. In the same way, if u is fixed, a reduction in p (more security with respect for restriction) will cause the straight line of constraint to move upwards while pivoting about the point $(0, u)$. In both cases, the section of the efficient frontier that obeys the restriction is limited.

One can also, by making use of these properties, determine the optimal portfolio on the basis of one of the two criteria by using the straight line tangential to the efficient frontier.

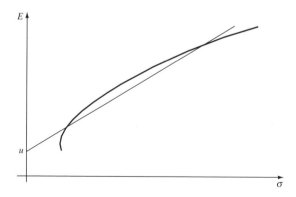

Figure 3.24   Deficit constraint

---

[38] If $u = 0$, this restriction means that except in a low probability event, the capital invested must be at least maintained.

3.2.8   The market model

Some developments in the market model now include the reasoning contained in the construction of Sharpe's model, where the index is replaced by the market in its totality. This model, however, contains more of a macroeconomic thought pattern than a search for efficient portfolios.

3.2.8.1   Systematic risk and specific risk

We have already encountered the concept of a systematic security risk in Section 3.1.1:

$$\beta_j = \frac{\sigma_{jM}}{\sigma_M^2}$$

This measures the magnitude of the risk of the security (j) in comparison to the risk of the average security on the market. It appears as a regression coefficient when the return on this security is expressed as a linear function of the market return: $R_{jt} = \alpha_j + \beta_j R_{Mt} + \varepsilon_{jt}$.

It is, of course, supposed that the residuals verify the classical hypotheses of the linear regression, establishing among other things that the residuals are of zero expectation and constant variance and are not correlated with the explanatory variable R_{Mt}.

Alongside the systematic risk β_j, which is the same for every period, another source of fluctuation in R_j is the residual ε_{jt}, which is specific to the period t. The term *specific risk* is given to the variance in the residuals: $\sigma_{\varepsilon_j}^2 = \mathrm{var}(\varepsilon_{jt})$.

Note

In practice, the coefficients α_j and β_j for the regression are estimated using the least square method. For example: $\hat{\beta}_j = s_{jM}/s_M^2$. The residuals are then estimated by $\hat{\varepsilon}_{jt} = R_{jt} - (\hat{\alpha}_j + \hat{\beta}_j R_{Mt})$ and the specific risk is estimated using its ergodic estimator $\frac{1}{T}\sum_{t=1}^{T} \hat{\varepsilon}_{jt}^2$. In the rest of this paragraph, we will omit the index t relating to time.

We will see how the risk σ_j^2 for a security consists of a systematic component and a specific component. We have:

$$\begin{aligned}
\sigma_j^2 &= \mathrm{var}(R_j) \\
&= E[(\alpha_j + \beta_j R_M + \varepsilon_j - E(\alpha_j + \beta_j R_M + \varepsilon_j))^2] \\
&= E[(\beta_j (R_M - E_M) + \varepsilon_j)^2] \\
&= \beta_j^2 E[(R_M - E_M)^2] + E(\varepsilon_j^2) + 2\beta_j E[(R_M - E_M)\varepsilon_j] \\
&= \beta_j^2 \,\mathrm{var}(R_M) + \mathrm{var}(\varepsilon_j)
\end{aligned}$$

Hence the announced decomposition relation of:

$$\sigma_j^2 = \beta_j^2 \sigma_M^2 + \sigma_{\varepsilon_j}^2$$

3.2.8.2 *Portfolio beta*

By using the regression expression for R_j, R_P can be developed easily:

$$R_P = \sum_{j=1}^{N} X_j R_j$$

$$= \sum_{j=1}^{N} X_j (\alpha_j + \beta_j R_M + \varepsilon_j)$$

$$= \sum_{j=1}^{N} X_j \alpha_j + \left(\sum_{j=1}^{N} X_j \beta_j \right) R_M + \sum_{j=1}^{N} X_j \varepsilon_j$$

This shows that as for the portfolio return, the portfolio beta is the average of the betas of all the constituent securities, weighted for the proportions expressed in terms of equity market capitalisation:

$$\beta_P = \sum_{j=1}^{N} X_j \beta_j$$

3.2.8.3 *Link between market model and portfolio diversification*

As for the simple index model, it is supposed here that the regression residuals relative to the various securities are not correlated: cov $(\varepsilon_i, \varepsilon_j) = 0$ for $i \neq j$. The portfolio risk is written as:

$$\sigma_P^2 = \text{var} \left(\sum_{j=1}^{N} X_j \alpha_j + \beta_P R_M + \sum_{j=1}^{N} X_j \varepsilon_j \right)$$

$$= \beta_P^2 \sigma_M^2 + \sum_{j=1}^{N} X_j^2 \sigma_{\varepsilon_j}^2$$

If, to simplify matters, one considers a portfolio consisting of N securities in equal proportions:

$$X_j = \frac{1}{N} \qquad j = 1, \ldots, N$$

the portfolio risk can develop as follows:

$$\sigma_P^2 = \text{var} \left(\sum_{j=1}^{N} X_j \alpha_j + \beta_P R_M + \sum_{j=1}^{N} X_j \varepsilon_j \right)$$

$$= \beta_P^2 \sigma_M^2 + \frac{1}{N^2} \sum_{j=1}^{N} \sigma_{\varepsilon_j}^2$$

$$= \beta_P^2 \sigma_M^2 + \frac{1}{N} \overline{\sigma_\varepsilon^2}$$

Here, the average residual variance has been introduced:

$$\overline{\sigma_\varepsilon^2} = \frac{1}{N} \sum_{j=1}^{N} \sigma_{\varepsilon_j}^2$$

The first term of the decomposition is independent of N, while the second tends towards 0 when N becomes very large. This analysis therefore shows that the portfolio risk σ_P^2 can be broken down into two terms:

- The systematic component $\beta_P^2 \sigma_M^2$ (non-diversifiable risk).
- The specific component $\sum X_j^2 \sigma_{\varepsilon_j}^2$ (diversifiable risk).

3.3 MODEL OF FINANCIAL ASSET EQUILIBRIUM AND APPLICATIONS

3.3.1 Capital asset pricing model

Unlike the previous models, this model, developed independently by W. Sharpe[39] and J. Lintner[40] and known as CAPM (MEDAF in French) is interested not in choosing a portfolio for an individual investor but in the behaviour of a whole market when the investors act rationally[41] and show an aversion to risk. The aim, in this situation, is to determine the exact value of an equity.

3.3.1.1 Hypotheses

The model being examined is based on a certain number of hypotheses. The hypotheses relating to investor behaviour are:

- They put together their portfolio using Markowitz's portfolio theory, that is, relying on the mean–variance pairing.
- They all have the same expectations, that is, none of them has any privileged information and they agree on the value of the parameters E_i, σ_i and σ_{ij} to be used.

Hypotheses can also be laid down with regard to the transactions:

- They are made without cost.
- The purchase, sale and holding times are the same for all investors.

Finally, it is assumed that the following conditions have been verified in relation to the market:

- There is no taxation either on increases in value, dividends or interest income.
- There are very many purchasers and sellers on the market and they do not have any influence on the market other than that exerted by the law of supply and demand.

---

[39] Sharpe W., Capital assets prices, *Journal of Finance*, Vol. 19, 1964, pp. 435–42.

[40] Lintner J., The valuation of risky assets and the selection of risky investments, *Review of Economics and Statistics*, Vol. 47, 1965, pp. 13–37.

[41] That is, according to the portfolio theory based on the mean–variance analysis.

- There is a risk-free interest rate, R_F, which is used for both borrowings and investments.
- The possibilities of borrowing and investing at this rate are not limited in terms of volume.

These hypotheses are of course not realistic. However, there are extensions of the model presented here, which make some of the hypotheses formulated more flexible. In addition, even the basic model gives good results, as do the applications that arise from it (see Sections 3.3.3, 3.3.4 and 3.3.5).

3.3.1.2 Separation theorem

This theorem states that under the conditions specified above, all the portfolios held by the investors are, in terms of equilibrium, combinations of a risk-free asset and a market portfolio.

According to the hypotheses, all the investors have the same efficient frontier for the equities and the same risk-free rate R_F. Therefore, according to the study of Markowitz's model with the risk-free security (Section 3.2.5), each investor's portfolio is located on the straight line issuing from point $(0, R_F)$ and tangential to the efficient frontier. This portfolio consists (see Figure 3.25) of:

- The risk-free equity, in proportion X.
- The portfolio A, corresponding to the tangent contact point, in proportion $1 - X$.

The risked portfolio A is therefore the same for all investors. The market will therefore, in accordance with the principle of supply and demand, adapt the prices so that the proportions in the portfolio are those of the whole market $(A = M)$ and the portfolios held by the investors are perfectly diversified.

The investor's choice will therefore be made only on the proportion X of the market portfolio (and therefore the $1 - X$ proportion of the risk-free equity). If the portfolio chosen is located to the left of the point M $(0 < X < 1)$, we are in fact looking at a combination of the two investments. If it is to the right of M $(X > 1)$, the investor borrows at the rate R_F in order to acquire more than 100 % of the market portfolio. The line in question is known as the *market straight line*.

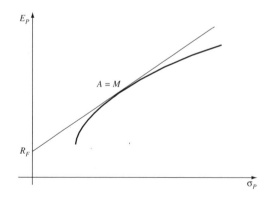

Figure 3.25   Separation theorem and market straight line

Interpretation of the separation theorem is simple. The market straight line passes through the points $(0, R_F)$ and (σ_M, E_M). Its equation is therefore given by:

$$E_P = R_F + \frac{E_M - R_F}{\sigma_M} \cdot \sigma_P$$

The expected return E_P on a portfolio is equal to the risk-free rate R_F plus the risk premium collected by the investor when he agrees to take a risk σ_P. The coefficient of σ_P (the slope of the market straight line) is therefore the increase in expected return obtained to support one unit of risk: this is the unit price of the risk on the market.

3.3.1.3 CAPM equation

We will now determine a relation very similar to the previous one – that is, a relation between expected return and risk – but in connection with a security instead of a portfolio.

For any portfolio of equities B, the straight line that connects the points $(0, R_F)$ and (σ_B, E_B) has the slope

$$\Psi_B = \frac{E_B - R_F}{\sigma_B}$$

This slope is clearly at its maximum when $B = M$ (see Figure 3.26) and, in the same way, the maximum value of Ψ_B^2 is Ψ_M^2. Therefore, if one terms the proportions of the various equities in the market portfolio $X_1, X_2, \ldots, X_N, (\Sigma X_i = 1)$ we will have:

$$(\Psi_M^2)_{X_k}{}' = 0 \qquad k = 1, \ldots, N$$

Like

$$\begin{cases} E_M - R_F = \sum_{j=1}^{N} X_j E_j - \left(\sum_{j=1}^{N} X_j \right) R_F = \sum_{j=1}^{N} X_j (E_j - R_F) \\ \sigma_M^2 = \sum_{i=1}^{N} \sum_{j=1}^{N} X_i X_j \sigma_{ij} \end{cases}$$

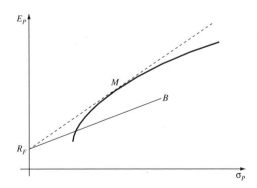

Figure 3.26 CAPM

the derivative of

$$\Psi_M^2 = \frac{(E_M - R_F)^2}{\sigma_M^2} = \frac{\left(\sum_{j=1}^{N} X_j (E_j - R_F) \right)^2}{\sum_{i=1}^{N} \sum_{j=1}^{N} X_i X_j \sigma_{ij}}$$

with respect to X_k is given by:

$$(\Psi_M^2)_{X_k}' = \frac{2 \left(\sum_{j=1}^{N} X_j (E_j - R_F) \right) (E_k - R_F) \cdot \sigma_M^2 - \left(\sum_{j=1}^{N} X_j (E_j - R_F) \right)^2 \cdot 2 \sum_{j=1}^{N} X_j \sigma_{kj}}{\sigma_M^4}$$

$$= \frac{2(E_M - R_F)(E_k - R_F)\sigma_M^2 - 2(E_M - R_F)^2 \sum_{j=1}^{N} X_j \sigma_{kj}}{\sigma_M^4}$$

$$= \frac{2(E_M - R_F) \cdot ((E_k - R_F)\sigma_M^2 - (E_M - R_F)\sigma_{kM})}{\sigma_M^4}$$

This will be zero if

$$E_k - R_F = (E_M - R_F)\frac{\sigma_{kM}}{\sigma_M^2}$$

or

$$E_k = R_F + \beta_k.(E_M - R_F)$$

This is termed the CAPM equation, which is interpreted in a similar way to the relation in the previous paragraph. The expected return E_k on the security (k) is equal to the risk-free rate R_F, plus a risk premium collected by the investor who agrees to take the risk. This risk premium is the increase in the expected return, to which more importance is given as the risk of the security within the market in question increases (β_k).

Note

As we have said, the hypotheses used as a basis for the model just developed are not realistic. Empirical studies have been carried out in order to determine whether the results obtained from the application of the CAPM model are valid. One of the most detailed analyses is that carried out by Fama and Macbeth,[42] which, considering the relation $E_k = R_F + \beta_k(E_M - R_F)$ as an expression of E_k according to β_k, tested the following hypotheses on the New York Stock Exchange (Figure 3.27):

- The relation $E_k = f(\beta_k)$ is linear and increasing.
- β_k is a complete measurement of the risk of the equity (k) on the market; in other words, the specific risk $\sigma_{\varepsilon_k}^2$ is not a significant explanation of E_k.

---

[42] Fama E. and Macbeth J., Risk, return and equilibrium: empirical tests, *Journal of Political Economy*, Vol. 71, No. 1, 1974, pp. 606–36.

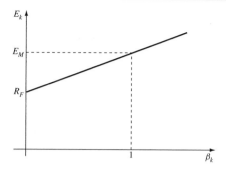

Figure 3.27   CAPM test

To do this, they used generalisations of the equation $E_k = f(\beta_k)$, including powers of β_k of a degree greater than 1 and a term that takes the specific risk into consideration. Their conclusion is that the CAPM model is in most cases acceptable.

3.3.2   Arbitrage pricing theory

In the CAPM model, the risk premium $E_k - R_F$ for an equity is expressed as a multiple of the risk premium $E_M - R_F$ for the market:

$$E_k - R_F = \beta_k(E_M - R_F)$$

The proportionality coefficient is the β of the security. It can therefore be considered that this approach allows the risk premium for an equity to be expressed on the basis of the risk premium for a single explanatory macroeconomic factor, or, which amounts to the same thing, on the basis of an aggregate that includes all the macroeconomic factors that interact with the market.

The arbitrage pricing theory[43] or APT allows a more refined analysis of the portfolio than does the CAPM, as breaking down the risk according to the single market factor, namely the beta, may prove insufficient to describe all the risks in a portfolio of equities. Hence the interest in resorting to risk breakdowns on the basis of several factors F_1, F_2, ..., F_P.

$$E_k - R_F = \sum_{j=1}^{p} \alpha_{kj}(E_{F_j} - R_F)$$

The APT theory shows that in an efficient market the quoted equity prices will be balanced by successive arbitrages, through the involvement of actors on the market. If one makes a point of watching developments in relative prices, it is possible to extract from the market a small number of arbitrage factors that allow the prices to balance out. This is precisely what the APT model does.

---

[43] Ross S. A., The arbitrage theory of capital asset pricing, *Journal of Economic Theory*, 1976, pp. 343–62.

The early versions[44] of the APT model relied on a previously compiled list of basic factors such as an industrial activity index, the spread between short-term and long-term interest rates, the difference in returns on bonds with very different ratings (see Section 4.2.1) etc. The coefficients α_{k1}, ..., α_{kp} are then determined by a regression technique based on historical observations R_{kt} and $R_{F_j,t}$ ($j = 1, \ldots, p$).

The more recent versions are based on more empirical methods that provide factors not correlated by a statistical technique[45] (factorial analysis), without the number of factors being known beforehand and even without them having any economic interpretation at all.

The factors obtained[46] from temporal series of returns on asset prices are purely statistical. Taken individually, they are not variables that are commonly used to describe a portfolio construction process or management strategy. None of them represents an interest, inflation or exchange rate. They are the equivalent of an orthogonal axis system in geometry.

The sole aim is to obtain a referential that allows a description of the interrelations between the assets studied on a stable basis over time. Once the referential is established, the risk on any asset quoted (equities, bonds, investment funds etc.) is broken down into a systematic part (common to all assets in the market) that can be represented in the factor space, and a specific part (particular to the asset). The systematic part is subsequently explained by awareness coefficients (α_{kj}) for the different statistical factors.

The explanatory power of the model can be explained by the fact that the different standard variables (economic, sectorial, fundamental etc.) used to understand the way in which it behaves are also represented in the referential for the factors provided an associated quoted support exists (price history).

The relation that links the return on a security to the various factors allows a breakdown of its variance into a part linked to the systematic risk factors (the explicative statistical factors) and a part that is specific to the securities and therefore diversifiable (regression residues etc.), that is:

$$\sigma_k^2 = \sum_{j=1}^{p} \alpha_{kj}^2 \operatorname{var}(R_{F_j}) + \sigma_{\varepsilon_k}^2$$

Example

A technically developed version of this method, accompanied by software, has been produced by Advanced Portfolio Technologies Inc. It extracts a series of statistical factors (represented by temporal series of crossed returns on assets) from the market, using a form search algorithm. In this way, if the left of Figure 3.28 represents the observed series of returns on four securities, the straight line on the same figure illustrates the three primary factors that allow reconstruction of the previous four series by linear combination.

For example, the first series breaks down into: $R_1 - R_F = 1 \cdot (R_{F_1} - R_F) + 1 \cdot (R_{F_2} - R_F) + 0.(R_{F_3} - R_F) + \varepsilon_1$.

[44] Dhrymes P. J., Friend I. and Gultekin N. B., A critical re-examination of the empirical evidence on the arbitrage pricing theory, *Journal of Finance*, No. 39, 1984, pp. 323–46. Chen N. F., Roll R. and Ross S. A., Economic forces of the stock market, *Journal of Business*, No. 59, 1986, pp. 383–403. More generally, Grinold C. and Kahn N., *Active Portfolio Management*, McGraw-Hill, 1998.

[45] See for example Saporta G., *Probabilities, Data Analysis and Statistics*, Technip, 1990; or Morrison D., *Multivariate Statistical Methods*, McGraw-Hill, 1976.

[46] Readers interested in the mathematical developments produced by extracting statistical factors from historical series of returns on assets should read Mehta M. L., *Random Matrices*, Academic Press, 1996. This work deals in depth with problems of proper values and proper vectors for matrices with very large numbers of elements generated randomly.

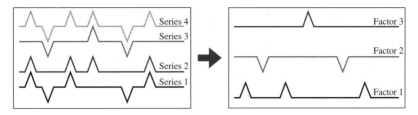

Figure 3.28 Arbitrage pricing theory

3.3.3 Performance evaluation

3.3.3.1 Principle

The portfolio manager,[47] of course, has an interest in the product that he manages. To do this properly, he will compare the return on his portfolio with the return on the market in which he is investing. From a practical point of view, this comparison will be made in relation to a market representative index for the sector in question.

Note

The return on a real portfolio between moments s and t is calculated simply using the relation $R_{P,[s;t]} = \dfrac{V_t - V_s}{V_s}$, provided there has been no movement within the portfolio during the interval of time in question. However, there are general flows (new securities purchased, securities sold etc.). It is therefore advisable to evaluate the return with the effect of these movements eliminated.

Note $t_1 < \ldots < t_n$ the periods in which these movements occur and propose that $t_0 = s$ and $t_{n+1} = t$. The return to be taken into consideration is therefore given by:

$$R_{P,]s;t]} = \prod_{k=0}^{n}(1 + R_{P,]t_k;t_{k+1}[}) - 1$$

Here, it is suggested that

$$R_{P,[t_k;t_{k+1}]} = \frac{V_{t_{k+1}}^{(-)} - V_{t_k}^{(+)}}{V_{t_k}^{(+)}}$$

$V_{t_j}^{(-)}$ and $V_{t_j}^{(+)}$ represent the value of the portfolio just before and just after the movement at moment t_j respectively.

In Section 3.2, it has been clearly shown that the quality of a security or a portfolio is not measured merely by its return. What should in fact be thought of those portfolios A and B in which the returns for a given period are 6.2 % and 6.3 % respectively but the attendant of B is twice that of A. The performance measurement indices presented below take into account not just the return, but also the risk on the security or portfolio.

---

[47] Management strategies, both active and passive, are dealt with in the following paragraph.

The indicators shown by us here are all based on relations produced by the financial asset valuation model and more particularly on the CAPM equation. They therefore assume that the hypotheses underlying this model are satisfied.

The first two indicators are based on the market straight-line equation and the CAPM equation respectively; the third is a variation on the second.

3.3.3.2 Sharpe index

The market straight-line equation is:

$$E_P = R_F + \frac{E_M - R_F}{\sigma_M} \cdot \sigma_P$$

which can be rewritten as follows:

$$\frac{E_P - R_F}{\sigma_P} = \frac{E_M - R_F}{\sigma_M}$$

This relation expresses that the excess return (compared to the risk-free rate), standardised by the standard deviation, is (in equilibrium) identical to a well-diversified portfolio and for the market. The term *Sharpe index* is given to the expression

$$SI_P = \frac{E_P - R_F}{\sigma_P}$$

which in practice is compared to the equivalent expression calculated for a market representative index.

Example

Let us take the data used for the simple Sharpe index model (Section 3.2.4):

$$E_1 = 0.05 \quad E_2 = 0.08 \quad E_3 = 0.10$$
$$\sigma_1 = 0.10 \quad \sigma_2 = 0.12 \quad \sigma_3 = 0.15$$
$$\rho_{12} = 0.3 \quad \rho_{13} = 0.1 \quad \rho_{23} = 0.4$$

Let us then consider the specific portfolio relative to the value $\lambda = 0.010$ for the risk parameter. In this case, we will have $X_1 = 0.4387$, $X_2 = 0.1118$ and $X_3 = 0.4496$, and therefore $E_P = 0.0758$ and $\sigma_P = 0.0912$. We will also have $E_I = 0.04$ and $\sigma_I = 0.0671$, and R_F is taken, as in Section 3.2.5, as 0.03.

The Sharpe index for the portfolio is therefore given as:

$$SI_P = \frac{0.0758 - 0.03}{0.0912} = 0.7982$$

The Sharpe index relative to the index equals:

$$SI_I = \frac{0.04 - 0.03}{0.0671} = 0.1490$$

This shows that the portfolio in question is performing better than the market.

Although Section 3.3.4 is given over to the portfolio management strategies for equities, some thoughts are also given on the role of the Sharpe index in the taking of investment (and disinvestment) decisions.

Suppose that we are in possession of a portfolio P and we are envisaging the purchase of an additional total of equities A, the proportions of P and A being noted respectively as X_P and X_A. Of course, $X_P + X_A = 1$ and X_A is positive or negative depending on whether an investment or a disinvestment is involved. The portfolio produced as a result of the decision taken will be noted as P' and its return will be given by $R_{P'} = X_P R_P + X_A R_A$.

The expected return and variance on return for the new portfolio are

$$E_{P'} = (1 - X_A)E_P + X_A E_A$$
$$\sigma_{P'}^2 = (1 - X_A)^2 \sigma_P^2 + X_A^2 \sigma_A^2 + 2X_A(1 - X_A)\sigma_P \sigma_A \rho_{AP}$$

We admit as the purchase criterion for A the fact that the Sharpe index for the new portfolio is at least equal to that of the old one: $SI_{P'} \geq SI_P$, which is expressed as:

$$\frac{(1 - X_A)E_P + X_A E_A - R_F}{\sigma_{P'}} \geq \frac{E_P - R_F}{\sigma_P}$$

By isolating the expected return on A, we obtain as the condition

$$E_A \geq E_P + \left(\frac{\sigma_{P'}}{\sigma_P} - 1\right)\frac{E_P - R_F}{X_A}$$

It is worth noting that if A does not increase the risk of the portfolio ($\sigma_{P'} \leq \sigma_P$), it is not even necessary for $E_A \geq E_P$ to purchase A.

Example

Suppose that one has a portfolio for which $E_P = 0.08$, that the risk-free total is $R_F = 0.03$ and that one is envisaging a purchase of A at the rate $X_A = 0.02$. The condition then becomes

$$E_A \geq 0.08 + \frac{5}{2}\left(\frac{\sigma_{P'}}{\sigma_P} - 1\right)$$

In the specific case where the management of risks is such that $\sigma_A = \sigma_P$, the ratio of the standard deviations is given by

$$\frac{\sigma_{P'}}{\sigma_P} = \sqrt{(1 - X_A)^2 + X_A^2 + 2X_A(1 - X_A)\rho_{AP}}$$

$$= \sqrt{0.9608 + 0.0392\rho_{AP}}$$

This allows the conditions of investment to be determined according to the correlation coefficient value: if $\rho_{AP} = -1$, 0 or 1, the condition becomes $E_A \geq 0.02$, $E_A \geq 0.0305$ and $E_A \geq 0.08$ respectively.

3.3.3.3 Treynor index

The CAPM equation for the kth equity in the portfolio, $E_k = R_F + \beta_k (E_M - R_F)$, allows the following to be written:

$$\sum_{k=1}^{N} X_k E_k = \left(\sum_{k=1}^{N} X_k\right) \cdot R_F + \left(\sum_{k=1}^{N} X_k \beta_k\right) \cdot (E_M - R_F)$$

or, $E_P = R_F + \beta_P (E_M - R_F)$

Taking account of the fact that $\beta_M = 1$, this last relation can be written as:

$$\frac{E_P - R_F}{\beta_P} = \frac{E_M - R_F}{\beta_M}$$

The interpretation is similar to that of the Sharpe index. The Treynor index is therefore defined by:

$$TI_P = \frac{E_P - R_F}{\beta_P}$$

which will be compared to the similar expression for an index.

Example

Let us take the data above, with the addition of (see Section 3.2.4): $\beta_1 = 0.60$, $\beta_2 = 1.08$, $\beta_3 = 1.32$. This will give $\beta_P = 0.9774$.

The Treynor index for this portfolio is therefore obtained by:

$$TI_P = \frac{0.0758 - 0.03}{0.9774} = 0.0469$$

meanwhile, the index relative to the index is

$$TI_I = \frac{0.04 - 0.03}{1} = 0.0100$$

This will lead to the same conclusion.

3.3.3.4 Jensen index

According to the reasoning in the Treynor index, we have $E_P - R_F = \beta_P (E_M - R_F)$.

This relation being relative (in equilibrium) for a well-diversified portfolio, a portfolio P will present an excess of return in relation to the market if there is a number $\alpha_P > 0$ so that: $E_P - R_F = \alpha_P + \beta_P (E_M - R_F)$.

The Jensen index, $JI_P = \hat{\alpha}$, is the estimator for the constant term of the regression:

$$E_{P,t} - R_{F,t} = \alpha + \beta (E_{I,t} - R_{F,t}).$$

For this, the variable to be explained (explanatory) is the excess of return of portfolio in relation to the risk-free rate (excess of return of market representative index). Its value is, of course, compared to 0.

Example

It is easy to verify that with the preceding data, we have
$JI_P = (0.0758 - 0.03) - 0.9774 \cdot (0.04 - 0.03) = 0.0360$, which is strictly positive.

3.3.4 Equity portfolio management strategies

3.3.4.1 Passive management

The aim of passive management is to obtain a return equal to that of the market. By the definition of the market, the gains (returns higher than market returns) realised by certain investors will be compensated by losses (returns lower than market returns) suffered by other investors:[48] the average return obtained by all the investors is the market return. The reality is a little different: because of transaction costs, the average return enjoyed by investors is slightly less than the market return.

The passive strategy therefore consists of:

- Putting together a portfolio of identical (or very similar) composition to the market, which corresponds to optimal diversification.
- Limiting the volume of transactions as far as is possible.

This method of operation poses a number of problems. For example, for the management of some types of portfolio, regulations dictate that each security should only be present to a fixed maximum extent, which is incompatible with passive management if a security represents a particularly high level of stock-exchange capitalisation on the market. Another problem is that the presence of some securities that not only have high rates but are indivisible, and this may lead to the construction of portfolios with a value so high that they become unusable in practice.

These problems have led to the creation of 'index funds', collective investment organisations that 'imitate' the market. After choosing an index that represents the market in which one wishes to invest, one puts together a portfolio consisting of the same securities as those in the index (or sometimes simply the highest ones), in the same proportions.

Of course, as and when the rates of the constituent equities change, the composition of the portfolio will have to be adapted, and this presents a number of difficulties. The reaction time inevitably causes differences between the return on the portfolio and the market return; these are known as 'tracking errors'. In addition, this type of management incurs a number of transaction costs, for adapting the portfolio to the index, for reinvesting dividends etc. For these reasons, the return on a certain portfolio will in general be slightly lower than that of the index.

3.3.4.2 Active management

The aim of active management is to obtain a return higher than the market return.

A fully efficient market can be beaten only temporarily and by chance: in the long term, the return cannot exceed the market return. Active management therefore suggests that the market is fully efficient.

---

[48] This type of situation is known in price theory as a *zero total game*. Refer for example to Binmore K., *Jeux et théorie des jeux*, De Boeck & Larcier, 1999.

Two main principles allow the target set to be achieved.

1) Asset allocation, which evolves over time and is also known as *market timing*, consists of putting together a portfolio consisting partly of the market portfolio or an index portfolio and partly of a risk-free asset (or one that is significantly less risk than equities, such as a bond). The respective proportions of these two components are then changed as time passes, depending on whether a rise or a fall in the index is anticipated.
2) Stock picking consists of putting together a portfolio of equities by choosing the securities considered to be undervalued and likely to produce a return higher than the market return in the near or more distant future (market reaction).

In practice, professionals use strategies based on one of the two approaches or a mixture of the two.

In order to assess the quality of active management, the portfolio put together should be compared with the market portfolio from the point of view of expected return and of risk incurred. These portfolio performance indexes have been studied in Section 3.3.3.

Let us now examine some methods of market timing and a method of stock picking: the application of the *dividend discount model*.

3.3.4.3 Market timing

This technique therefore consists of managing a portfolio consisting of the market portfolio (M) for equities and a bond rate (O) in the respective proportions X and $1 - X$, X being adapted according to the expected performance of the two components.

These performances, which determine a market timing policy, may be assessed using different criteria:

- The price-earning ratio, introduced in Section 3.1.3: PER = rate/profit.
- The yield gap, which is the ratio between the return on the bond and the return on the equities (dividend/rate).
- The earning yield, which is the product of the PER by the bond rate.
- The risk premium, which is the difference between the return on the market portfolio and the return on the bond: $RP = E_M - E_O$. It may be estimated using a history, but it is preferable to use an estimation produced beforehand by a financial analyst, for example using the DDM (see below).

Of course, small values for the first three criteria are favourable to investment in equities; the situation is reversed for the risk premium.

The first method for implementing a market timing policy is recourse to *decision channels*. If one refers to one of the four criteria mentioned above as c, for which historical observations are available (and therefore an estimation c for its average and s_c for its standard deviation), we choose, somewhat arbitrarily, to invest a certain percentage of equities depending on the observed value of c compared to c, the difference between the two being modulated by s_c. We may choose for example to invest 70 %, 60 %, 50 %, 40 %

Figure 3.29   Fixed decision channels

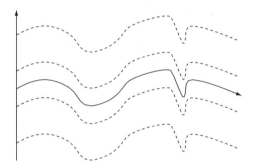

Figure 3.30   Moving decision channels

or 30 % in equities depending on the position of c in relation to the limits:[49] $\overline{c} - \frac{3}{2}s_c, \overline{c} - \frac{1}{2}s_c, \overline{c} + \frac{1}{2}s_c$ and $\overline{c} + \frac{3}{2}s_c$ (Figure 3.29).

This method does not take account of the change of the c parameter over time. The $\overline{c}$ and s_c parameters can therefore be calculated over a sliding history (for example, one year) (Figure 3.30).

Another, more rigorous method can be used with the risk premium only. In the search for the efficient frontier, we have looked each time for the minimum with respect to the proportions of the expression $\sigma_P^2 - \lambda E_P$ in which the λ parameter corresponds to the risk ($\lambda = 0$ for a cautious portfolio, $\lambda = +\infty$ for a speculative portfolio). This parameter is equal to the slope of the straight line in the plane (E, σ^2) tangential to the efficient frontier and coming from the point $(R_F, 0)$. According to the separation theorem (see Section 3.3.1), the contact point for this tangent corresponds to the market portfolio (see Figure 3.31) and in consequence we have: $\lambda = \dfrac{\sigma_M^2}{E_M - R_F}$.

In addition, the return on portfolio consisting of a proportion X of the market portfolio and a proportion $1 - X$ of the bond rate is given by $R_P = X R_M + (1 - X) R_O$, which

---

[49] The order of the channels must be reversed for the risk premium.

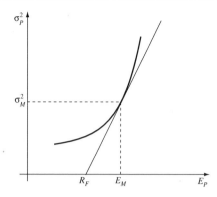

Figure 3.31 Separation theorem

allows the following to be determined:

$$E_P = XE_M + (1 - X)E_O$$
$$\sigma_P^2 = X^2\sigma_M^2 + 2X(1 - X)\sigma_{MO} + (1 - X)^2\sigma_O^2$$

The problem therefore consists of determining the value of X, which minimises the expression:

$$Z(X) = \sigma_P^2 - \lambda E_P = X^2\sigma_M^2 + 2X(1 - X)\sigma_{MO} + (1 - X)^2\sigma_O^2 - \lambda[XE_M + (1 - X)E_O].$$

The derivative of this function:

$$Z'(X) = 2X\sigma_M^2 + 2(1 - 2X)\sigma_{MO} - 2(1 - X)\sigma_O^2 - \lambda(E_M - E_O)$$
$$= 2X(\sigma_M^2 - 2\sigma_{MO} + \sigma_O^2) + 2\sigma_{MO} - 2\sigma_O^2 - \lambda \cdot RP$$

provides the proportion sought:

$$X = \frac{\lambda \cdot RP - 2(\sigma_{MO} - \sigma_O^2)}{2(\sigma_M^2 - 2\sigma_{MO} + \sigma_O^2)}$$

or, in the same way, replacing λ and RP by their value:

$$X = \frac{\dfrac{E_M - E_0}{E_M - R_F} \cdot \sigma_M^2 - 2(\sigma_{MO} - \sigma_O^2)}{2(\sigma_M^2 - 2\sigma_{MO} + \sigma_O^2)}$$

Example

If we have the following data:

$$
\begin{array}{ll}
E_M = 0.08 & \sigma_M = 0.10 \\
E_O = 0.06 & \sigma_O = 0.02 \\
R_F = 0.04 & \rho_{MO} = 0.6
\end{array}
$$

we can calculate successively:

$$\sigma_{MO} = 0.10 \cdot 0.02 \cdot 0.6 = 0.0012$$

$$\lambda = \frac{0.10^2}{0.08 - 0.04} = 0.25$$

$$PR = 0.08 - 0.06 = 0.02$$

and therefore:

$$X = \frac{0.25 \cdot 0.02 - 2 \cdot (0.0012 - 0.02^2)}{2 \cdot (0.10^2 - 2 \cdot 0.0012 + 0.02^2)} = 0.2125$$

Under these conditions, therefore, it is advisable to invest 21.25 % in equities (market portfolio) and 78.75 % in bonds.

3.3.4.4 Dividend discount model

The aim of the dividend discount model, or DDM, is to compare the expected return of an equity and its equilibrium return, which will allow us to determine whether it is overvalued or undervalued.

The expected return, $\tilde{R}_k$, is determined using a model for updating future dividends. A similar reasoning to the type used in the Gordon–Shapiro formula (Section 3.1.3), or a generalisation of that reasoning, can be applied. While the Gordon–Shapiro relation suggests a constant rate of growth for dividends, more developed models (two-rate model) use, for example, a rate of growth constant over several years followed by another, lower rate for subsequent years. Alternatively, a three-rate model may be used with a period of a few years between the two constant-rate periods in which the increasing rate reduces linearly in order to make a continuous connection.

The return to equilibrium E_k is determined using the CAPM equation (Section 3.3.1). This equation is written $E_k = R_F + \beta_k(E_M - R_F)$.

If one considers that it expresses E_k as a function of β_k, we are looking at a straight-line equation; the line passes through the point $(0, R_F)$ and since $\beta_M = 1$, through the point $(1, E_M)$. This straight line is known as the *financial asset evaluation line* or the *security market line*.

If the expected return $\tilde{R}_k$ for each security is equal to its return on equilibrium E_k, all the points $(\beta_k, \tilde{R}_k)$ will be located on the security market line. In practice, this is not the case because of certain inefficiencies in the market (see Figure 3.32).

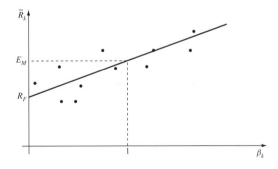

Figure 3.32 Security market line

This technique considers that the $\tilde{R}_k$ evaluation made by the analysts is correct and that the differences noted are due to market inefficiency. Therefore, the securities whose representative point is located above the security market line are considered to be undervalued, and the market should sooner or later rectify the situation and produce an additional return for the investor who purchased the securities.

3.4 EQUITY DYNAMIC MODELS

The above paragraphs deal with static aspects, considering merely a 'photograph' of the situation at a given moment. We will now touch on the creation of models for developments in equity returns or rates over time.

The notation used here is a little different: the value of the equity at moment t is noted as S_t. This is a classic notation (indicating 'stock'), and in addition, the present models are used among other things to support the development of option valuation models for equities (see Section 5.3), for which the notation C_t is reserved for equity options (indicating 'call').

Finally, we should point out that the following, unless specified otherwise, is valid only for equities that do not give rise to the distribution of dividends.

3.4.1 Deterministic models

3.4.1.1 Discrete model

Here, the equity is evaluated at moments $t = 0$, 1, etc. If it is assumed that the return on the equity between moments t and $t + 1$ is i, we can write: $i = \dfrac{S_{t+1} - S_t}{S_t}$, which leads to the evolution equation $S_{t+1} = S_t \cdot (1 + i)$.

If the rate of return i is constant and the initial value S_0 is taken into account, the equation (with differences) above will have the solution: $S_t = S_0 \cdot (1 + i)^t$.

If the rate varies from period to period (i_k for the period] $k - 1$; k]), the previous relation becomes $S_t = S_0 . (1 + i_1) (1 + i_2) \ldots (1 + i_t)$.

3.4.1.2 Continuous model

We are looking here at an infinitesimal development in the value of the security. If it is assumed that the return between moments t and $t + \Delta t$ (with 'small' Δt) is proportional to the duration Δt with a proportionality factor δ:

$$\delta \cdot \Delta t = \frac{S_{t+\Delta t} - S_t}{S_t}$$

the evolution equation is a differential equation[50] $S'_t = S_t \cdot \delta$.
The solution to this equation is given by $S_t = S_0 \cdot e^{\delta t}$.

The link will be noted between this relation and the relation corresponding to it for the discrete case, provided $\delta = \ln (1 + i)$.

---

[50] Obtained by making Δt tend towards 0.

If the rate of return δ is not constant, the differential development equation will take the form $S'_t = S_t \cdot \delta(t)$, thus leading to the more complex solution $S_t = S_0 \cdot e^{\int_0^t \delta(t)\,dt}$.

Note

The parameters appear in the above models (the constant rates i and δ, or the variable rates i_1, i_2, ... and $\delta(t)$) should of course for practical use be estimated on the basis of historical observations.

3.4.1.3 Generalisation

These two aspects, discrete and continuous, can of course be superimposed. We therefore consider:

- A continuous evolution of the rate of return, represented by the function $\delta(t)$. On top of this:
- A set of discrete variations occurring at periods τ_1, τ_2, ..., τ_n so that the rate of return between τ_{k-1} and τ_k is equal to i_k.

If n is the greatest integer so that $\tau_n \leq t$, the change in the value is given by

$$S_t = S_0 \cdot (1+i_1)^{\tau_1} (1+i_2)^{\tau_2-\tau_1} \ldots (1+i_n)^{\tau_n-\tau_{n-1}} (1+i_{n+1})^{t-\tau_n} \cdot e^{\int_0^t \delta(t)\,dt}.$$

This presentation will allow the process of dividend payment, for example, to be taken into consideration in a discrete or continuous model. Therefore, where the model includes only the continuous section represented by $\delta(t)$, the above relation represents the change in the value of an equity that pays dividends at periods τ_1, τ_2 etc. with a total D_k paid in τ_k and linked to i_k by the relation

$$i_k = -\frac{D_k}{S_k^{(-)}}$$

Here, $S_k^{(-)}$ is the value of the security just before payment of the kth dividend.

3.4.2 Stochastic models

3.4.2.1 Discrete model

It is assumed that the development from one period to another occurs as follows: equity at moment t has the (random) value S_t and will at the following moment $t+1$ have one of the two values $S_t.u$ (higher than S_t) or $S_t.d$ (lower than S_t) with the respective probabilities of α and $(1-\alpha)$.

We therefore have $d \leq 1 \leq u$, but it is also supposed that $d \leq 1 < 1 + R_F \leq u$, without which the arbitrage opportunity will clearly be possible. In practice, the parameters u, d and α should be estimated on the basis of observations.

Generally speaking, the following graphic representation is used for evolutions in equity prices:

$$S_t \nearrow \quad S_{t+1} = S_t \cdot u \quad (\alpha)$$
$$\searrow \quad S_{t+1} = S_t \cdot d \quad (1 - \alpha)$$

It is assumed that the parameters u, d and α remain constant over time and we will no longer clearly show the probability α in the following graphs; the rising branches, for example, will always correspond to the increase (at the rate u) in the value of the security with the probability α.

Note that the return of the equity between the period t and $(t + 1)$ is given by

$$\frac{S_{t+1} - S_t}{S_t} = \begin{cases} u - 1 & (\alpha) \\ d - 1 & (1 - \alpha) \end{cases}$$

Between the moments $t + 1$ and $t + 2$, we will have, in the same way and according to the branch obtained at the end of the previous period:

$$S_{t+1} \nearrow \quad S_{t+2} = S_{t+1} \cdot u = S_t \cdot u^2$$
$$\searrow \quad S_{t+2} = S_{t+1} \cdot d = S_t \cdot ud$$

or

$$S_{t+1} \nearrow \quad S_{t+2} = S_{t+1} \cdot u = S_t \cdot ud$$
$$\searrow \quad S_{t+2} = S_{t+1} \cdot d = S_t \cdot d^2$$

It is therefore noted that a rise followed by a fall leads to the same result as a fall followed by a rise. Generally speaking, a graph known as a *binomial trees* can be constructed (see Figure 3.33), rising from period 0 (when the equity has a certain value S_0) to the period t.

It is therefore evident that the (random) value of the equity at moment t is given by $S_t = S_0 \cdot u^N d^{t-N}$, in which the number N of rises is of course a random binomial variable[51] with parameters $(t; \alpha)$:

$$\Pr[N = k] = \binom{t}{k} \alpha^k (1 - \alpha)^{t-k}$$

The following property can be demonstrated:

$$E(S_t) = S_0 \cdot (\alpha u + (1 - \alpha)d)^t$$

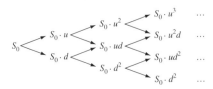

Figure 3.33   Binomial tree

---

[51] See Appendix 2 for the development of this concept and for the properties of the random variable.

In fact, what we have is:

$$E(S_t) = \sum_{k=0}^{t} S_0 \cdot u^k d^{t-k} \cdot \binom{t}{k} \alpha^k (1-\alpha)^{t-k}$$

$$= S_0 \cdot \sum_{k=0}^{t} \binom{t}{k} (\alpha u)^k ((1-\alpha)d)^{t-k}$$

This leads to the relation declared through the Newton binomial formula.

Note that this property is a generalisation for the random case of the determinist formula $S_t = S_0 \cdot (1+i)^t$.

3.4.2.2 Continuous model

The method of equity value change shown in the binomial model is of the *random walk* type. At each transition, two movements are possible (rise or fall) with unchanged probability. When the period between each transaction tends towards 0, this type of random sequence converges towards a standard Brownian motion or SBM.[52] Remember that we are looking at a stochastic process w_t (a random variable that is a function of time), which obeys the following processes:

- $w_0 = 0$.
- w_t is a process with independent increments : if $s < t < u$, then $w_u - w_t$ is independent of $w_t - w_s$.
- w_t is a process with stationary increments : the random variables $w_{t+h} - w_t$ and w_h are identically distributed.
- Regardless of what t may be, the random variable w_t is distributed according to a normal law of zero mean and standard deviation $\sqrt{t}$:

$$f_{w_t}(x) = \frac{1}{\sqrt{2\pi t}} e^{-x^2/2t}$$

The first use of this process for modelling the development in the value of a financial asset was produced by L. Bachelier.[53] He assumed that the value of a security at a moment t is a first-degree function of the SBM: $S_t = a + bw_t$. According to the above definition, a is the value of the security at $t = 0$ and b is a measure of the volatility σ of the security for each unit of time. The relation used was therefore $S_t = S_0 + \sigma \cdot w_t$.

The shortcomings of this approach are of two types:

- The same absolute variation (€10 for example) corresponds to variations in return that are very different depending on the level of price (20 % for a quotation of €50 and 5 % for a value of €200).
- The random variable S_t follows a normal law with mean S_0 and standard deviation $\sigma \sqrt{t}$; this model therefore allows for negative prices.

---

[52] Appendix 2 provides details of the results, reasoning and properties of these stochastic processes.

[53] Bachelier L., *Théorie de la spéculation*, Gauthier-Villars, 1900. Several more decades were to pass before this reasoning was finally accepted and improved upon.

For this reason, P. Samuelson[54] proposed the following model. During the short interval of time $[t; t + dt]$, the return (and not the price) alters according to an *Itô process* :

$$\frac{S_{t+dt} - S_t}{S_t} = \frac{dS_t}{S_t} = E_R \cdot dt + \sigma_R \cdot dw_t$$

Here, the non-random term (the trend) is proportional to the expected return and the stochastic term involves the volatility for each unit of time in this return. This model is termed a geometric Brownian motion.

Example

Figure 3.34 shows a simulated trajectory (development over time) for 1000 very short periods with the values $E_R = 0.1$ and $\sigma_R = 0.02$, based on a starting value of $S_0 = 100$.

We can therefore establish the first property in the context of this model: the stochastic process S_t showing the changes in the value of the equity can be written as

$$S_t = S_0 \cdot \exp\left[\left(E_R - \frac{\sigma_R^2}{2}\right) \cdot t + \sigma_R \cdot w_t\right]$$

This shows that S_t follows a log-normal distribution (it can only take on positive values).

In fact, application of the Itô formula[55] to the function $f(x, t) = \ln \cdot x$ where $x = S_t$, we obtain:

$$d(\ln S_t) = \left[0 + \frac{1}{S_t} E_R S_t - \frac{1}{2S_t^2}\sigma_R^2 S_t^2\right] \cdot dt + \frac{1}{S_t}\sigma_R S_t \cdot dw_t$$

$$= \left(E_R - \frac{\sigma_R^2}{2}\right) \cdot dt + \sigma_R \cdot dw_t$$

This equation resolves into: $\ln S_t = C^* + \left(E_R - \frac{\sigma_R^2}{2}\right) \cdot t + \sigma_R \cdot w_t$

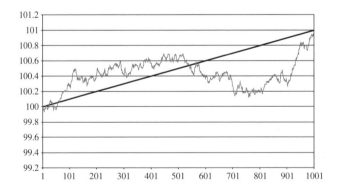

Figure 3.34   Geometric Brownian motion

---

[54] Samuelson P., Mathematics on speculative price, *SIAM Review*, Vol. 15, No. 1, 1973.
[55] See Appendix 2.

The integration constant C^* is of course equal to $\ln S_0$ and the passage to the exponential gives the formula declared.

It is then easy to deduce the moments of the random variable S_t:

$$E(S_t) = S_0 \cdot e^{E_R t}$$

$$\text{var}(S_t) = S_0^2 \cdot e^{2E_R t} (e^{\sigma_R^2 t} - 1)$$

The first of these relations shows that the average return $E(S_t/S_0)$ on this equity over the interval $[0; t]$ is equivalent to a capitalisation at the instant rate, E_R.

A second property can be established, relative to the instant return on the security over the interval $[0; t]$. This return obeys a normal distribution with mean and standard deviation, shown by

$$\left(E_R - \frac{\sigma_R^2}{2} ; \frac{\sigma_R}{\sqrt{t}} \right)$$

This result may appear paradoxical, as the average of the return is not equal to E_R. This is because of the structure of the stochastic process and is not incompatible with the intuitive solution, as we have $E(S_t) = S_0 \cdot e^{E_R t}$.

To establish this property, expressing the stochastic instant return process as δ_t, we can write $S_t = S_0 \cdot e^{\delta_t \cdot t}$, that is, according to the preceding property,

$$\delta_t = \frac{1}{t} \cdot \ln \left(\frac{S_t}{S_0} \right)$$

$$= \left(E_R - \frac{\sigma_R^2}{2} \right) + \sigma_R \cdot \frac{w_t}{t}$$

This establishes the property.

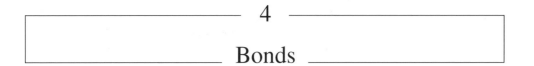

4

Bonds

4.1 CHARACTERISTICS AND VALUATION

To an investor, a *bond* is a financial asset issued by a public institution or private company corresponding to a loan that confers the right to interest payments (known as *coupons*) and repayment of the loan upon maturity. It is a negotiable security and its issue price, redemption value, coupon total and life span are generally known and fixed beforehand.

4.1.1 Definitions

A bond is characterised by various elements:

1. The *nominal value* or NV of a bond is the amount printed on the security, which, along with the *nominal rate* of the bond, allows the coupon total to be determined.
2. The bond *price* is shown as P. This may be the *price at issue* ($t = 0$) or at any subsequent moment t. The *maturity price* is of course identical to the *redemption value* or R mentioned above.
3. The *coupons* C_t constitute the interest paid by the issuer. These are paid at various periods, which are assumed to be both regular and annual ($t = 1, 2, \ldots, T$).
4. The maturity T represents the period of time that separates the moment of issue and the time of reimbursement of the security.

The financial flows associated with a bond are therefore:

- From the purchaser, the payment of its price; this may be either the issue price paid to the issuer or the rate of the bond paid to any seller at a time subsequent to the issue.
- From the issuer, the payment of coupons from the time of acquisition onwards and the repayment on maturity.

The issue price, nominal value and repayment value are not necessarily equal. There may be premiums (positive or negative) on issue and/or on repayment.

The bonds described above are those that we will be studying in this chapter; they are known as *fixed-rate bonds*. There are many variations on this simple bond model.

It is therefore possible for no coupons to be paid during the bond's life span, the return thus being only the difference between the issue price and the redemption value. This is referred to as a *zero-coupon bond*.[1] This kind of security is equivalent to a fixed-rate investment.

There are also bonds more complex than those described above, for example:[2]

- *Variable rate bonds*, for which the value of each coupon is determined periodically according to a parameter such as an index.

---

[1] A debenture may therefore, in a sense, be considered to constitute a superimposition of zero-coupon debentures.
[2] Read for example Colmant B., Delfosse V. and Esch L., *Obligations, Les notions financières essentielles*, Larcier, 2002. Also: Fabozzi J. F., *Bond Markets, Analysis and Strategies*, Prentice-Hall, 2000.

- *Transition* bonds, which authorise repayment before the maturity date.
- *Lottery bonds*, in which the (public) issuer repays certain bonds each year in a draw.
- *Convertible* bonds (convertible into equities) etc.

4.1.2 Return on bonds

The return on a bond can of course be calculated by the *nominal rate* (or *coupon rate*) r_n, which is defined as the relation between the total value of the coupon and the nominal value

$$r_n = \frac{C}{NV}$$

This definition, however, will only make sense if all the different coupons have the same value. It can be adapted by replacing the denominator with the price of the bond at a given moment. The nominal rate is of limited interest, as it does not include the life span of the bond at any point; using it to describe two bonds is therefore rather pointless.

For a fixed period of time (such as one year), it is possible to use a rate of return equivalent to the return on one equity:

$$\frac{P_t + C_t - P_{t-1}}{P_{t-1}}$$

This concept is, however, very little used in practice.

4.1.2.1 Actuarial rate on issue

The actuarial rate on issue, or more simply the actuarial rate (r) of a bond is the rate for which there is equality between the discounted value of the coupons and the repayment value on one hand and the issue price on the other hand:

$$P = \sum_{t=1}^{T} C_t (1+r)^{-t} + R(1+r)^{-T}$$

Example

Consider for example a bond with a period of six years and nominal value 100, issued at 98 and repaid at 105 (issue and reimbursement premiums 2 and 5 respectively) and a nominal rate of 10 %. The equation that defines its actuarial rate is therefore:

$$98 = \frac{10}{1+r} + \frac{10}{(1+r)^2} + \frac{10}{(1+r)^3} + \frac{10}{(1+r)^4} + \frac{10}{(1+r)^5} + \frac{10+105}{(1+r)^6}$$

This equation (sixth degree for unknown r) can be resolved numerically and gives $r = 0.111044$, that is, $r =$ approximately 11.1 %.

The actuarial rate for a zero-coupon bond is of course the rate for a risk-free investment, and is defined by

$$P = R(1+r)^{-T}$$

The rate for a bond issued and reimbursable at par ($P = NV = R$), with coupons that are equal ($C_t = C$ for all t) is equal to the nominal rate: $r = r_n$. In fact, for this particular type of bond, we have:

$$P = \sum_{t=1}^{T} C(1+r)^{-t} + P(1+r)^{-T}$$

$$= C\frac{(1+r)^{-1} - (1+r)^{-T-1}}{1 - (1+r)^{-1}} + P(1+r)^{-T}$$

$$= C\frac{1 - (1+r)^{-T}}{r} + P(1+r)^{-T}$$

From this, it can be deduced that $r = C/P = r_n$.

4.1.2.2 Actuarial return rate at given moment

The actuarial rate as defined above is calculated when the bond is issued, and is sometimes referred to as the *ex ante* rate. It is therefore assumed that this rate will remain constant throughout the life of the security (and regardless of its maturity date).

A major principle of financial mathematics (the principle of *equivalence*) states that this rate does not depend on the moment at which the various financial movements are 'gathered in'.

Example

If, for the example of the preceding paragraph (bond with nominal value of 100 issued at 98 and repaid at 105), paying an annual coupon of 10 at the end of each of the security's six years of life) and with an actuarial rate of 11.1 %, one examines the value acquired for example on the maturity date, we have:

- for the investment, $98 \cdot (1 + r)^6$;
- for the generated financial flows: $10 \cdot [(1+r)^5 + (1+r)^4 + (1+r)^3 + (1+r)^3 + (1+r)^2 + (1+r)^1 + 1] + 105$.

The equality of these two quantities is also realised for $r = 11.1\%$.

If we now place at a given moment t anywhere between 0 and T, and are aware of the change in the market rate between 0 and t, the actuarial rate of return at the moment[3] t, which we will call[4] $r(t)$, is the rate for which there is equality between:

1. The value of the investment acquired at t, calculated at this rate $r(t)$.
2. The sum of:
   — The value of the coupons falling due acquired at t, reinvested at the current rate observed between 0 and t.

---

[3] This is sometimes known as the *ex post* rate.
[4] $r(0) = r$ is of course the actuarial rate at issue.

— The discounted value in t of the financial flows generated subsequent to t, calculated using the market rate at the moment t.

Example

Let us take the same example as above. Suppose that we are at the moment in time immediately subsequent to payment of the third coupon ($t = 3$) and the market rate has remained at 11.1 % for the first two years and has now changed to 12 %. The above definition gives us the equation that defines the actuarial rate of return for the specific moment $t = 3$.

$$98 \cdot (1 + r(3))^3 = (10 \cdot 1.111 \cdot 1.12 + 10 \cdot 1.12 + 10) + \left(\frac{10}{1.12} + \frac{10}{1.12^2} + \frac{115}{1.12^3} \right)$$

$$= 35.33 + 98.76$$

$$= 134.09$$

This gives $r(3) = 11.02 \%$.

It will of course be evident that if the rate of interest remains constant (and equal to 11.1) for the first three years, the above calculation would have led to $r(3) = 11.1 \%$, this being consistent with the principle of equivalence.

This example clearly shows the phenomenon of bond risk linked to changes in interest rates. This phenomenon will be studied in greater detail in Section 4.2.1.

4.1.2.3 Accrued interest

When a bond is acquired between two coupon payment dates, the purchaser pays not only the value of the bond for that specific moment but also the portion of the coupon to come, calculated in proportion to the period that has passed since payment of the last coupon. The seller, in fact, has the right to partial interest relating to the period from the last coupon payment to the moment of the deal. This principle is called the *accrued interest system* and the price effectively paid is the *dirty price*, as opposed to the *clean price*, which represents merely the rate for the bond at the time of the deal.

Let us consider a bond of maturity T and non integer moment $t + \theta$ (integer t and $0 \leq \theta < 1$) (Figure 4.1).

The dirty price $P^{(d)}$ of the bond is linked to the clean price P by the relation $P^{(d)}_{t+\theta} = P_{t+\theta} + \theta \cdot C_{t+1}$.

The accrued interest system affects the rate of return, as the purchaser, at the moment of the transaction, pre-finances part of the next coupon. A slight reduction in the actuarial rate therefore occurs, and will be smaller the closer the moment of the deal is (before or after) to a coupon payment date. For this reason, it is known as the *festoon effect*.

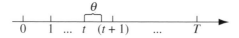

Figure 4.1   Accrued interest

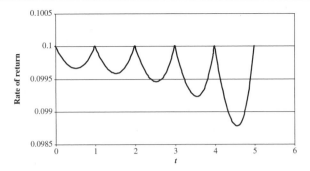

Figure 4.2 Festoon effect

The actuarial rate of return is calculated in the classic way, and is defined implicitly by the relation:

$$P_{t+\theta} + \theta \cdot C_{t+1} = \sum_{k=t+1}^{T} C_k(1+r)^{-k+t+\theta} + R(1+r)^{-T+t+\theta}$$

Example

Let us consider a bond, issued and repayable at par, with a price at a constant 100, which presents annual coupons at 10 for five years and clearly has an actuarial rate at issue of 10 %. This will produce the graph shown in Figure 4.2.

4.1.3 Valuing a bond

The value of a bond at any given moment (that is, its price) is the discounted value of the financial flows generated (residual coupons and final repayment), the discounting rate being the market rate[5] for bonds of the same nature and the same residual time (we will term it r_m).

On the day after the payment of the tth coupon, the valuation is made using the equation:

$$P_t = \sum_{k=t+1}^{T} C_k(1+r_m)^{-k+t} + R(1+r_m)^{-T+t}$$

At a given moment $t + \theta$ (integer t and $0 \leq \theta < 1$), we will, taking the accrued interest into account, have:

$$P_{t+\theta} = -\theta \cdot C_{t+1} + \sum_{k=t+1}^{T} C_k(1+r_m)^{-k+t+\theta} + R(1+r_m)^{-T+t+\theta}$$

4.2   BONDS AND FINANCIAL RISK

4.2.1 Sources of risk

A bond is a financial asset generally considered to be low risk in comparison to equities or derivatives with high leverage effect. This does not mean, however, that holding bonds does not pose certain risks.

---

[5] This arises from the law of supply and demand.

4.2.1.1 Default risk

The *default risk*, which relates to cases in which the issuer fails to honour his undertaking, can be described as late payment of coupons, bankruptcy with consequent nonpayment of coupons, and nonrepayment at maturity date.

This default risk cannot, of course, be quantified. Note, however, that bond market professionals attach considerable importance to ratings allocated to issuers through certain agencies such as Moody's and Standard & Poor's, with the aim of determining the quality of the issuers and therefore 'estimating' the probability of default. This means that for the same maturity date, a coupon for an issuer rating of AAA (the highest) will be less than the coupon offered by a B-rated issuer; the concept intuitively recognised here is that of market price of risk. In addition, the rating will have a direct influence on another nonquantifiable risk, the liquidity of the security in question.

4.2.1.2 Rate fluctuation risk

Another type of risk associated with bonds, this one quantifiable, is the risk linked to fluctuations in interest rates.

For certain specific bonds (known as call-associated bonds), the issuer has the right to repay the bond before its maturity date. If the repayment is made just after a fall in interest rates, it will not be possible for the investor to reinvest the total repaid at a rate equivalent to that of the security, and the investor therefore suffers a loss of income.

However, as we stated in the introduction (Section 4.1.1), we are not looking at this type of product here. We will therefore limit ourselves to analysing the risk of a 'classic' bond. Two aspects of this risk, which in one sense are contradictory, may be taken into consideration.

First, there is the *risk of reinvestment*. In the event of a change in market rates, the coupons (and sometimes the repayment value itself) will be reinvested at a different rate. In this instance, an increase (decrease) in the interest rate will be favourable (unfavourable) to the investor.

Then, there is the *risk of realisation* if the bond is sold before its maturity date. The sale price is determined by the discounted value of the term coupons (at the rate in force on the market at the time) and by the repayment value. In this case, an increase (decrease) in the interest rate will of course be unfavourable (favourable) to the investor.

Example

Let us consider a bond with nominal value of 1000, without issue or repayment premium ($NV = P = R = 1000$), with a period of eight years and a coupon constant of 100. In this case, the actuarial rate at issue r is equal to the nominal return rate, that is, 10 %. Let us suppose also that at the end of the second year, the market rate changes from 10 % to 12 %.

What will happen if the investor wants to resell the bond after four years? To analyse the situation, we will determine the actuarial rate of return $r(4)$ at moment 4.

Reinvesting the coupons (at 10 % during the first two years and at 12 % afterwards) gives, in $t = 4$, a purchase value of[6] $A_4 = 100 \cdot 1.1 \cdot 1.12^2 + 100 \cdot 1.12^2 + 100 \cdot 1.12 + 100 = 475.424$.

---

[6] While without a rate change, we would have obtained $A_4 = 464.1$, which clearly shows that a rise in rates is favourable.

In addition, the resale value at $t = 4$ is given by the discounted value (12 %) of the term coupons and the repayment:[7]

$$B_4 = \frac{100}{1.12} + \frac{100}{1.12^2} + \frac{100}{1.12^3} + \frac{1100}{1.12^4} = 939.253$$

The *ex post* return rate is defined by the relation $P \cdot (1 + r(4))^4 = 1414.677$, which ultimately leads to $r(4) = 9.06\%$. This rate is lower than the one found by replacing A_4 with B_4 by 1464.1, as we would be using 10 %, the actuarial rate of the bond at its issue.

By applying the same reasoning to an investor who resells his bond after seven years, we obtain for a reinvestment value $A_7 = 1005.376$ and for a realisation value $B_7 = 982.143$ (instead of 948.717 and 1000 respectively if the rate had not changed). The *ex post* rate of return is then given by $r(7) = 10.31$ (instead of 10 %). This time, the combination of the two effects is reversed and favours the investor.

4.2.2 Duration

4.2.2.1 Definition

The observations made in the above example raise the question of identifying at which the increase/decrease in the interest rate is unfavourable/favourable to the investor and at which point it becomes favourable/unfavourable to the investor.

The answer to this question is found in the concept of *duration*.[8] Let us consider a bond at the moment of its issue[9] with actuarial rate r. Its duration, termed D, is defined as follows:

$$D = \frac{\sum_{t=1}^{T} t \cdot C_t (1 + r)^{-t} + T \cdot R(1 + r)^{-T}}{\sum_{t=1}^{T} C_t (1 + r)^{-t} + R(1 + r)^{-T}}$$

The concept of *modified duration* is also entered, as is the *sensitivity coefficient*, defined by:

$$D_m = \frac{D}{1 + r}$$

Note

In addition to this 'simple' concept of duration, a more developed concept of 'stochastic duration' will be issued in Section 4.6.

4.2.2.2 Interpretations

The concept of duration can be interpreted in several different ways; the two best known follow.

---

[7] While with an initial rate of 10 %, we would have obtained $B_4 = 1000$. This time, the rise in interest rates clearly does not favour the investor.

[8] This concept was introduced in Macauley F., *Some Theoretical Problems Suggested by the Movement of Interest Rates, Bond Yields and Stock Prices in the United States since 1856*, National Bureau of Economic Research, 1938, pp. 44–53.

[9] This concept can easily be generalised at any time, provided it is assumed that the rate r stays constant.

Duration can first of all be considered as the average life span of the bond, the weighting coefficients for this average being proportional to the discounted values for the rate r of the financial flows (coupons and repayment) at the corresponding times. In fact, given that the denominator is none other than the price P on issue, we can write:

$$D = \sum_{t=1}^{T} t \frac{C_t(1+r)^{-t}}{P} + T \frac{R(1+r)^{-T}}{P}$$

$$= 1 \cdot \frac{C_1(1+r)^{-1}}{P} + \cdots + (T-1) \cdot \frac{C_{T-1}(1+r)^{-(T-1)}}{P} + T \cdot \frac{(C_T + R)(1+r)^{-T}}{P}$$

Duration can also be interpreted in terms of sensitivity of prices to interest rates. When two economic variables x and y are linked by a relation $y = y(x)$, one way of describing the way in which y depends on x is to use the derivative $y'(x)$.

The relation that defines the actuarial rate, $P = \sum_{t=1}^{T} C_t(1+r)^{-t} + R(1+r)^{-T}$, defines a function $P(r)$. The derivative of this function can be written

$$P'(r) = - \sum_{t=1}^{T} t \cdot C_t(1+r)^{-t-1} - T \cdot R(1+r)^{-T-1}$$

$$= -(1+r)^{-1} \left\{ \sum_{t=1}^{T} t \cdot C_t(1+r)^{-t} + T \cdot R(1+r)^{-T} \right\}$$

$$= -(1+r)^{-1} D \cdot P(r)$$

This shows how the duration works in the measurement of changes in P according to r. This relation can also be written:

$$D = -(1+r)\frac{P'(r)}{P(r)}$$

or:

$$D_m = -\frac{P'(r)}{P(r)}$$

By taking a small variation in the Δr rate into account instead of the infinitesimal variation, and noting that $\Delta P = P(r + \Delta r) - P(r)$, the previous relation is written as:

$$D = -(1+r)\frac{\frac{\Delta P}{\Delta r}}{P}$$

$$= -\frac{\frac{\Delta P}{P}}{\frac{\Delta(1+r)}{1+r}}$$

$$= \varepsilon(P/1+r)$$

because the variation Δr is the same as $\Delta(1+r)$.

We are looking here at the classic economic concept of *elasticity*. Generally speaking, the elasticity $\varepsilon(y/x)$ of y with respect to x,

$$\varepsilon(y/x) = \frac{\dfrac{\Delta y}{y}}{\dfrac{\Delta x}{x}}$$

is interpreted as follows: if x increases by 1 %, y will vary (increase or decrease according to the sign of Δy) by $|\varepsilon(y/x)|$ %.

Duration is therefore shown as elasticity (with minus sign) of the price of the bond with respect to $(1 + r)$, and a relative increase of 1 % in $(1 + r)$ will lead to a relative decrease in P of D %.

Example

Let us take the data used above (a bond issued and repaid at par, 1000 in value, eight years in maturity and coupon constant at 100; $r = 10$ %). It is easily shown that $D = 5.868$.

If the relative increase in $(1 + r)$ is 1 % (that is, if $(1 + r)$ changes from 1.1 to 1.1 $\times 1.01 = 1.111$, or if r changes from 10 % to 11.1 %), it is easy to see from the direct calculation that the price changes from $P(10\%) = 1000$ to:

$$P(11.1\%) = \sum_{t=1}^{8} 100 \cdot 1.111^{-t} + 1000 \cdot 1.111^{-8} = 943.59$$

This total therefore decreases by 5.64 %, the difference with respect to duration arising simply because we have not used an infinitesimal increase.

4.2.2.3 Duration of specific bonds

The duration of a zero-coupon bond is equal to its maturity. In fact, it is given by:

$$D = \frac{T \cdot R(1 + r)^{-T}}{R(1 + r)^{-T}} = T$$

In all other cases, duration is strictly less than maturity; we are looking in fact at a weighted average of the numbers 1, 2, ..., T.

A *perpetual bond* is a security that goes on issuing coupons *ad infinitum* (and issues no repayment). It is supposed here that the coupons are for the same total C.

Here, the relation that defines the actual rates on return takes the form[10]

$$P = C \sum_{t=1}^{\infty} (1 + r)^{-t} = \frac{C}{r}$$

---

[10] By using the concept of the *geometric series*.

This allows the duration of a perpetual bond to be calculated:

$$D = -(1+r)\frac{P'(r)}{P(r)} = -(1+r)\frac{-\dfrac{C}{r^2}}{\dfrac{C}{r}} = \frac{1+r}{r}$$

4.2.2.4 Duration and characteristics of a bond

Duration is a function of the parameters r_n (nominal rate), r (actuarial rate) and T (maturity). Here we show the way in which it depends on these three parameters, without strict supporting calculations.[11]

Duration is a decreasing function of r_n, the two parameters r and T being fixed. In the same way, it is a decreasing function of r, the two parameters r and T being fixed.

The dependency of D on T (r and r_n being fixed) is more complex. We have already indicated that the duration of a zero-coupon bond is equal to its maturity and that of a perpetual obligation is equal to $(1+r)/r$. For a bond repayable at par and with constant coupons, it can be shown that:

- If it is issued at par or above par, D increases concavely along with T, with:

$$\lim_{T \to \infty} D(T) \begin{Bmatrix} = \\ < \end{Bmatrix} \frac{1+r}{r}$$

  depending on whether the bond is issued at par or above par.
- If it is issued below par, D shows an increase according to T until a certain moment passes, and then decreases.

4.2.2.5 Immunisation of bonds

The most important aspect of duration is that the reinvestment risk and the sale risk will balance if the bond is sold at moment D. Interest rate changes will not have any more influence on the actuarial *ex post* rate of return. The bond is said to be *immunised* at horizon D against the interest-rate risk.

This result is not in fact accurate unless the interest-rate changes are of low magnitude and occur just after the security is purchased.

Let us therefore suppose that a small change Δr in the market rate (that is, the actuarial rate on issue) occurs just after the security is issued; this rate changes from r to $r + \Delta r$.

Let us now go to a time $t + \theta$ (integer t and $0 \le \theta < 1$) in the life of the bond. We have to prove that if the security is immunised at the horizon $t + \theta$ (that is, if the actuarial rate of return $r(t + \theta)$ is equal to the rate r at issue), $t + \theta$ is equal to the *duration D* of the bond.

The reinvestment and sale values at the moment $t + \theta$ are given respectively by:

$$A_{t+\theta} = \sum_{k=1}^{t} C_k (1 + r + \Delta r)^{t+\theta-k}$$

$$B_{t+\theta} = \sum_{k=t+1}^{T} C_k (1 + r + \Delta r)^{-k+t+\theta} + R(1 + r + \Delta r)^{-T+t+\theta}$$

---

[11] The reasoning is not very complicated, but is quite demanding.

Their sum is therefore equal to:

$$A_{t+\theta} + B_{t+\theta} = (1+r+\Delta r)^{t+\theta}\left[\sum_{k=1}^{T} C_k(1+r+\Delta r)^{-k} + R(1+r+\Delta r)^{-T}\right]$$

Let us express the powers shown in this expression using a Taylor development to the first degree:

$$(1+r+\Delta r)^m = (1+r)^m + m(1+r)^{m-1}\Delta r + O((\Delta r)^2)$$

This allows the following to be written:

$$A_{t+\theta} + B_{t+\theta}$$

$$= [(1+r)^{t+\theta} + (t+\theta)(1+r)^{t+\theta-1}\Delta r + O((\Delta r)^2)]$$

$$\cdot\left\{\sum_{k=1}^{T} C_k[(1+r)^{-k} - k(1+r)^{-k-1}\Delta r + O((\Delta r)^2)]\right.$$

$$\left. + R[(1+r)^{-T} - T(1+r)^{-T-1}\Delta r + O((\Delta r)^2)]\right\}$$

$$= (1+r)^{t+\theta}\left[1 + \frac{t+\theta}{1+r}\Delta r + O((\Delta r)^2)\right]$$

$$\cdot\left\{\left[\sum_{k=1}^{T} C_k(1+r)^{-k} + R(1+r)^{-T}\right]\right.$$

$$\left. - \left[\sum_{k=1}^{T} k \cdot C_k(1+r)^{-k-1} + T \cdot R(1+r)^{-T-1}\right]\Delta r + O((\Delta r)^2)\right\}$$

$$= (1+r)^{t+\theta}\left[1 + \frac{t+\theta}{1+r}\Delta r + O((\Delta r)^2)\right] \cdot \left\{P - \frac{D \cdot P}{1+r}\Delta r + O((\Delta r)^2)\right\}$$

$$= (1+r)^{t+\theta} P \cdot \left[1 + \frac{t+\theta-D}{1+r}\Delta r + O((\Delta r)^2)\right]$$

By definition of the actuarial rate at moment t, we also have

$$A_{t+\theta} + B_{t+\theta} = P \cdot (1 + r(t+\theta))^{t+\theta}$$

This is only possible if the coefficient $\dfrac{t+\theta-D}{1+r}$ is zero, that is, if $t+\theta = D$, which we wished to prove.

Example

Let us take the data used above (a bond issued and repaid at par, value 1000, maturity eight years and coupon constant at 100, $r = 10\%$ and $D = 5.868$), and assume that immediately after its issue the rate of interest changes from 10 % to 9 % and remains at that level subsequently.

The reinvestment and sale values at moment D will be given respectively by:

$$A_D = 100 \cdot (1.09^{D-1} + 1.09^{D-2} + 1.09^{D-3} + 1.09^{D-4} + 1.09^{D-5}) = 644.98$$

$$B_D = \frac{100}{1.09^{6-D}} + \frac{100}{1.09^{7-D}} + \frac{1100}{1.09^{8-D}} = 1104.99$$

The actuarial rate of return at moment D will be given by:

$$1000 \cdot (1 + r(D))^D = 1104.99 + 644.98$$

We therefore find that $r(D) = 10.005 \%$, which clearly shows that the two sources of risk vanish at a horizon that is equal to the duration.[12]

4.2.2.6 Approximation of a bond price

Applying the Taylor formula to the expression $P(r + \Delta r)$ gives

$$P(r + \Delta r) = P(r) + P'(r) \cdot \Delta r + O((\Delta r)^2)$$

$$= P(r) - \frac{D \cdot P(r)}{1 + r} \Delta r + O((\Delta r)^2)$$

This allows an approximate formula to be written for evaluating $P(r + \Delta r)$:

$$P(r + \Delta r) \approx P(r) \left[1 - \frac{D}{1 + r} \Delta r \right]$$

$$\approx P(r)[1 - D_m \cdot \Delta r]$$

Example

Following the previous example (a bond issued and repaid at par, value 1000, maturity eight years and coupon constant at 1000, $r = 10 \%$ and $D = 5.868$), we have for this modified duration:

$$D_m = \frac{5.868}{1.1} = 5.335$$

Let us verify the interpretation of this parameter for an increase of 0.8 % in r. The new price (exact development) is then given by

$$P(0.108) = 100 \cdot \sum_{t=1}^{8} 1.108^{-t} + 1000 \cdot 1.108^{-8} = 958.536$$

---

[12] The very slight difference between $r(D)$ and the actuarial rate of return at issue ($r = 10\%$) arises because the result that we have given (demonstrated using the Taylor formula) is only valid for an infinitesimal variation in the rate of interest, while in our example the variation is 1 %.

While the above approximation gives:

$$P(0.108) \approx 1000 \cdot (1 - 5.335 \cdot 0.008) = 957.321$$

The relation $P(r + \Delta r) - P(r) \approx -D_m P(r) \cdot \Delta r$ used with $\Delta r = 0.0001$ (this one-hundredth per cent is termed the *basis point*), gives the price variation for a bond as triggered by an increase in the actuarial rate. This variation is known as the *value of one basis point* and termed the VBP.

4.2.3 Convexity

4.2.3.1 Definition

The duration (or modified duration) allows the variations in price to be understood in terms of interest rates, but only in a linear way. This linear variation is clearly shown by the first-degree relation:

$$P(r + \Delta r) \approx P(r) \cdot \left[1 - D \frac{\Delta r}{1 + r} \right]$$

It is, however, easy to show that the price curve is not in fact linear (see Figure 4.3). In order to take this curve into consideration, a new parameter is reduced.

In this way, the *convexity* of a bond, termed C, is defined by the relation:

$$C = \frac{\displaystyle\sum_{t=1}^{T} t(t+1)C_t(1+r)^{-t} + T(T+1)R(1+r)^{-T}}{(1+r)^2 \cdot \left[\displaystyle\sum_{t=1}^{T} C_t(1+r)^{-t} + R(1+r)^{-T} \right]}$$

Example

Let us take once again the data used above (a bond issued and repaid at par, value 1000, maturity eight years and coupon constant at 1000, $r = 10\%$).

$$C = \frac{100 \cdot [1 \cdot 2 \cdot 1.1^{-1} + 2 \cdot 3 \cdot 1.1^{-2} + \cdots + 8 \cdot 9 \cdot 1.1^{-8}] + 1000 \cdot 8 \cdot 9 \cdot 1.1^{-8}}{1.1^2 \cdot \{100 \cdot [1.1^{-1} + 1.1^{-2} + \cdots + 1.1^{-8}] + 1000 \cdot 1.1^{-8}\}} = 38.843$$

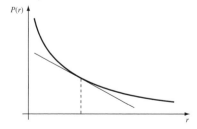

Figure 4.3   Price of a bond

4.2.3.2 Interpretation

The mathematical concept that allows this curve to be taken into consideration is the second derivative of the function. We therefore have:

$$P''(r) = \sum_{t=1}^{T} t(t+1) \cdot C_t (1+r)^{-t-2} + T(T+1) \cdot R(1+r)^{-T-2}$$

$$= (1+r)^{-2} \left\{ \sum_{t=1}^{T} t(t+1) \cdot C_t (1+r)^{-t} + T(T+1) \cdot R(1+r)^{-T} \right\}$$

$$= C \cdot P(r)$$

This allows us to write: $C = \dfrac{P''(r)}{P(r)}$.

4.2.3.3 Approximating a bond price

We can now apply the Taylor formula to the expression $P(r + \Delta r)$ up to order 2:

$$P(r + \Delta r) = P(r) + P'(r) \cdot \Delta r + \frac{P''(r)}{2}(\Delta r)^2 + O\left((\Delta r)^3\right)$$

$$= P(r) - \frac{D \cdot P(r)}{1+r}\Delta r + \frac{C \cdot P(r)}{2}(\Delta r)^2 + O\left((\Delta r)^3\right)$$

This gives us the approximation formula

$$P(r + \Delta r) \approx P(r)[1 - D_m \cdot \Delta r + \tfrac{1}{2}C \cdot (\Delta r)^2]$$

Example

Let us continue with the previous example (a bond issued and repaid at par, value 1000, maturity eight years and coupon constant at 100; $r = 10\,\%$, $D = 5.868$ and $C = 38.843$. Assuming once again an increase of 0.8 % in r, we have the following price valuation:

$$P(0.108) \approx 1000 \cdot [1 - 5.335 \cdot 0.008 + \tfrac{1}{2}38.843 \cdot 0.008^2] = 958.564$$

This is a much more accurate approximation than the one that uses only duration, as duration only will give a value of 957.321 when the precise value is 958.536.

As the second-degree term $C(\Delta r)^2/2$ of the approximation formula is always positive, it therefore appears that when one has to choose between two bonds with the same return (actuarial rate) and duration, it will be preferable to choose the one with the greater convexity regardless of the direction of the potential variation in the rate of return.

4.3 DETERMINISTIC STRUCTURE OF INTEREST RATES[13]

4.3.1 Yield curves

The actuarial rate at the issue of a bond, as defined in Section 4.1.2 is obviously a particular characteristic to the security in question. The rate will vary from one bond to another, depending mainly on the quality of the issuer (assessed using the ratings issued by public rating companies) and the maturity of the security.

The first factor is of course very difficult to model, and we will not be taking account of it, assuming throughout this section 4.3 that we are dealing with a public issuer who does not carry any risk of default. As for the second factor, it can be assumed that for equal levels of maturity, the rate is the same for all securities in accordance with the law of supply and demand. In reality, the coupon policies of the various issuers introduce additional differences; in the following paragraphs, therefore, we will only be dealing with zero-coupon bonds whose rate now depends only on their maturities. This simplification is justified by the fact that a classic bond is a simple 'superimposition' of zero-coupon securities, which will be valuated by discounting of the various financial flows (coupons and repayment) at the corresponding rate.[14]

We are only dealing with deterministic structures for interest rates; random cases are dealt with in Section 4.5.

If we describe $P(s)$ as the issue price of a zero-coupon bond with maturity s and $R(s)$ as the rate observed on the market at moment 0 for this type of security, called the *spot rate*, these two values are clearly linked by the relation $P(s) = (1 + R(s))^{-s}$.

The value $R(s)$, for all the values of $s > 0$, constitutes the *term interest-rate structure* at moment 0 and the graph for this function is termed the *yield curve*.

The most natural direction of the yield curve is of course upwards; the investor should gain more if he invests over a longer period. This, however, is not always the case; in practice we frequently see flat curves (constant $R(s)$ value) as well as increasing curves, as well as inverted curves (decreasing $R(s)$ value) and humped curves (see Figure 4.4).

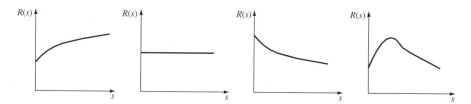

Figure 4.4   Interest rate curves

---

[13] A detailed presentation of these concepts can be found in Bisière C., *La Structure par Terme des Taux d'intérêt*, Presses Universitaires de France, 1997.

[14] This justifies the title of this present section, which mentions 'interest rates' and not bonds.

4.3.2   Static interest rate structure

The static models examine the structure of interest rates at a fixed moment, which we will term 0, and deal with a zero-coupon bond that gives rise to a repayment of 1, which is not a restriction.

In this and the next paragraph, we will detail the model for the discrete case and then generalise it for the continuous case. These are the continuous aspects that will be used in Section 4.5 for the stochastic dynamic models.

4.3.2.1   Discrete model

The price at 0 for a bond of maturity level s is termed[15] $P_0(s)$ and the associated spot rate is represented by $R_0(s)$. We therefore have: $P_0(s) = (1 + R_0(s))^{-s}$.

The spot interest rate at $R_0(s)$ in fact combines all the information on interest rates relative to period [0,1], [1, 2] ..., [s − 1, s]. We will give the symbol $r(t)$ and the term *term interest rate* or *short-term interest rate* to the aspects relative to the period [t − 1; t]. We therefore have: $(1 + R_0(s))^s = (1 + r(1)). (1 + r(2)). .... (1 + r(s))$.

Reciprocally, it is easy to express the terms according to the spot-rate terms:

$$\begin{cases} r(1) = R_0(1) \\ 1 + r(s) = \dfrac{(1 + R_0(s))^s}{(1 + R_0(s - 1))^{s-1}} & s = 2, 3, \ldots \end{cases}$$

In the same way, we have:

$$r(s) = \frac{P_0(s - 1)}{P_0(s)} - 1 \quad (s > 0)$$

To sum up, we can easily move from any one of the following three structures to another; the price structure $\{R_0(s) : s = 1, 2, \ldots\}$ and the term interest structure $\{r(s) : s = 1, 2, \ldots\}$.

Example

Let us consider a spot rate structure defined for maturity dates 1−6 shown in Table 4.1.

This (increasing) structure is shown in Figure 4.5.

From this, it is easy to deduce prices and term rates: for example:

$$P_0(5) = 1.075^{-5} = 0.6966$$

$$r(5) = 1.075^5 / 1.073^4 - 1 = 0.0830$$

This generally gives data shown in Table 4.2.

Table 4.1   Spot-rate structure

s	1	2	3	4	5	6
$R_0(s)$	6.0%	6.6%	7.0%	7.3%	7.5%	7.6%

[15] Of course, $P_0(0) = 1$.

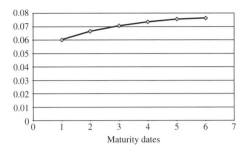

Figure 4.5   Spot-rate structure

Table 4.2   Price and rate structures at 0

s	$R_0(s)$	$P_0(s)$	$r(s)$
0		1.0000	
1	0.060	0.9434	0.0600
2	0.066	0.8800	0.0720
3	0.070	0.8163	0.0780
4	0.073	0.7544	0.0821
5	0.075	0.6966	0.0830
6	0.076	0.6444	0.0810

4.3.2.2   *Continuous model*

If the time set is $[0; +\infty]$, we retain the same definitions and notations for the price structures and spot rates: $\{P_0(s): s > 0\}$ and $\{R_0(s) : s > 0\}$. This last will be an instant rate; after a period s, a total 1 will become, at this rate : $e^{s \cdot R_0(s)}$.

We will also note, before taking limits, $R_0^d(s)$ being the spot rate for the discrete model (even applied to a non integer period). It is therefore linked to the spot rate for the continuous model by the relation $R_0(s) = \ln(1 + R_0^d(s))$.

With regard to the term rate, we are provisionally introducing the notation $r(t_1, t_2)$ to represent the interest rate relative to the period $[t_1; t_2]$ and we define the *instant term interest rate* by:

$$r(t) = \lim_{s \to t+} \frac{1}{s - t} \int_t^s r(t, u)\, du$$

We can readily obtain, as above:

$$(1 + r(s, s + \Delta s))^{\Delta s} = \frac{\left(1 + R_0^d(s + \Delta s)\right)^{s + \Delta s}}{\left(1 + R_0^d(s)\right)^s}$$

Thanks to the Taylor formula, this is written:

$$[1 + \Delta s.r(s, s + \Delta s) + O((\Delta s)^2)].(1 + R_0^d(s))^s = (1 + R_0^d(s + \Delta s))^{s + \Delta s}$$

This relation can be rewritten as:

$$r(s, s + \Delta s) \cdot \left(1 + R_0^d(s)\right)^s + O(\Delta s) = \frac{\left(1 + R_0^d(s + \Delta s)\right)^{s+\Delta s} - \left(1 + R_0^d(s)\right)^s}{\Delta s}$$

After taking the limit, this becomes:

$$r(s) = \frac{\left[(1 + R_0^d(s))^s\right]'}{\left(1 + R_0^d(s)\right)^s} = \left[\ln\left(1 + R_0^d(s)\right)^s\right]' = \left[s \cdot \ln\left(1 + R_0^d(s)\right)\right]' = [s \cdot R_0(s)]'$$

This relation, which expresses the spot rate according to the instant term rate, can easily be inverted by integrating:

$$R_0(s) = \frac{1}{s} \int_0^s r(u)\, du$$

It can also be expressed easily by saying that the spot rate for the period [0; s] is the average of the instant term rate for the same period. The price is of course linked to the two rates by the relations:

$$P_0(s) = e^{-s \cdot R_0(s)} = e^{-\int_0^s r(u)\, du}$$

Note

For a flat rate structure (that is, $R_0(s)$ independent of s), it is easy to see, by developing the relation $[s \cdot R_0(s)]' = r_0(s)$, that

$$R_0(s) = r(s) = r \text{ for every } s$$

and that the price structure is given, $P_0(s) = e^{-rs}$.

4.3.3 Dynamic interest rate structure

The dynamic models examine the structure of the interest rates at any given moment t. They always deal with zero-coupon bonds, issued at 0 and giving rise to a repayment of 1.

They may allow the distortions in the rate curve to be taken into account; in fact, we will be studying the link that exists between price and rate structures for the various observation periods.

4.3.3.1 Discrete model

The price at the moment t for the bond issued at 0 and maturing at s is termed[16] $P_t(s)$. The term $R_t(s)$ is given to the spot rate relative to the interval] t; s]. Finally, the term rate relative to the period] $t - 1$; t] is termed $r(t)$.

---

[16] It is of course supposed that $0 < t < s$.

Following reasoning similar in every way to that used for the static models, we will readily obtain the relations

$$P_t(s) = (1 + R_t(s))^{-(s-t)}$$

$$(1 + R_t(s))^{s-t} = (1 + r(t+1)) \cdot (1 + r(t+2)) \cdot \ldots \cdot (1 + r(s))$$

This will invert readily to

$$\begin{cases} r(t+1) = R_t(t+1) \\ 1 + r(s) = \dfrac{(1 + R_t(s))^s}{(1 + R_t(s-1))^{s-1}} \quad s = t+2, t+3, \ldots \end{cases}$$

We also have, between the structure of the prices and that of the interest rates:

$$r(s) = \frac{P_t(s-1)}{P_t(s)} - 1 \quad (s > t)$$

The link between the price structures at different observation times is expressed by the following relation:

$$P_t(s) = [(1 + r(t+1)) \cdot (1 + r(t+2)) \cdot \ldots \cdot (1 + r(s))]^{-1}$$

$$= \left[\frac{(1 + r(t)) \cdot (1 + r(t+1)) \cdot (1 + r(t+2)) \cdot \ldots \cdot (1 + r(s))}{(1 + r(t))} \right]^{-1}$$

$$= \frac{(1 + R_{t-1}(s))^{-(s-t+1)}}{(1 + R_{t-1}(t))^{-1}}$$

$$= \frac{P_{t-1}(s)}{P_{t-1}(t)}$$

This result can easily be generalised, whatever u may be, placed between t and s ($t \le u \le s$), we have:

$$P_t(s) = \frac{P_u(s)}{P_u(t)}$$

From this relation it is possible to deduce a link, which, however, has a rather ungainly expression, between the spot-rate structures at the various times.

Example

Let us take once again the spot interest-rate structure used in the previous paragraph: 6 %, 6.6 %, 7 %, 7.3 %, 7.5 % and 7.6 % for the respective payment dates at 1, 2, 3, 4, 5 and 6 years. Let us see what happens to the structure after two years. We can find easily:

$$P_2(5) = \frac{P_0(5)}{P_0(2)} = \frac{0.69656}{0.88001} = 0.7915$$

$$R_2(5) = P_2(5)^{\frac{-1}{5-2}} - 1 = 0.7915^{-1/3} - 1 = 0.0810$$

Table 4.3   Price and rate structures at 2

s	$P_2(s)$	$R_2(s)$
2	1.0000	
3	0.9276	0.0780
4	0.8573	0.0800
5	0.7915	0.0810
6	0.7322	0.0810

and more generally as shown in Table 4.3.

Note that we have:

$$r(5) = \frac{P_0(4)}{P_0(5)} - 1 = \frac{P_2(4)}{P_2(5)} - 1 = 0.0830$$

4.3.3.2   Continuous model

The prices $P_t(s)$ and the spot rates $R_t(s)$ are defined as for the static models, but with an observation at moment t instead of 0. The instant term rates $r(t)$ are defined in the same way.

It can easily be seen that the relations that link the two are:

$$r(s) = [(s - t) \cdot R_t(s)]'_s \qquad \forall t$$

$$R_t(s) = \frac{1}{s - t} \int_t^s r(u) \, du$$

Meanwhile, the relations that link rates to prices are given by:

$$P_t(s) = e^{-(s-t) \cdot R_t(s)} = e^{-\int_t^s r(u) \, du}$$

4.3.4   Deterministic model and stochastic model

The relations mentioned above have been established in a deterministic context. Among other things, the short instant rate and the term rate have been assimilated. More generally (stochastic model), the following distinction should be made.

1. The instant term rate, defined by: $r(t) = \lim\limits_{s \to t+} R_t(s)$.
2. The instant term or forward rate, defined as follows: if $f_t(s_1, s_2)$ represents the rate of interest seen since time t for a bond issued at s_1 and with maturity at s_2, the forward rate (in s seen from t, with $t < s$) is: $f_t(s) = \lim\limits_{u \to s+} f_t(s, u)$.

In a general model, this forward rate must be used to find the price and spot-rate structures:

$$P_t(s) = e^{-\int_t^s f_t(u) \, du}$$

$$R_t(s) = \frac{1}{s - t} \int_t^s f_t(u) \, du$$

It can easily be seen that these two rates (instant term and forward) are linked by the relation $r(t) = f_t(t)$.

It can be demonstrated that in the deterministic case, $f_t(s)$ is independent of t and the two rates can therefore be identified: $f_t(s) = r(s)$. It is therefore only in this context that we have:

$$P_t(s) = e^{-\int_t^s r(u)\,du}$$

$$R_t(s) = \frac{1}{s-t} \int_t^s r(u)\,du$$

$$P_t(s) = \frac{P_u(s)}{P_u(t)}$$

4.4   BOND PORTFOLIO MANAGEMENT STRATEGIES

4.4.1   Passive strategy: immunisation

The aim of passive management is to neutralise the portfolio risk caused by fluctuations in interest rates.

4.4.1.1   Duration and convexity of portfolio

Let us consider a bond portfolio consisting at moment 0 of N securities ($j = 1, \ldots, N$), each characterised by:

- a maturity (residual life) T_j;
- coupons yet to come C_j, t ($t = 1, \ldots, T_j$);
- a repayment value R_j;
- an actuarial rate on issue r_j;
- a price P_j.

The highest of the maturity values T_j will be termed T, and $F_{j,t}$ the financial flow generated by the security j at the moment t:

$$F_{j,t} = \begin{cases} C_j & \text{if } t < T_j \\ C_{T_j} + R_j & \text{if } t = T_j \\ 0 & \text{if } t > T_j \end{cases}$$

The duration of the jth security is given by

$$D_j = \frac{\displaystyle\sum_{t=1}^{T_j} t \cdot C_{j,t}(1+r_j)^{-t} + T_j \cdot R_j(1+r_j)^{-T_j}}{\displaystyle\sum_{t=1}^{T_j} C_{j,t}(1+r_j)^{-t} + R_j(1+r_j)^{-T_j}} = \frac{\displaystyle\sum_{t=1}^{T} t \cdot F_{j,t}(1+r_j)^{-t}}{P_j}$$

Finally, let us suppose that the jth security is present within the portfolio in the number n_j. The discounted financial flow generated by the portfolio at moment t totals:

$$\sum_{j=1}^{N} n_j F_{j,t}(1+r_j)^{-t}$$

Its price totals: $\sum_{j=1}^{N} n_j P_j$.

The duration of the portfolio can therefore be written as:

$$D_P = \frac{\displaystyle\sum_{t=1}^{T} t \cdot \sum_{j=1}^{N} n_j F_{j,t}(1+r_j)^{-t}}{\displaystyle\sum_{k=1}^{N} n_k P_k}$$

$$= \sum_{j=1}^{N} \frac{n_j}{\displaystyle\sum_{k=1}^{N} n_k P_k} \sum_{t=1}^{T_j} t \cdot F_{j,t}(1+r_j)^{-t}$$

$$= \sum_{j=1}^{N} \frac{n_j P_j}{\displaystyle\sum_{k=1}^{N} n_k P_k} \cdot \frac{\displaystyle\sum_{t=1}^{T_j} t \cdot F_{j,t}(1+r_j)^{-t}}{P_j}$$

$$= \sum_{j=1}^{N} X_j D_j$$

Where: $X_j = \dfrac{n_j P_j}{\sum_{k=1}^{N} n_k P_k}$ represents the proportion of the jth security within the portfolio, expressed in terms of capitalisation.

The same reasoning will reveal the convexity of the portfolio:

$$C_P = \sum_{j=1}^{N} X_j C_j$$

4.4.1.2 Immunising a portfolio

A portfolio is said to be immunised at horizon H if its value at that date is at least the value that it would have had if interest rates had remained constant during the period $[0; H]$. By applying the result arrived at in Section 4.2.2 for a bond in the portfolio, we obtain the same result: a bond portfolio is immunised at a horizon that corresponds to its duration.

Of course, whenever the interest rate changes, the residual duration varies suddenly. A careful bond portfolio manager wishing to immunise his portfolio for a horizon H that he has fixed must therefore:

- Put together a portfolio with duration H.
- After each (significant) interest rate change, alter the composition of the portfolio by making sales and purchases (that is, alter the proportions of X_j) so that the residual duration can be 'pursued'.

Of course these alterations to the portfolio composition will incur transaction charges, which should be taken into consideration and balanced against the benefits supplied by the immunising strategy.

Note

It was stated in Section 4.2.3 that of two bonds that present the same return (actuarial rate) and duration, the one with the higher convexity will be of greater interest. This result remains valid for a portfolio, and the manager must therefore take it into consideration whenever revising his portfolio.

4.4.2   Active strategy

The aim of active management is to obtain a return higher than that produced by immunisation, that is, higher than the actuarial return rate on issue.

In the case of increasing rates (the commonest case), when the rate curve remains unchanged over time, the technique is to purchase securities with a higher maturity than the investment horizon and to sell them before their maturity date.[17]

Example

Let us take once again the rate structure shown in the previous section (Table 4.4).

Let us suppose that the investor fixes a two-year horizon. If he simply purchases a security with maturity in two years, he will simply obtain an annual return of 6.6%. In addition, the return over two years can be calculated by

$$\frac{1 - 0.8800}{0.8800} = 0.1364 \text{ and } \sqrt{1.1364} = 1.066$$

Table 4.4   Price and rate structures

S	$R_0(s)$	$P_0(s)$	$r(s)$
0		1.0000	
1	0.060	0.9434	0.06000
2	0.066	0.8800	0.07203
3	0.070	0.8163	0.07805
4	0.073	0.7544	0.08205
5	0.075	0.6966	0.08304
6	0.076	0.6444	0.08101

---

[17] If the rate curve is flat and remains flat, the strategy presented will produce the same return as the purchase of a security with a maturity equivalent to the investment horizon.

If he purchases a security with maturity in five years (at a price of 0.6966) and sells it on after two years (at the three-year security price if the rate curves remain unchanged, that is 0.8163), he will realise a total return of

$$\frac{0.8163 - 0.6966}{0.6966} = 1.1719$$

This will give $\sqrt{1.1719} = 1.0825$, that is, an annual return of 8.25 %, which is of considerably greater interest than the return (6.6 %) obtained with the two-year security.

Note that we have an interpretation of the term rate here, as the total return for the period [3; 5], effectively used, is given by $(1 + r(4)) \cdot (1 + r(5)) = 1.0821 \cdot 1.0830 = 1.1719$.

The interest rate obtained using this technique assumes that the rate curve remains unchanged over time. If, however the curve, and more specifically the spot rate used to calculate the resale price, fluctuates, the investor will be exposed to the interest-rate fluctuation risk. This fluctuation will be favourable (unfavourable) to him if the rate in question falls (rises).

In this case, the investor will have to choose between a safe return and a higher but potentially more risky return.

Example

With the same information, if after the purchase of a security with maturity in five years the spot rate for the three-year security shifts from 7.6 % to 8 %, the price of that security will fall from 0.8163 to 0.7938 and the return over the two years will be

$$\frac{0.7938 - 0.6966}{0.6966} = 1.1396$$

We therefore have $\sqrt{1.1396} = 1.0675$, which corresponds to an annual return of 6.75 %.

4.5   STOCHASTIC BOND DYNAMIC MODELS

The models presented here are actually generalisations of the deterministic interest-rate structures. The aim is to produce relations that govern changes in price $P_t(s)$ and spot rates $R_t(s)$. There are two main categories of these models: distortion models and arbitrage models.

The *distortion models* examine the changes in the price $P_t(s)$ when the interest-rate structure is subject to distortion. A simple model is that of Ho and Lee,[18] in which the distortion of the rate curve shows in two possible movements in each period; it is therefore a binomial discrete type of model. A more developed model is the Heath, Jarrow and Morton model,[19] which has a discrete and a continuous version and in which the distortions to the rate curve are more complex.

The *arbitrage models* involve the compilation, and where possible the resolution, of an equation with partial derivatives for the price $P_t(s, v_1, v_2, \ldots)$ considered as a function of $t, v_1, v_2, \ldots$ (s fixed), using:

[18] Ho T. and Lee S., Term structure movement and pricing interest rate contingent claims, *Journal of Finance*, Vol. 41, No. 5., 1986, pp. 1011–29.

[19] Heath D., Jarrow R. and Morton A., *Bond Pricing and the Term Structure of Interest Rates: a New Methodology*, Cornell University, 1987. Heath D., Jarrow R. and Morton A., Bond pricing and the term structure of interest rates: discrete time approximation, *Journal of Financial and Quantitative Analysis*, Vol. 25, 1990, pp. 419–40.

- the absence of arbitrage opportunity;
- hypotheses relating to stochastic processes that govern the evolutions in the state variables v_1, v_2 etc.

The commonest of the models with just one state variable are the Merton model,[20] the Vasicek model[21] and the Cox, Ingersoll and Ross model;[22] all these use the instant term rate $r(t)$ as the state variable. The models with two state variables include:

- The Brennan and Schwarz model,[23] which uses the instant term rate r and the long rate l as variables.
- The Nelson and Schaefer model[24] and the Schaefer and Schwartz model,[25] for which the state variables are the long rate l and the spread $s = l - r$.
- The Richard model,[26] which uses the instant term rate and the rate of inflation.
- The Ramaswamy and Sundaresan model,[27] which takes the instant market price of risk linked to the risk of default alongside the instant term rate.

In this section we will be dealing with only the simplest of arbitrage models: after a general introduction to the principle of these models (Section 4.5.1), we will examine in succession the Vasicek model (Section 4.5.2) and the Cox, Ingersoll and Ross model[28] (Section 4.5.3). Finally, in Section 4.5.4, we will deal with the concept of 'stochastic duration'.

4.5.1 Arbitrage models with one state variable

4.5.1.1 General principle

It is once again stated (see Section 4.3) that the stochastic processes of interest to us here are:

- The price $P_t(s)$ in t of a zero-coupon bond (unit repayment value) maturing at the moment s (with $t < s$). The spot rate $R_t(s)$, linked to the price by the relation

$$P_t(s) = e^{-(s-t)R_t(s)}$$

---

[20] Merton R., Theory of rational option pricing, *Bell Journal of Economics and Management Science*, Vol. 4, No. 1, 1973, pp. 141–83.

[21] Vasicek O., An equilibrium characterisation of the term structure, *Journal of Financial Economics*, Vol. 5, No. 2, 1977, pp. 177–88.

[22] Cox K., Ingersoll J. and Ross J., A theory of the term structure of interest rates, *Econometrica*, Vol. 53, No. 2, 1985, pp. 385–406.

[23] Brennan M. and Schwartz E., A continuous time approach to the pricing of bonds, *Journal of Banking and Finance*, Vol. 3, No. 2, 1979, pp. 133–55.

[24] Nelson J. and Schaefer S., The dynamics of the term structure and alternative portfolio immunization strategies, in Bierwag D., Kayfman G. and Toevs A., *Innovations in Bond Portfolio Management: Duration Analysis and Immunization*, JAI Press, 1983.

[25] Schaefer S. and Schwartz E., A two-factor model of the term structure: an approximate analytical solution, *Journal of Financial and Quantitative Analysis*, Vol. 19, No. 4, 1984, pp. 413–24.

[26] Richard S., An arbitrage model of the term structure of interest rates, *Journal of Financial Economics*, Vol. 6, No. 1, 1978, pp. 33–57.

[27] Ramaswamy K. and Sundaresan M., The valuation of floating-rate instruments: theory and evidence, *Journal of Financial Economics*, Vol. 17, No. 2, 1986, pp. 251–72.

[28] The attached CD-ROM contains a series of Excel files that show simulations of these stochastic processes and its rate curves for the various models, combined together in the 'Ch4' file.

- The instant term rate, which we will refer hereafter as r_t[29] or r if there is no risk of confusion, and which is the instant rate at moment t, being written as

$$r_t = \lim_{s \to t+} R_t(s) = \lim_{s \to t+} \frac{1}{s-t} \int_t^s f_t(u) \, du$$

It is this instant term rate that will be the state variable. The price and spot rate will be written as $P_t(s, r)$ and $R_t(s, r)$ and will be considered as functions of the variables t and r alone, the maturity date s being fixed. In addition, it is assumed that these expressions are random via the intermediary of r_t only.

It is assumed here that the changes in the state variable r_t are governed by the general stochastic differential equation[30] $dr_t = a(t, r_t) \, dt + b(t, r_t) \, dw_t$, where the coefficients a and b respectively represent the average instant return of the instant term rate and the volatility of that rate, and w_t is the standard Brownian motion.

Applying the Itô formula to the function $P_t(s, r_t)$ leads to the following, with simplified notations:

$$dP_t(s, r_t) = (P_t' + P_r'a + \tfrac{1}{2}P_{rr}''b^2) \cdot dt + P_r'b \cdot dw_t$$
$$= P_t(s, r_t) \cdot \mu_t(s, r_t) \cdot dt - P_t(s, r_t) \cdot \sigma_t(s, r_t) \cdot dw_t$$

Here, we have:

$$\begin{cases} \mu_t = \dfrac{P_t' + P_r'a + \tfrac{1}{2}P_{rr}''b^2}{P} \\[2ex] \sigma_t = -\dfrac{P_r'b}{P} \end{cases}$$

(Note that $\sigma_t > 0$ as $P_r' < 0$). The expression $\mu_t(s, r_t)$ is generally termed the *average instant return* of the bond.

Let us now consider two fixed maturity dates s_1 and $s_2(> t)$ and apply an arbitrage reasoning by putting together, at the moment t, a portfolio consisting of:

- The issue of a bond with maturity date s_1.
- The purchase of X bonds with maturity date s_2.

The X is chosen so that the portfolio does not contain any random components; the term involving dw_t therefore has to disappear.

The value of this portfolio at moment t is given by $V_t = -P_t(s_1) + XP_t(s_2)$, and the hypothesis of absence of opportunity for arbitrage allows us to express that the average return on this portfolio over the interval $[t; t + dt]$ is given by the instant term rate r_t:

$$\frac{dV_t}{V_t} = r_t \cdot dt + 0 \cdot dw_t$$

---

[29] Instead of $r(t)$ as in Section 4.3, for ease of notation.
[30] See Appendix 2.

By differentiating the value of the portfolio, we have:

$$dV_t = -P_t(s_1)(\mu_t(s_1)\,dt - \sigma_t(s_1)\,dw_t) + X \cdot P_t(s_2)(\mu_t(s_2)\,dt - \sigma_t(s_2)\,dw_t)$$

$$= [-P_t(s_1)\mu_t(s_1) + XP_t(s_2)\mu_t(s_2)] \cdot dt + [P_t(s_1)\sigma_t(s_1) - XP_t(s_2)\sigma_t(s_2)] \cdot dw_t$$

The arbitrage logic will therefore lead us to

$$\begin{cases} \dfrac{-P_t(s_1)\mu_t(s_1) + XP_t(s_2)\mu_t(s_2)}{-P_t(s_1) + XP_t(s_2)} = r_t \\ \dfrac{P_t(s_1)\sigma_t(s_1) - XP_t(s_2)\sigma_t(s_2)}{-P_t(s_1) + XP_t(s_2)} = 0 \end{cases}$$

In other words:

$$\begin{cases} XP_t(s_2) \cdot (\mu_t(s_2) - r_t) = P_t(s_1) \cdot (\mu_t(s_1) - r_t) \\ XP_t(s_2) \cdot \sigma_t(s_2) = P_t(s_1) \cdot \sigma_t(s_1) \end{cases}$$

We can eliminate X, for example by dividing the two equations member by member, which gives:

$$\frac{\mu_t(s_1) - r_t}{\sigma_t(s_1)} = \frac{\mu_t(s_2) - r_t}{\sigma_t(s_2)}$$

This shows that the expression $\lambda_t(r_t) = \dfrac{\mu_t(s) - r_t}{\sigma_t(s)}$ is independent of s; this expression is known as the *market price of the risk.*

By replacing μ_t and σ_t with their value in the preceding relation, we arrive at

$$P_t' + (a + \lambda b)P_r' + \frac{b^2}{2}P_{rr}'' - rP = 0$$

What we are looking at here is the partial derivatives equation of the second order, which together with the initial condition $P_s(s, r_t) = 1$, defines the price process. This equation must be resolved for each specification of $a(t, r_t)$, $b(t, r_t)$ and $\lambda_t(r_t)$.

4.5.1.2   The Merton model[31]

Because of its historical interest,[32] we are showing the simplest model, the Merton model. This model assumes that the instant term rate follows a random walk model: $dr_t = \alpha \cdot dt + \sigma \cdot dw_t$ with α and σ being constant and the market price of risk being zero ($\lambda = 0$).

The partial derivatives equation for the prices takes the form:

$$P_t' + \alpha P_r' + \frac{\sigma^2}{2}P_{rr}'' - rP = 0.$$

---

[31] Merton R., Theory of rational option pricing, *Bell Journal of Economics and Management Science*, Vol. 4, No. 1, 1973, pp. 141–83.

[32] This is in fact the first model based on representation of changes in the spot rate using a stochastic differential equation.

It is easy to verify that the solution to this equation (with the initial condition) is given by

$$P_t(s, r_t) = \exp\left[-(s-t)r_t - \frac{\alpha}{2}(s-t)^2 + \frac{\sigma^2}{6}(s-t)^3\right]$$

The average instant return rate is given by

$$\mu_t(s, r_t) = \frac{P_t' + \alpha P_r' + \frac{\sigma^2}{2}P_{rr}''}{P} = \frac{r_t \cdot P}{P} = r_t$$

which shows that in this case, the average return is independent of the maturity date.
    The spot rate totals:

$$R_t(s, r_t) = -\frac{1}{s-t}\ln P_t(s, r_t)$$

$$= r_t + \frac{\alpha}{2}(s-t) - \frac{\sigma^2}{6}(s-t)^2$$

This expression shows that the spot rate is close to the instant term rate in the short term, which is logical, but also (because of the third term) that it will invariably finish as a negative for distant maturity dates; this is much less logical.

Note

If one generalises the Merton model where the market price of risk λ is a strictly positive constant, we arrive at an average return μ_t that grows with the maturity date, but the inconvenience of the R_t spot rate remains.
    The Merton model, which is unrealistic, has now been replaced by models that are closer to reality; these models are covered in the next two paragraphs.

4.5.2   The Vasicek model[33]

In this model, the state variable r_t develops according to an Ornstein–Uhlenbeck process $dr_t = \delta(\theta - r_t) \cdot dt + \sigma \cdot dw_t$ in which the parameters δ, θ and σ are strictly positive constants and the rate risk unit premium is also a strictly positive constant $\lambda_t(r_t) = \lambda > 0$.
    The essential property of the Ornstein–Uhlenbeck process is that the variable r_t is 'recalled' back towards θ if it moves too far away and that δ represents the 'force of recall'.

Example

Figure 4.6 shows a simulated trajectory (evolution over time) for such a process over 1000 very short time periods with the values $\delta = 100$, $\theta = 0.1$ and $\sigma = 0.8$ with a start value for r_0 of 10%.

---

[33] Vasicek O., An equilibrium characterisation of the term structure, *Journal of Financial Economics*, Vol. 5, No. 2, 1977, pp. 177–88.

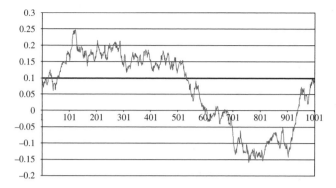

Figure 4.6 Ornstein–Uhlenbeck process

The partial derivatives equation for the price is shown here:

$$P_t' + (\delta(\theta - r) + \lambda\sigma)P_r' + \frac{\sigma^2}{2}P_{rr}'' - rP = 0$$

The solution to this equation and its initial condition is given by

$$P_t(s, r_t) = \exp\left[-k(s-t) + \frac{k-r_t}{\delta}(1 - e^{-\delta(s-t)}) - \frac{\sigma^2}{4\delta^3}(1 - e^{-\delta(s-t)})^2\right]$$

where we have:

$$k = \theta + \frac{\lambda\sigma}{\delta} - \frac{\sigma^2}{2\delta^2}$$

The average instant return rate is given by:

$$\mu_t(s, r_t) = \frac{P_t' + \delta(\theta - r_t)P_r' + \frac{\sigma^2}{2}P_{rr}''}{P}$$

$$= \frac{r_t \cdot P - \lambda\sigma \cdot P_r'}{P}$$

$$= r_t + \frac{\lambda\sigma}{\delta}(1 - e^{-\delta(s-t)})$$

This average return increases depending on the maturity date, and presents a horizontal asymptote in the long term (Figure 4.7).

The spot rate is given by:

$$R_t(s, r_t) = -\frac{1}{s-t}\ln P_t(s, r_t)$$

$$= k - \frac{k-r_t}{\delta(s-t)}(1 - e^{-\delta(s-t)}) + \frac{\sigma^2}{4\delta^3(s-t)}(1 - e^{-\delta(s-t)})^2$$

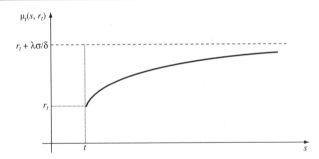

Figure 4.7   The Vasicek model: average instant return

On one hand, this expression shows that the spot rate is stabilised for distant maturity dates and regardless of the initial value of the spot rate: $\lim_{(s-t)\to+\infty} R_t(s, r_t) = k$.

On the other hand, depending on the current value of the spot rate in relation to the parameters, we can use this model to represent various movements of the yield curve. Depending on whether r_t belongs to the

$$\left[0; k - \frac{\sigma^2}{4\delta^2}\right], \quad \left]k - \frac{\sigma^2}{4\delta^2}; k + \frac{\sigma^2}{2\delta^2}\right[, \quad \left[k + \frac{\sigma^2}{2\delta^2}; +\infty\right[$$

we will obtain a rate curve that is increasing, humped or decreasing.

Example

Figure 4.8 shows spot-rate curves produced using the Vasicek model for the following parameter values: $\delta = 0.2, \theta = 0.08, \sigma = 0.05$ and $\lambda = 0.02$. The three curves correspond, from bottom to top, to $r_0 = 2\%$, $r_0 = 6\%$ and $r_0 = 10\%$.

The Vasicek model, however, has two major inconvenients. On one hand, the Ornstein–Uhlenbeck process $dr_t = \delta(\theta - r_t) \cdot dt + \sigma \cdot dw_t$, on the basis of which is constructed, sometimes, because of the second term, allows the instant term rate to assume negative values. On the other hand, the function of the spot rate that it generated, $R_t(s)$, may in some case also assume negative values.

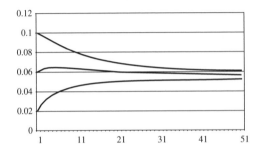

Figure 4.8   The Vasicek model: yield curves

4.5.3   The Cox, Ingersoll and Ross model[34]

This model is part of a group also known as the equilibrium models as they are based on a macroeconomic type of reasoning, based in turn on the hypothesis that the consumer will show behaviour consistently aimed at maximising expected utility.

These considerations, which we will not detail, lead (as do the other arbitrage models) to a specific definition of the stochastic process that governs the evolution of the instant term rate r_t as well as the market price of risk $\lambda_t(r_t)$.

If within the Ornstein–Uhlenbeck process the second term is modified to produce $dr_t = \delta(\theta - r_t) \cdot dt + \sigma r^\alpha_t \cdot dw_t$, with $\alpha > 0$, we will avoid the inconvenience mentioned earlier: the instant term rate can no longer become negative. In fact, as soon as it reaches zero, only the first term will subsist and the variation in rates must therefore necessarily be upwards; the horizontal axis then operates as a 'repulsing barrier'.

Using the macroeconomic reasoning on which the Cox, Ingersoll and Ross model is based, we have a situation where $\alpha = 1/2$ and the stochastic process is known as the *square root process*:

$$dr_t = \delta(\theta - r_t) \cdot dt + \sigma\sqrt{r_t} \cdot dw_t$$

The same reasoning leads to a rate risk unit premium given by $\lambda_t(r_t) = \dfrac{\gamma}{\sigma}\sqrt{r_t}$, where γ is a strictly positive constant; the market price of risk therefore increases together with the instant term rate in this case.

Example

Figure 4.9 represents a square root process with the parameters $\delta = 100$, $\theta = 0.1$ and $\sigma = 0.8$.

The partial derivative equation for the price is given by

$$P'_t + (\delta(\theta - r) + \gamma r)P'_r + \frac{\sigma^2}{2}r P''_{rr} - rP = 0$$

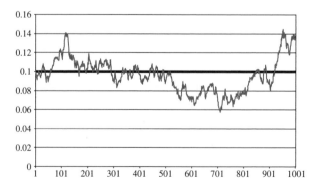

Figure 4.9   Square root process

[34] Cox J., Ingersoll J. and Ross J., A theory of the term structure of interest rates, *Econometrica*, Vol. 53, No. 2, 1985, pp. 385–406.

The solution to this equation and its initial condition is given by

$$P_t(s, r_t) = x_t(s) \cdot e^{-y_t(s)r}$$

where we have:

$$
\begin{cases}
x_t(s) = \left(\dfrac{2k e^{\frac{1}{2}(\delta - \gamma + k)(s-t)}}{z_t(s)} \right)^{\frac{2\delta\theta}{\sigma^2}} \\[2em]
y_t(s) = \dfrac{2(e^{k(s-t)} - 1)}{z_t(s)} \\[1em]
z_t(s) = 2k + (\delta - \gamma + k)(e^{k(s-t)} - 1) \\[0.5em]
k = \sqrt{(\delta - \gamma)^2 + 2\sigma^2}
\end{cases}
$$

The average instant rate return is given by:

$$
\begin{aligned}
\mu_t(s, r_t) &= \frac{P_t' + \delta(\theta - r_t)P_r' + \dfrac{\sigma^2}{2} r P_{rr}''}{P} \\[1em]
&= \frac{r_t \cdot P - \gamma r_t \cdot P_r'}{P} \\[1em]
&= r_t(1 + \gamma y_{t(s)})
\end{aligned}
$$

In this case, the average rate of return is proportional to the instant term rate.
Finally, the spot rate is given by:

$$
\begin{aligned}
R_t(s, r_t) &= -\frac{1}{s-t} \ln P_t(s, r_t) \\[1em]
&= -\frac{1}{s-t} (\ln x_t(s) - r_t y_t(s))
\end{aligned}
$$

Example

Figure 4.10 shows the spot-rate curves produced using the Cox, Ingersoll and Ross model for the following parameter values: $\delta = 0.2$, $\theta = 0.08$, $\sigma = 0.05$ and $\gamma = 0.02$. The three curves, from bottom to top, correspond to $r_0 = 2\%$, $r_0 = 6\%$ and $r_0 = 10\%$.

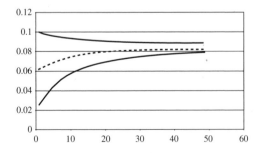

Figure 4.10   The Cox, Ingersoll and Ross model: rate curves

Finally, we should point out that in contrast to the Vasicek model, the Cox, Ingersoll and Ross model can never produce a negative spot rate. In addition, as with the Vasicek model, the spot rate stabilises for distant maturity dates regardless of the initial value of the spot rate:

$$\lim_{(s-t)\to+\infty} R_t(s, r_t) = \frac{2\delta\theta}{\delta - \gamma + k}$$

4.5.4 Stochastic duration

Finally, to end this section dedicated to random models, we turn to a generalisation of the concept of duration.

Duration and convexity of rate products are ongoing techniques used to assess the sensitivity and alteration of the price of an asset following an alteration to its rate. Duration allows the variation in value to be estimated for more significant variations. These concepts are used not only in bond portfolio management but also in asset and liability management in the context of immunisation of interest margins. What happens is that part of the balance-sheet margin is produced by a spread between the interest paid on assets (long-term deposits) and interest received on assets (the bank's own portfolio with a fixed income). This margin is immunised against variations in rate if convexity and duration are identical on both sides of the balance sheet. This identity of duration and convexity, also known as *mutual support*, does not necessarily mean that cash flows are identical in assets and liabilities. In this case, distortion of the rate curve could lead to non-identical alterations in asset and liability values.

The transition from a deterministic rate curve to a stochastic rate model provides the solution to this problem. The random evolution of rates allows the *stochastic duration* to be calculated. There are several stochastic rate models (see Sections 4.5.1–4.5.3), but the type most frequently used in financial literature is the classical Vasicek model.

4.5.4.1 Random evolution of rates

The classical Vasicek model is based on changes in the instant term rate governed by an Ornstein–Uhlenbeck process: $dr_t = \delta(\theta - r_t) \cdot dt + \sigma \cdot dw_t$.

The forward long rate $r_{+\infty fw}$ is of course a function of the parameters δ, θ and σ of the model. Variations in a bond's price depend on the values taken by the random variable r_t and the alterations to the model's parameters. The natural way of approaching stochastic duration is to adjust the parameters econometrically on rate curves observed.

4.5.4.2 Principle of mutual support

The total variation in value at the initial moment t is obtained by developing Taylor in the first order:

$$dV_t(s, r_t, r_{+\infty fw}, \sigma) = V'_{r_t} dr_t + V'_{r_{+\infty fw}} dr_{+\infty fw} + V'_\sigma d\sigma$$

The principle of mutual support between assets and liabilities requires two restrictions to be respected: first, equality of values between assets and liabilities:

$$V_{A,t}(s, r_t, r_{+\infty fw}, \sigma) = V_{L,t}(s, r_t, r_{+\infty fw}, \sigma)$$

and second, equality of total variations: regardless of what the increases in dr_t, $dr_{+\infty fw}$ and $d\sigma$ may be, we have

$$dV_{A,t}(s, r_t, r_{+\infty fw}, \sigma) = dV_{L,t}(s, r_t, r_{+\infty fw}, \sigma)$$

This second condition therefore requires that:

$$V'_{A,r_t}(s, r_t, r_{+\infty fw}, \sigma) = V'_{L,r_t}(s, r_t, r_{+\infty fw}, \sigma)$$
$$V'_{A,r_{+\infty fw}}(s, r_t, r_{+\infty fw}, \sigma) = V'_{L,r_{+\infty fw}}(s, r_t, r_{+\infty fw}, \sigma)$$
$$V'_{A,\sigma}(s, r_t, r_{+\infty fw}, \sigma) = V'_{L,\sigma}(s, r_t, r_{+\infty fw}, \sigma)$$

4.5.4.3 Extension of the concept of duration

Generally speaking, it is possible to define the duration D that is a function of the variation in long and short rates:

$$D_t(s, r_t, r_{+\infty fw}) = \frac{1}{2V}(V'_{r_t} + V'_{r_{+\infty fw}})$$

This expression allows us to find the standard duration when the rate curve is deterministic and tends towards a constant curve with $\sigma = 0$ and $\theta = r_t$, with the initial instant term rate for the period t:

$$D_t(s, r_t, r_{+\infty fw}) = \frac{1}{V} \cdot V'_{r_t}$$

Generally, the duration is sensitive to the spread S between the short rate and the long rate. Sensitivity to spread allows the variation in value to be calculated for a spread variation:

$$S_t(s, r_t, r_{+\infty fw}) = \frac{1}{2V}(-V'_{r_t} + V'_{r_{+\infty fw}}) = \frac{1}{V} \cdot V'_{r_t}$$

In this case, if s is stable and considered to be a constant, the mutual support will correspond to the equality of stochastic distribution and of sensitivity of spread for assets and liabilities.

The equality $dV_{A,t}(s, r_t, r_{+\infty fw}) = dV_{L,t}(s, r_t, r_{+\infty fw})$, valid whatever the increases in dr_t and $dr_{+\infty fw}$ is equivalent to:

$$\begin{cases} D_A = D_L \\ S_A = S_L \end{cases}$$

5

Options

5.1 DEFINITIONS

5.1.1 Characteristics

An *option*[1] is a contract that confers on its purchaser, in return for a *premium*, the right to purchase or sell an asset (the *underlying* asset) on a future date at a price determined in advance (the *exercise price* of the option). Options for purchasing and options for selling are known respectively as *call* and *put* options. The range of assets to which options contracts can be applied is very wide: ordinary equities, bonds, exchange rates, commodities and even some derivative products such as FRAs, futures, swaps or options.

An option always represents a right for the holder and an obligation to buy or sell for the issuer. This option right may be exercised when the contract expires (a *European* option) or on any date up to and including the expiry date (an *American* option). The holder of a call option will therefore exercise his option right if the price of the underlying equity exceeds the exercise price of the option or *strike*; conversely, a put option will be exercised in the opposite case.

The assets studied in the two preceding chapters clearly show a degree of random behaviour (mean-variance theory for equities, interest-rate models for bonds). They do, however, also allow deterministic approaches (Gordon-Shapiro formula, duration and convexity). With options, the random aspect is much more intrinsic as everything depends on a decision linked to a future event.

This type of contract can be a source of profit (with risks linked to speculation) and a means of hedging. In this context, we will limit our discussion to European call options.

Purchasing this type of option may lead to an attractive return, as when the price of the underlying equity on maturity is lower than the exercise price, the option will not be exercised and the loss will be limited to the price of the option (the premium). When the price of the underlying equity on maturity is higher than the exercise price, the underlying equity is received for a price lower than its value.

The sale (issue) of an equity option, on the other hand, is a much more speculative operation. The profit will be limited to the premium if the price of the underlying equity remains lower than the exercise price, while considerable losses may arise if the rise is higher than the price of the underlying equity. This operation should therefore only be envisaged if the issuer has absolute confidence in a fall (or at worst a reduced rise) in the price of the underlying equity.

Example

Let us consider a call option on an equity with a current price of 100, a premium of 3 and an exercise price of 105. We will calculate the profit made (or the loss suffered)

---

[1] Colmant B. and Kleynen G., *Gestion du risque de taux d'intérêt et instruments financiers dérivés*, Kluwer, 1995. Hull J. C., *Options, Futures and Other Derivatives*, Prentice Hall, 1997. Hicks A., *Foreign Exchange Options*, Woodhead, 1993.

Table 5.1 Profit on option according to price of underlying equity

Price of underlying equity	Gain	
	Purchaser	Issuer
90	−3	3
95	−3	3
100	−3	3
105	−3	3
106	−2	2
107	−1	1
108	0	0
109	1	−1
110	2	−2
115	7	−7
120	12	−12

by the purchaser and by the issuer of the contract according to the price reached by the underlying equity on maturity. See Table 5.1.

Of course, issuers who notice the price of the underlying equity rising during the contractual period can partly protect themselves by purchasing the same option and thus closing their position. Nevertheless, because of the higher underlying equity price, the premium for the option purchased may be considerably higher than that of the option that was issued.

The price (premium) of an option depends on several different factors:

- the price of the underlying equity S_t at the moment t (known as the *spot*);
- the exercise price of the option K (known as the *strike*);
- the duration $T - t$ remaining until the option matures;[2]
- the volatility σ_R of the return on the underlying equity;
- the risk-free rate R_F.[3]

The various ways of specifying the function f (which will be termed C or P depending on whether a call or a put is involved) give rise to what are termed models of valuation. These are dealt with in Section 5.3.

5.1.2 Use

The example shown in the preceding paragraph corresponds to the situation in which the purchaser can hope for an attractive gain. The profit realised is shown in graphic form in Figure 5.1.

---

[2] This residual duration $T - t$ is frequently referred to simply as τ

[3] This description corresponds, for example, to an option on an equity (with which we will mostly be dealing in this chapter). For an exchange option, the rate of interest will be divided in two, into domestic currency and foreign currency. In addition, this rate, which will be used in making updates, may be considered either discretely (discounting factor $(1 + R_F)^{-t}$) or continuously (the notation r: e^{-rt} will then be used).

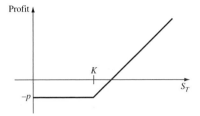

Figure 5.1 Acquisition of a call option

Alongside this speculative aspect, the issue of a call option can become attractive if it is held along with the underlying equity. In fact, if the underlying equity price falls (or rises little), the loss suffered on that equity will be partly offset by receipt of the premium, whereas if the price rises greatly, the profit that would have been realised will be limited to the price of the option plus the differential between the exercise price and the price of the underlying equity at the start of the contract.

Example 1

Following the example shown above, we calculated the profit realised (or the loss suffered) when the underlying equity alone is held and when it is covered by the call option (Table 5.2).

Example 2

Let us now look at a more realistic example. A European company X often has invoices expressed in US dollars payable on delivery. The prices are of course fixed at the moment of purchase (long before the delivery). If the rate for the dollar rises between the moment of purchase and the moment of delivery, the company X will suffer a loss if it purchases its dollars at the moment of payment.

Table 5.2 Profit/loss on equity covered by call option

Price of underlying equity	Profit/loss	
	Purchaser	Issuer
90	−3	3
95	−3	3
100	−3	3
105	−3	3
106	−2	2
107	−1	1
108	0	0
109	1	−1
110	2	−2
115	7	−7
120	12	−12

Let us assume, more specifically, that the rate for the dollar at the moment t is S_t (US\$1 = €S_t) and that X purchases goods on this day ($t = 0$) valued at US\$1000, the rate being $S_0 = x$ (US\$1 = €x), for delivery in $t = T$. The company X, on $t = 0$, acquires 1000 European US\$/€ calls maturing on T, the exercise price being $K = €x$ for US\$1.

If $S_T > x$, the option will be exercised and X will purchase its dollars at rate x (the rate in which the invoice is expressed) and the company will lose only the total of the premium. If $S_T \leq X$, the option will not be exercised and X will purchase its dollars at the rate S_T and the business will realise a profit of $1000 \cdot (x - S_T)$ less the premium.

The purchase of the option acts as insurance cover against changes in rates. Of course it cannot be free of charge (consider the point of view of the option issuer); its price is the option premium.

The case envisaged above corresponds to the acquisition of a call option. The same kind of reasoning can be applied to four situations, corresponding to the purchase or issue of a call option on one hand or of a put option on the other hand. Hence we have Figures 5.2 and 5.3.

In addition to the simple cover strategy set out above, it is possible to create more complex combinations of subsequent equity, call options and put options. These more involved strategies are covered in Section 5.4.

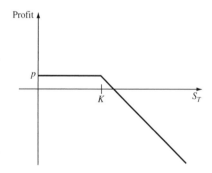

Figure 5.2   Issue of a call option

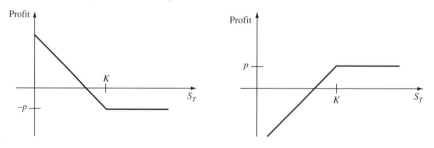

Figure 5.3   Acquisition and issue of a put option

5.2 VALUE OF AN OPTION

5.2.1 Intrinsic value and time value

An option premium can be spilt into two terms: its intrinsic value and its time value.

The *intrinsic value* of an option at a moment t is simply the profit realised by the purchaser (without taking account of the premium) if the option was exercised at t. More specifically, for a call option it is the difference, if that difference is positive,[4] between the price of the underlying equity S_t at that moment and the exercise price[5] K of the option. If the difference is negative, the intrinsic value is by definition 0. For a put option, the intrinsic value will be the difference between the exercise price and the underlying equity price.[6] Therefore, if the intrinsic value of the option is termed VI, we will have $VI_t = $ max $(0, S_t - K) = (S_t - K)^+$ for a call option and $VI_t = $ max $(0, K - S_t) = (K - S_t)^+$ for a put option, with the graphs shown in Figure 5.4.

The price of the option is of course at least equal to its intrinsic value. The part of the premium over and above the intrinsic value is termed *time value* and shown as VT, hence: $VT_t = p_t - VI_t$.

This time value, which is added to the intrinsic value to give the premium, represents payment in anticipation of an additional profit for the purchaser. From the point of view of the issuer, it therefore represents a kind of risk premium.

The time value will of course decrease as the time left to run decreases, and ends by being cancelled out at the maturity date (see Figure 5.5).

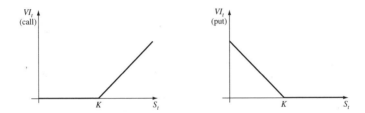

Figure 5.4 Intrinsic value of a call option and put option

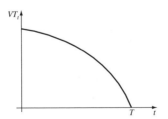

Figure 5.5 Time value according to time

---

[4] The option is then said to be 'in the money'. If the difference is negative, the option is said to be 'out of the money'. If the subjacent share price is equal or close to the exercise price, it is said to be 'at the money'. These definitions are inverted for put options.

[5] The option cannot in fact be exercised immediately unless it is of the American type. For a European option, the exercise price should normally be discounted for the period remaining until the maturity date.

[6] This definition is given for an American option. For a European option, it is sufficient, within the interpretation of S_t, to replace the price at the moment t by the maturity date price.

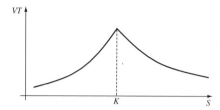

Figure 5.6 Time value according to underlying equity price

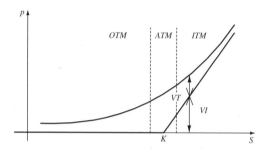

Figure 5.7 Splitting of call option premium

It is easy to see, as the other parameters are constant, that the time value will be greater as the underlying equity price comes near to the exercise price, as shown in Figure 5.6.

To understand this property, let us view things from the call issuer's point of view to lay down the ideas. If the option is out of the money, it will probably not be exercised and the issuer may dispense with acquiring the underlying equity; his risk (steep rise in the underlying equity price) will therefore be low and he will receive very little reward. In the same way, an in-the-money option will probably be exercised, and the issuer will therefore have an interest in acquiring the underlying equity; a sharp drop in the underlying equity price represents a highly improbable risk and the time value will also be low. Conversely, for an at-the-money option the issuer will have no degree of certainty with regard to whether or not the option should be exercised, or how the underlying equity price will develop; the risk of the underlying equity price falling after he acquires the equity (or of a price surge without the underlying equity being acquired) is therefore high and a risk premium will be requested in consequence. This phenomenon is shown in Figure 5.7.

In addition, it is evident that the longer the period remaining until the option contract matures, the higher the risk and the greater the time value (see Figure 5.8).

Of course, the value of an option at maturity is identical to its intrinsic value:

$$\begin{cases} C_T = (S_T - K)^+ \\ P_T = (K - S_T)^+ \end{cases}$$

5.2.2 Volatility

Of the parameters that define the price of an option, let us now look more specifically at the volatility σ_R of the return of the underlying equity. The *volatility* of an option

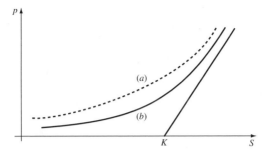

Figure 5.8 Call premium and high (*a*) and brief (*b*) maturity

is defined as a measurement of the dispersion of the return of the underlying equity. In practice, it is generally taken for a reference period of one year and expressed as a percentage. This concept of volatility can be seen from two points of view: historical volatility and implied volatility.

Historical volatility is simply the annualised standard deviation on the underlying equity return, obtained from daily observations of the return in the past:

$$\sigma_R = \sqrt{J \cdot \frac{1}{n} \sum_{t=1}^{n} (R_t - \overline{R})^2}$$

Here, the factor J represents the number of working days in the year; n is the number of observations and R_t is the return on the underlying equity. It is easy to calculate, but the major problem is that it is always 'turned towards the past' when it really needs to help analyse future developments in the option price.

For this reason, the concept of *implied volatility* has been introduced. This involves using a valuation model to estimate the dispersion of the return of the underlying equity for the period remaining until the contract matures. The value of the option premium is determined in practice by the law of supply and demand. In addition, this law is linked to various factors through a binomial model of valuation: $p_t = f(S_t, K, T - t, \sigma_R, R_F)$ or through Black and Scholes (see Section 5.3). The resolution of this relation with respect to σ_R defines the implied volatility. Although the access is more complicated, this concept is preferable and it is this one that will often be used in practice.

5.2.3 Sensitivity parameters

5.2.3.1 'Greeks'

The premium is likely to vary when each of the parameters that determine the price of the option (spot price, exercise price, maturity etc.) change. The aim of this paragraph is to study the indices,[7] known as 'Greeks', which measure the sensitivity of the premium to fluctuations in some of these characteristics through the relation $p_t = f(S_t, K, \tau, \sigma_R, R_F)$.

---

[7] In the same way as duration and convexity, which measure the sensitivity of the value of a bond following changes in interest rates (see Chapter 4).

Here, we will restrict ourselves to examining the most commonly used sensitivity coefficients: those that bring the option price and namely the underlying equity price time, volatility and risk-free rate into relation. In addition, the sign indications given are valid for a non-dividend-paying equity option.

The coefficient Δ (*delta*) represents the sensitivity of the option price with respect to the underlying equity price. It is measured by dividing the variations in these two prices for a small increase δS_t in the underlying equity price:

$$\Delta = \frac{f(S_t + \delta S_t, K, \tau, \sigma_R, R_F) - f(S_t, K, \tau, \sigma_R, R_F)}{\delta S_t}$$

Or, more specifically:

$$\Delta = \lim_{\delta S_t \to 0} \frac{f(S_t + \delta S_t, K, \tau, \sigma_R, R_F) - f(S_t, K, \tau, \sigma_R, R_F)}{\delta S_t}$$
$$= f'_S(S_t, K, \tau, \sigma_R, R_F)$$

Thus, for a call, if the underlying equity price increases by €1, the price of the option will increase by €Δ. It will be between 0 and 1 for a call and between -1 and 0 for a put.

Another coefficient expresses the sensitivity of the option price with respect to the underlying equity price, but this time in the second order. This is the coefficient Γ (*gamma*), which is expressed by the ratio of variations in Δ on one hand and the price S_t on the other hand.

$$\Gamma = f''_{SS}(S_t, K, \tau, \sigma_R, R_F)$$

If one wishes to compare the dependency of the option premium *vis-à-vis* the underlying equity price and the price of a bond according to the actuarial rate, it can be said that Δ is to the duration what Γ is to convexity. This coefficient Γ, which is always positive, is the same for a call option and for a put option.

The following coefficient, termed Θ (*theta*), measures the dependence of the option price according to time:

$$\Theta = f'_t(S_t, K, T - t, \sigma_R, R_F)$$

or, by introducing the residual life span $\tau = T - t$ of the contract,

$$\Theta = -f'_\tau(S_t, K, \tau, \sigma_R, R_F)$$

When the maturity date for the option contract is approaching, the value of the contract will diminish, implying that Θ is generally negative.

The coefficient V (*vega*)[8] measures the sensitivity of the option premium with respect to volatility:

$$V = f'_\sigma(S_t, K, \tau, \sigma_R, R_F)$$

It is always positive and has the same value for a call and for a put. It is of course interpreted as follows: if the volatility increases by 1 %, the option price increases by V.

---

[8] Also termed κ (*kappa*) on occasions – possibly because vega is not a Greek letter!

Finally, the coefficient ρ (*rho*) expresses the manner in which the option price depends on the risk-free rate R_F:

$$\rho = f'_{R_F}(S_t, K, \tau, \sigma_R, R_F)$$

This coefficient will be positive or negative depending on whether we are dealing with a call or a put.

5.2.3.2 *'Delta hedging'*

As these coefficients have now been defined, we can move onto an interesting interpretation of the delta. This element plays its part in hedging a short-term position (issue) of a call option (referred to as 'delta hedging'). The question is: how many units of the underlying equity must the issuer of a call acquire in order to hedge his position? This quantity is referred to as X. Although the current value of the underlying equity is X, the value of its portfolio, consisting of the purchase of X units of the underlying equity and the issue of one call on that equity, is:

$$V(S) = X \cdot S - C(S)$$

If the price of the underlying equity changes from S to $S + \delta S$, the value of the portfolio changes to:

$$V(S + \delta S) = X \cdot (S + \delta S) - C(S + \delta S)$$

As $\Delta \approx \dfrac{C(S + \delta S) - C(S)}{\delta S}$, the new value of the portfolio is:

$$V(S + \delta S) = X \cdot (S + \delta S) - [C(S) + \Delta \cdot \delta S]$$
$$= X \cdot S - C(S) + (X - \Delta) \cdot \delta S$$
$$= V(S) + (X - \Delta) \cdot \delta S$$

The position will therefore be hedged against a movement (up or down) of the underlying equity price if the second term is zero ($X = \Delta$), that is, if the issuer of the call holds Δ units in the underlying equity.

5.2.4 General properties

5.2.4.1 *Call–put parity relation for European options*

We will now draw up the relation that links a European call premium and a European put premium, both relating to the same underlying equity and both with the same exercise price and maturity date: this is termed the 'call–put parity relation'.

We will establish this relation for a European equity option that does not distribute a dividend during the option contract period.

Let us consider a portfolio put together at moment t with:

- the purchase of the underlying equity, whose value is S_t;
- the purchase of a put on this underlying equity, with exercise price K and maturity T; its value is therefore $P_t(S_t, K, \tau, \sigma_R, R_F)$;

- the sale of a call on the same underlying equity, with exercise price K and maturity T; its value is therefore $C_t(S_t, K, \tau, \sigma_R, R_F)$;
- the borrowing (at risk-free rate R_F) of a total worth K at time T; the amount is therefore $K \cdot (1 + R_F)^{-\tau}$.

The value of the portfolio at maturity T will be $S_T + P_T - C_T - K$. As we have shown previously that $C_T = (S_T - K)^+$ and that $P_T(K - S_T)^+$, this value at maturity will equal:

$$\text{if } S_T > K, \qquad S_T + 0 - (S_T - K) - K = 0$$

$$\text{if } S_T \le K, \qquad S_T + (K - S_T) - 0 - K = 0$$

This portfolio, regardless of changes to the value of the underlying equity between t and T and for constant K and R_F, has a zero value at moment T. Because of the hypothesis of absence of arbitrage opportunity,[9] the portfolio can only have a zero value at moment t.

The zero value of this portfolio at moment t is expressed by: $S_t + P_t - C_t - K \cdot (1 + R_F)^{-\tau} = 0$.

Or, in a more classic way, by:

$$C_t + K \cdot (1 + R_F)^{-\tau} = P_t + S_t$$

This is the relation of parity declared.

Note

The 'call–put' parity relation is not valid for an exchange option because of the interest rate spread between the two currencies. If the risk-free interest rate for the domestic currency and that of the foreign currency are referred to as $R_F^{(D)}$ and $R_F^{(F)}$ (they are assumed to be constant and valid for any maturity date), it is easy to see that the parity relation will take the form $C_t + K \cdot (1 + R_F^{(D)})^{-\tau} = P_t + S_t \cdot (1 + R_F^{(F)})^{-\tau}$.

5.2.4.2 Relation between European call and American call

Let us now establish the relation that links a European call to an American call, both for the same underlying equity and with the same exercise price and maturity date. As with the parity relation, we will deal only with equity options that do not distribute a dividend during the option contract period.

As the American option can be exercised at any moment prior to maturity, its value will always be at least equal to the value of the European option with the same characteristics:

$$C_t^{(a)}(S_t, K, T - t, \sigma_R, R_F) \ge C_t^{(e)}(S_t, K, T - t, \sigma_R, R_F)$$

The parity relation allows the following to be written in succession:

$$C_t^{(e)} + K \cdot (1 + R_F)^{-\tau} = P_t^{(e)} + S_t$$

$$C_t^{(e)} \ge S_t - K \cdot (1 + R_F)^{-\tau} > S_t - K$$

$$C_t^{(a)} \ge C_t^{(e)} > (S_t - K)^+$$

---

[9] Remember that no financial movement has occurred between t and T as we have excluded the payment of dividends.

As $(S_t - K)^+$ represents what the American call would return if exercised at moment t, its holder will be best advised to retain it until moment T. At all times, therefore, this option will have the same value as the corresponding European option:

$$C_t^{(a)} = C_t^{(e)} \qquad \forall t \in [0; T]$$

We would point out that the identity between the American and European calls does not apply to puts or to other kinds of option (such as exchange options).

5.2.4.3 Inequalities on price

The values of calls and puts obey the following inequalities:

$$[S_t - K(1 + R_F)^{-\tau}]^+ \le C_t \le S_t$$
$$[K(1 + R_F)^{-\tau} - S_t]^+ \le P_t^{(e)} \le K(1 + R_F)^{-\tau}$$
$$[K - S_t]^+ \le P_t^{(a)} \le K$$

These inequalities limit the area in which the graph for the option according to the underlying equity price can be located. This leads to Figure 5.9 for a European or American call and Figure 5.10 for puts.

The right-hand inequalities are obvious: they state simply that an option cannot be worth more than the gain it allows. A call cannot therefore be worth more than the underlying equity whose acquisition it allows. In the same way, a put cannot be worth more than the

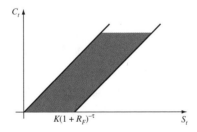

Figure 5.9   Inequalities for a call value

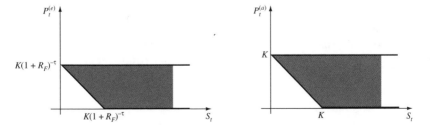

Figure 5.10   Inequalities for the value of a European put and an American put

exercise price K at which it allows the underlying equity to be sold; and for a European put, it cannot exceed the discounted value of the exercise price in question (the exercise can only occur on the maturity date).

Let us now justify the left-hand inequality for a call. To do this, we set up at moment t a portfolio consisting of:

- the purchase of one call;
- a risk-free financial investment worth K at maturity: $K(1 + R_F)^{-\tau}$;
- the sale of one unit of the underlying equity.

Its value at moment t will of course be: $V_t = C_t + K(1 + R_F)^{-\tau} - S_t$.

Its value on maturity will depend on the evolution of the underlying equity:

$$V_T = \begin{cases} \text{if } S_T > K, & (S_T - K) + K - S_T = 0 \\ \text{if } S_T \leq K, & 0 + K - S_T \end{cases}$$

In other words, $V_T = (K - S_T)^+$, which is not negative for any of the possible evolution scenarios. In the absence of arbitrage opportunity, we also have $V_t \geq 0$, that is, $C_t \geq S_t - K(1 + R_F)^{-\tau}$.

As the price of the option cannot be negative, we have the inequality declared.

The left-hand inequality for a European put is obtained in the same way, by arbitrage-based logic using the portfolio consisting of:

- the purchase of one put;
- the purchase of one underlying equity unit;
- the purchase of an amount worth K at maturity: $K(1 + R_F)^{-\tau}$.

The left-hand inequality for an American put arises from the inequality for a European put. It should be noted that there is no need to discount the exercise price as the moment at which the option right will be exercised is unknown.

5.3   VALUATION MODELS

Before touching on the developed methods for determining the value of an option, we will show the basic principles for establishing option pricing using an example that has been deliberately simplified as much as possible.

Example

Consider a European call option on the US\$/€ exchange rate for which the exercise price is $K = 1$. Then suppose that at the present time ($t = 0$) the rate is $S_0 = 0.95$ (US\$1 = €0.95). We will be working with a zero risk-free rate ($R_F = 0$) in order to simplify the developments.

Let us suppose also that the random changes in the underlying equity between moments $t = 0$ and $t = T$ can correspond to two scenarios s_1 and s_2 for which S_T is €1.1 and €0.9 respectively, and that the scenarios occur with the respective probabilities of 0.6 and 0.4.

$$S_T = \begin{cases} 1.1 & \Pr(s_1) = 0.6 \\ 0.9 & \Pr(s_2) = 0.4 \end{cases}$$

The changes in the exchange option, which is also random, can therefore be described as:

$$C_T = \begin{cases} 0.1 & \Pr(s_1) = 0.6 \\ 0.0 & \Pr(s_2) = 0.4 \end{cases}$$

Let us consider that at moment $t = 0$, we have a portfolio consisting of:

- the issue of a US\$/€ call (at the initial price of C_0);
- a loan of €X;
- the purchase of US\$$Y$.

so that:

- The initial value V_0 of the portfolio is zero: the purchase of the US\$$Y$ is made exactly with what is generated by the issue of the call and the loan.
- The portfolio is risk-free, and will undergo the same evolution whatever the scenario (in fact, its value will not change as we have assumed R_F to be zero).

The initial value of the portfolio in € is therefore $V_0 = -C_0 - X + 0.95Y = 0$.
Depending on the scenario, the final value will be given by:

$$V_T(s_1) = -0.1 - X + 1.1 \cdot Y$$

$$V_T(s_2) = -X + 0.9 \cdot Y$$

The hypothesis of absence of opportunity for arbitrage allows confirmation that $V_T(s_1) = V_T(s_2) = 0$ and the consequent deduction of the following values: $X = 0.45$ and $Y = 0.5$. On the basis of the initial value of the portfolio, the initial value of the option is therefore deduced:

$$C_0 = -X + 0.95Y = 0.025$$

It is important to note that this value is totally independent of the probabilities 0.6 and 0.4 associated with the two development scenarios for the underlying equity price, otherwise we would have $C_0 = 0.1 \times 0.6 + 0 \times 0.4 = 0.06$.
If now we determine another law of probability

$$\Pr(s_1) = q \qquad \Pr(s_2) = 1 - q$$

for which $C_0 = E_q(C_T)$, we have $0.025 = 0.01 \cdot q + 0 \cdot (1 - q)$, that is: $q = 0.25$.
We are in fact looking at the law of probability for which $S_0 = E_q(S_T)$:

$$E_q(S_T) = 1.1 \cdot 0.25 + 0.9 \cdot 0.75 = 0.95 = S_0$$

We have therefore seen, in a very specific case where there is a need for generalisation, that the current value of the option is equal to the mathematical expectation of its future value, with respect to the law of probability for which the current value of the underlying equity is equal to the expectation of its future value.[10] This law of probability is known as the *risk-neutral probability*.

5.3.1 Binomial model for equity options

This model was produced by Cox, Ross and Rubinstein.[11] In this discrete model we look simply at a list of times 0, 1, 2, ..., T separated by a unit of time (the period), which is usually quite short.

Placing ourselves in a perfect market, we envisage a European equity option that does not distribute any dividends during the contract period and with a constant volatility during the period in question.

In addition, we assume that the risk-free interest does not change during this period, that it is valid for any maturity (flat, constant yield curve), and that it is the same for a loan and for an investment. This interest rate, termed R_F, will be expressed according to a duration equal to a period; and the same will apply for other parameters (return, volatility etc.).

Remember (Section 3.4.2) that the change in the underlying equity value from one time to another is dichotomous in nature: equity has at moment t the value S_t, but at the next moment $t + 1$ will have one of the two values $S_t \cdot u$ (greater than S_t) or $S_t \cdot d$ (less than S_t) with respective probabilities of α and $(1 - \alpha)$. We have $d \leq 1 < 1 + R_F \leq u$ and the parameters u, d and α, which are assumed to be constant over time, should be estimated on the basis of observations.

We therefore have the following graphic representation of the development in equity prices for a period:

$$S_t \begin{array}{l} \nearrow S_{t+1} = S_t \cdot u \quad (\alpha) \\ \searrow S_{t+1} = S_t \cdot d \quad (1 - \alpha) \end{array}$$

and therefore, more generally speaking, as shown in Figure 5.11.

Now let us address the issue of evaluating options at the initial moment. Our reasoning will be applied to a call option.

It is known that the value of the option at the end of the contract will be expressed according to the value of the equity by $C_T = (S_T - K)^+$.

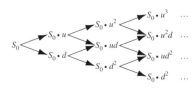

Figure 5.11 Binomial tree for underlying equity

---

[10] When the risk-free rate is zero, remember.

[11] Cox J., Ross S. and Rubinstein M., Option pricing: a simplified approach, *Journal of Financial Economics*, No. 7, 1979, pp. 229–63

After constructing the tree diagram for the equity from moment 0 to moment T, we will now construct the tree from T to 0 for the option, from each of the ends in the equity tree diagram, to reconstruct the value C_0 of the option at 0. This reasoning will be applied in stages.

5.3.1.1 One period

Assume that $T = 1$. From the equity tree diagram it can be clearly seen that the call C_0 (unknown) can evolve into two values with the respective probabilities of α and $(1 - \alpha)$:

$$C_0 \begin{cases} \nearrow C_1 = C(u) = (S_0 \cdot u - K)^+ \\ \searrow C_1 = C(d) = (S_0 \cdot d - K)^+ \end{cases}$$

As the value of C_1 (that is, the value of $C(u)$ and $C(d)$) is known, we will now determine the value of C_0. To do this, we will construct a portfolio put together at $t = 0$ by:

- the purchase of X underlying equities with a value of S_0;
- the sale of one call on this underlying equity, with a value of C_0.

The value V_0 of this portfolio, and its evolution V_1 in the context described, are given by:

$$V_0 = X \cdot S_0 - C_0 \begin{cases} \nearrow V_1 = X \cdot S_0 \cdot u - C(u) \\ \searrow V_1 = X \cdot S_0 \cdot d - C(d) \end{cases}$$

We then choose X so that the portfolio is risk-free (the two values of V_1 will then be identical). The hypothesis of absence of arbitrage opportunity shows that in this case, the return on this portfolio must be given by the risk-free rate R_F.

We therefore obtain:

$$\begin{cases} V_1 = X \cdot S_0 \cdot u - C(u) = X \cdot S_0 \cdot d - C(d) \\ V_1 = (X \cdot S_0 - C_0)(1 + R_F) \end{cases}$$

The first equation readily provides:

$$X \cdot S_0 = \frac{C(u) - C(d)}{u - d}$$

and therefore:

$$V_1 = \frac{d \cdot C(u) - u \cdot C(d)}{u - d}$$

The second equation then provides:

$$\frac{d \cdot C(u) - u \cdot C(d)}{u - d} = \left(\frac{C(u) - C(d)}{u - d} - C_0 \right)(1 + R_F)$$

This easily resolves with respect to C_0:

$$C_0 = (1 + R_F)^{-1} \left[\frac{(1 + R_F) - d}{u - d} C(u) + \frac{u - (1 + R_F)}{u - d} C(d) \right]$$

The coefficients for $C(u)$ and $C(d)$ are clearly between 0 and 1 and total 1. We therefore introduce:

$$q = \frac{(1 + R_F) - d}{u - d} \qquad 1 - q = \frac{u - (1 + R_F)}{u - d}$$

They constitute the *neutral risk* law of probability.

We therefore have the value of the original call:

$$C_0 = (1 + R_F)^{-1} [q \cdot C(u) + (1 - q) \cdot C(d)]$$

Note 1

As was noted in the introductory example, the probability of growth α is not featured in the above relation. The only law of probability involved is the one relating to the risk-neutral probability q, with respect to which C_0 appears as the discounted value of the average value of the call at maturity ($t = 1$).

The term 'risk-neutral probability' is based on the logic that the expected value of the underlying equity at maturity ($t = 1$) with respect to this law of probability is given by:

$$E_q(S_1) = q \cdot S_0 \cdot u + (1 - q) \cdot S_0 \cdot d$$

$$= S_0 \left[\frac{(1 + R_F) - d}{u - d} u + \frac{u - (1 + R_F)}{u - d} d \right]$$

$$= S_0(1 + R_F)$$

The change in the risk-free security is the same as the expected change in the risked security (for this law of probability).

Note 2

When using the binomial model practically, it is simpler to apply the reasoning with respect to one single period for each node on the tree diagram, progressing from T to 0. We will, however, push this analysis further in order to obtain a general result.

5.3.1.2   Two periods

Let us now suppose that $T = 2$. The binomial tree diagram for the option will now be written as:

$$C_0 \begin{cases} C_1 = C(u) \begin{cases} C_2 = C(u, u) = (S_0 \cdot u^2 - K)^+ \\ C_2 = C(u, d) = C(d, u) = (S_0 \cdot ud - K)^+ \end{cases} \\ C_1 = C(d) \begin{cases} C_2 = C(d, d) = (S_0 \cdot d^2 - K)^+ \end{cases} \end{cases}$$

The previous reasoning will allow transition from time 2 to time 1:

$$\begin{cases} C(u) = (1 + R_F)^{-1}[q \cdot C(u, u) + (1 - q) \cdot C(u, d)] \\ C(d) = (1 + R_F)^{-1}[q \cdot C(d, u) + (1 - q) \cdot C(d, d)] \end{cases}$$

And from time 1 to time 0:

$$C_0 = (1 + R_F)^{-1} \left[q \cdot C(u) + (1 - q) \cdot C(d) \right]$$

$$= (1 + R_F)^{-2} \left[q^2 \cdot C(u, u) + 2q(1 - q) \cdot C(u, d) + (1 - q)^2 \cdot C(d, d) \right]$$

Consideration of the coefficients for $C(u,u)$, $C(u,d)$ and $C(d, d)$ allows the above note to be specified: C_0 is the discounted value for the expected value of the call on maturity $(t = 2)$ with respect to a binomial law of probability[12] for parameters $(2; q)$.

5.3.1.3 *T periods*

To generalise what has already been said, it is seen that C_0 is the discounted value of the expected value of the call on maturity $(t = T)$ with respect to a binomial law of probability for parameters $(T; q)$. We can therefore write:

$$C_0 = (1 + R_F)^{-T} \sum_{j=0}^{T} \binom{T}{j} q^j (1 - q)^{T-j} C(\underbrace{u, \ldots, u}_{j}, \underbrace{d, \ldots, d}_{T-j})$$

$$= (1 + R_F)^{-T} \sum_{j=0}^{T} \binom{T}{j} q^j (1 - q)^{T-j} (S_0 u^j d^{T-j} - K)^+$$

As $u^j d^{T-j}$ is an increasing function of j, if one introduces $j = \min \{j : S_0 u^j d^{T-j} - K > 0\}$, that is, the smallest value of j that is strictly higher than $\dfrac{\ln K - \ln(S_0 d^T)}{\ln u - \ln d}$, the evaluation of the call takes the form:

$$C_0 = (1 + R_F)^{-T} \sum_{j=J}^{T} \binom{T}{j} q^j (1 - q)^{T-j} (S_0 u^j d^{T-j} - K)$$

$$= S_0 \sum_{j=J}^{T} \binom{T}{j} \left(\frac{uq}{1 + R_F} \right)^j \left(\frac{d(1 - q)}{1 + R_F} \right)^{T-j} - K(1 + R_F)^{-T} \sum_{j=J}^{T} \binom{T}{j} q^j (1 - q)^{T-j}$$

Because:

$$\frac{uq}{1 + R_F} + \frac{d(1 - q)}{1 + R_F} = \frac{u[(1 + R_F) - d] + d[u - (1 + R_F)]}{(1 + R_F)(u - d)} = 1$$

we introduce:

$$q' = \frac{uq}{1 + R_F} \qquad 1 - q' = \frac{d(1 - q)}{1 + R_F}$$

---

[12] See Appendix 2.

By introducing the notation $B(n; p)$ for a binomial random variable with parameters (n, p), we can therefore write:

$$C_0 = S_0 \cdot \Pr\left[B(T; q') \geq J\right] - K(1 + R_F)^{-T} \cdot \Pr\left[B(T; q) \geq J\right]$$

The 'call–put' parity relation $C_0 + K(1 + R_F)^{-T} = P_0 + S_0$ allows the evaluation formula to be obtained immediately for the put with the same characteristics:

$$P_0 = -S_0 \cdot \Pr[B(T; q') < J] + K(1 + R_F)^{-T} \cdot \Pr[B(T; q) < J]$$

Note

The parameters u and d are determined, for example, on the basis of the volatility σ_R of the return of the underlying equity. In fact, as the return relative to a period takes the values $(u - 1)$ or $(d - 1)$ with the respective probabilities α and $(1 - \alpha)$, we have:

$$E_R = \alpha(u - 1) + (1 - \alpha)(d - 1)$$
$$\sigma_R^2 = \alpha(u - 1)^2 + (1 - \alpha)(d - 1)^2 - [\alpha(u - 1) + (1 - \alpha)(d - 1)]^2$$
$$= \alpha(1 - \alpha)(u - d)^2$$

By choosing $\alpha = 1/2$, we arrive at $u - d = 2\sigma_R$. Cox, Ross and Rubinstein suggest taking $d = 1/u$, which leads to an easily solved second-degree equation or, with a Talor approximation, $u = e^{\sigma_R}$ and $d = e^{-\sigma_R}$.

Example

Let us consider a call option of seven months' duration, relating to an equity with a current value of €100 and an exercise price of €110. It is assumed that its volatility is $\sigma_R = 0.25$, calculated on an annual basis, and that the risk-free rate is 4 % per annum.

We will assess the value of this call at $t = 0$ by constructing a binomial tree diagram with the month as the basic period. The equivalent volatility and risk-free rate as given by:

$$\sigma_R = \sqrt{\frac{1}{12} \cdot 0.25} = 0.07219$$

$$R_F = \sqrt[12]{1.04} - 1 = 0.003274$$

We therefore have $u - 1/u = 0.1443$, for which the only positive root is[13] $u = 1.07477$ (and therefore $d = 0.93043$). The risk-neutral probability is:

$$q = \frac{1.003274 - 0.93043}{1.07477 - 0.93043} = 0.5047$$

---

[13] If we had chosen $\alpha = 1/3$ instead of $1/2$, we would have found that $u = 1.0795$, that is, a relatively small difference; the estimation of u therefore only depends relatively little on α.

Let us first show the practical method of working: the construction of two binomial tree diagrams (forward for the equity and backward for the bond). For example, we have for the two values of S_1:

$$S_0 \cdot u = 100 \cdot 1.07477 = 107.477$$

$$S_0 \cdot d = 100 \cdot 0.93043 = 93.043$$

The binomial tree for the underlying equity is shown in Table 5.3.

The binomial tree diagram for the option is constructed backwards. The last column is therefore constructed on the basis of the relation $C_T = (S_T - K)^+$.

The first component of this column is max $(165.656 - 110; 0) = 55.656$, and the elements in the preceding columns can be deduced from it, for example:

$$\frac{1}{1.003274}[0.5047 \cdot 55.656 + 0.4953 \cdot 33.409] = 44.491$$

This gives us Table 5.4.

The initial value of the call is therefore $C_0 = €4.657$.

Let us now show the calculation of the value of the option based on the final formula. The auxiliary probability is given by:

$$q' = \frac{1.07477 \cdot 0.5047}{1.003274} = 0.5406$$

Table 5.3 Binomial tree for underlying equity

0	1	2	3	4	5	6	7
100	107.477	115.513	124.150	133.432	143.409	154.132	165.656
	93.043	100.000	107.477	115.513	124.150	133.432	143.409
		86.570	93.043	100.000	107.477	115.513	124.150
			80.548	86.570	93.043	100.000	107.477
				74.944	80.548	86.570	93.043
					69.731	74.944	80.548
						64.880	69.731
							60.366

Table 5.4 Binomial tree for option

0	1	2	3	4	5	6	7
4.657	7.401	11.462	17.196	24.809	34.126	44.491	55.656
	1.891	3.312	5.696	9.555	15.482	23.791	33.409
		0.456	0.906	1.801	3.580	7.118	14.150
			0	0	0	0	0
				0	0	0	0
					0	0	0
						0	0
							0

In addition, as $\dfrac{\ln 110 - \ln(100 \cdot d^7)}{\ln u - \ln d} = 4.1609$, we find that $J = 5$. This will allow us to calculate:

$$\Pr[B(7; p) \geq 5] = \binom{7}{5} p^5 (1-p)^2 + \binom{7}{6} p^6 (1-p) + \binom{7}{7} p^7$$

$$= p^5 (21 - 35p + 15p^2)$$

and therefore: $\Pr[B(7; q) \geq 5] = 0.2343$ and $\Pr[B(7; q') \geq 5] = 0.2984$.

The price of the call therefore equals: $C_0 = 100 \cdot 0.2984 - 110 \cdot (1 + R_F)^{-7} \cdot 0.2343 = 4.657$.

Meanwhile, the premium for the put with the same characteristics is:

$$P_0 = 100 \cdot (1 - 0.2984) + 100 \cdot (1 + R_F)^{-7} \cdot (1 - 0.2343) = 12.168$$

Note that it is logical for the price of the put to be higher than that of the call, as the option is currently 'out of the money'.

5.3.1.4 Taking account of dividends

We have assumed until now that the underlying equity does not pay a dividend. Let us now examine a case in which dividends are paid.

If only one dividend is paid during the ith period (interval $[i - 1; i]$), and the rate of the dividend is termed δ (ratio of the dividend amount to the value of the security), the value of the security will be reduced to the rate δ when the dividend is paid and the binomial tree diagram for the underlying equity must therefore be modified as follows:

- up to the time $(i - 1)$, no change: the values carried by the nodes in the tree diagram for the period $j \leq i - 1$ will be $S_0 u^k d^{j-k} (k = 0, \ldots, j)$;
- from the time i onwards (let us say for $j \geq i$), the values become[14] $S_0(1 - \delta) u^k d^{j-k}$ $(k = 0, \ldots, j)$;
- the tree diagram for the option is constructed in the classic backward style from that point;
- if several dividends are paid at various times during the option contract, the procedure described above must be applied whenever a payment is made.

5.3.2 Black and Scholes model for equity options

We now develop the well-known continuous time model compiled by Black and Scholes.[15] In this model the option, concluded at moment 0 and maturing at moment T, can be evaluated at any moment $t \in [0; T]$, and as usual, we note $\tau = T - t$.

We further assume that the risk-free rate of interest does not change during this period, that it is valid for any maturity date (flat and constant yield curve) and that it is the same

---

[14] This means that when the tree diagram is constructed purely numerically, taking account of the factor $(1 - \delta)$ will only be effective for the passage from the time $i - 1$ to the time i.

[15] Black F. and Scholes M., The pricing of options and corporate liabilities, *Journal of Political Economy*, Vol. 81, 1973, pp. 637–59.

for an investment as for a loan. The annual rate of interest, termed R_F up until now, is replaced in this continuous model by the corresponding instant rate $r = \ln(1 + R_F)$, so that a unitary total invested during a period of t years becomes $(1 + R_F)^t = e^{rt}$.

Remember (see Section 3.4.2) that the evolution of the underlying equity value is governed by the stochastic differential equation

$$\frac{dS_t}{S_t} = E_R \cdot dt + \sigma_R \cdot dw_t$$

We will initially establish[16] the Black and Scholes formula for a call option the value of which is considered to be a function of the value S_t of the underlying equity and of time t, the other parameters being considered to be constant: $C_t = C(S_t, t)$.

By applying Itô's formula to the function $C(S_t, t)$, we obtain:

$$dC(S_t, t) = \left(C'_t + E_R S_t C'_S + \frac{\sigma_R^2}{2} S_t^2 C''_{SS} \right) \cdot dt + \sigma_R S_t C'_S \cdot dw_t$$

Let us now put together a portfolio that at moment t consists of:

- the purchase of X underlying equities with a value of S_t;
- the sale of one call on then underlying equity, with value $C(S_t, t)$.

The value V_t of this portfolio is given by $V_t = X \cdot S_t - C(S_t, t)$. This, by differentiation, gives:

$$dV_t = X \cdot [E_R S_t \cdot dt + \sigma_R S_t \cdot dw_t] - \left[\left(C'_t + E_R S_t C'_S + \frac{\sigma_R^2}{2} S_t^2 C''_{SS} \right) \cdot dt + \sigma_R S_t C'_S \cdot dw_t \right]$$

$$= \left[X \cdot E_R S_t - \left(C'_t + E_R S_t C'_S + \frac{\sigma_R^2}{2} S_t^2 C''_{SS} \right) \right] \cdot dt + [X \cdot \sigma_R S_t - \sigma_R S_t C'_S] \cdot dw_t$$

We then choose X so that the portfolio no longer has any random components (the coefficient of dw_t in the preceding relation must be zero). The hypothesis of absence of arbitrage opportunity shows that if possible, the return on the portfolio should be given by the risk-free rate r:

$$\frac{dV_t}{V_t} = r \cdot dt + 0 \cdot dw_t$$

We therefore arrive at:

$$\begin{cases} \dfrac{X \cdot E_R S_t - \left(C'_t + E_R S_t C'_S + \dfrac{\sigma_R^2}{2} S_t^2 C''_{SS} \right)}{X \cdot S_t - C(S_t, t)} = r \\[2ex] \dfrac{X \cdot \sigma_R S_t - \sigma_R S_t C'_S}{X \cdot S_t - C(S_t, t)} = 0 \end{cases}$$

---

[16] We will only develop the financial part of the logic, as the end of the demonstration is purely analytical. Readers interested in details of calculations can consult the original literature or Devolder P., *Finance Stochastique*, Éditions de l'ULB, 1993.

or, in the same way:

$$\begin{cases} X \cdot (E_R - r)S_t - \left(C_t' + E_R S_t C_S' + \dfrac{\sigma_R^2}{2} S_t^2 C_{SS}'' - rC(S_t, t) \right) = 0 \\ X - C_S' = 0 \end{cases}$$

The second equation provides the value of X, which cancels out the random component of the portfolio: $X = C'_S$. By making a substitution in the first equation, we find:

$$(E_R - r)S_t \cdot C_S' - \left(C_t' + E_R S_t C_S' + \frac{\sigma_R^2}{2} S_t^2 C_{SS}'' - rC(S_t, t) \right) = 0$$

In other words:

$$C_t' + r S_t C_S' + \frac{\sigma_R^2}{2} S_t^2 C_{SS}'' - rC(S_t, t) = 0$$

In this equation, the instant mean return E_R has disappeared.[17]

We are looking at a partial derivative equation (in which none of the elements are now random) of the second order for the unknown function $C(S_t, t)$. It allows a single solution if two limit conditions are imposed:

$$\begin{cases} C(0, t) = 0 \\ C(S_T, T) = (S_T - K)^+ \end{cases}$$

Through a change in variables, this equation can be turned into an equation well known to physicists: the heat equation.[18] It is in fact easy, although demanding, to see that if the new unknown function $u(x, s) = C(S_t, t)e^{rt}$ is introduced where the change of variables occurs:

$$\begin{cases} S_t = K \cdot \exp \left(\dfrac{\sigma_R^2 (x - s)}{2\left(r - \dfrac{\sigma_R^2}{2} \right)} \right) \\ t = T - \dfrac{s\sigma_R^2}{2\left(r - \dfrac{\sigma_R^2}{2} \right)^2} \end{cases}$$

which inverts to:

$$\begin{cases} x = \dfrac{2}{\sigma_R^2} \left(r - \dfrac{\sigma_R^2}{2} \right) \cdot \left[\ln \dfrac{S_t}{K} + \left(r - \dfrac{\sigma_R^2}{2} \right) \tau \right] \\ s = \dfrac{2}{\sigma_R^2} \left(r - \dfrac{\sigma_R^2}{2} \right)^2 \tau \end{cases}$$

---

[17] In the same way as the independence of the result obtained by the binomial model with respect to the probability α governing the evolution of the subjacent share price was noted.

[18] See for example: Krasnov M., Kisilev A., Makarenko G. and Chikin E., *Mathématique supérieures pour ingénieurs et polytechniciens*, De Boeck, 1993. Also: Sokolnikov I. S. and Redheffer R. M., *Mathematics of Physics and Modern Engineering*, McGraw-Hill, 1966.

The equation obtained turns into: $u''_{xx} = u'_s$.

With the conditions limit:

$$
\begin{cases}
\lim_{x \to -\infty} u(x, s) = 0 \\
\\
u(x, 0) = v(x) =
\begin{cases}
K \cdot \left[\exp \left(\dfrac{x \dfrac{\sigma_R^2}{2}}{r - \dfrac{\sigma_R^2}{2}} \right) - 1 \right] & \text{if } x \geq 0 \\
\\
0 & \text{if } x < 0
\end{cases}
\end{cases}
$$

this heat equation has the solution:

$$
u(x, s) = \frac{1}{2\sqrt{\pi s}} \int_{-\infty}^{+\infty} v(y) e^{-(x-y)^2/4s} \, dy
$$

By making the calculations with the specific expression of $v(y)$, and then making the inverse change of variables, we obtain the Black and Scholes formula for the call option

$$
C(S_t, t) = S_t \Phi(d_1) - K e^{-r\tau} \Phi(d_2),
$$

where we have:

$$
\left. \begin{matrix} d_1 \\ d_2 \end{matrix} \right\} = \frac{\ln \dfrac{S_t}{K} + \left(r \pm \dfrac{\sigma_R^2}{2} \right) \tau}{\sigma_R \sqrt{\tau}}
$$

and the function Φ represents the standard normal distribution function:

$$
\Phi(t) = \frac{1}{\sqrt{2\pi}} \int_{-\infty}^{t} e^{-x^2/2} dx
$$

The price P_t of a put option can be evaluated on the basis of the price of the call option, thanks to the relation of 'call–put' parity: $C_t + K \cdot e^{-rT} = P_t + S_t$.

In fact:

$$
\begin{aligned}
P(S_t, t) &= C(S_t, t) + K e^{-r\tau} - S_t \\
&= S_t \Phi(d_1) - K e^{-r\tau} \Phi(d_2) + K e^{-r\tau} - S_t \\
&= -S_t [1 - \Phi(d_1)] + K e^{-r\tau} [1 - \Phi(d_2)]
\end{aligned}
$$

and therefore:

$$
P(S_t, t) = -S_t \Phi(-d_1) + K e^{-r\tau} \Phi(-d_2)
$$

because:

$$
1 - \Phi(t) = \Phi(-t)
$$

Example

Consider an option with the same characteristics as in Section 5.3.1: $S_0 = 100$, $K = 110$, $t = 0$, $T = 7$ months, $\sigma_R = 0.25$ on an annual basis and $R_F = 4\%$ per year.

We are working with the year as the time basis, so that: $\tau = 7/12, r = \ln 1.04 = 0.03922$.

$$\left.\begin{array}{c} d_1 \\ d_2 \end{array}\right\} = \frac{\ln\dfrac{100}{110} + \left(0.03922 \pm \dfrac{0.25^2}{2}\right)\cdot\dfrac{7}{12}}{0.25\cdot\sqrt{\dfrac{7}{12}}} = \left\{\begin{array}{l} -0.2839 \\ -0.4748 \end{array}\right.$$

Hence $\Phi(d_1) = 0.3823$ and $\Phi(d_2) = 0.3175$. This allows the price of the call to be calculated:

$$C = C(S_0, 0) = 100 \cdot \Phi(d_1) - 110 \cdot e^{-0.03922\cdot\frac{7}{12}} \cdot \Phi(d_2) = 4.695$$

As the put premium has the same characteristics, it totals:

$$P = P(S_0, 0) = -100 \cdot [1 - \Phi(d_1)] + 110 \cdot e^{-0.03922\cdot\frac{7}{12}} \cdot [1 - \Phi(d_2)] = 12.207$$

The similarity of these figures to the values obtained using the binomial model (4.657 and 12.168 respectively) will be noted.

5.3.2.2 Sensitivity parameters

When the price of an option is calculated using the Black and Scholes formula, the sensitivity parameters or 'Greeks' take on a practical form.

Let us examine first the case of a call option delta. If the reduced normal density is termed ϕ

$$\phi(x) = \Phi'(x) = \frac{1}{\sqrt{2\pi}}e^{-x^2/2}$$

we arrive, by derivation, at:

$$\Delta(C) = C_S' = \Phi(d_1) + \frac{1}{S_t\sigma_R\sqrt{\tau}}\left[S_t\phi(d_1) - Ke^{-r\tau}\phi(d_2)\right]$$

It is easy to see that the quantity between the square brackets is zero and that therefore $\Delta(C) = \Phi(d_1)$, and that by following a very similar logic, we will arrive at a put of: $\Delta(P) = \Phi(d_1) - 1$.

The above formula provides a very simple means of determining the number of equities that should be held by a call issuer to hedge his risk (the delta hedging). This is a common use of the Black and Scholes relation: the price of an option is determined by the law of supply and demand and its 'inversion' provides the implied volatility. The latter is therefore used in the relation $\Delta(C) = \Phi(d_1)$, which is then known as the *hedging formula*.

The other sensitivity parameters (gamma, theta, vega and rho) are obtained in a similar way:

$$\Gamma(C) = \Gamma(P) = \frac{\phi(d_1)}{S_t \sigma_R \sqrt{\tau}}$$

$$\begin{cases} \Theta(C) = -\dfrac{S_t \sigma_R \phi(d_1)}{2\sqrt{\tau}} - rKe^{-r\tau}\Phi(d_2) \\[2mm] \Theta(P) = -\dfrac{S_t \sigma_R \phi(d_1)}{2\sqrt{\tau}} + rKe^{-r\tau}\Phi(-d_2) \end{cases}$$

$$V(C) = V(P) = \tau S_t \phi(d_1)$$

$$\begin{cases} \rho(C) = \tau Ke^{-r\tau}\Phi(d_2) \\ \rho(C) = -\tau Ke^{-r\tau}\Phi(-d_2) \end{cases}$$

In finishing, let us mention a relationship that links the delta, gamma and theta parameters. The partial derivative equation obtained during the demonstration of the Black and Scholes formula for a call is also valid for a put (the price therefore being referred to as p without being specified):

$$p'_t + rS_t p'_S + \frac{\sigma_R^2}{2} S_t^2 p''_{SS} - rp(S_t, t) = 0$$

This, using the sensitivity parameters, will give:

$$\Theta + rS_t \Delta + \frac{\sigma_R^2}{2} S_t^2 \Gamma = r \cdot p$$

5.3.2.3 Taking account of dividends

If a continuous rate dividend[19] δ is paid between t and T and the underlying equity is worth S_t (resp. S_T) at the moment t (resp. T), it can be said that had it not paid a dividend, it would have passed from value S_t to value $e^{\delta\tau} S_T$. It can also be said that the same equity without dividend would pass from value $e^{-\delta\tau} S_t$ at moment t to value S_T at moment T. In order to take account of the dividend, therefore, it will suffice within the Black and Scholes formula to replace S_t by $e^{-\delta\tau} S_t$, thus giving:

$$C(S_t, t) = S_t e^{-\delta\tau}\Phi(d_1) - Ke^{-r\tau}\Phi(d_2)$$

$$P(S_t, t) = -S_t e^{-\delta\tau}\Phi(-d_1) + Ke^{-r\tau}\Phi(-d_2).$$

where, we have:

$$\left.\begin{array}{c} d_1 \\ d_2 \end{array}\right\} = \frac{\ln\dfrac{S_t}{K} + \left(r - \delta \pm \dfrac{\sigma_R^2}{2}\right)\tau}{\sigma_R \sqrt{\tau}}$$

---

[19] An discounting/capitalisation factor of the exponential type is used here and throughout this paragraph.

5.3.3 Other models of valuation

5.3.3.1 Options on bonds

It is not enough to apply the methods shown above (binomial tree diagram or Black and Scholes formula) to options on bonds. In fact:

- Account must be taken of coupons regularly paid.
- The constancy of the underlying equity volatility (a valid hypothesis for equities) does not apply in the case of bonds as their values on maturity converge towards the repayment value R.

The binomial model can be adapted to suit this situation, but is not an obvious generalisation of the method set out above.[20]

Adapting the Black and Scholes model consists of replacing the geometric Brownian motion that represents the changes in the value of the equity with a stochastic process that governs the changes in interest rates, such as those used as the basic for the Vasicek and Cox, Ingersoll and Ross models (see Section 4.5). Unfortunately, the partial derivatives equation deduced therefrom does not generally allow an analytical solution and numeric solutions therefore have to be used.[21]

5.3.3.2 Exchange options

For an exchange option, two risk-free rates have to be taken into consideration: one relative to the domestic currency and one relative to the foreign currency.

For the discrete model, these two rates are referred to respectively as $R_F^{(D)}$ and $R_F^{(F)}$. By altering the logic of Section 5.3.1 using this generalisation, it is possible to determine the price of an exchange option using the binomial tree diagram technique. It will be seen that the principle set out above remains valid with a slight alteration of the close formulae: C_0 is the discounted expected value of the call on maturity (for a period):

$$C_0 = (1 + R_F^{(D)})^{-1} \left[q \cdot C(u) + (1 - q) \cdot C(d) \right]$$

with the neutral risk probability:

$$q = \frac{\left(1 + (R_F^{(D)} - R_F^{(F)})\right) - d}{u - d} \qquad 1 - q = \frac{u - \left(1 + (R_F^{(D)} - R_F^{(F)})\right)}{u - d}$$

For the continuous model, the interest rates in the domestic and foreign currencies are referred to respectively as $r^{(D)}$ and $r^{(F)}$. Following a logic similar to that accepted for options on dividend-paying equities, we see that the Black and Scholes formula is still valid provided the underlying equity price S_t is replaced by $S_t e^{-r^{(F)}\tau}$, which gives the formulae:

$$C(S_t, t) = S_t e^{-r^{(F)}\tau} \Phi(d_1) - K e^{-r^{(D)}\tau} \Phi(d_2)$$

$$P(S_t, t) = -S_t e^{-r^{(F)}\tau} \Phi(-d_1) + K e^{-r^{(D)}\tau} \Phi(-d_2)$$

---

[20] Read for example Copeland T. E. and Weston J. F., *Financial Theory and Corporate Policy*, Addison-Wesley, 1988.

[21] See for example Cortadon G., The pricing of options on default-free bonds, *Journal of Financial and Quantitative Analysis*, Vol. 17, 1982, pp. 75–100.

where, we have:

$$
\left.\begin{array}{c} d_1 \\ d_2 \end{array}\right\} = \frac{\ln \dfrac{S_t}{K} + \left((r^{(D)} - r^{(F)}) \pm \dfrac{\sigma_R^2}{2} \right) \tau}{\sigma_R \sqrt{\tau}}
$$

This is known as the Garman–Kohlhagen formula.[22]

5.4 STRATEGIES ON OPTIONS[23]

5.4.1 Simple strategies

5.4.1.1 Pure speculation

As we saw in Section 5.1, the asymmetrical payoff structure particular to options allows investors who hold them in isolation to profit from the fall in the underlying equity price while limiting the loss (on the reduced premium) that occurs when a contrary variation occurs.

The issue of a call/put option, on the other hand, is a much more speculative operation. The profit will be limited to the premium if the underlying equity price remains lower/higher than the exercise price, while considerable losses may arise if the price of the underlying equity rises/falls more sharply. This type of operation should therefore only be envisaged if the issuer is completely confident that the price of the underlying equity will fall/rise.

5.4.1.2 Simultaneous holding of put option and underlying equity

As the purchase of a put option allows one to profit from a fall in the underlying equity price, it seems natural to link this fall to the holding of the underlying equity, in order to limit the loss inflicted by the fall in the price of the equity held alone.

5.4.1.3 Issue of a call option with simultaneous holding of underlying equity

We have also seen (Example 1 in Section 5.1.2) that it is worthwhile issuing a call option while holding the underlying equity at the same time. In fact, when the underlying equity price falls (or rises slightly), the loss incurred thereon is partly compensated by encashment of the premium, whereas when the price rises steeply, the profit that would have been realised on the underlying equity is limited to the price of the option increased by the difference between the exercise price and the underlying equity price at the beginning of the contract.

5.4.2 More complex strategies

Combining options allows the creation of payoff distributions that do not exist for classic assets such as equities or bonds. These strategies are usually used by investors trying to turn very specific forecasts to profit. We will look briefly at the following:

- straddles;
- strangles;

---

[22] Garman M. and Kohlhagen S., Foreign currency option values, *Journal of International Money and Finance*, No. 2, 1983, pp. 231–7.
[23] Our writings are based on Reilly F. K. and Brown K. C., *Investment Analysis and Portfolio Management*, South-Western, 2000.

- spreads;
- range forwards.

5.4.2.1 Straddles

A straddle consists of simultaneously purchasing (resp. selling) a call option and a put option with identical underlying equity, exercise price and maturity date. The concomitant call (resp. put) corresponds to a *long* (resp. *short*) *straddle*.

Clearly it is a question of playing volatility, as in essence, it is contradictory to play the rise and the fall in the underlying equity price at the same time.

We saw in Section 5.2.3 (The Greeks: vega) that the premium of an option increases along with volatility. As a result, the *short straddle* (resp. *long straddle*) is the action of an investor who believes that the underlying equity price will vary more (resp. less) than historically regardless of direction of variation.

It is particularly worth mentioning that with the *short straddle*, it is possible to make money with a zero variation in underlying equity price.

Finally, note that the *straddle* (Figure 5.12) is a particular type of option known as the chooser option.[24]

5.4.2.2 Strangles

The *strangle* is a *straddle* except for the exercise price, which is not identical for the call option and the put option, the options being 'out of the money'. As a result:

- The premium is lower.
- The expected variation must be greater than that associated with the *straddle*.

Certainly, this type of strategy presents a less aggressive risk-return profile in comparison with the straddle. A comparison is shown in Figure 5.13.

5.4.2.3 Spreads

Option *spreads* consist of the concomitant purchases of two contracts that are identical but for just one of their characteristics:

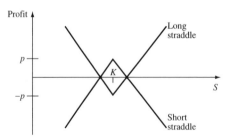

Figure 5.12 Long straddle and short straddle

---

[24] Reilly F. K. and Brown K. C., suggest reading Rubinstein M., Options for the Undecided, in From Black–Scholes to black holes, *Risk Magazine*, 1992.

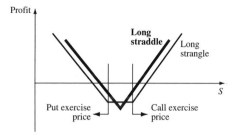

Figure 5.13   Long strangle compared with long straddle

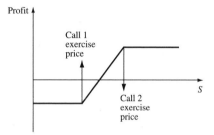

Figure 5.14   Bull money spread

- The *money spread* consists of the simultaneous sale of an out of the money call option and the purchase of the same option in the money. The term *bull money spread* (resp. *bear money spread*) is used to describe a *money spread* combination that gains when the underlying equity price rises (resp. falls) (see Figure 5.14). The term *butterfly money spread* is used to define a combination of *bear* and *bull money spreads* with hedging (limitation) for potential losses (and, obviously, reduced opportunities for profit).
- The *calendar spread* consists of the simultaneous sale and purchase of call or put options with identical exercise prices but different maturity dates.

Spreads are used when a contract appears to have an aberrant value in comparison with another contract.

5.4.2.4   Range forwards

For memory, range forwards consist of a combination of two optional positions. This combination is used for hedging, mainly for options on exchange rates.

Part III

General Theory of VaR

Introduction

As we saw in Part II, the sheer variety of products available on the markets, linear and otherwise, together with derivatives and underlying products, implies *a priori* a multi-faceted understanding of risk, which by nature is difficult to harmonise.

Ideally, therefore, we should identify a single risk indicator that estimates the loss likely to be suffered by the investor with the level of probability of that loss arising. This indicator is *VaR*.

There are three classic techniques for estimating *VaR*:

1. The estimated variance–covariance matrix method.
2. The Monte Carlo simulation method.
3. The historical simulation method.

An in-depth analysis of each of these methods will show their strong and weak points from both a theoretical and a practical viewpoint.

We will now show, in detail, how *VaR* can be calculated using the historical simulation method. This method is the subject of the following chapter as well as a file on the accompanying CD-ROM entitled 'Ch 8', which contains the Excel spreadsheets relating to these calculations.

6
Theory of *VaR*

6.1 THE CONCEPT OF 'RISK PER SHARE'

6.1.1 Standard measurement of risk linked to financial products

The various methods for measuring risks associated with an equity or portfolio of equities have been studied in Chapter 3. Two types of measurement can be defined: the intrinsic method and the relative method.

The intrinsic method is the variance (or similarly, the standard deviation) in the return of the equity. In the case of a portfolio, we have to deal not only with variances but also with correlations (or covariances) two by two. They are evaluated practically by their ergodic estimator, that is, on the basis of historical observations (see Section 3.1).

The relative method takes account of the risk associated with the equity or portfolio of equities on the basis of how it depends upon market behaviour. The market is represented by a stock-exchange index (which may be a sector index). This dependence is measured using the beta for the equity or portfolio and gives rise to the CAPM type of valuation model (see Section 3.3).

The risk measurement methods for the other two products studied (bonds and options) fall into this second group.

Among the risks associated with a bond or portfolio of bonds, those that are linked to interest-rate fluctuations can be expressed as models. In this way (see Section 4.1) we see the behaviour of the two components of the risk posed by selling the bond during its lifetime and reinvesting the coupons, according to the time that elapses between the issue of the security and its repayment. If we wish to summarise this behaviour in a simple index, we have to consider the duration of the bond; as we are looking in this context at a first-level approximation, a second measurement, that of *convexity* (see Section 4.2) will define the duration more precisely.

Finally, the value of an option depends on a number of variables: underlying equity price, exercise price, maturity, volatility, risk-free rate.[1] The most important driver is of course the underlying equity price, and for this reason two parameters, one of the first order (delta) and another of the second order (gamma), are associated with it. The way in which the option price depends on the other variables gives rise to other sensitivity parameters. These indicators are known as 'the Greeks' (see Section 5.2).

6.1.2 Problems with these approaches to risk

The ways of measuring the risks associated with these products or a portfolio of them, whatever they may make to the management of these assets, bring features with them that do not allow for immediate generalisation.

---

[1] Possibly in two currencies if an exchange option is involved.

1. The representation of the risk associated with an equity through the variance in its returns (or through its square root, the standard deviation), or of the risk associated with an option through its volatility, takes account of both good and bad risks. A significant variance corresponds to the possibility of seeing returns vastly different from the expected return, i.e. very small values (small profits and even losses) as well as very large values (significant profits).

   This method does not present many inconveniences in portfolio theory (see Section 3.2), in which equities or portfolios with significant variances are volatile elements, little appreciated by investors who prefer 'certainty' of return with low risk of loss and low likelihood of significant profit. It is no less true to say that in the context of risk management, it is the downside risk that needs to be taken into consideration. Another parameter must therefore be used to measure this risk.

2. The approach to the risks associated with equities in Markowitz's theory limits the description of a distribution to two parameters: a measure of return and a measure of deviation. It is evident that an infinite number of probability laws correspond to any one expected return–variance pairing. We are, in fact, looking at *skewed distributions*: Figure 6.1 shows two distributions that have the same expectation and the same variance, but differ considerably in their skewness.

   In the same way, distributions with the same expectation, variance and *skewness coefficient* γ_1 may show different levels of kurtosis, as shown in Figure 6.2.

   The distributions with higher peaks towards the middle and with fatter tails than a normal distribution[2] (and therefore less significant for intermediate values) are described as *leptokurtic* and characterised by a positive *kurtosis coefficient* γ_2 (for the

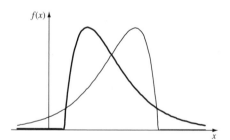

Figure 6.1   Skewness of distributions

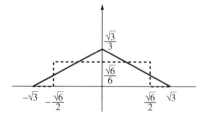

Figure 6.2   Kurtosis of distributions

---

[2] The definition of this law is given in Point (3) below.

distributions in Figure 6.2, this coefficient totals -0.6 for the triangular and -1.2 for the rectangular).

Remember that this variance of expected returns approach is sometimes justified through utility theory. In fact, when the utility function is quadratic, the expected utility of the return on the portfolio is expressed solely from the single-pair expectation variance (see Section 3.2.7).

3. In order to justify the mean-variance approach, the equity portfolio theory deliberately postulates that the return follows a *normal* probability law, which is characterised specifically by the two parameters in question; if μ and σ respectively indicate the mean and the standard deviation for a normal random variable, this variable will have the density of:

$$f(x) = \frac{1}{\sqrt{2\pi}\sigma} \exp\left[-\frac{1}{2}\left(\frac{x-\mu}{\sigma}\right)^2\right]$$

This is a symmetrical distribution, very important in probability theory and found everywhere in statistics because of the central limit theorem. The graph for this density is shown in Figure 6.3.

A series of studies shows that normality of return of equities is a hypothesis that can be accepted, at least in an initial approximation, provided the period over which the return is calculated is not too short. It is admitted that weekly and monthly returns do not diverge too far from a normal law, but daily returns tend to diverge and follow a leptokurtic distribution instead.[3]

If one wishes to take account of the skewness and the leptokurticity of the distribution of returns, one solution is to replace the normal distribution with a distribution that depends on more parameters, such as the Pearson distribution system,[4] and to estimate the parameters so that μ, σ^2, γ_1 and γ_2 correspond to the observations. Nevertheless, the choice of distribution involved remains wholly arbitrary.

Finally, for returns on securities other than equities, and for other elements involved in risk management, the normality hypothesis is clearly lacking and we do not therefore need to construct a more general risk measurement index.

4. Another problem, by no means insignificant, is that concepts such as duration and convexity of bonds, variances of returns on equities, or the delta, gamma, rho or theta

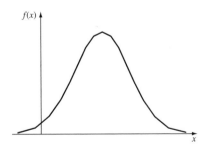

Figure 6.3   Normal distribution

[3] We will deal again with the effects of kurtosis on risk evaluation in Section 6.2.2.
[4] Johnson N. L. and Kotz S., *Continuous Univariate Distributions*, John Wiley and Sons, Ltd, 1970.

option parameters do not, despite their usefulness, actually 'say' very much as risk measurement indices. In fact, they do not state the kind of loss that one is likely to suffer, or the probability of it occurring. At the very most, the loss–probability pairing will be calculated on the basis of variance in a case of normal distribution (see Section 6.2.2).

5. In Section 6.1.1 we set out a number of classical risk analysis models associated with three types of financial products: bonds, equities and options. These are specific models adapted to specific products. In order to take account of less 'classical' assets (such as certain sophisticated derivatives), we will have to construct as many adapted models as are necessary and take account in those models of exchange-rate risks, which cannot be avoided on international markets.

Building this kind of structure is a mammoth task, and the complexity lies not only in building the various blocks that make up the structure but also in assembling these blocks into a coherent whole. A new technique, which combines the various aspects of market risk analysis into a unified whole, therefore needs to be elaborated.

6.1.3   Generalising the concept of 'risk'

The *market risk* is the risk with which the investor is confronted because of his lack of knowledge of future changes in basic market variables such as security rates, interest rates, exchange rates etc. These variables, also known as *risk factors*, determine the price of securities, conditional assets, portfolios etc.

If the price of an asset is expressed as p and the risk factors that explain the price as $X_1, X_2, \ldots, X_n$, we have the wholly general relation $p = f(X_1, X_2, \ldots, X_n) + \varepsilon$, in which the residue ε corresponds to the difference between reality (the effective price p) and the *valuation model* (the function f).

If the price valuation model is a *linear model* (as for equities), the risk factors combine, through the central limit theorem, to give a distribution of the variable p that is normal (at least in an rough approximation) and is therefore defined only by the two expectation–variance parameters.

On the other hand, for some types of security such as options, the valuation model ceases to be linear. The above logic is no longer applicable and its conclusions cease to be valid.

We would point out that alongside the risk factors that we have just mentioned, the following can be added as factors in market risk:

- the imperfect nature of valuation models;
- imperfect knowledge of the rules and limits particular to the institution;
- the impossibility of anticipating regulatory and legislative changes.

Note

As well as market risk, investors are confronted with other types of risk that correspond to the occurrence of exceptional events such as wars, oil crises etc. This group of risks cannot of course be estimated using techniques designed for market risk. The techniques shown in this Part III do not therefore deal with these 'event-related' risks. This should not, however, prevent the wise risk manager from analysing his positions using value at risk theory, or from using 'catastrophe scenarios', in an effort to understand this type of exceptional risk.

6.2   *VaR* FOR A SINGLE ASSET

6.2.1   Value at Risk

In view of what has been set out in the previous paragraph, an index that allows estimation of the market risks facing an investor should:

- be independent of any distributional hypothesis;
- concern only downside risk, namely the risk of loss;
- measure the loss in question in a certain way;
- be valid for all types of assets and therefore either involve the various valuation models or be independent of these models.

Let us therefore consider an asset the price[5] of which is expressed as p_t at moment t. The variation observed for the asset in the period $[s; t]$ is expressed as $\Delta p_{s,t}$ and is therefore defined as $\Delta p_{s,t} = p_t - p_s$. Note that if $\Delta p_{s,t}$ is positive, we have a profit; a negative value, conversely, indicates a loss.

The only hypothesis formulated is that the value of the asset evolves in a stationary manner; the random variable $\Delta p_{s,t}$ has a probability law that only depends on the interval in which it is calculated through the duration $(t - s)$ of that interval. The interval $[s; t]$ is thus replaced by the interval $[0; t - s]$ and the variable Δp will now only have the duration of the interval as its index. We therefore have the following definitive definition: $\Delta p_t = p_t - p_0$.

The '*value at risk*' of the asset in question for the duration t and the probability level q is defined as an amount termed *VaR*, so that the variation Δp_t observed for the asset during the interval $[0; t]$ will only be less than *VaR* with a probability of $(1 - q)$:

$$\Pr[\Delta p_t \leq VaR] = 1 - q$$

Or similarly:

$$\Pr[\Delta p_t > VaR] = q$$

By expressing as $F_{\Delta p}$ and $f_{\Delta p}$ respectively the distribution function and density function of the random variable Δp_t, we arrive at the definition of *VaR* in Figures 6.4 and 6.5.

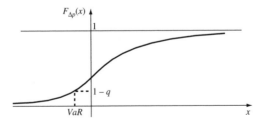

Figure 6.4   Definition of *VaR* based on distribution function

---

[5] In this chapter, the theory is presented on the basis of the value, the price of assets, portfolios etc. The same developments can be made on the basis of returns on these elements. The following two chapters will show how this second approach is the one that is adopted in practice.

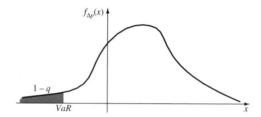

Figure 6.5   Definition of *VaR* based on density function

It is evident that two parameters are involved in defining the concept of *VaR*: duration t and probability q. In practice, it is decided to fix t once for everything (one day or one week, for example), and *VaR* will be calculated as a function of q and expressed VaR_q if there is a risk of confusion. It is in fact possible to calculate *VaR* for several different values of q.

Example

If *VaR* at 98 % equals $-500\,000$, this means that there are 98 possibilities out of 100 of the maximum loss for the asset in question never exceeding $500\,000$ for the period in question.

Note 1

As we will see in Chapter 7, some methods of estimating *VaR* are based on a distribution of value variation that does not have a density. For these random variables, as for the discrete values, the definition that we have just given is lacking in precision. Thus, when $1 - q$ corresponds to a jump in the distribution function, no suitable value for the loss can be given and the definition will be adapted as shown in Figure 6.6.

In the same way, when q corresponds to a plateau in the distribution function, an infinite number of values will be suitable; the least favourable of these values, that is the smallest, is chosen as a safety measure, as can be seen in Figure 6.7.
In order to take account of this note, the very strict definition of *VaR* will take the following form:

$$VaR_q = \min \{V : \Pr[\Delta p_t \leq V] \geq 1 - q\}$$

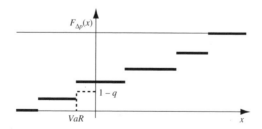

Figure 6.6   Case involving jump

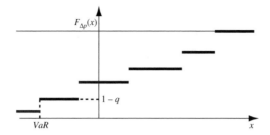

Figure 6.7   Case involving plateau

Table 6.1   Probability distribution of loss

Δp	Pr
−5	0.05
−4	0.05
−3	0.05
−2	0.10
−1	0.15
0	0.10
1	0.20
2	0.15
3	0.10
4	0.05

Example

Table 6.1 shows the probability law for the variation in value.
   For this distribution, we have $VaR_{0.90} = -4$ and $VaR_{0.95} = -5$.

Note 2

Clearly *VaR* is neither the loss that should be expected nor the maximum loss that is likely to be incurred, but is instead a level of loss that will only be exceeded with a level of probability fixed *a priori*. It is a parameter that is calculated on the basis of the probability law for the variable ('variation in value') and therefore includes all the parameters for that distribution. *VaR* is not therefore suitable for drawing up a classification of securities because, as we have seen for equities, the comparison of various assets is based on the simultaneous consideration of two parameters: the expected return (or loss) and a measure of dispersion of the said return.

Note 3

On the other hand, it is essential to be fully aware when defining *VaR* of the duration on the basis of which this parameter is evaluated. The parameter, calculated for several different portfolios or departments within an institution, is only comparable if the reference period is the same. The same applies if *VaR* is being used as a comparison index for two or more institutions.

Note 4

Sometimes a different definition of *VaR* is found,[6] one that takes account not of the variation in the value itself but the difference between that variation and the expected variation. More specifically, this value at risk (for the duration t and the probability level q) is defined as the amount (generally negative) termed VaR^*, so that the variation observed during the interval $[0; t]$ will only be less than the average upward variation in $|VaR^*|$ with a probability of $(1 - q)$. Thus, if the expected variation is expressed as $E(\Delta p_t)$, the definition $\Pr[\Delta p_t - E(\Delta p_t) \leq VaR^*] = 1 - q$. Or, again: $\Pr[\Delta p_t > VaR^* + E(\Delta p_t)] = q$.

It is evident that these two concepts are linked, as we evidently have
$$VaR = VaR^* + E(\Delta p_t).$$

6.2.2   Case of a normal distribution

In the specific case where the random variable Δp_t follows a *normal law* with mean $E(\Delta p_t)$ and standard deviation $\sigma(\Delta p_t)$, the definition can be changed to:

$$\Pr\left[\frac{\Delta p_t - E(\Delta p_t)}{\sigma(\Delta p_t)} \leq \frac{VaR_q - E(\Delta p_t)}{\sigma(\Delta p_t)}\right] = 1 - q$$

This shows that the expression $\dfrac{VaR_q - E(\Delta p_t)}{\sigma(\Delta p_t)}$ is the *quantile* of the standard normal distribution, ordinarily expressed as z_{1-q}. As $z_{1-q} = -z_q$, this allows *VaR* to be written in a very simple form $VaR_q = E(\Delta p_t) - z_q \cdot \sigma(\Delta p_t)$ according to the expectation and standard deviation for the loss. In the same way, the parameter VaR^* is calculated simply, for a normal distribution, $VaR_q{}^* = -z_q \cdot \sigma(\Delta p_t)$.

The values of z_q are found in the normal distribution tables.[7] A few examples of these values are given in Table 6.2.

Table 6.2   Normal distribution quantiles

q	z_q
0.500	0.0000
0.600	0.2533
0.700	0.5244
0.800	0.8416
0.850	1.0364
0.900	1.2816
0.950	1.6449
0.960	1.7507
0.970	1.8808
0.975	1.9600
0.980	2.0537
0.985	2.1701
0.990	2.3263
0.995	2.5758

[6] Jorion P., *Value At Risk*, McGraw-Hill, 2001.
[7] Pearson E. S. and Hartley H. O., *Biometrika Tables for Statisticians*, Biometrika Trust, 1976, p. 118.

Example

If a security gives an average profit of 100 over the reference period with a standard deviation of 80, we have $E(\Delta p_t) = 100$ and $\sigma(\Delta p_t) = 80$, which allows us to write:

$$VaR_{0.95} = 100 - (1.6449 \times 80) = -31.6$$

$$VaR_{0.975} = 100 - (1.9600 \times 80) = -56.8$$

$$VaR_{0.99} = 100 - (2.3263 \times 80) = -86.1$$

The loss incurred by this security will only therefore exceed 31.6 (56.8 and 86.1 respectively) five times (2.5 times and once respectively) in 100 times.

Note

It has been indicated in Section 6.1.2 that the normality hypothesis was far from being valid in all circumstances. In particular, it has been shown that the daily returns on equities are better represented by a Pareto or Student distribution,[8] that is, leptokurtic distributions. Thus, for a *Student distribution* with ν degrees of freedom (where $\nu > 2$), the variance is

$$\sigma^2 = 1 + \frac{2}{\nu - 2}$$

and the kurtosis coefficient (for $\nu > 4$) will then be:

$$\gamma_2 = \frac{6}{\nu - 4}$$

This last quantity is always positive, and this proves that the Student distribution is leptokurtic in nature. With regard to the number of degrees of freedom ν, Table 6.3 shows the coefficient γ_2 and the quantiles z_q for $q = 0.95$, $q = 0.975$ and $q = 0.99$ relative to these Student distributions,[9] reduced beforehand (the variable is divided by its standard deviation) in order to make a useful comparison between these figures and those obtained on the basis of the reduced normal law.

Table 6.3   Student distribution quantiles

ν	γ_2	$z_{0.95}$	$z_{0.975}$	$z_{0.99}$
5	6.00	2.601	3.319	4.344
10	1.00	2.026	2.491	3.090
15	0.55	1.883	2.289	2.795
20	0.38	1.818	2.199	2.665
25	0.29	1.781	2.148	2.591
30	0.23	1.757	2.114	2.543
40	0.17	1.728	2.074	2.486
60	0.11	1.700	2.034	2.431
120	0.05	1.672	1.997	2.378
normal	0	1.645	1.960	2.326

---

[8] Blattberg R. and Gonedes N., A comparison of stable and student distributions as statistical models for stock prices, *Journal of Business*, Vol. 47, 1974, pp. 244–80.

[9] Pearson E. S. and Hartley H. O., *Biometrika Tables for Statisticians*, Biometrika Trust, 1976, p. 146.

This clearly shows that when the normal law is used in place of the Student laws, the *VaR* parameter is underestimated unless the number of degrees of freedom is high.

Example

With the same data as above, that is, $E(\Delta p_t) = 100$ and $\sigma(\Delta p_t) = 80$, and for 15 degrees of freedom, we find the following evaluations of *VaR*, instead of 31.6, 64.3 and 86.1 respectively.

$$VaR_{0.95} = 100 - (1.883 \times 80) = -50.6$$

$$VaR_{0.975} = 100 - (2.289 \times 80) = -83.1$$

$$VaR_{0.99} = 100 - (2.795 \times 80) = -123.6$$

6.3   *VaR* FOR A PORTFOLIO

6.3.1   General results

Consider a portfolio consisting of N assets in respective quantities[10] $n_1, \ldots, n_N$. If the price of the jth security is termed p_j, the price p_P of the portfolio will of course be given by:

$$p_P = \sum_{j=1}^{N} n_j p_j$$

The price variation will obey the same relation:

$$\Delta p_P = \sum_{j=1}^{N} n_j \Delta p_j$$

Once the distribution of the various Δp_j elements is known, it is not easy to determine the distribution of the Δp_P elements: the probability law of a sum of random variables will only be easy to determine if these variables are independent, and this is clearly not the case here. It is, however, possible to find the expectation and variance for Δp_P on the basis of expectation, variance and covariance in the various Δp_j elements:

$$E(\Delta p_P) = \sum_{j=1}^{N} n_j E(\Delta p_j)$$

$$\text{var}(\Delta p_P) = \sum_{i=1}^{N} \sum_{j=1}^{N} n_i n_j \text{cov}(\Delta p_i, \Delta p_j)$$

---

[10] It can be shown that when prices are replaced by returns, the numbers n_j of assets in the portfolio must be replaced by proportions X_j (positive numbers the sum of which is 1), representing the respective stock-exchange capitalisation levels of the various securities (see Chapter 3).

where we have, when the two indices are equal:

$$\text{cov}(\Delta p_i, \Delta p_i) = \text{var}(\Delta p_i)$$

The relation that gives var (Δp_P) is the one that justifies the principle of diversification in portfolio management: the imperfect correlations (<1) between the securities allows the portfolio risk to be diminished (see Section 3.2).

Under the hypothesis of normality, the *VaR* of the portfolio can thus be calculated on the basis of these two elements using the formula:

$$VaR_q = E(\Delta p_P) - z_q \cdot \sigma(\Delta p_P)$$

A major problem with using these relations is that they require knowledge not only of the univariate parameters $E(\Delta p_i)$ and $\text{var}(\Delta p_i)$ for each security, but also of the bivariate parameters $\text{cov}(\Delta p_i, \Delta p_j)$ for each pair of securities. If the portfolio contains $N = 100$ different securities, for example, the first parameters will be $2N = 200$ in number, while the second parameters will be much more numerous ($N(N-1)/2 = 4950$) and it will not be easy to determine whether they have all been obtained or whether they are accurate. Thankfully, some models allow these relations to be simplified considerably under certain hypotheses.

Thus, for a portfolio of equities, it is possible to use Sharpe's simple index model (see Section 3.2.4) and consider that the relative variations in price[11] of the various equities are first-degree functions of the relative variation in a single market index:

$$\frac{\Delta p_j}{p_j} = a_j + b_j \frac{\Delta I}{I} + \varepsilon_j \qquad j = 1, \dots, N$$

Remember that this model, the parameters of which are estimated using linear regression, relies on the following hypotheses: the variables $\varepsilon_1, \dots, \varepsilon_N$ and $(\Delta I / I)$ are not correlated and $E(\varepsilon_j) = 0$ for $j = 1, \dots, N$.

By using the notations:

$$E\left(\frac{\Delta I}{I}\right) = E_I \qquad \text{var}\left(\frac{\Delta I}{I}\right) = \sigma_I^2 \qquad \text{var}(\varepsilon_j) = \sigma_{\varepsilon_j}^2$$

we have, for the expectation and variance of the Δp_j elements:

$$E\left(\frac{\Delta p_j}{p_j}\right) = a_j + b_j E_I$$

$$\text{var}\left(\frac{\Delta p_j}{p_j}\right) = b_j^2 \sigma_I^2 + \sigma_{\varepsilon_j}^2$$

The covariances are calculated in the same way:

$$\text{cov}\left(\frac{\Delta p_i}{p_i}, \frac{\Delta p_j}{p_j}\right) = b_i b_j \sigma_I^2$$

---

[11] That is, the returns.

By making a substitution in the formulae that give the expectation and variance for Δp_P, we find successively:

$$E(\Delta p_P) = \sum_{j=1}^{N} n_j(a_j p_j + b_j p_j E_I)$$

$$= \left(\sum_{j=1}^{N} n_j a_j p_j \right) + \left(\sum_{j=1}^{N} n_j b_j p_j \right) E_I$$

$$= a_P + b_P E_I$$

and:

$$\text{var}(\Delta p_P) = \sum_{j=1}^{N} n_j^2 (b_j^2 p_j^2 \sigma_I^2 + p_j^2 \sigma_{\varepsilon_j}^2) + \sum_{i=1}^{N} \sum_{\substack{j=1 \\ j \neq i}}^{N} n_i n_j b_i b_j p_i p_j \sigma_I^2$$

$$= \left(\sum_{i=1}^{N} \sum_{j=1}^{N} n_i n_j b_i b_j p_i p_j \right) \sigma_I^2 + \sum_{j=1}^{N} n_j^2 p_j^2 \sigma_{\varepsilon_j}^2$$

$$= b_P^2 \sigma_I^2 + \sum_{j=1}^{N} n_j^2 p_j^2 \sigma_{\varepsilon_j}^2$$

The *VaR* relative to this portfolio is therefore given by:

$$VaR_q = a_P + b_P E_I - z_q \sqrt{b_P^2 \sigma_I^2 + \sum_{j=1}^{N} n_j^2 p_j^2 \sigma_{\varepsilon_j}^2}$$

Example

Let us take the example of Section 3.2.4 again and consider a portfolio consisting of three securities in the following numbers: $n_1 = 3$, $n_2 = 6$, $n_3 = 1$.

The relative price variations of these securities are expressed on the basis of the prices in a stock-exchange index for the following regressive relations:

$$R_1 = 0.014 + 0.60R_I \qquad (\sigma_{\varepsilon_1}^2 = 0.0060)$$

$$R_2 = -0.020 + 1.08R_I \qquad (\sigma_{\varepsilon_2}^2 = 0.0040)$$

$$R_3 = 0.200 + 1.32R_I \qquad (\sigma_{\varepsilon_3}^2 = 0.0012)$$

The index is characterised by $E_I = 0.0031$ and $\sigma_I = 0.0468$. If the current prices of these securities are $p_1 = 120$, $p_2 = 15$ and $p_3 = 640$, we have:

$$a_P = 3 \times 0.014 \times 120 - 6 \times 0.020 \times 15 + 1 \times 0.200 \times 640 = 131.24$$

$$b_P = 3 \times 0.60 \times 120 + 6 \times 1.08 \times 15 + 1 \times 1.32 \times 640 = 1158.00$$

$$\sum_{j=1}^{N} n_j^2 p_j^2 \sigma_{\varepsilon_j}^2 = 3^2 \times 120^2 \times 0.0060 + 6^2 \times 15^2 \times 0.0040 + 1^2 \times 640^2 \times 0.0012 = 1283.52$$

and therefore:

$$VaR_{0.99} = 131.24 + 1158.00 \times 0.04 - 2.3263\sqrt{1158.00^2 \times 0.0045 + 1283.52}$$

$$= -21.4421$$

Note

Once more, the results obtained in this paragraph assume that we are in the context of the hypothesis of normality and that the distributions are therefore characterised entirely by the expectation–variance pairing. If one requires an estimation of the *VaR* that is entirely independent from this hypothesis, the problem will need to be approached in a different way, that is, without going through an evaluation of the various assets separately.

6.3.2   Components of the *VaR* of a portfolio

In this and the following paragraph, we will be working under the hypothesis of normality and with the version of *VaR* that measures the risk in relation to the average variation in value:[12]

$$VaR^* = VaR - E(\Delta p) = -z_q \cdot \sigma(\Delta p)$$

The argument developed in the previous paragraph expressed the portfolio on the basis of n_j numbers $(j = 1, \ldots, N)$ of securities of each type in the portfolio. Here, we will use the presentation used in Chapter 3 and introduce the proportions of the various securities expressed in terms of stock-exchange capitalisation: $X_j (j = 1, \ldots, N)$. We can therefore write:

$$\frac{\Delta p_P}{p_P} = \sum_{j=1}^{N} X_j \frac{\Delta p_j}{p_j}$$

with:

$$X_j = \frac{n_j p_j}{\sum_{k=1}^{N} n_k p_k}$$

By using the return notation as in Chapter 3, the variable being studied for the *VaR* is therefore:

$$\Delta p_P = p_P \cdot \sum_{j=1}^{N} X_j R_j$$

The average and the variances for this are given by:

$$E(\Delta p_P) = p_P \cdot \sum_{j=1}^{N} X_j E_j = p_P \cdot E_P$$

$$\text{var}(\Delta p_P) = p_P^2 \cdot \sum_{i=1}^{N} \sum_{j=1}^{N} X_i X_j \sigma_{ij} = p_P^2 \cdot \sigma_P^2$$

---

[12] We will also be omitting the index q relative to probability, so as not to make the notation too laborious.

where we have, as usual:

$$E_j = E(R_j) \qquad \sigma_j^2 = \mathrm{var}(R_j) \qquad \sigma_{ij} = \mathrm{cov}(R_i, R_j)$$

This will allow the *VaR* for the portfolio to be written as:

$$VaR_P{}^* = -p_P \cdot z_q \cdot \sigma_P = -p_P \cdot z_q \cdot \sqrt{\sum_{i=1}^{N} \sum_{j=1}^{N} X_i X_j \sigma_{ij}}$$

6.3.2.1 Individual VaR

The *individual VaR* of the security (j) within the portfolio is the *VaR* of all of these securities; if their number is n_j, we will have:

$$VaR_j{}^* = -z_q \cdot \sigma \left(\Delta(n_j p_j) \right)$$
$$= -z_q \cdot n_j p_j \cdot \sigma_j$$
$$= -p_P \cdot z_q \cdot X_j \sigma_j$$

As $\sigma_{ij} \le \sigma_i \sigma_j$ (the correlation coefficient is always 1 or less), we have:

$$VaR_P{}^* \ge -p_P \cdot z_q \cdot \sqrt{\sum_{i=1}^{N} \sum_{j=1}^{N} X_i X_j \sigma_i \sigma_j}$$
$$= -p_P \cdot z_q \cdot \sum_{j=1}^{N} X_j \sigma_j$$
$$= \sum_{j=1}^{N} VaR_j{}^*$$

The right-hand member, which can be interpreted as the nondiversified *VaR* of the portfolio, is therefore always lower (that is, more pessimistic) than the *VaR* diversified into *VaR**$_P$.

6.3.2.2 Marginal VaR

The *marginal VaR* measures the alteration to the *VaR* of a portfolio following a minor variation in its composition. More specifically, it relates to the variation rate $VaR_P{}^* = -p_P \cdot z_q \cdot \sigma_P$, explained by the variation in σ_P brought about by an infinitesimal increase in the proportion X_j of the security (j) while the other proportions remain constant. It is therefore equal to:

$$\Delta VaR_j{}^* = -p_P \cdot z_q \cdot (\sigma_P)_{X_j}{}'$$

As $(\sigma_P^2)_{X_j}{}' = 2\sigma_P(\sigma_P)_{X_j}{}'$ and:

$$(\sigma_P^2)_{X_j}{}' = 2X_j\sigma_j^2 + 2\sum_{\substack{i=1 \\ i \neq j}}^{N} X_i\sigma_{ij}$$

$$= 2\sum_{i=1}^{N} X_i \, \text{cov}(R_i, R_j)$$

$$= 2 \, \text{cov}(R_P, R_j)$$

$$= 2\sigma_{jP}$$

we finally obtain:

$$\Delta VaR_j{}^* = -p_P \cdot z_q \cdot \frac{\sigma_{jP}}{\sigma_P}$$

$$= -p_P \cdot z_q \cdot \sigma_P \beta_{jP}$$

$$= VaR_P{}^* \cdot \beta_{jP}$$

6.3.2.3 Components of VaR

We have seen that it is not possible to split the *VaR* on the basis of individual *VaR* values, as these values do not 'benefit' from the diversification effect. The solution is to define the *VaR component* that relates to the security (j) through the marginal *VaR* affected by a weight equal to the X_j proportion of (j) within the portfolio:

$$CVaR_j{}^* = X_j \cdot \Delta VaR_j{}^*$$

What we have, in fact, is:

$$\sum_{j=1}^{N} CVaR_j{}^* = \sum_{j=1}^{N} X_j \cdot \Delta VaR_j{}^*$$

$$= VaR_P{}^* \cdot \sum_{j=1}^{N} X_j \beta_{jP}$$

$$= \frac{VaR_P{}^*}{\sigma_P^2} \cdot \sum_{j=1}^{N} X_j \text{cov}(R_j, R_P)$$

$$= VaR_P{}^*$$

6.3.3 Incremental *VaR*

6.3.3.1 Definition

Assume that we are in possession of a portfolio P and are anticipating the purchase of an additional set of equities A, the values of P and A being expressed as p_P and p_A

respectively. It is considered that p_A is positive or negative depending on whether an investment or disinvestment is involved. The portfolio produced by this decision will be expressed as P' with value $p_{P'} = p_P + p_A$.

The *incremental VaR* following the acquisition of A is defined as:

$$IVaR_A{}^* = VaR_{P'}{}^* - VaR_P{}^*$$

Together with the use of the definition, the practical use of the incremental *VaR* can be simplified if the proportion of A is low. The proportions of A and P within P' are respectively:

$$X_A = \frac{p_A}{p_{P'}} \qquad X_P = \frac{p_P}{p_{P'}} = 1 - X_A$$

The variance in the new portfolio, if the second-degree terms in X_A can be ignored, is:

$$\sigma_{P'}^2 = (1 - X_A)^2 \sigma_P^2 + X_A^2 \sigma_A^2 + 2X_A(1 - X_A)\sigma_{AP}$$
$$\approx (1 - 2X_A)\sigma_P^2 + 2X_A\sigma_{AP}$$

With the same approximation, we have:

$$VaR_{P'}^{*2} - VaR_P^{*2} \approx 2VaR_P{}^* \cdot IVaR_A{}^*$$

In addition, we have:

$$VaR_{P'}^{*2} - VaR_P^{*2} = -p_{P'}^2 \cdot z_q^2 \cdot \sigma_{P'}^2 + p_P^2 \cdot z_q^2 \cdot \sigma_P^2$$
$$\approx -p_P^2 \cdot z_q^2 \cdot (\sigma_{P'}^2 - \sigma_P^2)$$
$$= VaR_P^{*2}\left(\frac{\sigma_{P'}^2}{\sigma_P^2} - 1\right)$$
$$\approx 2X_A \cdot VaR_P^{*2}\left(\frac{\sigma_{AP}}{\sigma_P^2} - 1\right)$$
$$= 2X_A \cdot VaR_P^{*2}(\beta_{AP} - 1)$$

Therefore:

$$IVaR_A \approx \frac{VaR_{P'}^{*2} - VaR_P^{*2}}{2VaR_P^*} \approx X_A \cdot VaR_P{}^*(\beta_{AP} - 1)$$

6.3.3.2 Hedging investment

Now that the portfolio P and the composition of A have been defined, we look for the ideal amount of A to acquire. The need, therefore, is to determine p_A in order for the risk to be minimised, that is, on order for $IVaR^*{}_A$ to be as high as possible or again, as P is fixed, for VaR_P^* to be as high as possible.

As:

$$\sigma_{P'}^2 = X_P^2 \sigma_P^2 + X_A^2 \sigma_A^2 + 2X_P X_A \sigma_{AP}$$

$$= \frac{1}{p_{P'}^2}[p_P^2 \sigma_P^2 + p_A^2 \sigma_A^2 + 2p_P p_A \sigma_{AP}]$$

we have:

$$VaR_{P'}{}^* = -p_{P'} \cdot z_q \cdot \sigma_{P'}$$

$$= -z_q \sqrt{p_P^2 \sigma_P^2 + p_A^2 \sigma_A^2 + 2p_P p_A \sigma_{AP}}$$

This quantity will be maximised if the expression under the root is minimised; as the derivative of this last quantity with respect to p_A is equal to $2p_A\sigma^2{}_A + 2p_P\sigma_{AP}$. the total of A to be acquired in order to minimise[13] the risk is shown as

$$p_A = -p_P \frac{\sigma_{AP}}{\sigma_A^2}$$

6.3.3.3   Link to Sharp index

We saw in Section 3.3.3 that by using the Sharp index as an acquisition criterion for A $(SI'_p \geq SI_P)$, we obtain the condition:

$$E_A \geq E_P + \left(\frac{\sigma_{P'}}{\sigma_P} - 1\right) \frac{E_P - R_F}{X_A}$$

By replacing the standard deviation with the *VaR* in the Sharpe's index (and by changing the sign):

$$SI'_p = -\frac{E_P - R_F}{VaR_P{}^*}$$

the condition becomes:

$$E_A \geq E_P + \left(\frac{VaR_{P'}{}^*}{VaR_P{}^*} - 1\right) \frac{E_P - R_F}{X_A}$$

$$= E_P + \frac{IVaR_A{}^*}{VaR_P{}^*} \cdot \frac{E_P - R_F}{X_A}$$

that is, finally,

$$E_A \geq E_P + \varepsilon(E_P - R_F)$$

in which we have:

$$\varepsilon = \frac{1}{X_A} \cdot \frac{IVaR_A{}^*}{VaR_P{}^*} = \frac{\dfrac{VaR_{P'}{}^* - VaR_P{}^*}{VaR_P{}^*}}{\dfrac{X_{P'} - X_P}{1}}$$

When X_A is low (and X_P therefore close to 1), this quantity is none other than the elasticity of *VaR* with respect to X_P.

---

[13] The sign of the second derivative clearly shows that the total found constitutes a minimum.

VaR Estimation Techniques

7.1 GENERAL QUESTIONS IN ESTIMATING *VaR*

7.1.1 The problem of estimation

The definition of the *VaR* parameter given in Section 6.2, $\Pr[\Delta p_t \leq VaR] = 1 - q$, or more precisely, $VaR_q = \min\{V : \Pr[\Delta p_t \leq V] \geq 1 - q\}$, clearly shows that knowledge of the distribution function $F_{\Delta p}(v) = \Pr[\Delta p_t \leq v]$ for the random variable 'variation in value', $\Delta p_t = p_t - p_0$ allows the *VaR* to be determined:

- either directly (by determining the quantile[1] for the variable Δp_t);
- or, assuming that the price of the assets follows a normal law, on the basis of the expectation and the standard deviation for the variable: $VaR_q = E(\Delta p_t) - z_q \cdot \sigma(\Delta p_t)$.

The aim of this chapter is therefore to present the standard methods for estimating the distribution of the variable Δp_t for a portfolio.

The possible inputs for this estimation are:

- the *mathematical valuation models* for the prices of the various assets; these are presented in brief in Section 3.3;
- the *histories*, that is, the observations of the various equity prices for a certain number of past periods.

The problem of estimating the probability distribution for Δp_t and the *VaR* may therefore be summarised in the diagram shown in Figure 7.1.

The *VaR* can be calculated just as readily for an isolated position or single risk factor as for a whole portfolio, and indeed for all the assets held by a business. Let us take the case of a risk factor to lay down the ideas: if the value of this risk factor at a moment t can be expressed as $X(t)$, we will use the relative variation on X

$$\Delta(t) = \frac{X(t) - X(t-1)}{X(t-1)},$$

for the period $[t-1; t]$[2] instead of the absolute variation $X(t) - X(t-1)$. Using Δp_t presents the twofold advantage of:

- making the magnitudes of the various factors likely to be involved in evaluating an asset or portfolio relative;
- supplying a variable that has been shown to be capable of possessing certain distributional properties (normality or quasi-normality for returns on equities, for example).

---

[1] Estimating quantiles is often a complex problem, especially for arguments close to 0 or 1. Interested readers should read Gilchrist W. G., *Statistical Modelling with Quantile Functions*, Chapman & Hall/CRC, 2000.

[2] If the risk factor X is a share price, we are looking at the return on that share (see Section 3.1.1).

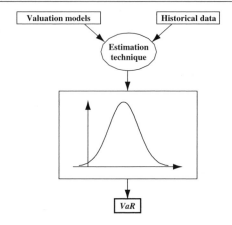

Figure 7.1   Estimating *VaR*

Note

In most calculation methods, a different expression is taken into consideration:

$$\Delta^*(t) = \ln \frac{X(t)}{X(t-1)}$$

As we saw in Section 3.1.1, this is in fact very similar to $\Delta(t)$ and has the advantage that it can take on any real value[3] and that the logarithmic return for several consecutive periods is the sum of the logarithmic return for each of those periods.

We will use the following notations:

- The risk factors are represented by $X_1, X_2, \ldots, X_n$, and the price of the equity therefore obeys a relation of the type $p = f(X_1, X_2, \ldots, X_n) + \varepsilon$.
- The combined duration of the histories is represented by $T + 1$. If the current moment is expressed as 0, it is therefore assumed that the observations $X(-T)$, $X(-T+1), \ldots, X(-1), X(0)$ are obtainable for the risk factor X. On the basis of these values, therefore, we can calculate first of all $\Delta(-T+1), \ldots, \Delta(-1)$ or the corresponding Δ^* values (we will refer to them hereafter as Δ).
- In addition, we suppose that the duration between two consecutive observation times (a day, for example) is also the horizon for which the *VaR* is calculated. The current value of the risk factor X is therefore $X(0)$ and we wish to estimate $X(1)$.

7.1.2   Typology of estimation methods

The *VaR* estimation techniques presented differ according to whether or not:

- distribution hypotheses have been formulated on the share prices;
- one is relying on the share price valuation models;

---

[3] Something that is useful when relying on the hypothesis of normality.

- stationarity is assumed (the observed distribution of variations in price and/or the parameters estimated on the basis of the histories are still valid for the horizon for which the *VaR* is being estimated).

Three methods are presented in detail, namely:

- Estimated variance–covariance matrix method (VC).
- Monte Carlo simulation (MC).
- Historical simulation (SH).

These techniques are described in the following three sections, being presented from the point of view of the underlying 'philosophy' and giving a high-level view of the calculations, without going into detail about the refinements and specific treatments introduced by the institutions that have defined them more precisely. The methodologies developed are shown in diagrammatic form in Figure 7.2.[4]

Note

If we wish to estimate the weekly *VaR* parameter, for example, on the basis of daily observations (five working days), the loss variable will be calculated by:

$$\Delta p^{(w)} = \Delta p_1^{(d)} + \Delta p_2^{(d)} + \Delta p_3^{(d)} + \Delta p_4^{(d)} + \Delta p_5^{(d)}$$

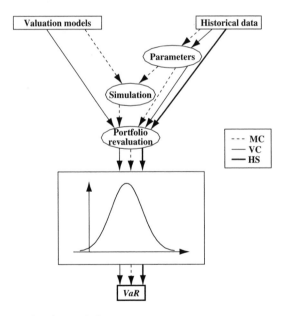

Figure 7.2   The three estimation techniques

---

[4] In fact, historical simulation uses evaluation models, as do the other two methods. However, it only uses them for certain types of product (nonlinear optionals, for example) and only at the re-evaluation stage.

The distribution of the variation in the weekly value is therefore calculated from there, because working on the hypothesis that the successive daily variations are independent, we have:

$$E(\Delta p^{(w)}) = E(\Delta p_1^{(d)}) + E(\Delta p_2^{(d)}) + E(\Delta p_3^{(d)}) + E(\Delta p_4^{(d)}) + E(\Delta p_5^{(d)})$$

$$\text{var}(\Delta p^{(w)}) = \text{var}(\Delta p_1^{(d)}) + \text{var}(\Delta p_2^{(d)}) + \text{var}(\Delta p_3^{(d)}) + \text{var}(\Delta p_4^{(d)}) + \text{var}(\Delta p_5^{(d)})$$

The calculation of the *VaR* parameter based on the expectation and standard deviation for the probability law will use the values:

$$E(\Delta p^{(w)}) = 5 \cdot E(\Delta p^{(d)})$$

$$\sigma(\Delta p^{(w)}) = \sqrt{5} \cdot \sigma(\Delta p^{(d)})$$

The same reasoning can be applied to any other combination of durations, provided, however, that the horizon considered is not too long, as any flaws in the hypothesis of independence will then become too important.

7.2 ESTIMATED VARIANCE–COVARIANCE MATRIX METHOD

The method of calculating the *VaR* using the estimated variance–covariance matrix system is the method proposed and developed by J. P. Morgan[5] using its RiskMetrics™ system. This is currently the most complete form of *VaR* calculation technique, from an operational point of view; it is also the system that has brought the *VaR* concept into prominence.

The method consists essentially of three stages, which are covered in the following three paragraphs:

- The identification of primary risk factors into which the financial asset portfolio can be split.
- The distribution of cashflows associated with these primary risk factors into simpler cashflows, corresponding to standard maturity dates.[6]
- The effective calculation of the *VaR*.

In its early versions,[7] this method of determining the VAR was based essentially on three hypotheses:

- The hypothesis of stationarity: the statistical parameters measured on the observed distribution of the price variations (or of the returns) are good estimations of these same (unknown) parameters for which the *VaR* is estimated.
- Returns on the various assets (or risk factors) obey a normal law.
- Asset prices depend on the risk factors in linear manner.

---

[5] J. P. Morgan, *RiskMetrics™ – Technical Document, 4th Edition*, Morgan Guaranty Trust Company, 1996. Also: Mina J. and Yi Xiao J., *Return to RiskMetrics: The Evolution of a Standard*, RiskMetrics, 2001.

[6] This distribution is known as *mapping*, and we will use this term in the sequel.

[7] Up until the third edition of RiskMetrics™.

The drawbacks of these hypotheses, which may be restrictive, led J. P. Morgan to generalise the framework of the method. This means that the third hypothesis (linearity) is no longer essential because of the way in which optional products are treated (see Section 7.2.3). In the same way, the hypothesis of normality has been made more flexible, as follows.

The hypothesis of normality allowed developments in the return on an asset to be described using a *random walk* model, written as: $R_t = \mu + \sigma \varepsilon_t$. In this model, the ε_t random variables are assumed to be independent and identically distributed (iid), with zero expectation and variance of 1. The μ and σ parameters are therefore given by:

$$E(R_t) = \mu$$

$$\mathrm{var}(R_t) = \sigma^2$$

The hypothesis of normality is therefore less of a problem if one assumes that:

- the returns have a volatility that varies over time $R_t = \mu + \sigma_t \varepsilon_t$;
- they are self-correlated, as in the GARCH[8] models or even in the random volatility models.

More generally, for the N assets within a portfolio, the hypothesis becomes $R_{jt} = \mu_j + \sigma_t \varepsilon_{jt}$, where the ε_{jt} follows a multi-normal law with zero expectations and of variance–covariance matrix V_t dependent on time. Returns that obey this condition are said to verify the hypothesis of *conditional normality*.

To generalise further, it is also possible to choose a law other than the normal law for the ε_t variable, such as the generalised law of errors that allows the leptokurtic distributions to be taken into account.[9]

In addition, even by generalising the normality hypothesis, it is possible to calculate $VaR_q^* = -z_q \cdot \sigma(\Delta p_t)$ in this methodology, and if one wishes, it is possible to come back to the concept of *VaR* that corresponds to an absolute variation, via $VaR_q = VaR_q^* + E(\Delta p_t)$.

In essence, this method of working[10] simply brings the problem of determining *VaR* down to estimating the variance in the portfolio loss.

7.2.1   Identifying cash flows in financial assets

The first stage therefore consists of converting the various positions in the portfolio into linear combinations of a certain number of risk factors that are easy to measure and have a variance (and therefore a *VaR*) that can be easily calculated.

$$p = f(X_1, X_2, \ldots, X_n) + \varepsilon$$
$$= a_1 X_1 + a_2 X_2 + \cdots + a_n X_n + \varepsilon$$

---

[8] Interested readers will find further information on this subject in Gourieroux C., *Modéles ARCH et applications financières*, Economica, 1992 and in Appendix 7.

[9] Readers are referred to Appendix 2 for developments on this law of probability.

[10] In reality, RiskMetrics™ simply calculates *VaR**. In other words, it assumes that the expectation loss is zero, or rather that the subsequent movements in the portfolio prices show no trends; the parameter μ is merely equal to 0.

Each of the risk factors is a cashflow:

- characterised by a certain amount;
- expressed in a certain currency;
- paid on a certain date.

These cashflows must of course be discounted on the date on which *VaR* is calculated (this date is termed 0).

The choice of risk factors is somewhat arbitrary and faces the following dilemma: representation of an asset as a number of elementary risks ensures very accurate results, but is costly in terms of calculation and data needed to supply the model. We now examine a number of decomposition models to support our statement.

7.2.1.1 Fixed-income securities

Let us consider a security that brings in certain income in amounts $X_1, X_2, \ldots, X_T$ at the respective times $t_1, t_2, \ldots, t_T$. Some of these income amounts may be positive and others negative. The full range of the risk factors on which the security depends is expressed as:

$$\begin{pmatrix} X_1(1+r_1)^{-t_1} & X_2(1+r_2)^{-t_2} & \cdots & X_T(1+r_T)^{-t_T} \\ t_1 & t_2 & \cdots & t_T \end{pmatrix}$$

Here, r_j represents the market interest rate for the corresponding period.

We are therefore looking at the breakdown of a fixed-income security into a total of zero-coupon bonds and the statistical data required will therefore relate to these bonds.

This type of decomposition will therefore apply to most products with interest rates, such as simple and variable-rate bonds, interest swaps, FRAs, futures with interest rates etc.

7.2.1.2 Exchange positions

For an exchange position at the current time, the two cashflows to be taken into consideration are the two amounts that are the subject of the transaction. They are merely linked by the exchange rate for the two currencies in question.

For an exchange position concluded for a future date T at a current (forward) rate F, we are required to consider not just the exchange rate on T (spot rate), but also S, the interest rate on the two currencies. The principle of exchange rate parity in fact states that the purchase of a currency X with a currency Y (the exchange rates being expressed as 'Y per X') is the same as borrowing the currency Y at the present time at rate r_Y and reselling it at T for X or exchanging Y for X at the present time and investing it at rate r_X: $(1+r_Y) \cdot S = F \cdot (1+r_X)$.

The purchase and sale of the two currencies at the time T can therefore be split into a loan, an investment and an exchange deal at moment 0. The same type of reasoning can also be applied to exchange swaps.

7.2.1.3 Other assets

For equities, the cashflows correspond simply to spot positions, which may be adapted according to an exchange rate if the security is quoted on the foreign market.

Raw materials are treated in the same way as fixed-income securities, on the basis of spot prices and the principle of discounting.

7.2.2 Mapping cashflows with standard maturity dates

Once the cashflows have been determined, application of the VaR calculation $VaR_q^* = -z_q \cdot \sigma(\Delta p_t)$ requires the variances in each of the cashflows and of all the two-by-two covariances to be known. If one looks at all the different possible dates, the task is quite clearly impossibly large; such a set of data does not exist and even if it did, processing the data would be far too unwieldy a process.

This is the reason for carrying out mapping – redistributing the various cashflows across a limited, previously determined range of standard maturity dates. In this way, RiskMetrics™ supplies the data that allows the VaR to be calculated for 14 *standard maturity dates*:[11] 1 month, 3 months, 6 months, 1 year, 2 years, 3 years, 4 years, 5 years, 7 years, 9 years, 10 years, 15 years, 20 years and 30 years.

For a cashflow that corresponds to one of the vertices, no mapping will be necessary. On the other hand, a cashflow that occurs between two vertices should be divided between the two neighbouring vertices, one directly above and the other directly below. Suppose that a cashflow with current value V_0 and maturity date t_0 has to be divided between the vertices t_1 and t_2 with $t_1 < t_0 < t_2$ (see Figure 7.3).

The problem is that of determining the current values V_1 and V_2 of the cashflows associated with the maturity dates t_1 and t_2. A number of procedures, based on slightly different principles, can be applied to make this division.

7.2.2.1 Elementary mapping

The first way of carrying out the mapping appears *a priori* to be very natural, as it relies on the most frequently applied principles of financial calculations. In fact, it requires:

- Preservation of the current value, $V_0 = V_1 + V_2$.
- Preservation of the duration $\dfrac{t_0 V_0}{V_0} = \dfrac{t_1 V_1 + t_2 V_2}{V_1 + V_2}$, or also: $t_0 V_0 = t_1 V_1 + t_2 V_2$.

The system put together by these two conditions is very easy to resolve:

$$V_1 = \frac{t_2 - t_0}{t_2 - t_1} V_0 \qquad V_2 = \frac{t_0 - t_1}{t_2 - t_1} V_0.$$

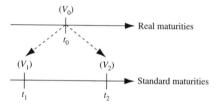

Figure 7.3 Mapping

---

[11] Better known as *vertices*.

Example

Let us consider a cashflow with a maturity date of $t_0 = 12$ years and a total 1000 (at that moment). The standard neighbouring maturity dates are $t_1 = 10$ years and $t_2 = 15$ years, and we assume that the interest rates for the two periods are $r_1 = 7\%$ and $r_2 = 8\%$. From that, the rate of interest corresponding to the duration of the cashflow to be processed ($r_0 = 7.4\%$) is determined by linear interpolation and the current value is: $V_0 = 1000 \cdot (1 + 0.074)^{-12} = 424.57$.

As the data have been specified thus, the divided current values can easily be calculated:

$$V_1 = \frac{15 - 12}{15 - 10} \cdot 424.57 = 254.74$$

$$V_2 = \frac{12 - 10}{15 - 10} \cdot 424.57 = 169.83$$

If one expresses the returns associated with each cashflow as R_0, R_1 and R_2, we clearly have:

$$R_0 V_0 = R_1 V_1 + R_2 V_2$$

hence the following expression for the variance:

$$\sigma_0^2 V_0^2 = \sigma_1^2 V_1^2 + \sigma_2^2 V_2^2 + 2\sigma_{12} V_1 V_2$$
$$= \sigma_1^2 V_1^2 + \sigma_2^2 V_2^2 + 2\sigma_1 \sigma_2 \rho_{12} V_1 V_2$$

Because of the presence of the correlation coefficient ρ_{12}, which is less than 1, the variance thus calculated may be underestimated:

$$\sigma_0^2 V_0^2 \leq \sigma_1^2 V_1^2 + \sigma_2^2 V_2^2 + 2\sigma_1 \sigma_2 V_1 V_2$$
$$= (\sigma_1 V_1 + \sigma_2 V_2)^2$$

In addition, with the values found for V_1 and V_2, the maximum value of the standard deviation can be written as:

$$\sigma_0 V_0 = \sigma_1 V_1 + \sigma_2 V_2$$
$$= \sigma_1 \frac{t_2 - t_0}{t_2 - t_1} V_0 + \sigma_2 \frac{t_0 - t_1}{t_2 - t_1} V_0$$

This shows that σ_0 is obtained by linear interpolation on the basis of σ_1 and σ_2.

7.2.2.2 Mapping according to RiskMetrics™

The problem of possibly underestimating the standard deviation (and therefore the VaR) will be overcome if the standard deviation is determined by linear interpolation. The mapping suggested by RiskMetrics™ is therefore defined by:

- Preservation of the current value: $V_0 = V_1 + V_2$.

- Preservation of the risk $\sigma_0^2 V_0^2 = \sigma_1^2 V_1^2 + \sigma_2^2 V_2^2 + 2\sigma_1\sigma_2\rho_{12} V_1 V_2$ where σ_1, σ_2 and ρ_{12} are data and σ_0 is obtained by linear interpolation.

Because of the first relation, it is possible to introduce the parameter α, for which

$$\alpha = \frac{V_1}{V_0} \qquad 1 - \alpha = \frac{V_2}{V_0}$$

This gives, in the second relation: $\sigma_0^2 = \sigma_1^2\alpha^2 + \sigma_2^2(1 - \alpha)^2 + 2\sigma_1\sigma_2\rho_{12}\alpha(1 - \alpha)$.

This can also be written: $\alpha^2(\sigma_1^2 + \sigma_2^2 - 2\sigma_1\sigma_2\rho_{12}) + 2\alpha(\sigma_1\sigma_2\rho_{12} - \sigma_2^2) + (\sigma_2^2 - \sigma_0^2) = 0$.

This second-degree equation will allow two solution couples to be found (V_1, V_2) and the couple consisting of two numbers of the same sign as V_0 will be preserved.

Example

Let us take the previous example, for which the cashflow to be divided was $V_0 = 424.57$ and the respective maturity dates were $t_1 = 10$, $t_0 = 12$ and $t_2 = 15$.

Let us assume that we have the following additional data: $\sigma_1 = 0.6\,\%$, $\sigma_2 = 0.9\,\%$, $\rho_{12} = 0.94$.

We note first of all a slight underestimation[12] of the risk caused by the diversification effect when the mapping is applied, on the basis of preservation of duration. The variance formula gives $\sigma^2{}_0 V^2{}_0 = 9.0643$.

Hence $\sigma_0 = 0.7091\,\%$ instead of the value $\sigma_0 = 0.72\,\%$ obtained by linear interpolation. With this latter value for σ_0, the mapping equation based on preservation of risk allows us to write:

$$1548\alpha^2 - 6048\alpha + 2916 = 0$$

We therefore obtain the two solutions $\alpha = 3.3436$ and $\alpha = 0.5634$. Only the second will guarantee cashflows with the same sign as V_0, and allows the following to be calculated:

$$V_1 = \alpha V_0 = 239.19$$

$$V_2 = (1 - \alpha) V_0 = 185.37$$

7.2.2.3 Alternative mapping

The mapping suggested by RiskMetrics™ has the advantage over the previous form of guaranteeing the preservation of risk (and it is exactly that parameter that interests us here).

It does, however, have an adverse effect: it compensates for the diversification effect by allocating the greater part of the cashflow to the vertex with the greater volatility, even though the actual maturity date may be closer to the vertex with the lower volatility. This phenomenon is evident in the figures in the example that we have just developed, but it can be verified generally.[13]

---

[12] The correlation coefficient here is in fact very close to 1.

[13] Schaller P., *On Cashflow Mapping in VaR Estimation*, Creditanstalt-Bankverein, CA-RISC-19960227, 1996.

The phenomenon would not be of great import if mapping only had to be produced for a single cashflow. It becomes much more problematic, however, if two cashflows are considered simultaneously: one with a total X corresponding to a vertex t_1 and another with a total $-X$ with a maturity date close to t_1. P. Schaller[13], shows that by varying the second maturity date continually on one side or another of t_1, the parameter α shows a discontinuity at t_1.

Schaller's proposal is therefore to retain the condition of risk preservation, in order to prevent underestimation of the risk through the diversification effect, and to replace the other condition by expressing that the proportion $\dfrac{V_1}{V_1 + V_2}$, allocated to the vertex t_1 tends towards $100\,\%$ (resp. $0\,\%$) when the actual maturity date t_0 tends towards t_1 (resp. t_2). More specifically, he proposes that the proportion in question should be a linear function f of the variable t_0 so that $f(t_1) = 1$ and $f(t_2) = 0$.

It is easy to see that $\dfrac{V_1}{V_1 + V_2} = f(t_0) = \dfrac{t_2 - t_0}{t_2 - t_1}$, and therefore that $t_2 V_1 - t_1 V_1 = t_2 V_1 + t_2 V_2 - t_0(V_1 + V_2)$.

To sum up, Schaller's mapping is defined by

- Preservation of the quasi-duration: $t_0(V_1 + V_2) = t_1 V_1 + t_2 V_2$.
- Preservation of the risk: $\sigma^2{}_0 V^2{}_0 = \sigma^2{}_1 V^2{}_1 + \sigma^2{}_2 V^2{}_2 + 2\sigma_1\sigma_2\rho_{12}V_1 V_2$, where σ_1, σ_2 and ρ_{12} are data and σ_0 is obtained by linear interpolation.

By introducing $\beta = \dfrac{V_1}{V_1 + V_2} = \dfrac{t_2 - t_0}{t_2 - t_1}$, which corresponds to the first condition, the second can be written:

$$\sigma_0^2 \frac{V_0^2}{(V_1 + V_2)^2} = \sigma_1^2\beta^2 + \sigma_2^2(1 - \beta)^2 + 2\sigma_1\sigma_2\rho_{12}\beta(1 - \beta)$$

This allows $(V_1 + V_2)$ and therefore V_1 and V_2 to be calculated.

Example

With the data from the example already used for the first two mappings, we find successively that:

$$\beta = \frac{15 - 12}{15 - 10} = 0.6$$

$$0.0072^2 \cdot \frac{424.57^2}{(V_1 + V_2)^2} = 0.00005028$$

$$V_1 + V_2 = 431.08$$

From this, it can be deduced that:

$$V_1 = \beta(V_1 + V_2) = 258.65$$

$$V_2 = (1 - \beta)(V_1 + V_2) = 172.43$$

Note

It may seem surprising that Schaller's mapping is made without preserving the current value. In reality, this is less serious than it may appear, because unlike normal financial calculations, we are not looking at the value of a portfolio but at its risk. In addition, in his paper, the author provides a thorough justification (through geometric logic) for his method of work.

7.2.3 Calculating *VaR*

7.2.3.1 Data

One reason why the estimated variance–covariance matrix method leads to mapping of elementary risk positions associated with a standard finite set of maturity dates is because it would be unthinkable to obtain this matrix for all the possible positions. We are thinking about:

- the various families of available securities;
- the full range of securities in each group (number of quoted equities, for example), in various stock-exchange locations;
- the consideration of various exchange rates between these financial locations;
- the abundance of derivatives, which have an infinite number of possible combinations;
- the various maturity dates of all the products.

The numerical values supplied for using this method are therefore the evaluations of the expected values and variances of the various risk factors, as well as the covariances relating to the corresponding couples.

It has therefore been agreed to use these parameters for the following risk factors:

- exchange rates (RiskMetrics™ uses 30 currencies);
- interest rates for the representation of fixed-rate instruments, such as bonds with mapping with a zero-coupon bond total (RiskMetrics™ uses 14 levels of maturity varying from one month to 30 years);
- national stock-exchange indices for representing equities using the 'beta' model (Risk-Metrics™ uses 30 national indices);
- a representative panel of raw materials.

Note 1

In Section 2.2.2 we introduce two concepts of volatility relative to one option: historical and implicit. Of course the same can be applied here for all the variances and covariances. It has also been said that the implicit parameters are more reliable than the historical parameters. However, because of the huge volume and frequency of data obtained, it is the historical variances and covariances that will be adopted in practice.

Note 2

The estimates of the variances and covariances can be calculated using the usual descriptive statistical formulae. If the estimation of such a parameter for the period t uses observations relative to periods $t-1, t-2, t-T$, these formulae are:

$$\sigma_{R,t}^2 = \frac{1}{T} \sum_{j=1}^{T} (R_{t-j} - \overline{R})^2$$

$$\sigma_{12,t} = \frac{1}{T} \sum_{j=1}^{T} (R_{1,t-j} - \overline{R}_1)(R_{2,t-j} - \overline{R}_2)$$

In actual fact, RiskMetrics™ does not use these formulae, but instead transforms the equally weighted averages into averages whose weight decreases geometrically in order to give greater weight to recent observations. For λ positioned between 0 and 1[15], we calculated:

$$\sigma_{R,t}^2 = (1-\lambda) \sum_{j=1}^{T} \lambda^{j-1} (R_{t-j} - \overline{R})^2$$

$$\sigma_{12,t} = (1-\lambda) \sum_{j=1}^{T} \lambda^{j-1} (R_{1,t-j} - \overline{R}_1)(R_{2,t-j} - \overline{R}_2)$$

These formulae are justified by the fact that if T is high, the weights will have a sum equal to 1 as:[14]

$$\sum_{j=1}^{\infty} \lambda^{j-1} = \frac{1}{1-\lambda}$$

In addition, they present the advantage of not requiring all the data involved in the formulae to be memorised, as they are included in the calculation by recurrence:

$$\sigma_{R,t+1}^2 = (1-\lambda) \sum_{j=1}^{T} \lambda^{j-1} (R_{t+1-j} - \overline{R})^2$$

$$= \lambda(1-\lambda) \sum_{j=0}^{T-1} \lambda^{j-1} (R_{t-j} - \overline{R})^2$$

$$= \lambda(1-\lambda) \left[\sum_{j=1}^{T} \lambda^{j-1} (R_{t-j} - \overline{R})^2 - \lambda^{T-1} (R_{t-T} - \overline{R})^2 + \frac{1}{\lambda}(R_t - \overline{R})^2 \right]$$

$$= \lambda \sigma_{R,t}^2 + (1-\lambda)(R_t - \overline{R})^2$$

---

[14] This concept, known as a 'geometric series', is dealt with in Appendix 1.

since λ^{T-1} is negligible if T is sufficiently high. In the same way, we have:

$$\sigma_{12,t+1} = \lambda\sigma_{12,t} + (1 - \lambda)(R_{1t} - \overline{R}_1)(R_{2t} - \overline{R}_2)$$

7.2.3.2 Calculations for a portfolio of linear shares

Let us consider a portfolio consisting of N assets in respective numbers $n_1, \ldots, n_N$, the value of each asset being expressed on the basis of risk factors $X_1, X_2, \ldots, X_n$ through a linear relation:

$$p_j = a_{j1}X_1 + \cdots + a_{jn}X_n \quad j = 1, \ldots, N$$

This is the case with securities such as bonds, equities, exchange positions, raw materials, interest and exchange swaps, FRAs etc.

The value of the portfolio can therefore be written as:

$$p_P = \sum_{j=1}^{N} n_j p_j$$

$$= \sum_{j=1}^{N} n_j \sum_{k=1}^{n} a_{jk} X_k$$

$$= \sum_{k=1}^{n} \left(\sum_{j=1}^{N} n_j a_{jk} \right) X_k$$

Here, if one wishes to take account of time:[15]

$$p_P(t) = \sum_{k=1}^{n} \left(\sum_{j=1}^{N} n_j a_{jk} \right) X_k(t)$$

The variation in the portfolio's value can therefore be written:

$$\Delta p_P(t) = p_P(t) - p_P(t-1)$$

$$= \sum_{k=1}^{n} \left(\sum_{j=1}^{N} n_j a_{jk} \right) (X_k(t) - X_k(t-1))$$

$$= \sum_{k=1}^{n} \left(\sum_{j=1}^{N} n_j a_{jk} X_k(t-1) \right) \frac{X_k(t) - X_k(t-1)}{X_k(t-1)}$$

$$= \sum_{k=1}^{n} x_k(t-1)\Delta_k(t)$$

---

[15] It is assumed that the influence of the risk factors (measured by a_{jk}) and the composition of the portfolio (n_j) does not change at the *VaR* calculation horizon.

Here, Δ_k has the standard interpretation, and $x_k(t-1) = \sum_{j=1}^{N} n_j a_{jk} X_k(t-1)$ can be interpreted as the total invested in $(t-1)$ in the kth risk factor.

We are interested in the changes to the portfolio between time 0 (now) and time 1 (*VaR* calculation horizon). It is therefore assumed that we have the following observations:

- The current positions in the various risk factors $x_k(0)$ $(k = 1, \ldots, n)$, which we will subsequently express simply as x_k.
- The estimation, based on historical periods, of the expected relative variations for the various risk factors $E(\Delta_k(1)) = E_k(k = 1, \ldots, n)$.
- The estimation, also based on historical periods, of the variances and covariances for the risk factors:

$$\text{var}(\Delta_k(1)) = \sigma_k^2 = \sigma_{kk} \qquad k = 1, \ldots, n$$
$$\text{cov}(\Delta_k(1), \Delta_l(1)) = \sigma_{kl} \qquad k, l = 1, \ldots, n$$

These data can be expressed in matrix form:

$$\vec{x} = \begin{pmatrix} x_1 \\ x_2 \\ \vdots \\ x_n \end{pmatrix} \qquad \vec{E} = \begin{pmatrix} E_1 \\ E_2 \\ \vdots \\ E_n \end{pmatrix} \qquad V = \begin{pmatrix} \sigma_1^2 & \sigma_{12} & \cdots & \sigma_{1n} \\ \sigma_{21} & \sigma_2^2 & \cdots & \sigma_{2n} \\ \vdots & \vdots & \ddots & \vdots \\ \sigma_{n1} & \sigma_{n2} & \cdots & \sigma_n^2 \end{pmatrix}$$

The fluctuations in the variation in value can be written as (see Section 3.1.1):

$$\sigma^2(\Delta p_P(1)) = \text{var}(\Delta p_P(1))$$

$$= \sum_{k=1}^{n} \sum_{l=1}^{n} x_k x_l \sigma_{kl}$$

$$= \vec{x}^t V \vec{x}$$

This allows the following calculation:

$$VaR_q^* = -z_q \sigma(\Delta p_P(1)) = -z_q \sqrt{\vec{x}^t V \vec{x}}.$$

And therefore:

$$VaR_q = VaR_q^* + E(\Delta p_P(1))$$

$$= \vec{x}^t \vec{E} - z_q \sqrt{\vec{x}^t V \vec{x}}$$

Note 1

In actual fact, the RiskMetrics™ system does not produce the matrix V for the variances and covariances, but two equivalent elements.

- The value $z_q \sigma_k$ $(k = 1, \ldots, n)$ of the *VaR* parameter for each risk factor, where q is chosen as equalling 0.95 and therefore $z_q = 1.6465$. On the basis of these data, we construct the matrix:

$$S = \text{diag}(-z_q \sigma_1, \ldots, -z_q \sigma_n) = -z_q \text{diag}(\sigma_1, \ldots, \sigma_n).$$

- The matrix for the correlations $\rho_{kl} = \dfrac{\sigma_{kl}}{\sigma_k \sigma_l}$:

$$C = \begin{pmatrix} 1 & \rho_{12} & \cdots & \rho_{1n} \\ \rho_{21} & 1 & \cdots & \rho_{2n} \\ \vdots & \vdots & \ddots & \vdots \\ \rho_{n1} & \rho_{n2} & \cdots & 1 \end{pmatrix}$$

Here, we clearly have: $V = [\text{diag}(\sigma_1, \ldots, \sigma_n)]^t C \, \text{diag}(\sigma_1, \ldots, \sigma_n)$.

We can therefore calculate the *VaR* by:

$$VaR_q^* = -\sqrt{z_q^2 \vec{x}^t [\text{diag}(\sigma_1, \ldots, \sigma_n)]^t C \, \text{diag}(\sigma_1, \ldots, \sigma_n) \vec{x}}$$

$$= -\sqrt{\vec{x}^t S^t C S \vec{x}}$$

$$= -\sqrt{(S\vec{x})^t C (S\vec{x})}$$

Note 2

This method shows the effect of diversification on risk with particular clarity; if there were no diversification, the elements in the matrix C would all be worth 1. In reality, however, they are worth 1 or less, which improves the value of the *VaR*. In addition, without the effects of diversification, all the components of $C(Sx)$ would be equal to $\sum_{k=1}^{n} (S\vec{x})_k$, and the *VaR* parameter would be given by:

$$VaR_q^* = \sum_{k=1}^{n} (S\vec{x})_k$$

$$= -z_q \sum_{k=1}^{n} x_k \sigma_k$$

7.2.3.3 The specific case of equities

If one is considering a portfolio of equities, it is no longer possible to use the variance–covariance matrix, which would be too bulky. For this reason, equities are dealt with on an approximation basis – a diagonal model. This model is comparable to Sharpe's simple index model presented in Section 3.2.4, but its index must be representative of the market.[16]

The only statistical elements needed in this case are the expected return E_I and the standard deviation σ_I for the index, the coefficients a_j and b_j of the model for the jth security

$$\frac{\Delta p_j}{p_j} = a_j + b_j \frac{\Delta I}{I} + \varepsilon_j$$

and the variances for the residuals from the various regressions:

$$\sigma_{\varepsilon_j}^2 \qquad (j = 1, \ldots, N)$$

---

[16] Sharpe's model, depending on the type of asset in question, may involve a sectorial index.

In fact, it is known that the expected return and the portfolio variance are given in this case by:

$$E(\Delta p_P) = a_P + b_P E_I$$

$$\text{var}(\Delta p_P) = b_P^2 \sigma_I^2 + \sum_{j=1}^{N} n_j^2 p_j \sigma_{\varepsilon_j}^2$$

where we have:

$$a_P = \sum_{j=1}^{N} n_j a_j p_j$$

$$b_P = \sum_{j=1}^{N} n_j b_j p_j$$

Note that this model, in which correlations between securities do not appear, nevertheless takes account of them as the various equities are linked to the same index. It can also be shown that:

$$\text{cov}\left(\frac{\Delta p_i}{p_i}, \frac{\Delta p_j}{p_j}\right) = b_i b_j \sigma_I^2$$

To make things easier, the RiskMetrics™ system actually uses a variance on this diagonal model, which differs only from the model we have just presented by the absence of the term $\sum_{j=1}^{N} n_j^2 p_j \sigma_{\varepsilon_j}^2$ from the second member of the formula that gives the variance for the portfolio.

This term takes account of the differences between the returns observed on the various securities and those shown by the model. This method of working therefore gives a slightly underestimated value for the *VaR* parameter, which according to the previous section, is:

$$VaR_q^* = -z_q b_P \sigma_I$$

7.2.3.4 Calculations for a portfolio of nonlinear values

For nonlinear products (essentially options[17]), the situation is much more complicated because of their nonlinear nature. Linearity is in fact essential for applying the estimated variance–covariance matrix method, as a linear combination of multinormal variables (correlated or otherwise) is itself distributed according to a normal law. We will assume only that the variances in underlying prices are distributed according to a normal law with zero expectation and standard deviation σ_I. As for the distribution of the variation in option price, we will show how this is determined.

Let us approach the case of an isolated option first. The method involves Taylor's development of the valuation model. The importance of the underlying equity price over the option price is such that for this variable, we develop up to order 2 and the variation

---

[17] For other methods of approach to *VaR* for options products, read Rouvinez C., Going Greek with VaR, *Risk Magazine*, February 1997, pp. 57–65.

in the premium is therefore obtained according to the option's various sensitivity coefficients:[18]

$$\Delta p_t = f'_S(S_t, K, \tau, \sigma_t, R_F)\Delta S_t + \tfrac{1}{2} f''_{SS}(S_t, K, \tau, \sigma_t, R_F)(\Delta S_t)^2$$
$$+ f'_K(S_t, K, \tau, \sigma_t, R_F)\Delta K + f'_\tau(S_t, K, \tau, \sigma_t, R_F)\Delta \tau$$
$$+ f'_\sigma(S_t, K, \tau, \sigma_t, R_F)\Delta \sigma_t + f'_R(S_t, K, \tau, \sigma_t, R_F)\Delta R_F$$
$$= \Delta \cdot \Delta S_t + \tfrac{1}{2}\Gamma \cdot (\Delta S_t)^2 + f'_K \cdot \Delta K - \Theta \cdot \Delta \tau + V \cdot \Delta \sigma_t + \rho \cdot \Delta R_F$$

As in RiskMetrics™, we will limit our analysis to the Δ, Γ and Θ parameters only:

$$\Delta p_t = \Delta \cdot \Delta S_t + \tfrac{1}{2}\Gamma \cdot (\Delta S_t)^2 - \Theta \cdot \Delta \tau$$

It can be demonstrated on that basis that the expectation, variance, skewness coefficient γ_1 and kurtosis coefficient γ_2 of Δp_t are obtained by:

$$E(\Delta p_t) = \tfrac{1}{2}\Gamma\sigma_t^2 - \Theta(\Delta \tau)$$

$$\text{var}(\Delta p_t) = \Delta^2\sigma_t^2 + \tfrac{1}{2}\Gamma^2\sigma_t^4$$

$$\gamma_1(\Delta p_t) = \frac{\Gamma\sigma_t(3\Delta^2 + \Gamma^2\sigma_t^2)}{(\Delta^2 + \tfrac{1}{2}\Gamma^2\sigma_t^2)^{3/2}}$$

$$\gamma_2(\Delta p_t) = \frac{3\Gamma^2\sigma_t^2(4\Delta^2 + \Gamma^2\sigma_t^2)}{(\Delta^2 + \tfrac{1}{2}\Gamma^2\sigma_t^2)^2}$$

To evaluate the parameters involved in the formulae, Δ, Γ and Θ are determined using the Black and Scholes valuation model through suitably adapted pricing software and σ_t is calculated on the basis of historical observations, as explained in the previous section.

The distribution of Δp_t is then determined as follows: from among a series of probability laws, known as the *Johnson Distributions*,[19] we look for the one for which the above four parameters correspond best, More specifically, from among the following relations:

$$\Delta S_t = a + b\frac{\Delta p_t - c}{d}$$

$$\Delta S_t = a + b \cdot \ln\left(\frac{\Delta p_t - c}{d}\right)$$

$$\Delta S_t = a + b \cdot \text{arcsh}\left(\frac{\Delta p_t - c}{d}\right)$$

$$\Delta S_t = a + b \cdot \ln\left(\frac{\Delta p_t - c}{c + d - \Delta p_t}\right)$$

which define respectively normal, log-normal, bounded and unbounded laws, the law and parameters a, b, c and d can be determined[20] so that for the four parameters mentioned above, ΔS_t follows a normal law with zero expectation and standard deviation σ_t.

---

[18] In fact, $\Delta t = 1$ when the *VaR* calculation horizon is 1 day.

[19] Johnson N. L., Systems of frequency curves generated by methods of translation, *Biometrika*, Vol. 36., 1949, pp. 149–75.

[20] Using the algorithm described in Hill I. D., Hill R. and Holder R. L., Fitting Johnson curves by moments (Algorithm AS 99), *Applied Statistics*, Vol. 25 No. 2, 1976, pp. 180–9.

As the aim here was to take account of nonlinearity (and therefore skewness and kurtosis among other properties), we are no longer looking at calculating *VaR* using the formula $VaR_q^* = -z_q \cdot \sigma(\Delta p_t)$.

In this case, take once again the initial definition, based on the quantile $\Pr[\Delta p_t \leq VaR] = 1 - q$ and therefore, for the law determined, write the equation $\Delta S_t = z_q$ and resolve it with respect to Δp_t.

In the case of a portfolio of optional products, the method shown above is generalised using the matrix calculation. Thus, for a portfolio consisting of N optional assets in respective numbers n_1, ..., n_N, the first two distribution parameters for the variance $\Delta p_{P,t}$ in the portfolio price are written as:

$$E(\Delta p_{P,t}) = \frac{1}{2} \text{tr}(\Gamma V) - \sum_{j=1}^{N} n_j \Theta_j(\Delta \tau)$$

$$\text{var}(\Delta p_{P,t}) = \vec{\Delta}^t V \vec{\Delta} + \frac{1}{2} \text{tr}(\Gamma V \Gamma V)$$

where V is the variance–covariance matrix for the returns of the various underlying equities, and:

$$\Gamma = \begin{pmatrix} n_1 \Gamma_1 & 0 & \cdots & 0 \\ 0 & n_2 \Gamma_2 & \cdots & 0 \\ \vdots & \vdots & \ddots & \vdots \\ 0 & 0 & \cdots & n_N \Gamma_N \end{pmatrix} \qquad \vec{\Delta} = \begin{pmatrix} n_1 \Delta_1 \\ n_2 \Delta_2 \\ \vdots \\ n_N \Delta_N \end{pmatrix}$$

Note 1

For optional products, RiskMetrics™ also proposes the use of the Monte Carlo methodology, as described in Section 7.3, alongside the approach based on Taylor's development of the valuation model.

Note 2

This *VaR* evaluation method is a local method, as it first determines the *VaR* parameter for each of the risk factors separately (the matrix S from Note for linear assets), and then aggregates them through the estimated variance–covariance method.

Conversely, the Monte Carlo and historical simulation methods introduced in Sections 7.3 and 7.4 initially determine the future value of the portfolio, and then deduce the *VaR* value compared to the current value of the portfolio.

7.3   MONTE CARLO SIMULATION

7.3.1   The Monte Carlo method and probability theory

7.3.1.1   Generation of probability distribution

Let us examine first of all the problem of generating values for a random variable X distributed according to a probability law whose distribution function F_X is known.[21]

---

[21] Vose D., *Quantitative Risk Analysis*, John Wiley & Sons, Ltd, 1996.

It is relatively easy to obtain the values for a *uniform random variable* within the interval [0; 1]. One can, for example, choose the list for a particular figure (the units figure or the last informed decimal) in a sequence of numbers taken within a table: a table of mathematical or statistical values, mortality table, telephone directory etc. One can also use a table of *random numbers*, available in most formula collections.[22] It is also possible to use software that generates pseudo-random numbers.[23]

As the full range of values for the distribution function F_X is precisely the interval [0; 1], it is sufficient for the purpose of generating the values of X to transform the values obtained for a uniform random variable U within [0; 1], using the reciprocal function of F_X. This function is the quantile Q_X for the variable X, and we will calculate $Q_X(u)$ for each value u generated within [0; 1].

The variable $Q_X(U)$ (random through the channel of U) is properly distributed according to the law of X, as, through definition of the uniform random variable,

$$\Pr[Q_X(U) \leq t] = \Pr[F_X(Q_X(U)) \leq F_X(t)]$$
$$= \Pr[U \leq F_X(t)]$$
$$= F_X(t)$$

This property is also illustrated in Figure 7.4.

7.3.1.2 *Using the variables generated*

The Monte Carlo simulation is a statistical method used when it is very difficult to determine a probability distribution by mathematical reasoning alone. It consists of 'fabricating' this distribution through the generation of a large number of pseudo-random samples extracted from the distribution, whether it is:

- known theoretically with parameters of a specified numerical value (by estimation, for example);
- the result of observations or calculations on observations.

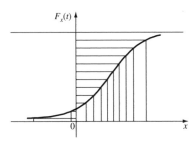

Figure 7.4 Monte Carlo simulation

---

[22] For example, Abramowitz M. and Stegun A., *Handbook of Mathematical Functions*, Dover, 1972.

[23] A method for generating pseudo-random numbers uniformly distributed within the interval [0; 1] is developed in Appendix 2.

Suppose for example that one wishes to find the distribution of samples through a random variable X for which the law of probability is known but not normal. A sample is extracted from this law by the procedure explained above, and the average of this procedure is a value that we will call x_1. If one then generates not one but many samples M in the same way, a distribution will be built up: $(\overline{x}_1, \overline{x}_2, \ldots, \overline{x}_M)$. This, with a good approximation if the size of the samples and M are sufficiently large, is the distribution of sampling for the expectation of X.

7.3.2 Estimation method

For the problem of constructing the distribution of the variation in value and estimating the *VaR*, the Monte Carlo simulation method is recommended by Bankers Trust in its RaRoc 2020™ system.

7.3.2.1 Risk factor case

Let us take first of all the very simple case in which the value for which the *VaR* is required is the risk factor X itself (the price for an equity, for example). The random variable

$$\Delta = \frac{X(1) - X(0)}{X(0)}$$

is distributed according to a certain law of probability. This law can of course be evaluated on the basis of observations:

$$\Delta(t) = \frac{X(t) - X(t-1)}{X(t-1)} \qquad t = -T+1, \ldots, -1, 0$$

However, as this variable will have to be generated using the Monte Carlo technique, it is essential for the distribution used not to present any irregularities corresponding to differences with respect to the real distribution. The Monte Carlo method is in fact very sensitive to these irregularities and they are especially likely to show themselves for extreme values, which are precisely the values of interest to us.

The solution adopted is therefore a valuation model that is adapted to the risk factor X. Thus, for the return on an equity, a normal or more leptokurtic (see Section 6.1.2) distribution will be chosen; if one wishes to take account of a development over time, an adapted stochastic process known as *geometric Brownian motion* (see Section 4.3.2) may be used. It expresses a relative variance in the price S_t at time t according to the expected return E_R and the volatility σ_R of the security in a two-term sum:

$$\frac{S_{t+dt} - S_t}{S_t} = \frac{dS_t}{S_t} = E_R \cdot dt + \sigma_R \cdot dw_t$$

Only the second term is random, dw_t being distributed according to a normal law of zero expectation and standard deviation $\sqrt{dt}$.

If the general form of the valuation model is the result of theoretical reasoning,[24] the parameters (expectation and standard deviation in the cases mentioned above) for this model shall be evaluated directly on the basis of observations.

---

[24] Reasoning for which the suitability needs to be verified using observations.

Through Monte Carlo simulation of the underlying random variable and use of the adapted valuation model, we therefore generate a large number M of pseudo-observations[25] $\Delta^{(t)}$ ($t = 1, \ldots, M$) for the random variable Δ.

The relation $X(1) - X(0) = \Delta$. $X(0)$ allows the future value of the risk factor X to be estimated by:

$$X^{(t)}(1) = X(0) + \Delta^{(t)} \cdot X(0) \quad t = 1, 2, \ldots, M$$

The distribution of the variation in value can therefore be estimated by:

$$\Delta p^{(t)} = X^{(t)}(1) - X(0) = \Delta^{(t)} \cdot X(0). \quad t = 1, 2, \ldots, M$$

7.3.2.2 Isolated asset case

Let us now consider the case in which the asset for which one wishes to determine the VaR depends on several risk factors $X_1, X_2, \ldots, X_n$. The value of this asset is therefore expressed by a relation of the type $p = f(X_1, X_2, \ldots, X_n)$.

The observations of these risk factors $X_k(t)$, ($k = 1, \ldots, n, t = -T + 1, \ldots, -1, 0$), allow the valuation model parameters and the stochastic processes relative to these risk factors to be estimated.

If the Δ_k variables ($k = 1, \ldots, n$) are generated independently of each other, the correlation that links the various risk factors exerting an influence on the price of the equity will be lost completely. Also, the Monte Carlo simulation method has to be adapted in order for various variables to be generated simultaneously while respecting the associated variance and covariance matrix. This matrix will of course also be calculated on the basis of available observations.

Let us begin by reasoning over the case of two risk factors. We wish to generate Δ_1 and Δ_2 according to a given law, so that:

$$E(\Delta_1) = \mu_1 \quad E(\Delta_2) = \mu_2$$

$$\mathrm{var}(\Delta_1) = \sigma_1^2 \quad \mathrm{var}(\Delta_2) = \sigma_2^2$$

$$\mathrm{cov}(\Delta_1, \Delta_2) = \sigma_{12}$$

If we generate two other variables δ_1 and δ_2 that obey the same theory, but so that

$$E(\delta_1) = 0 \quad E(\delta_2) = 0$$

$$\mathrm{var}(\delta_1) = 1 \quad \mathrm{var}(\delta_2) = 1$$

δ_1 and δ_2 are independent
It is sufficient to define:

$$\begin{cases} \Delta_1 = \sigma_1 \delta_1 + \mu_1 \\ \Delta_2 = \sigma_2 \rho \delta_1 + \sigma_2 \sqrt{1 - \rho^2} \delta_2 + \mu_2 \end{cases}$$

---

[25] We use (t) in the upper index when it no longer represents time but instead constitutes a numbering for various estimations of a random variable.

where we have introduced the correlation coefficient

$$\rho = \mathrm{corr}(\Delta_1, \Delta_2) = \frac{\sigma_{12}}{\sigma_1 \sigma_2}$$

to obtain the variables Δ_1 and Δ_2 with the desired properties.[26]

The definition of the Δ_k variables can also be written as:

$$\begin{pmatrix} \Delta_1 \\ \Delta_2 \end{pmatrix} = \begin{pmatrix} \sigma_1 & 0 \\ \sigma_2 \rho & \sigma_2 \sqrt{1 - \rho^2} \end{pmatrix} \begin{pmatrix} \delta_1 \\ \delta_2 \end{pmatrix} + \begin{pmatrix} \mu_1 \\ \mu_2 \end{pmatrix}$$

The matrix for the δ_k coefficients, which we will call L, is such that:

$$\begin{aligned} LL^t &= \begin{pmatrix} \sigma_1 & 0 \\ \sigma_2 \rho & \sigma_2 \sqrt{1 - \rho^2} \end{pmatrix} \begin{pmatrix} \sigma_1 & \sigma_2 \rho \\ 0 & \sigma_2 \sqrt{1 - \rho^2} \end{pmatrix} \\ &= \begin{pmatrix} \sigma_1^2 & \sigma_1 \sigma_2 \rho \\ \sigma_1 \sigma_2 \rho & \sigma_2^2 \rho^2 + \sigma_2^2 (1 - \rho^2) \end{pmatrix} \\ &= \begin{pmatrix} \sigma_1^2 & \sigma_{12} \\ \sigma_{12} & \sigma_2^2 \end{pmatrix} \end{aligned}$$

We are looking at the variance–covariance matrix for the Δ_k variables, and the matrix L for the coefficients is therefore deduced by the *Choleski factorisation*.[27]

In the general case of n risk factors, the process is generalised: the Δ_k variables ($k = 1, \ldots, n$) may be written as a vector that is defined on the basis of the independent δ_k variables ($k = 1, \ldots, n$) with zero expectations and variances equal to 1, through the relation:

$$\vec{\Delta} = L\vec{\delta} + \vec{\mu}$$

Here, L is the Choleski factorisation matrix and the variance–covariance matrix for the Δ_k variables.

Once the Δ_k variables ($k = 1, \ldots, n$) are generated:

$$\Delta_k^{(t)} \qquad (k = 1, \ldots, n \quad t = 1, \ldots, M)$$

The future values of the risk factors are determined on the basis of the values currently observed $X_1(0), \ldots, X_n(0)$:

$$X_k^{(t)}(1) = X_k(0) \cdot (1 + \Delta_k^{(t)}) \quad (k = 1, \ldots, n \quad t = 1, \ldots, M)$$

From this, the future price of the asset can be easily deduced:

$$p^{(t)}(1) = f(X_1^{(t)}(1), X_2^{(t)}(1), \ldots, X_n^{(t)}(1)) \qquad t = 1, \ldots, M$$

---

[26] It is not generally true that such first-degree expressions give random variables Δ arising from the same distribution as that of δ. It is, however, true for multinormal distributions.

[27] This factorisation can only be made under certain conditions. Among other things, it is essential for the number T of observations to exceed the number n of risk factors. Refer to Appendix 1 for further details on this method.

so that, by difference with:

$$p(0) = f(X_1(0), X_2(0), \ldots, X_n(0)).$$

the variation in value can be estimated: $\Delta_p{}^{(t)} = p^{(t)}(1) - p(0) \quad (t = 1, \ldots, M)$.

Note

It is possible to simplify the approach somewhat for some specific risk factors for which a stochastic process of evolution is difficult to obtain. Thus, for the volatility of an option (vega risk), one can for different values of this parameter σ_R apply the methodology as presented above and then group together all the results of the simulations carried out for these values.

7.3.2.3 *Portfolio case*

Let us deal finally with the general case in which one wishes to determine the *VaR* for a portfolio consisting of N assets in respective numbers[28] $n_1, \ldots, n_N$, the value of each of these assets expressed on the basis of several different risk factors $X_1, X_2, \ldots, X_N$. The value p_P of this portfolio is expressed according to the p_j values ($j = 1, \ldots, N$) for the various assets through the relation $p_P = \sum_{j=1}^{N} n_j p_j$.

Even where *VaR* is calculated on the basis of a normal distribution hypotheses using the expectation and standard deviation (and the Monte Carlo method, if it uses theoretical models, does not rely on this distributional hypothesis), we then have to use a variance-covariance matrix again (that for all the couples of securities in the portfolio[29]), as it has been seen in Section 3.1.1 that:

$$\text{var}(\Delta p_P) = \sum_{i=1}^{N} \sum_{j=1}^{N} n_i n_j \text{cov}(\Delta p_i, \Delta p_j).$$

It is preferable here to determine the distribution of the portfolio loss directly on the basis of the effect of variations in the various risk factors on the value of the portfolio itself.

7.3.2.4 *Synthesis*

This approach consists of the following stages:

1. A group of valuation models is chosen for the various risk factors or the assets in the portfolio (choice to be validated by suitable statistical tests). This may refer to normal or log-normal laws or more complex models for certain derived products; or more generally, it may relate to any distribution that has been adjusted on the basis of historical observations. One can also consider the relations that express the way in which the prices of various assets behave according to common risk factors, like a general market index (for Sharpe's simple index model for equities), sectorial indices (for multiple-index models), interest rates or exchange rates.

---

[28] Remember (see Section 3.1.1) that in cases where prices are replaced by returns, the numbers n_j of assets in the portfolio must be replaced by the proportions that correspond to the respective stock-exchange capitalisations for the various securities.

[29] This variance-covariance matrix is much larger (it may concern hundreds of different assets) than the matrix mentioned in the previous paragraph relating to just a few explicative risk factors for an isolated asset.

2. On the basis of historical periods for present equities and risk factors, the following are estimated:
   - the distribution of the various risk factors, as well as the parameters associated with them, the expectations and the variance and covariance matrix.
   - the parameters for the relations[30] that link the prices of the assets with the risk factors. Generally, these are estimations made using regressive techniques.
3. For the full range of risk factors, the combined use of probability models obtained in (1) and the distribution parameters determined in (2) allows construction, using the Monte Carlo method, of a large number M (5000–10 000) of pseudo-random samples extracted from each of the risk factor variance distributions in question.

$$\Delta_k^{(t)} \qquad k = 1, \ldots, n \qquad t = 1, \ldots, M.$$

The future values of the risk factors are then obtained from the values currently observed: $X_1(0), \ldots, X_n(0)$:

$$X_k^{(t)}(1) = X_k(0) \cdot (1 + \Delta_k^{(t)}) \qquad k = 1, \ldots, n \qquad t = 1, \ldots, M.$$

Here we have as many evaluation scenarios as there are prices. It is obvious that the simulations must be carried out on the basis of parameters that each describe a risk factor individually, but also on the basis of correlations that link them to each other (Choleski factorisation).

4. The results of these simulations are then introduced into the relations for the assets, according to the common risk factors:

$$p_j = f_j(X_1, X_2, \ldots, X_n) \qquad j = 1, \ldots, N$$

These relations may be very simple (such as risk factor equivalent to asset) or much more complex (such as in the case of optional assets). They allow the future price distributions to be simulated for the various assets:

$$p_j^{(t)} = f_j(X_1^{(t)}(1), X_2^{(t)}(1), \ldots, X_n^{(t)}(1)) \qquad j = 1, \ldots, N \qquad t = 1, \ldots, M$$

The calculation of the portfolio value according to the value of its components for each of the M simulations

$$p_P^{(t)}(1) = \sum_{j=1}^{N} n_j p_j^{(t)}(1) \qquad t = 1, \ldots, M$$

assumes that the distributions of the various prices can simply be added together to give the portfolio price distribution. It is known, however, that this is only possible if the joint price distribution is multi-normal. Because the Monte Carlo method aims to avoid this demanding hypothesis, the components of the portfolio can thus be aggregated by a new simulation, taking account this time of the correlation structure between the various assets in the portfolio. This is much more laborious.

---

[30] These are often stochastic processes.

5. The confrontation with the current value of the portfolio, $p_P(0) = \sum_{j=1}^{N} n_j p_j(0)$, where:

$$p_j(0) = f_j(X_1(0), X_2(0), \ldots, X_n(0)) \quad j = 1, \ldots, N$$

allows the distribution of the value variance in the portfolio to be estimated:

$$\Delta p^{(t)} = p_P^{(t)}(1) - p_P(0) \qquad t = 1, \ldots, M$$

After the M results have been ordered and grouped where necessary, the value of the *VaR* parameter can be easily deduced.

Note 1

Another method consists of using the results of the simulations to construct not the distribution of the portfolio variation in value as above, but the expectation and variance of that variation. The *VaR* is then calculated more simply, using the formula $VaR_q = E(\Delta p_t) - z_q \cdot \sigma(\Delta p_t)$. This, alongside the calculation facilities, presents the very disadvantage of the normality hypothesis that the Monte Carlo method attempts to avoid.

Note 2

It may appear surprising to have to carry out so many simulations (5000 to 10 000), when the statistical limit theorems (law of large numbers, central limit theorem, etc.) are generally applicable to a very much smaller number of observations. It must be borne in mind that what we are interested in here is not a 'globalising' notion of a law of probability, such as expectation or variance for example, but an 'extreme' notion, which corresponds to a phenomenon that occurs only rarely. Much more significant numbers are therefore necessary, in the same way that estimation of a proportion p per interval of confidence with a fixed relative error will require many more observations to estimate that $p = 0.01$ than $p = 0.4$.[31]

Note 3

Just like the Monte Carlo simulation, *stress testing*, which is covered in Section 2.1.2, is based on the scenario concept. In this method, however, the distribution parameters are not estimated on the basis of historical periods and no future prices are generated through simulation. We simply envisage the specific potential developments[32] of the prices and the portfolio value is reassessed in this context.

This method of working will of course help to understand phenomena not found in the historical periods (through a wide experience of financial markets, for example). However, it does not allow the distribution of the loss to be determined, as the scenarios are chosen on one hand and the correlation structure is practically ignored by definition on the other hand. We are therefore looking at a useful (maybe even a necessary) complement rather than a competing or substitute method.

---

[31] We will deal with the estimation of these extreme values in greater detail in Section 7.4.2.
[32] The catastrophe scenarios are part of these developments.

7.4 HISTORICAL SIMULATION

The third method of estimating *VaR* is based on the hypothesis of stationarity: the joint (theoretical and unknown) distribution of the price variations for the different risk factors for the horizon for which the *VaR* is being estimated is properly estimated by observing the variations in these prices during the available history. In this case, the quality of the parameter estimation (expectations, variances, covariances) for this distribution is also guaranteed.[33]

The method of estimating *VaR* by historical simulation is the method used by Chase Manhattan[34] with the Charisma™ and Risk$™ systems.

7.4.1 Basic methodology

The principle applied is that of estimating the distribution of the variations of risk factors through the distribution observed on the basis of historical periods. Assimilating the frequency of variations in value less than the *VaR* parameter value on one hand and the corresponding probability on the other hand is a direct consequence of the *law of large numbers*.

7.4.1.1 Risk factor case

Let us deal first of all with the very simple case where the *VaR* required to be determined is the risk factor X itself (the rate for an equity, for example). It is therefore assumed that the distribution of the random variable

$$\Delta = \frac{X(1) - X(0)}{X(0)}$$

is properly represented by the observations:

$$\Delta(t) = \frac{X(t) - X(t - 1)}{X(t - 1)} \qquad t = -T + 1, \ldots, -1, 0$$

The relation $X(1) - X(0) = \Delta \cdot X(0)$ allows the future value of the risk factor to be established through:

$$X^{(t)}(1) = X(0) + \Delta(t) \cdot X(0) \qquad t = -T + 1, \ldots, -1, 0$$

The distribution of the value variation is therefore assessed as:

$$\Delta p^{(t)} = X^{(t)}(1) - X(0) = \Delta(t) \cdot X(0) \qquad t = -T + 1, \ldots, -1, 0$$

7.4.1.2 Isolated asset case

Let us now consider a case in which the asset for which the *VaR* is required to be determined depends on a number of risk factors $X_1, X_2, \ldots, X_n$. The value of this asset is therefore expressed by a relation of the type $p = f(X_1, X_2, \ldots, X_n)$.

---

[33] We deal very briefly in Section 7.4.2 with a methodology that can be applied in cases of non-stationariness (due for example to the presence of aberrant observations). It is based on historical observations but gives models of the distribution tails.

[34] Chase Manhattan Bank NA., *Value at Risk: its Measurement and Uses*, Chase Manhattan Bank, n/d. Chase Manhattan Bank NA., *The Management of Financial Price Risk*, Chase Manhattan Bank NA., 1996. Stambaugh F., *Value at Risk*, S.Ed., 1996.

We have observations available for these risk factors, for which the relative variations can be determined:

$$\Delta_k(t) = \frac{X_k(t) - X_k(t-1)}{X_k(t-1)} \qquad k = 1, \ldots, n \qquad t = -T+1, \ldots, -1, 0$$

On the basis of the values currently observed $X_1(0), \ldots, X_n(0)$ for the various risk factors, the distribution of the future values is estimated by:

$$X_k^{(t)}(1) = X_k(0) \cdot (1 + \Delta_k(t)) \qquad k = 1, \ldots, n \qquad t = -T+1, \ldots, -1, 0$$

From that, the estimation of the future distribution price of the asset in question can be deduced easily:

$$p^{(t)}(1) = f(X_1^{(t)}(1), X_2^{(t)}(1), \ldots, X_n^{(t)}(1)) \qquad t = -T+1, \ldots, -1, 0$$

Thus, by difference from:

$$p(0) = f(X_1(0), X_2(0), \ldots, X_n(0))$$

The distribution of the variation of value is estimated as:

$$\Delta p^{(t)} = p^{(t)}(1) - p(0) \qquad t = -T+1, \ldots, -1, 0$$

7.4.1.3 Portfolio case

Here, the reasoning is very similar to that followed in the Monte Carlo simulation. To determine the *VaR* of a portfolio consisting of N assets in respective numbers[35] $n_1, \ldots, n_N$, the value of each asset is expressed on the basis of a number of risk factors $X_1, X_2, \ldots, X_n$. The value p_P of the portfolio is expressed according to p_j $(j = 1, \ldots, N)$ for the various assets by:

$$p_P = \sum_{j=1}^{N} n_j p_j$$

Even in cases where *VaR* is calculated on the basis of a normal distribution by the $VaR_q = E(\Delta p_t) - z_q \cdot \sigma(\Delta p_t)$ (and the historical simulation method is independent of this distributional hypothesis), a problem is encountered in the case of a portfolio as the variance of value within that portfolio depends on the covariances between the prices of the various assets:

$$\text{var}(\Delta p_P) = \sum_{i=1}^{N} \sum_{j=1}^{N} n_i n_j \text{cov}(\Delta p_i, \Delta p_j)$$

Therefore, we are also directly determining the distribution of the variation of value for the portfolio on the basis of the effect exerted by the variations in the various risk factors

---

[35] Remember (see Section 3.4) that in cases where prices are replaced by returns, the numbers n_j of assets in the portfolio must be replaced by the proportions that correspond to the respective stock-exchange capitalisations for the various securities.

on the value of the portfolio itself. The impact will of course be determined in the same
way as just shown for an isolated asset.

7.4.1.4 Synthesis

The different stages can therefore be isolated as follows.

1. The various risk factors X_1, X_2, ..., X_n are identified, determining the value of the
   various assets in the portfolio: indices, security rates, interest rates, exchange rates etc.
2. The methodology shown above is applied to each risk factor. Therefore, on the basis
   of observations of the various risk factors for the times $-T$, $-T+1$, ..., -1, 0, the
   relative variations or the corresponding $\Delta_k(t)$ are deduced:

$$\Delta_k(t) = \frac{X_k(t) - X_k(t-1)}{X_k(t-1)} \qquad k = 1, \ldots, n \quad t = -T+1, \ldots, -1, 0$$

The current observations $X_1(0), \ldots, X_n(0)$ for these risk factors allow the distribution
of the future values to be obtained:

$$X_k^{(t)}(1) = X_k(0) \cdot (1 + \Delta_k(t)) \qquad k = 1, \ldots, n \quad t = -T+1, \ldots, -1, 0$$

3. The prices of the various assets are expressed on the basis of risk factors through the
   relations:
$$p_j = f_j(X_1, X_2, \ldots, X_n) \qquad j = 1, \ldots, N$$

These relations may be very simple (such as risk factor equivalent to asset) or much
more complex (for example, Black and Scholes formula for valuing an option on the
basis of risk factors as 'underlying price' and 'risk-free security return'). They allow
the distributions of the future prices of the various assets to be determined:

$$p_j^{(t)}(1) = f_j(X_1^{(t)}(1), X_2^{(t)}(1), \ldots, X_n^{(t)}(1)) \quad j = 1, \ldots, N \quad t = -T+1, \ldots, -1, 0$$

The future value distribution of the portfolio can therefore be determined:

$$p_P^{(t)}(1) = \sum_{j=1}^{N} n_j p_j^{(t)}(1)$$

4. In addition, we have the current value of the portfolio

$$p_P(0) = \sum_{j=1}^{N} n_j p_j(0)$$

where:
$$p_j(0) = f_j(X_1(0), X_2(0), \ldots, X_n(0)) \qquad j = 1, \ldots, N$$

From there, the variation in value of the portfolio can be easily deduced:

$$\Delta p^{(t)} = p_P^{(t)}(1) - p_P(0) \qquad t = -T+1, \ldots, -1, 0$$

Note 1

Instead of determining the *VaR* directly from the estimated distribution of the loss, this loss can be used to calculate the expectation and variance for the variable and thus to evaluate the *VaR* through the relation

$$VaR_q = E(\Delta p_t) - z_q \cdot \sigma(\Delta p_t)$$

We would not of course recommend this method, which is based on the normality hypothesis, as the historical simulation method (in the same way as the Monte Carlo simulation method) is independent of this hypothesis.

Note 2

It should be noted that in the tth estimation of the future value of the portfolio, we use the estimations of the future values of the various assets relative to period t, which are themselves evaluated on the basis of the differences $\Delta_k(t)$ measured at that time. The *VaR* for the portfolio is therefore estimated according to the variations in the portfolio's value during the period of observation, and not determined for each asset on the basis of the least favourable combination of risk factors followed by aggregation of the least favourable combination of *VaR* parameters. This method of working leads to the consideration that the unfavourable variations in the assets making up the portfolio are all produced at the same time; this is a 'catastrophe scenario' that does not take account of the correlation between the various assets and therefore of the effects of diversification. The method shown above takes this structure into consideration by using concomitant observations of risk factors and aggregations of concomitant values for the constituent assets.

Note 3

The methodology as presented above uses the valuation models $p_j = f_j(X_1, X_2, \ldots, X_n)$ $j = 1, \ldots, N$ to estimate the future value of the various prices (and thus the future value of the portfolio price) on the basis of estimation of the future value of the elementary risk factors $X_1, X_2, \ldots, X_n$. Another method is to use the observations of these elementary risk factors to put together the database for the price p_j for the various assets using these valuation models (in practice, by using suitable pricing software). These assets then become risk factors, their future value being estimated using the method presented, and the portfolio can be re-evaluated on the basis of these estimations.

Because for an efficient market the prices reflect all the information available on that market, this method of working is economically coherent; the individual items of information supply the valuation models (that is, they make up the pricer input) and the database used by the *VaR* estimation technique is that of the price deduced therefrom. This technique is all the more homogeneous as the concept of price is its common denominator. This approach is therefore preferable and easier to implement; it will be used in the practical applications in Chapter 8.

Finally, we would point out that this kind of adaptation can only be partly envisaged for the Monte Carlo simulation. In this method, in fact, the stochastic processes used for the simulations are essentially valid to represent developments in elementary risks. Thus, for an option price, it is the underlying price values that will be simulated; the price of the option is thus reconstituted by a valuation model such as Black and Scholes. Of course this means that the Monte Carlo method will have to have access to very large databases from the beginning (all the elementary risk factors, multiplied by the number of possible maturity dates) and to carry out many different simulations for all the components.

Note 4

In its Risk$™ system, Chase Manhattan considers a *VaR* calculation horizon of one day and daily observations relating to a historical period of $T = 100$ days.

Example

Let us consider a portfolio[36] consisting of three equities with respective numbers: $n_1 = 3$, $n_2 = 3$ and $n_3 = 5$, for which the rates have been observed at 11 separate times (from -10 to 0, we therefore have $T = 10$ see Table 7.1).

The relative variations $\Delta_k(t)$ are calculated for $t = -9, \ldots, 0$:

$$\Delta_1(-9) = \frac{13\,150 - 12\,800}{12\,800} = 0.0273$$

The values for the next period can be deduced therefrom, on the basis of the observations for $t = 0$ (see Table 7.2):

$$X_1^{(-9)}(1) = 14\,800 \times (1 + 0.0273) = 15\,204.7$$

The value of the portfolio is then determined at $t = 0$:

$$p_P(0) = 3 \times 14\,800 + 2 \times 25\,825 + 5 \times 1530 = 1\,03\,700$$

Table 7.1 Historical rates

t	$C_1(t)$	$C_2(t)$	$C_3(t)$
-10	12 800	23 475	1238
-9	13 150	23 150	1236
-8	12 150	21 875	1168
-7	11 100	21 400	1234
-6	11 725	22 100	1310
-5	11 950	21 650	1262
-4	12 025	22 650	1242
-3	12 325	21 000	1170
-2	13 675	23 625	1260
-1	14 300	24 150	1342
0	14 800	25 825	1530

[36] A detailed, real-life application of this historical simulation technique for different types of financial products is shown in Chapter 8.

Table 7.2   Historical returns and portfolio estimations

	Variations			Estimations		
t	$\Delta_1(t)$	$\Delta_2(t)$	$\Delta_3(t)$	$X_1^{(t)}(1)$	$X_2^{(t)}(1)$	$X_3^{(t)}(1)$
−9	0.0273	−0.0138	−0.0016	15 204.7	25 467.5	1527.5
−8	−0.0760	−0.0551	−0.0550	13 674.5	24 402.7	1445.8
−7	−0.0864	−0.0217	0.0565	13 521.0	25 264.2	1616.5
−6	0.0563	0.0327	0.0616	15 633.3	26 669.7	1624.2
−5	0.0192	−0.0204	−0.0366	15 084.0	25 299.2	1473.9
−4	0.0063	0.0462	−0.0158	14 892.9	27 017.8	1505.8
−3	0.0249	−0.0728	−0.0580	15 169.2	23 943.7	1441.3
−2	0.1095	0.1250	0.0769	16 421.1	29 053.1	1647.7
−1	0.0457	0.0222	0.0651	15 467.4	26 398.9	1629.6
0	0.0350	0.0694	0.1401	15 317.5	27 616.2	1744.3

The future value estimations for the portfolio are:

$$p_P^{(-9)}(1) = 3 \times 15\,204.7 + 2 \times 25\,467.5 + 5 \times 1527.5 = 104\,186.6$$

The variations in value are (see Table 7.3):

$$\Delta p^{(-9)} = 104 \times 186.6 - 103.700 = 486.6$$

Classifying the value variations in decreasing order (from the lowest −6, 642.0 to the highest 11,908.0) (in Table 7.4 – classification) shows the estimated distribution of the future value variation, which can be represented by the distribution function shown in Figure 7.5.

It is readily apparent from here that $VaR_{0.95} = -6624.0$. Note that if the *VaR* is calculated separately for three equities from the same historical periods, we find the following shown in Table 7.5.

These values should not be aggregated with the weight n_j, as this would give $VaR = -3 \times 1279.0 - 2 \times 1881.3 - 5 \times 88.7 = -8611.9$ for the portfolio, a value that does not take account of the correlation structure between the structures and thus overestimates the loss suffered.

Table 7.3   Future values and losses incurred

t	$p_P^{(t)}(1)$	$\Delta p^{(t)}$
−9	104 186.6	486.6
−8	97 058.0	−6642.0
−7	99 173.7	−4526.3
−6	108 360.6	4660.6
−5	103 220.0	−480.0
−4	106 243.1	2543.1
−3	100 601.6	−3098.4
−2	115 608.0	11 908.0
−1	107 374.9	3674.9
0	109 906.5	6206.5

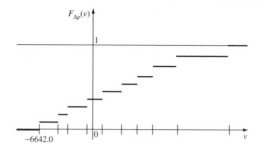

Figure 7.5 Estimated distribution of value variation

Table 7.4 Classification

−6642.0
−4526.3
−3098.4
−480.0
486.6
2543.1
3674.9
4660.6
6206.5
11908.0

Table 7.5 *VaR* per asset

(1)	(2)	(3)
−1279.0	−1881.3	−88.7

7.4.2 The contribution of extreme value theory

One criticism that can be made of the historical simulation method (see Section 7.5) is that a small number of outliers, whether these are true exceptional observations or whether they are caused by errors in measurement or processing etc., will heavily influence the value of the *VaR* for a long period (equal to the duration of the historical periods). Extreme value theory[37] can assist in resolving this problem.

7.4.2.1 Extreme value theorem

The *extreme value theorem* states[38] that as a series of independent and identically distributed random variables X_1, X_2, ..., X_n, for which two series of coefficients $\alpha_n > 0$

---

[37] Appendix 4 sets out the theoretical bases for this method in brief.
[38] Gnedenko B. V., On the limit distribution for the maximum term in a random series, *Annals of Mathematics*, Vol. 44, 1943, pp. 423–53.
Galambos J., *Advanced Probability Theory*, M. Dekker, 1988, Section 6.5.
Jenkinson A. F., The frequency distribution of the annual maximum (or minimum) value of meteorological elements, *Quarterly Journal of the Royal Meteorology Society*, Vol 87, 1955, pp. 145–58.

and β_n ($n = 1, 2, \ldots$) such as the limit (for $n \to \infty$) for the random variable

$$Y_n = \frac{\max(X_1, \ldots, X_n) - \beta_n}{\alpha_n}$$

is not degenerated, this variable will allow a law of probability that depends on a real parameter τ and defined by the distribution function:

$$F_Y(y) = \begin{cases} 0 & \text{if } y \leq \frac{1}{\tau} \text{ when } \tau < 0 \\ \exp\left[-(1 - \tau y)^{\frac{1}{\tau}}\right] & \text{if } \begin{cases} y > \frac{1}{\tau} \text{ when } \tau < 0 \\ y \text{ real when } \tau = 0 \\ y < \frac{1}{\tau} \text{ when } \tau > 0 \end{cases} \\ 1 & \text{if } y \geq \frac{1}{\tau} \text{ when } \tau > 0 \end{cases}$$

This is independently of the common distribution of the X_i totals.[39] The probability law involved is the *generalised Pareto distribution*.

The numbers α_n, β_n and τ are interpreted respectively as a dispersion parameter, a location parameter and a *tail parameter* (see Figure 7.6). Thus, $\tau < 0$ corresponds to X_i values with a fat tail distribution (decreasing less than exponential), $\tau = 0$ has a thin tail distribution (exponential decrease) and $\tau > 0$ has a zero tail distribution (bounded support).

7.4.2.2 Estimation of parameters by regression

The methods[40] that allow the α_n, β_n and τ parameters to be estimated by regression use the fact that this random variable Y_n (or more precisely, its distribution) can in practice be estimated by sampling on a historical basis: N periods each of a duration of n will supply N values for the loss variable in question.

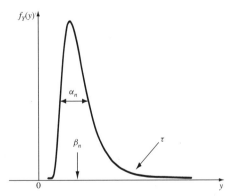

Figure 7.6   Distribution of extremes

---

[39] When $\tau = 0$, $(1 - \tau y)^{1/\tau}$ is interpreted as being equal to its limit e^{-y}.

[40] Gumbel F. J., *Statistics of Extremes*, Columbia University Press, 1958.

Longin F. M., Extreme value theory: presentation and first applications in finance, *Journal de la Société Statistique de Paris*, Vol. 136, 1995, pp. 77–97.

Longin F. M., The asymptotic distribution of extreme stock market returns, *Journal of Business*, No. 69, 1996, pp. 383–408.

Longin F. M., From value at risk to stress testing: the extreme value approach, *Journal of Banking and Finance*, No. 24, 2000, pp. 1097–130.

We express the successive observations of the variation in value variable as x_1, x_2, ..., x_{Nn}, and the extreme value observed for the ith 'section' of observations as $\hat{y}_{i,n}$ ($i = 1, \ldots, N$).

$$\hat{y}_{1,n} = \max(x_1, \ldots, x_n)$$
$$\hat{y}_{2,n} = \max(x_{n+1}, \ldots, x_{2n})$$
$$\ldots\ldots$$
$$\hat{y}_{N,n} = \max(x_{(N-1)n+1}, \ldots, x_{Nn})$$

Let us arrange these observations in order of increasing magnitude, expressing the values thus arranged y_i' ($i = 1, \ldots, N$):

$$y_1' \leq y_2' \leq \cdots \leq y_N'$$

It is therefore possible to demonstrate that if the extremes observed are in fact a representative sample of the law of probability given by the extreme value theorem, we have

$$F_Y\left(\frac{y_i' - \beta_n}{\alpha_n}\right) = \frac{i}{N+1} + u_i \quad i = 1, \ldots, N$$

where the u_i values correspond to a normal zero-expectation law. When this relation is transformed by taking the iterated logarithm (logarithm of logarithm) for the two expressions, we obtain:

$$-\ln\left[-\ln\left(\frac{i}{N+1}\right)\right] = -\ln\left[-\ln\left(F_Y\left(\frac{y_i' - \beta_n}{\alpha_n}\right)\right)\right] + \varepsilon_i$$

$$= -\ln\left[-\ln\left[\exp\left[-\left(1 - \tau\frac{y_i' - \beta_n}{\alpha_n}\right)^{\frac{1}{\tau}}\right]\right]\right] + \varepsilon_i$$

$$= -\ln\left[\left(1 - \tau\frac{y_i' - \beta_n}{\alpha_n}\right)^{\frac{1}{\tau}}\right] + \varepsilon_i$$

$$= \frac{1}{\tau}\{\ln\alpha_n - \ln[\alpha_n - \tau(y_i' - \beta_n)]\} + \varepsilon_i$$

This relation constitutes a nonlinear regressive equation for the three parameters α_n, β_n and τ.

Note that when we are dealing with a matter of distribution of extremes with a thin tail (τ parameter not significantly different from 0), we have: $F_Y(y) = \exp[-\exp(-y)]$, and another regressive relationship has to be used:

$$-\ln\left[-\ln\left(\frac{i}{N+1}\right)\right] = -\ln\left[-\ln\left(F_Y\left(\frac{y_i' - \beta_n}{\alpha_n}\right)\right)\right] + \varepsilon_i$$

$$= -\ln\left[-\ln\left[\exp\left[-\exp\left(-\frac{y_i' - \beta_n}{\alpha_n}\right)\right]\right]\right] + \varepsilon_i$$

$$= \frac{y_i' - \beta_n}{\alpha_n} + \varepsilon_i$$

7.4.2.3   Estimating parameters using the semi-parametric method

As well as the technique for estimating the α_n, β_n and τ parameters, there are non-parametric methods,[41] specifically indicated for estimating the tail parameter τ. They are, however, time consuming in terms of calculation, as an intermediate parameter has to be estimated using a Monte Carlo-type method. We show the main aspects here.

The ith observation is termed $x_{(i)}$ after the observations are arranged in increasing order: $x_{(1)} \leq \ldots \leq x_{(n)}$. The first stage consists of setting a limit M so that only the M highest observations from the sample (of size n) will be of interest in shaping the tail distribution. It can be shown[42] that an estimator (as termed by Hill) for the tail parameter is given by:

$$\hat{\tau} = \frac{1}{M} \sum_{k=1}^{M} \ln x_{(n-k+1)} - \ln x_{(n-M)}$$

The choice of M is not easy to make, as the quality of Hill's estimator is quite sensitive to the choice of this threshold. If this threshold is fixed too low, the distribution tail will be too rich and the estimator will be biased downwards; if it is fixed too high, there will only be a small number of observations to use for making the estimation. The optimal choice of M can be made using a graphic method[43] or the bootstrap method[44], which we will not be developing here.

An estimator proposed by Danielsson and De Vries for the limit distribution function is given by:

$$\hat{F}_Y(y) = 1 - \frac{M}{n} \left(\frac{x_{(n-M)}}{y} \right)^{\frac{1}{\hat{\tau}}}$$

This relation is variable for $y \geq x_{(n-M)}$ only.

7.4.2.4   Calculation of VaR

Once the parameters have been estimated, the *VaR* parameter can then be determined. We explain the procedure to be followed when the tail model is estimated using the semi-parametric method,[45] presenting a case of one risk factor only. Of course we will invert the process to some extent, given that it is the left extremity of the distribution that has to be used.

The future value of the risk is estimated in exactly the same way as for the historical simulation:

$$X^{(t)}(1) = X(0) + \Delta(t) \cdot X(0) \qquad t = -T+1, \ldots, -1, 0$$

[41] Beirland J., Teugels J. L. and Vynckier P., *Practical Analysis of Extreme Values*, Leuven University Press, 1996.

[42] Hill B. M., A simple general approach to inference about the tail of a distribution, *Annals of Statistics*, Vol. 46, 1975, pp. 1163–73. Pickands J., Statistical inference using extreme order statistics, Vol. 45, 1975, pp. 119–31.

[43] McNeil A. J., *Estimating the tails of loss severity distributions using extreme value theory*, Mimeo, ETH Zentrum Zurich. 1996.

[44] Danielsson J. and De Vries C., *Tail index and quantile estimation with very high frequency data*, Mimeo, Iceland University and Tinbergen Institute Rotterdam, 1997.

Danielsson J. and De Vries C., Tail index and quantile estimation with very high frequency data, *Journal of Empirical Finance*, No. 4, 1997, pp. 241–57.

[45] Danielsson J. and De Vries C., *Value at Risk and Extreme Returns*, LSE Financial Markets Group Discussion Paper 273, London School of Economics, 1997.

Embrechts P., Klüppelberg C. and Mikosch T., *Modelling Extreme Events for Insurance and Finance*, Springer Verlag, 1999. Reiss R. D. and Thomas M., *Statistical Analysis of Extreme Values*, Birkhauser Verlag, 2001.

The choice of M is made using one of the methods mentioned above, and the tail parameter is estimated by:

$$\hat{\tau} = \frac{1}{M} \sum_{k=1}^{M} \ln x_{(k)} - \ln x_{(M+1)}$$

The adjustment for the left tail of the distribution is made by

$$\hat{F}_Y(y) = \frac{M}{n} \left(\frac{x_{(M+1)}}{y} \right)^{\frac{1}{\hat{\tau}}}$$

This relation is valid for $y \geq x_{(M+1)}$ only.

The distribution tail is simulated[46] by taking a number of values at random from the re-evaluated distribution of the $X^{(t)}(1)$ values and by replacing each x value lower than $x_{(M+1)}$ by the corresponding value obtained from the distribution of the extremes, that is, for the level of probability p relative to x, through the $\hat{x}_p$ solution of the equation

$$p = \frac{M}{n} \left(\frac{x_{(M+1)}}{\hat{x}_p} \right)^{\frac{1}{\hat{\tau}}}$$

In other words:

$$\hat{x}_p = x_{(M+1)} \left(\frac{M}{np} \right)^{\tau}.$$

Note

Extreme value theory, which allows the adverse effects of one or more outliers to be avoided, has a serious shortcoming despite its impressive appearance. The historical period that has to be used must have a very long duration, regardless of the estimation method used. In fact:

- In the method based on nonlinear regression, Nn observations must be lodged in which the duration n on which an extreme value is measured must be relatively long. The extreme value theorem is an asymptotic theorem in which the number N of durations must be large if one wishes to work with a sample distribution that is representative of the actual distribution of the extremes.
- In the semi-parametric method, a large number of observations are abandoned as soon as the estimation process starts.

7.5 ADVANTAGES AND DRAWBACKS

We now move on to review the various advantages and drawbacks of each *VaR* estimation technique. To make things simpler, we will use the abbreviations shown in Figure 7.2: VC for the estimated variance–covariance matrix method, MC for the Monte Carlo simulation and HS for historical simulation.

---

[46] This operation can also be carried out by generating a uniform random variable in the interval [0; 1], taking the reciprocal for the observed distribution of $X^{(t)}(1)$ and replacing the observed values lower than $x_{(M+1)}$ by the value given by the extremes distribution.

7.5.1 The theoretical viewpoint

7.5.1.1 Hypotheses and limitations

(1) Let us envisage first of all the presence or absence of a distributional hypothesis and its likely impact on the method.

MC and HS do not formulate any distributional hypothesis. Only VC assumes that variations in price are distributed according to a normal law.[47] Here, this hypothesis is essential:

- because of the technique used to split the assets into cashflows: only multinormal distribution is such that the sum of the variables, even when correlated, is still distributed according to such a law;
- because the information supplied by RiskMetrics™ includes the $-z_q\sigma_k$ values ($k = 1, \ldots, n$) of the *VaR** parameter for each risk factor, and $z_q = 1.645$, that is, the normal distribution quantile for $q = 0.95$.

This hypothesis has serious consequences for certain assets such as options, as the returns are highly skewed and the method can no longer be applied. It is for this reason that RiskMetrics™ introduced a method based on the quantile concept for this type of asset, similar to MC and VC.

For simpler assets such as equities, it has been demonstrated that the variations in price are distributed according to a leptokurtic law (more pointed than the normal close to the expectation, with thicker tails and less probable intermediate values). The normality hypothesis asserts that the *VaR* value is underestimated for such leptokurtic distributions, because of the greater probability associated with the extreme values.

This phenomenon has already been observed for the Student distributions (see Section 6.2.2). It can also be verified for specific cases.

Example

Consider the two distributions in Figure 6.2 (Section 6.1.2), in which the triangular, defined by

$$f_1(x) = \frac{\sqrt{3} - |x|}{3} \qquad x \in \left[-\sqrt{3}; \sqrt{3}\right]$$

has thicker tails than the rectangular for which

$$f_2(x) = \frac{\sqrt{6}}{6} \qquad x \in \left[-\frac{\sqrt{6}}{2}; \frac{\sqrt{6}}{2}\right]$$

Table 7.6 shows a comparison of two distributions.

The phenomenon of underestimation of risk for leptokurtic distributions is shown by the fact that:

$$VaR_q(\text{triangular}) = \sqrt{6(1-q)} - \sqrt{3}$$

$$VaR_q(\text{rectangular}) = \sqrt{6(1-q)} - \frac{\sqrt{6}}{2} > VaR_q(\text{triangular})$$

---

[47] In any case, it formulates the conditional normality hypothesis (normality with changes in variation over time).

Table 7.6   Comparison of two distributions

	Triangular	Rectangular
μ	0	0
σ^2	0.5	0.5
γ_1	0	0
γ_2	-0.6	-1.2

In addition, numerical analyses carried out by F. M. Longin have clearly shown the underestimation of the *VaR* for leptokurtic distributions under normality hypothesis. They have also shown that the underestimation increases as q moves closer to the unit; in other words, we have an interest in extreme risks. Thus, for a market portfolio represented by an index, he calculated that:

$$VaR_{0.5}(\text{HS}) = 1.6 \; VaR_{0.5}(\text{VC})$$

$$VaR_{0.75}(\text{HS}) = 2.1 \; VaR_{0.75}(\text{VC})$$

$$VaR_{0.95}(\text{HS}) = 3.5 \; VaR_{0.95}(\text{VC})$$

$$VaR_{0.99}(\text{HS}) = 5.9 \; VaR_{0.99}(\text{VC})$$

This problem can be solved in VC by the consideration, in the evolution model for the variable return $R_{jt} = \mu_j + \sigma_t \varepsilon_{jt}$, for a residual distributed not normally but in accordance with a generalised law of errors smoother than the normal law.

In the MC and HS methods, the normality hypothesis is not formulated. In MC, however, if the portfolio is not re-evaluated by a new simulation, the hypothesis will be required but only for this section of the method.

(2) The VC method, unlike MC and HS, relies explicitly on the hypothesis of asset price linearity according to the risk factors. This hypothesis forms the basis for the principle of splitting assets into cashflows. It is, however, flawed for certain groups of assets, such as options: the linear link between the option price and the underlying equity price assumes that Δ is the only non-zero sensitivity parameter.

For this reason, RiskMetrics™ has abandoned the VC methodology and deals with this type of product by calling on Taylor's development. Another estimation technique, namely MC, is sometimes indicated for dealing with this group of assets.

(3) The hypothesis of stationarity can take two forms. In its more exacting form, it suggests that joint (theoretical and unknown) distribution of price variations in different risk factors, for the *VaR* calculation horizon, is well estimated in the observations of variations in these prices during the historical period available. The hypothesis of stationarity is formulated thus for the HS method. However, if it is not verified because of the presence of a trend in the observed data, it is easy to take account of the trend for estimating the future value of the portfolio.

A 'softer' form is recommended for applying the VC method, as this method no longer relates to the complete distribution; the statistical parameters measured on the observed distribution of the price (or return) variances are good estimations of these same (unknown) parameters for the horizon for which the *VaR* is being estimated. The VC method does, however, have the drawback of being unable to depart from this hypothesis if a trend is present in the data.

(4) In the presentation of the three estimation methods, it is assumed that the *VaR* calculation horizon was equal to the periodicity of the historical observations.[48] The usual use of *VaR* involves making this period equal to one day for the management of dealing room portfolios and 10 days according to prudential regulations,[49] although a longer period can be chosen when measuring the risk associated with stable products such as investment funds.

If, on the other hand, one wishes to consider a horizon (say one month) longer than the observation period (say one day), three methods may be applied:

- Estimating the *VaR* on the basis of monthly returns, even if the data are daily in nature. This leads to serious erosion of the accuracy of the initial observations.
- Using the formulae set out in the note in Section 7.1.2, which consist of multiplying the expectation loss and the loss variance respectively by the horizon (here, the number of working days in the month) and the square root of the horizon. This is of course only valid with a hypothesis of independence of daily variations and for methodologies that calculate the *VaR* on the basis of these two parameters only (case of normal distribution) such as VC. When HS cannot rely on the normality hypothesis, this method of working is incorrect[50] and the previous technique should be applied.
- For MC and for this method only, it is possible to generate not only a future price value but a path of prices for the calculation horizon.

We now explain this last case a little further, where, for example, the price evolution of an equity is represented by geometric Brownian motion (see Section 3.4.2):

$$S_{t+dt} - S_t = S_t \cdot (E_R \cdot dt + \sigma_R \cdot dw_t)$$

where the Wiener process (dw_t) obeys a law with a zero expectation and a variance equal to dt. If one considers a normal random variable ε with zero expectation and variance of 1, we can write:

$$S_{t+dt} - S_t = S_t \cdot (E_R \cdot dt + \sigma_R \cdot \varepsilon\sqrt{dt})$$

Simulation of a sequence of independent values for ε using the Monte Carlo method allows the variations $S_{t+dt} - S_t$ to be obtained, and therefore, on the basis of the last price observed S_0, allows the path of the equity's future price to be generated for a number of dates equal to the number of ε values simulated.[51]

7.5.1.2 Models used

(1) The valuation models play an important part in the VC and MC methods. In the case of VC, they are even associated with a conditional normality hypothesis. For MC, the

---

[48] The usual use of *VaR* involves making this period equal to one day. However, a longer period can be chosen when measuring the risk associated with stable products such as investment funds.

[49] This 10-day horizon may, however, appear somewhat unrealistic when the speed and volume of the deals conducted in a dealing room is seen.

[50] As is pointed out quite justifiably by Hendricks D., *Evaluation of value at risk models using historical data*, FRBNY Policy Review, 1996, pp. 39–69.

[51] The process that we have described for MC is also applicable, provided sufficient care is taken, for a one-day horizon, with this period broken down into a small number of subperiods.

search for a model is an essential (and difficult) part of the method; however, as there is a wide variety of models on offer, there is some guarantee as to the quality of results.

Conversely, the HS method is almost completely independent of these models; at the most, it uses them as a pricing tool for putting together databases for asset prices.

Here is one of the many advantages of this method, which have their source in the conceptual simplicity of the technique in question.

To sum up, the risk associated with the quality of the models used is:

- significant and untreatable for VC;
- significant but manageable for MC;
- virtually zero for HS.

(2) As VC and HS are based on a hypothesis of stationarity, the MC method is the only one to make intensive use of asset price development models over time (dynamic models). These models can improve the results of this method, provided the models are properly adapted to the data and correctly estimated.

7.5.1.3 Data

The data needed for supplying the VC methods in its RiskMetrics™ version are:

- the partial *VaR*s for each of the elementary risks;
- the correlation matrix for the various risk-factor couples.

Thus, for n risk factors, $n(n + 1)/2$ different data are necessary. If for example one is considering 450 elementary risk factors, 101 475 different data must be determined daily. Note that the RiskMetrics™ system makes all these data available to the user.

The MC method consumes considerably less data; in addition to the history of the various risk factors, a number of correlations (between risk factors that explain the same asset) are essential. However, if the portfolio is re-evaluated by a new simulation in order to avoid the normality hypothesis, the variance–covariance matrix for the assets in the portfolio will be essential.

Finally, the HS method is the least data consuming; as the historical periods already contain the structure of the correlation between risk factors and between assets, this last information does not need to be obtained from an outside body or calculated on the basis of historical periods.

7.5.2 The practical viewpoint

7.5.2.1 Data

Most of the data used in the VC method cannot be directly determined by an institution applying a *VaR* methodology. Although the institution knows the composition of its portfolio and pays close attention to changes in the prices of the assets making up the portfolio, it cannot know the levels of volatility and the correlations of basic risk factors, some of which can only be obtained by consulting numerous outside markets. The VC method can therefore only be effective if all these data are available in addition, which is the case if the RiskMetrics™ system is used. This will, however, place the business at a disadvantage as it is not provider of the data that it uses. It will not therefore be possible to analyse these data critically, or indeed make any corrections to them in case of error.

Conversely, the MC method and especially the HS method will use data from inside the business or data that can be easily calculated on the basis of historical data, with all the flexibility that this implies with respect to their processing, conditioning, updating and control.

7.5.2.2 Calculations

Of course, the three methods proposed require a few basic financial calculations, such as application of the principle of discounting. We now look at the way in which the three techniques differ from the point of view of calculations to be made.

The calculations required for the HS method are very limited and easily programmable on ordinary computer systems, as they are limited to arithmetical operations, sorting processes and the use of one or another valuation model when the price to be integrated into the historical process is determined.

The VC method makes greater use of the valuation models, since the principle of splitting assets and mapping cashflows is based on this group of models and since options are dealt with directly using the Black and Scholes model. Most notably, these valuation models will include regressions, as equity values are expressed on the basis of national stock-exchange indices. In addition, the matrix calculation is made when the portfolio is re-evaluated on the basis of the variance–covariance matrix.

In contrast to these techniques, which consume relatively little in terms of calculations (especially HS), the MC method requires considerable calculation power and time:

- valuation models (including regressions), taking account of changes over time and therefore estimations of stochastic process parameters;
- forecasting, on the basis of historical periods, of a number of correlations (between the risk factors that explain the same asset on one hand, and between assets in the same portfolio for the purpose of its re-valuation on the other hand);
- matrix algebra, including the Choleski decomposition method;
- finally and most significantly, a considerable number of simulations. Thus, if M is the number of simulations required in the Monte Carlo method to obtain a representative distribution and the asset for which a price must be generated depends on n risk factors, a total of nM simulations will be necessary for the asset in question. If the portfolio is also revalued by simulation (with a bulky variance–covariance matrix), the number of calculations increases still further.

7.5.2.3 Installation and use

The basic principles of the VC method, with splitting of assets and mapping of cashflows, cannot be easily understood at all levels within the business that uses the methodology; and the function of risk management cannot be truly effective without positive assistance from all departments within the business. In addition, this method has a great advantage: RiskMetrics™ actually exists, and the great number of data that supply the system are

Table 7.7 Advantages and drawbacks

	VC	MC	HS
Distributional hypothesis	Conditional normality	No	No
Linearity hypothesis	Taylor if options	No	No
Stationarity hypothesis	Yes	No	Method to be adapted if trend
Horizon	1 observation period	Paths (any duration)	1 observation period
Valuation models	Yes (unmanageable risk)	Yes (manageable risk)	External
Dynamic models	No	Yes	External
Required data	–Partial VaR^* –Correlation matrix	Histories (+ var-cov. of assets)	Historices
Source of data	External	In house	In house
Sensitivity	Average	Average	Outliers
Calculation	–Valuation models –Matrix calculation	–Valuation models –Statistical estimates –Matrix calculation –Simulations	External valuation models
Set-up	Easy	Difficult	Easy
Understanding	Difficult	Average	Easy
Flexibility	Low	Low	Good
Robustness	Too many hypotheses	Good	Good

also available. The drawback, of course, is the lack of transparency caused by the external origin of the data.

Although the basic ideas of the MC method are simple and natural, putting them into practice is much more problematic, mainly because of the sheer volume of the calculation.

The HS method relies on theoretical bases as simple and natural as those of the MC method. In addition, the system is easy to implement and its principles can be easily understood at all levels within a business, which will be able to adopt it without problems. In addition, it is a very flexible methodology: unlike the other methods, which appear clumsy because of their vast number of calculations, aggregation can be made at many different levels and used in many different contexts (an investment fund, a portfolio, a dealing room, an entire institution). Finally, the small number of basic hypotheses and the almost complete absence of complex valuation models makes the HS method particularly reliable in comparison with MC and especially VC.

Let us end by recalling one drawback of the HS method, inherent in the simplicity of its design: its great sensitivity to quality of data. In fact, one or a few more outliers (whether exceptional in nature or caused by an error) will greatly influence the *VaR* value over a long period (equal to the duration of the historical periods). It has been said that extreme value theory can overcome this problem, but unfortunately, the huge number of calculations that have to be made when applying it is prohibitive. Instead, we would recommend that institutions using the HS method set

up a very rigorous data control system and systematically analyse any exceptional observations (that is, *outliers*); this is possible in view of the internal nature of the data
used here.

7.5.3 Synthesis

We end by setting out a synoptic table[52] shown in Table 7.7 of all the arguments put forward.

---

[52] With regard to the horizon for the VC method, note that the VAR can be obtained for a longer horizon H than the
periodicity of observations, by multiplying the VAR for a period by $\sqrt{H}$, except in the case of optional products.

8

Setting Up a *VaR* Methodology

The aim of this chapter is to demonstrate how the *VaR* can be calculated using the historical simulation method. So that the reader can work through the examples specifically, we felt it was helpful to include a CD-ROM of Excel spreadsheets in this book. This file, called 'CH8.XLS', contains all the information relating to the examples dealt with below. No part of the sheets making up the file has been hidden so that the calculation procedures are totally transparent.

The examples presented have been deliberately simplified; the actual portfolios of banks, institutions and companies will be much more complex than what the reader can see here. The great variety of financial products, and the number of currencies available the world over, have compelled us to make certain choices.

In the final analysis, however, the aim is to explain the basic methodology so that the user can transpose historical simulation into the reality of his business. Being aware of the size of some companies' portfolios, we point out a number of errors to be avoided in terms of simplification.

8.1 PUTTING TOGETHER THE DATABASE

8.1.1 Which data should be chosen?

Relevant data is fundamental. As *VaR* dreals with extreme values in a series of returns, a database error, which is implicitly extreme, will exert its influence for many days. The person responsible for putting together the data should make a point of testing the consistency of the new values added to the database every day, so that it is not corrupted.

The reliability of data depends upon:

- the source (internal or external);
- where applicable, the sturdiness of the model and the hypotheses that allow it to be determined;
- awareness of the market;
- human intervention in the data integration process.

Where the source is external, market operators will be good reference points for specialist data sources (exchange, long term, short term, derivatives etc.). Sources may be printed (financial newspapers and magazines) or electronic (Reuters, Bloomberg, Telerate, Datastream etc.).

Prices may be chosen 'live' (what is the FRA 3–6 USD worth on the market?) or calculated indirectly (calculation of forward-forward on the basis of three and six months Libor USD, for example). The ultimate aim is to provide proof of consistency as time goes on.

On a public holiday, the last known price will be used as the price for the day.

8.1.2   The data in the example

We have limited ourselves to four currencies (EUR, PLN, USD and GBP), in weekly data. For each of these currencies, 101 dates (from 19 January 2001 to 20 December 2002) have been selected. For these dates, we have put together a database containing the following prices:

- 1, 2, 3, 6 and 12, 18, 24, 36, 48 and 60 months deposit and swap rates for EUR and PLN, and the same periods but only up to 24 months for USD and GBP.
- Spot rates for three currency pairs (EUR/GBP, EUR/PLN and EUR/USD).

The database contains 3737 items of data.

8.2   CALCULATIONS

8.2.1   Treasury portfolio case

The methodology assumes that historical returns will be applied to a current portfolio in order to estimate the maximum loss that will occur, with a certain degree of confidence, through successive valuations of that portfolio.

The first stage, which is independent of the composition of the portfolio, consists of determining the past returns (in this case, weekly returns).

8.2.1.1   Determining historical returns

As a reminder (see Section 3.1.1), the formula that allows the return to be calculated[1] is:

$$R_t = \frac{C_t - C_{t-1}}{C_{t-1}}$$

For example, the weekly return for three months' deposit USD between 19 January 2001 and 26 January 2001 is:

$$\frac{0.05500 - 0.05530}{0.05530} = -0.5425\,\%$$

The results of applying the rates of return to the databases are found on the 'Returns' sheet within CH8.XLS. For 101 rates, 100 weekly returns can be determined.

8.2.1.2   Composition of portfolio

The treasury portfolio is located on the 'Portfolios' sheet within CH8.XLS. This sheet is entirely fictitious, and has base in economic reality either for the dates covered by the sample and even less at the time you read these lines. The only reality is the prices and rates that prevail at the dates chosen (and *de facto* the historical returns).

The investor's currency is the euro. The term 'long' (or 'short') indicates:

- in terms of deposits, that the investor has borrowed (lent).

---

[1] We were able to use the other expression for the return, that is, $\ln \dfrac{C_t}{C_{t-1}}$ (see also Section 3.1.1).

- in terms of foreign exchange, that the investor has purchased (sold) the first currency (EUR in the case of EUR/USD) in exchange for the second currency in the pair.

We have assumed that the treasury portfolio for which the *VaR* is to be calculated contains only new positions for the date on which the maximum loss is being estimated: 20 December 2002.

In a real portfolio, an existing contract must of course be revalued in relation to the period remaining to maturity. Thus, a nine-month deposit that has been running for six months (remaining period therefore three months) will require a database that contains the prices and historical returns for three-month deposits in order to estimate the maximum loss for the currency in question.

In addition, some interpolations may need to be made on the curve, as the price for some broken periods (such as seven-month deposits running for four months and 17 days) does not exist in the market.

Therefore, for each product in the treasury portfolio, we have assumed that the contract prices obtained by the investor correspond exactly to those in the database on the date of valuation. The values in Column 'J' ('Initial Price') in the 'Portfolios' sheet in CH8.XLS for the treasury portfolio will thus correspond to the prices in the 'Rates' sheet in CH8.XLS for 20 December 2002 for the products and currencies in question.

8.2.1.3   Revaluation by asset type

We have said that historical simulation consists of revaluing the current portfolio by applying past returns to that portfolio; the *VaR* is not classified and determined until later.

Account should, however, be taken of the nature of the product when applying the historical returns. Here, we are envisaging two types of product:

- interest-rate products;
- FX products.

A. Exchange rate product: deposit

Introduction: Calculating the VBP

We saw in Section 2.1.2 that the value of a basis point (VBP) allowed the sensitivity of an interest rate position to a basis point movement to be calculated, whenever interest rates rise or fall.

Position 1 of the treasury portfolio (CH8.XLS, 'Portfolios' sheet, line 14) is a deposit (the investor is 'long') within a GBP deposit for a total of GBP50 000 000 at a rate of 3.9400 %.

The investor's interest here is in the three-month GBP rate increasing; he will thus be able to reinvest his position at a more favourable rate. Otherwise, the position will make a loss. More generally, however, it is better to pay attention to the sensitivity of one's particular position.

The first stage consists of calculating the interest on the maturity date:

$$I = C \cdot R \cdot \frac{ND}{DIV}$$

Here:

I represents the interest;
C represents the nominal;
R represents the interest rate;
ND represents the number of days in the period;
DIV represents the number of days in a year for the currency in question.

$$I = 50\,000\,000 \times 0.0394 \times 90/365 = 485\,753.42.$$

Let us now assume that the rates increase by one basis point. The interest cashflow at the maturity date is thus calculated on an interest rate base of: $0.0394 + 0.0001 = 0.0395$. We therefore obtain:

$$I = 50\,000\,000 \times 0.0395 \times 90/365 = 486\,986.30$$

As the investor in the example is 'long', that is, it is better for him to lend in order to cover his position, he will gain: $I = 50\,000\,000 \times 0.0001 \times 90/365 = |485\,753.42 - 486\,986.30| = 1\,232.88$ GBP every time the three-month GBP rate increases by one basis point.

Historical return case

The VBP assumes a predetermined variation of one basis point every time, either upwards or downwards. In the example, this variation equals a profit (rise) or loss (fall) of 1232.88 GBP.

In the same way, we can apply to the current rate for the position any other variation that the investor considers to be of interest: we stated in Section 2.1.2 that this was the case for simulations (realistic or catastrophic).

However, if the investor believes that the best forecast[2] of future variations in rates is a variation that he has already seen in the past, all he then needs to do is apply a series of past variations to the current rate (on the basis of past returns) and calculate a law of probability from that.

On 19 January 2001, the three-month GBP was worth 5.72 %, while on 26 January 2001 it stood at 5.55 %. The historical return is -2.9720 % ('Returns' sheet, cell AG4). This means that: $0.0572 \times (1 + (-0.02972)) = 0.0555$.

If we apply this past return to the current rate for the position ('Portfolios' sheet, cell J14), we will have: $0.0394 \times (1 + (-0.02972)) = 0.038229$.

This rate would produce interest of: $I = 50\,000\,000 \times 0.038229 \times 90/365 = 471\,316.70$.

As the investor is 'long', this drop in the three-month rate would produce a loss in relation to that rate, totalling: $471\,316.70 - 485\,753.42 = -14\,436.73$ GBP. The result is shown on the 'Treasury Reval' sheet, cell D3.

Error to avoid

Some people may be tempted to proceed on the basis of difference from past rate: $0.055500 - 0.057200 = -0.0017$. And then to add that difference to the current rate:

---

[2] The argument in favour of this assumption is that the variation has already existed. The argument against, however, is that it cannot be assumed that it will recur in the future.

$0.0394 - 0.0017 = 0.0377$. This would lead to a loss of: $I = 50\,000\,000 \times (-0.0017) \times 90/365 = -20\,958.90$. This is obviously different from the true result of $-14\,436.73$.

This method is blatantly false. To stress the concepts once again, if rates moved from 10% to 5% within one week (return of -50%) a year ago, with the differential applied to a current position valued at a rate of 2%, we would have a result of:

$0.02 \times (1 - 0.50) = 0.01$ with the right method.
$0.02 - (0.10 - 0.05) = -0.03$ with the wrong method.

In other words, it is best to stick to the relative variations in interest rates and FX rates and not to the absolute variations.

B. FX product: spot

Position 3 in the treasury portfolio (CH8.XLS, 'Portfolios' sheet, line 16) is a purchase (the investor is 'long') of EUR/USD for a total of EUR75\,000\,000 at a price of USD1.0267 per EUR.

Introduction: calculating the value of a 'pip'

A 'pip' equals one-hundredth of a USD cent in a EUR/USD quotation, that is, the fourth figure after the decimal point. The investor is 'long' as he has purchased euros and paid for the purchase in USD. A rise (fall) in the EUR/USD will therefore be favourable (unfavourable) for him.

In the same way as the VBP for rate products, the sensitivity of a spot exchange position can be valued by calculating the effect of a variation in a 'pip', upwards or downwards on the result for the position. The calculations are simple:

$$75\,000\,000 \times 1.0267 = 77\,002\,500$$

$$75\,000\,000 \times 1.0268 = 77\,010\,000$$

$$77\,010\,000 - 77\,002\,500 = 7500$$

Example of historical returns

On 19 January 2001, the spot EUR/USD was worth 0.9336, while on 26 January 2001 it stood at 0.9238. The historical return ('Returns' sheet, cell AO4) is -1.0497%. This means that: $0.9336 \times (1 + (-1.0497)) = 0.9238$.

By applying Position 3 of the treasury portfolio to the current rate, we have: $1.0267 \times (1 + (-1.0497)) = 1.01592273$.

The investor's position is 'long', so a fall in the EUR/USD rate will be unfavourable for him, and the loss (in USD) will be:

$$75\,000\,000 \times ((1.0267 \times (1 + (-1.0497))) - 1.0267))$$

$$= 75\,000\,000 \times (1.01592273 - 1.0267) = -808\,295.31$$

This result is displayed in cell F3 of the 'Treasury Reval' sheet.

8.2.1.4 Revaluation of the portfolio

The revaluation of the treasury portfolio is shown in the table produced by cells from B2 to G102, on the 'Treasury Reval' sheet.

For each of the positions, from 1–3, we have applied 100 historical returns (from 26 January 2001 to 20 December 2002) in the currency in question (GBP, USD, EUR). The total shown is the loss (negative total) or profit (positive total) as calculated above taking account of past returns.

Let us take as an example the first revaluation (corresponding to the 26 January 2001 return) for Position 1 of the portfolio (cell D3 in the 'Treasury Reval' sheet).

The formula that allows the loss or profit to be calculated consists of the difference in interest receivable at the current (initial) price of the position and the interest receivable in view of the application to the initial price of the corresponding historical return on 26 January 2001. We therefore have the general formula:

$$L = \left(C \cdot R \cdot (1 + HR) \cdot \frac{ND}{DIV}\right) - \left(C \cdot R \cdot \frac{ND}{DIV}\right)$$

$$= C \cdot \left(\left(R \cdot (1 + HR) \cdot \frac{ND}{DIV}\right) - \left(R \cdot \frac{ND}{DIV}\right)\right)$$

Here:

L is the loss;
C is the total to which the transaction relates;
L is the current rate (initial price) of the transaction;
HR is the historical return.

It is this last formula that is found in cells D3 to F102. Of course we could have simplified[3] it here:

$$L = C \cdot \left(\left(R \cdot (1 + HR) \cdot \frac{ND}{DIV}\right) - \left(R \cdot \frac{ND}{DIV}\right)\right)$$

$$= C \cdot R \cdot \frac{ND}{DIV} \cdot ((1 + HR) - 1)$$

$$= C \cdot R \cdot \frac{ND}{DIV} \cdot HR$$

If the investor is 'long', he has borrowed and will wish to cover himself by replacing his money at a higher rate than the initial price. Therefore, if HR is a negative (positive) total, and he has realised a loss (profit). This is the case for Position 1 of the portfolio on 26 January 2001.

On the other hand, if the investor is 'short', he has lent and will wish to cover himself by borrowing the money at a lower rate than the initial price. Therefore, if HR is a negative (positive) total, P must be positive (negative) and the preceding formula (valid if the investor is 'long') must be multiplied by -1.

For Position 2 of the portfolio, the investor is 'short' and we have (cell E3 of the 'Treasury Reval' sheet:

$$L = (-1) \cdot C \cdot \left(\left(R \cdot (1 + HR) \cdot \frac{ND}{DIV}\right) - \left(R \cdot \frac{ND}{DIV}\right)\right)$$

---

[3] We have not simplified it, so that the various components of the difference can be seen more clearly.)

On each past date, we have a loss or profit expressed in the currency of the operation for each position. As the investor has the euro for his national or accounting currency, we have summarised the three losses or gains in EUR equivalents at each date. The chosen FX rate for the euro against the other currencies is of course the rate prevailing on the date of calculation of the *VaR*, that is, 20 December 2002. The overall loss is shown in column G of the 'Treasury Reval' sheet.

8.2.1.5 Classifying the treasury portfolio values and determining the VaR

When all the revaluations have been carried out, we have (see 'Treasury Reval' sheet) a series of 100 losses or profits according to historical return date.

One has to classify them in increasing order, that is, from the greatest loss to the smallest. The reader will find column G of the 'Treasury Reval' sheet classified in increasing order on the 'Treasury *VaR*' sheet, in column B. To the right of this column, $1 - q$ appears.

A. Numerical interpretation

We think it important to state once again that when $1 - q$ corresponds to a plateau of the loss distribution function, we have chosen to define *VaR* as the left extremity of the said section (see Figure 6.7).

We therefore say that:

- There are 66 chances out of 100 that the actual loss will be −EUR360 822 or less $(1 - q = 0.34)$, or $VaR_{0.66} = -360\,822$.
- There are 90 chances out of 100 that the actual loss will be −EUR1 213 431 or less $(1 - q = 0.10)$, or $VaR_{0.90} = -1\,213\,431$.
- There are 99 chances out of 100 that the actual loss will be −EUR2 798 022 or less $(1 - q = 0.01)$, or $VaR_{0.99} = -2\,798\,022$.

B. Representation in graphical form

If the forecast of losses is shown on the *x*-axis and $1 - q$ is shown on the *y*-axis, the estimated loss distribution will be obtained. Figure 8.1, also appears on the 'Treasury *VaR*' sheet.

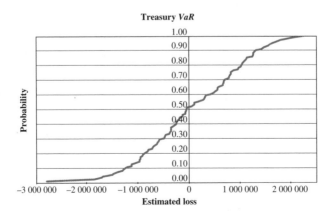

Figure 8.1   Estimated loss distribution of treasury portfolio

8.2.2   Bond portfolio case

The first stage once again consists of determining the past returns (in this case, weekly).

8.2.2.1   Past variations to be applied

The main difficulty connected with this type of asset, in terms of determining *VaR*, is the question of whether or not the historical prices or rates are available.

When a bond is first issued, for example, it has to be acknowledged that we do not have any historical prices.

As the aim of this chapter is merely to show how *VaR* can be calculated using the historical simulation method, using deliberately simplified examples, we have used a range of rates for deposits and swaps on the basis of which we will construct our example. We did not therefore wish to use bond historical prices as a basis.

A. Yield

The price of a bond is known on at least one date: that for which we propose to determine the *VaR* (in our example, 20 December 2002).

Using this price, and by taking into account the calculation date, the maturity date, coupon date, the price on maturity, the basis of calculation and the frequency of the coupon payments, the 'yield to maturity' or YTM, can be calculated as shown in Section 4.1.2.

Columns H3 to H9 of the 'Portfolios' sheet show the relative yields for the bond in our fictitious portfolio. As not all versions of Excel contain the 'yield' financial function, we have copied the values into columns I3 to I9.

It is to this yield to maturity that we intend to apply the variations relative to corresponding rates of deposit and/or swaps, in terms of maturity, for the remaining period of the corresponding bond.

We are of course aware that this method is open to criticism as the price, if we had used it, not only reflects general interest-rate levels, but also carries a dimension of credit risk and lack of liquidity.

B. Interpolation of rates

We cannot deduce from the 'Rates' sheet the returns to be applied to the yield to maturity; the remaining periods are in fact broken.

We have determined (in the 'Bonds Interp' sheet), the two maturity dates (columns I and J in that sheet) that straddle the remaining period, together with the portion of rate differential to be added to the lower rate (column F divided by column H).

Readers will find the value of the rates to be interpolated (taken from the 'Rates' sheet) in the 'Variation Bonds' sheet, the rate differential to which the rule of interpolation mentioned above is applied. For bond 1 in our portfolio, this calculation is found in column G. All that remains now is to determine the return relative to the series of synthetic rates in exactly the same way as shown in Section 8.2.1. The returns applicable to the yield to maturity for bond 1 in the portfolio are thus shown in column H of the 'Variation Bonds' sheet.

8.2.2.2   Composition of portfolio

The 'bond' portfolio is found on the 'Portfolios' sheet in CH8.XLS. This sheet, like the rest of the portfolio, is purely fictitious. The investor's national currency is the euro.

The portfolio is 'long', with six bonds, for which the following are given:

- currency;
- coupon;
- maturity date;
- ISIN code;
- last known price (this is the 'bid', because if the position is closed, one should expect to deal at the bid price);
- yield on maturity (in formula form in column H, in copied value in column I);
- basis of calculation (current/current or 30/360);
- frequency of payment of the coupon.

8.2.2.3 Portfolio revaluation

In Table B2–H9, the 'Losses Bonds' sheet summarises the portfolio data that we need in order to revalue it.

Remember that we propose to apply the relative variations in rates (column L for bond 1, column Q for bond 2 etc.), to the yield to maturity (column C) of each bond that corresponds, in terms of maturity, to the period still outstanding.

A new yield to maturity is therefore deduced (column M for bond 1); it is simply the current total to which a past variation has been applied.

We explained above that starting from the last known price of a bond, and taking account of the date of the calculation as well as the expiry date, the coupon date, the price on maturity, the basis of calculation and the frequency of the coupon, we deduce the yield to maturity.

It is possible, in terms of correlations, to start from our 'historical' yields to maturity in order to reconstruct a synthesised price (column N). The 'Price' function in Excel returns a price on the basis of the given yield to maturity (column M) and of course that of the date of the calculation as well as the expiry date, coupon date, price on maturity, basis of calculation and frequency of coupon. As not all versions of Excel contain the 'Price' function, we have copied the values from column N into column O for bond 1, from column S into column T for bond 2, etc.

All that now remains is to compare the new price to the last known price, and to multiply this differential by the nominal held in the portfolio in order to deduce the resulting profit or loss (column P for bond 1). As indicated in cell B11, we assume that we are holding a nominal of €100 million on each of the six bond lines.

Note

It may initially seem surprising that the nominal used for bond 1 (expressed in PLN) is also €100 million. In fact, rather than expressing the nominal in PLN, calculating the loss or profit and dividing the total again by the same EUR/PLN rate (that is, 3.9908 at 20 December 2002), we have immediately expressed the loss for a nominal expressed in euros.

It is then sufficient (column AP) to summarise the six losses and/or profits for each of the 100 dates on each line (with respect for the correlation structure).

8.2.2.4 Classifying bond portfolio values and determining VaR

Once all the new valuations have been made, a series of 100 losses or profits ('Losses Bonds' sheet) will be shown according to historical return date. One has to classify them

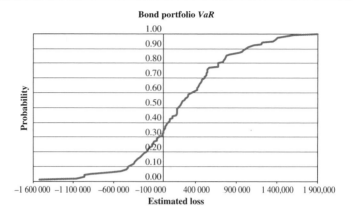

Figure 8.2 Estimated loss distribution of bond portfolio

in ascending order, that is, from the greatest loss to the smallest. Readers will find column AP in the 'Losses Bonds' sheet classified in ascending order on the 'Bonds *VaR*' sheet in column B. $1 - q$ is located to the right of that column.

A. Numerical interpretation

We say that:

- There are 66 chances out of 100 that the actual loss will be −EUR917 or less ($1 - q = 0.34$), or $VaR_{0.66} = -917$.
- There are 90 chances out of 100 that the actual loss will be −EUR426 740 or less ($1 - q = 0.10$), or $VaR_{0.90} = -426\,740$.
- There are 99 chances out of 100 that the actual loss will be −EUR1 523 685 or less ($1 - q = 0.01$), or $VaR_{0.99} = -1\,523\,685$.

B. Representation in graphical form

If the loss estimates are shown on the *x*-axis and $1 - q$ is shown on the *y*-axis, the estimated loss distribution will be obtained. Figure 8.2 also appears on the 'Bonds *VaR*' sheet.

8.3 THE NORMALITY HYPOTHESIS

We have stressed the hidden dangers of underestimating the risk where the hypothesis of normality is adopted. In fact, because of the leptokurtic nature of market observations, the normal law tails (*VaR* being interested specifically in extreme values) will report the observed historical frequencies poorly, as they will be too flat. It is prudent, when using theoretical forecasts to simplify calculations, to overstate market risks; here, however, the opposite is the case.

In order to explain the problem better we have compared the observed distribution for the bond portfolio in CH8.XLS with the normal theoretical distribution. The comparison is found on the 'Calc N' sheet (N = normal) and teaches us an interesting lesson with regard to the tails of these distributions.

We have used the estimated loss distribution of the bond portfolio (copied from the 'Bonds *VaR*' sheet). We have produced 26 categories (from −1 600 000 to −1 465 000, from −1 465 000 to −1 330 000 etc., up to 1 775 000 to 1 910 000) in which each of these 100 losses will be placed. For example, the loss of −1 523 685.01 (cell D4) will belong to the first class (from −1 600 000 to −1 465 000, column G).

The table G2−AF103 on the 'Calc N' sheet contains one class per column (lines G2−AF3) and 100 lines, that is, one per loss (column D4−D103). Where a given loss intersects with a class, there will be a figure of 0 (if the loss is not in the category in question) or 1 (if otherwise).

By finding the total of 1s in a column, we will obtain the number of losses per class, or the *frequency*. Thus, a loss of between −1 600 000 and −1 465 000 has a frequency of 1 % (cell G104) and a loss of between 425 000 and 560 000 has a frequency of 13 % (cell V104).

Cells AH2−AJ29 carry the category centres (−1 532 500 for the class −1 600 000 to −1 465 000), and the frequencies as a figure and a percentage.

If we look at AH2 to AI29 in bar chart form, we will obtain the observed distribution for the bond portfolio (Figure 8.3) located in AL2 to AQ19.

Now the normal distribution should be calculated. We have calculated the mean and standard deviation for the estimated distribution of the losses in D104 and D105, respectively. We have carried the losses to AS4 to AS103.

Next, we have calculated the value of the normal density function (already set out in Section 3.4.2 'Continuous model'), that is, $f(x) = \dfrac{1}{\sqrt{2\pi}\sigma} \exp\left[-\dfrac{1}{2}\left(\dfrac{x-\mu}{\sigma}\right)^2 \right]$, to each loss in the bond portfolio (AT4 to AT103). If we plot this data on a graph, we will obtain (Figure 8.4) the graph located from AV2 to BB19.

In order to compare these distributions (observed and theoretical), we have superimposed them; the calculations that allow this superimposition are located in the 'Graph N' sheet.

As can be seen in Figures 8.3 and 8.4, the coordinates are proportional (factor 135 000 for class intervals). We have summarised the following in a table (B2 to D31 of the 'Graph N' sheet):

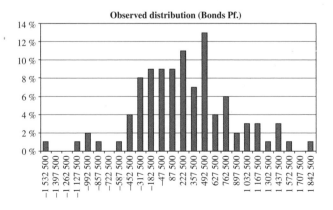

Figure 8.3 Observed distribution

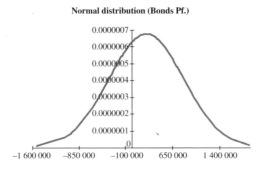

Figure 8.4   Normal distribution

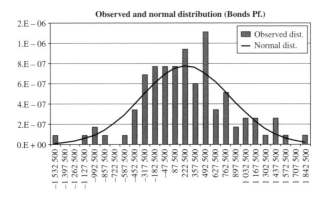

Figure 8.5   Normal and observed distributions

- the class centres;
- the observed frequencies relating to them;
- the normal coordinates relative to each class centre.

It is therefore possible (Figure 8.5) to construct a graph, located in E2 to N32, which is the result of the superimposition of the two types of distribution types.

We may observe an underestimation of the frequency through normal law in distribution tails, which further confirms the leptokurtic nature of the financial markets.

Part IV
From Risk Management
to Asset Management

Introduction

Although risk management methods have been used first and foremost to quantify market risks relative to market transactions, these techniques tend to be generalised especially if one wishes to gain a comprehensive understanding of the risks inherent in the management of institutional portfolios (investment funds, hedge funds, pension funds) and private portfolios (private banking and other wealth management methods).

In this convergence between asset management on the one hand and risk management on the other, towards what we term the discipline of 'asset and risk management', we are arriving, especially in the field of individual client portfolio management, at 'portfolio risk management', which is the subject of Chapter 9.

Next, we will look at methods for optimising asset portfolios that verify normal law hypotheses, which is especially the case with equities.[1] In particular, we will be adapting two known portfolio optimisation methods:

- Sharpe's simple index method (see Section 3.2.4) and the EGP method (see Section 3.2.6).
- *VaR* (see Chapter 6); we will be seeing the extent to which *VaR* improves the optimisation.

To close this fourth part, we will see how the APT model described in Section 3.3.2 allows investment funds to be analysed in behavioural terms.

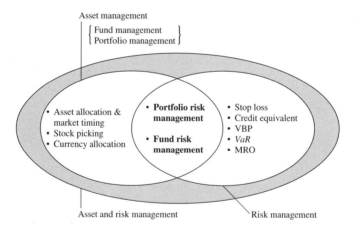

Figure P1   Asset and risk management

---

[1] In fact, the statistical distribution of an equity is leptokurtic but becomes normal over a sufficiently long period.

9

Portfolio Risk Management[1]

9.1 GENERAL PRINCIPLES

This involves application of the following:

- To portfolios managed traditionally, that is, using:
  — asset allocation with a greater or lesser risk profile (including, implicitly, market timing);
  — a choice of specific securities within the category of equities or options (stock picking);
  — currency allocation.
- To particularly high-risk portfolios (said to have a 'high leverage effect') falling clearly outside the scope of traditional management (the most frequent case), a fivefold risk management method that allows:
  — daily monitoring by the client (and intraday monitoring if market conditions require) of the market risks to which he or she is exposed given the composition of his or her portfolio.
  — monitoring of equal regularity by the banker (or wealth manager where applicable) of the client positions for which he or she is by nature the only person responsible.

Paradoxically (at least initially) it is this second point that is essential for the client, since this ability to monitor credit risk with the use of modern and online tools allows the banker to minimise the client's need to provide collateral, something that earns little or nothing.

9.2 PORTFOLIO RISK MANAGEMENT METHOD

Let us take the case of the particularly high-risk portfolios, including derivatives:

- linear portfolios (such as FRA, IRS, currency swaps and other forward FX);
- nonlinear portfolios (options); that is highly leveraged portfolios.

In order to minimise the need for collateral under this type of portfolio wherever possible, the pledging agreement may include clauses that provide for a risk-monitoring framework, which will suppose rights and obligations on the part of the contractual parties:

- The banker (wealth manager) reports on the market risks (interest rates, FX, prices etc.) thus helping the client to manage the portfolio.

---

[1] Lopez T., Delimiting portfolio risk, *Banque Magazine*, No. 605, July–August 1999, pp. 44–6.

- The client undertakes to respect the risk criteria (by complying with the limits) set out in the clauses, authorising the bank (under certain conditions) to act in his name and on his behalf if the limits in question are breached.

A portfolio risk management mandate generally consists of two parts:

- the investment strategy;
- the risk framework.

9.2.1 Investment strategy

This part sets out:

- The portfolio management strategy.
- The responsibilities of each of the parties.
- The maximum maturity dates of the transactions.
- The nature of the transactions.

9.2.2 Risk framework

In order to determine the risks and limits associated with the portfolio, the following four limits will be taken into consideration, each of which may not be exceeded.

1. The *stop loss* limit for the portfolio.
2. The maximum credit equivalent limit.
3. The upper VBP (value of one basis point) limit for the portfolio.
4. The upper *VaR* (Value at Risk) limit for the portfolio.

For each measure, one should be in a position to calculate:

- the limit;
- the outstanding to be compared to the limit.

9.2.2.1 The portfolio stop loss

With regard to the limit, the potential global loss on the portfolio (defined below) can never exceed x % of the cash equivalent of the portfolio, the portfolio being defined as the sum of:

- the available cash balances, on one hand;
- the realisation value of the assets included in the portfolio, on the other hand.

The percentage of the cash equivalent of the portfolio, termed the *stop loss*, is determined jointly by the bank and the client, depending on the client's degree of aversion to the risk, based in turn on the degree of leverage within the portfolio.

For the outstanding, the total potential loss on the portfolio is the sum of the differences between:

- the value of its constituent assets at the initiation of each transaction;
- the value of those same assets on the valuation date;

Each of these must be less than zero for them to apply.

Example

Imagine a portfolio of EUR100 invested in five equities ABC at EUR10 per share and five equities XYZ at EUR5 per share at 1 January.

If the value of ABC changes to EUR11 and that of XYZ to EUR4 on the next day, the potential decrease in value on XYZ (loss of EUR1 on 10 equities in XYZ) will be taken into account for determining the potential overall loss on the portfolio. The EUR5 increase in value on the ABC equities (gain of EUR1 on five equities ABC) will, however, be excluded. The overall loss will therefore be −EUR10.

The cash equivalent of the portfolio will total EUR95, that is, the total arising from the sale of all the assets in the portfolio. This produces a stop loss equal to 20 % of the portfolio cash equivalent (20 % of EUR95 or 19). See Table 9.1.

9.2.2.2 Maximum credit equivalent limit

The credit limit totals the cash equivalent of the portfolio (defined in the 'portfolio stop loss' section). The credit liabilities, which consist of the sum of the credit equivalents defined below, must be equal to or less than the cash equivalent of the portfolio. The credit equivalent calculation consists of producing an equivalent value weighting to base products or their derivatives; these may or may not be linear.

The weighting will be a function of the intrinsic risk relative to each product (Figure 9.1) and will therefore depend on whether or not the product:

- involves exchange of principal (for example, a spot FX involves an exchange of principal whereas a forward FX deal will defer this to a later date);
- involves a contingent obligation (if options are issued);
- involves a contingent right (if options are purchased);

Table 9.1 Stop loss

Stop loss	Potential loss	Use of limit
EUR19	−EUR10	52.63 %

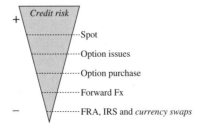

Figure 9.1 Weight of the credit equivalent

- the product price (if no exchange of principal is supposed) is linked to one variable (interest rate for FRA, IRS and currency swaps) or two variables (interest rates and spot in the case of forward FX).

We could for example determine credit usage per product as follows:

1. For spot cash payments, 100 % of the nominal of the principal currency.
2. For the sale of options, the notional for the underlying principal currency, multiplied by the forward delta.
3. For the purchase of options, 100 % of the premium paid.
4. For other products, each position opened in the portfolio would be the subject of a daily economic revaluation (mark-to-market). The total potential loss arising would be taken (gains being excluded) and multiplied by a weighting factor (taking account of the volatility of the asset value) equal to $100\% + x\% + y\%$ for future exchanges and $100\% + x\%$ for FRA, IRS and currency swaps, x and y always being strictly positive amounts.

Example

Here is a portfolio consisting of five assets (Tables 9.2 and 9.3).
The revaluation prices are shown in Table 9.4.

Table 9.2   FX products

Product	P/S	Currency	Nom.	P/S	Currency	Nom.	Spot	Forward
Spot	S	EUR	5 m	P	USD	5.5 million	1.1	–
Six-month future	P	USD	10 m	S	JPY	1170 million	120	117

Table 9.3   FX derivatives and FRA

Product	P/S	Currency	Nominal	Price/premium
Three-month call Strike 1.1	P	EUR/USD	EUR11 million	EUR220 000
Two-month put Strike 195.5	S	GBP/JPY	£5 million	GBP122 000
FRA 3–6	S	DKK	100 million	3.3 %

Table 9.4   Revaluation price

Product	Historical price	Current price	Loss (currency)	Potential loss (EUR)
Spot	1.1	1.12	−100 000	−89 285.71
FX forward	117	114.5	−25 million	−189 969.60
Long call	2.00 % nom. EUR	2.10 % nom. EUR	+11 000	+11 000
Short put	2.44 % nom. GBP	2.48 % nom. GBP	−2000	−3034.90
FRA	3.3 %	3.4 %	−25 000	−3363.38
Total				−274 653.59

Table 9.5   Credit equivalent agreements

Product	Credit equivalent
Spot	100 % of nominal of principal currency
FX forward	110 % of potential loss (<0)
FX options purchase	100 % of premium paid by client
FX options sale	Principal dev. notional $\times \Delta_{forward}$
FRA	103 % of potential loss (<0)

Table 9.6   Credit equivalent calculations

Product	Nominal/potential loss (EUR)	Credit equivalent (EUR)
Spot	5 000 000.00	5 000 000.00
FX forward	−189 969.60·110 %	208 966.56
Long call	220 000.00	220 000.00
Short put	7 587 253.41·60 %	4 552 352.05
FRA	−3363.38·103 %	3464.28
Total		9 984 782.89

Table 9.7   Outstanding in credit equivalent

Pf. cash equivalent	Credit outstanding	Use of limit
15 000 000	9 984 782.89	66.57 %

Given that:

- The following rules have been adopted (Table 9.5).
- The $\Delta_{forward}$ of the put totals −60 %, and the result is a credit equivalent calculation shown in Table 9.6.

Suppose that in view of the cash available in the portfolio, the cash equivalent of the portfolio is EUR15 million. Table 9.7 shows the results.

9.2.2.3   Maximum VBP of portfolio

As was shown in Section 2.1.2, the value of one basis point or VBP quantifies the portfolio's sensitivity to a parallel and unilateral upward movement of the interest rate curve for a unit of one-hundredth per cent (that is, a basis point).

With regard to the limit, the total VBP of the portfolio may not exceed EURx per million euros invested in the portfolio (in cash equivalent). The total x equals:

- one-hundredth of the stop loss expressed in currency;
- or, 10 000 times the stop loss expressed as a percentage, which means that in a case of maximum exposure according to the VBP criterion defined here, a variation of 1 % (100 basis points) in interest rates in an unfavourable direction in order to reach the stop loss.

Example

Assume that the cash equivalent of the portfolio is EUR1 000 000 and the stop loss equal to 20 % of that cash equivalent, that is EUR200 000.

The total VBP for this portfolio may not exceed:

- one-hundredth of the stop loss expressed in the currency, that is, EUR200 000 divided by 100, that is EUR2000, which equals:
- 10 000 times the stop loss expressed as a percentage, that is, 10 000 multiplied by 20 %.

With regard to the calculation of the outstanding:

- the total VBP per currency is equal to the sum of the VBPs of each asset making up the portfolio in that currency, and;
- the total VBP for the portfolio is equal to the sum of the VBP for each currency taken as an absolute value. As a measure of caution, therefore, the least favourable correlations are taken into consideration.

Example

Assume a portfolio consisting of two positions (see Tables 9.2 and 9.3), both subject to a VBP calculation (Tables 9.8 and 9.9).

Let us first calculate the VBPs relative to the equivalent loan and borrowing for the FX forward, and of course the VBP for the FRA.

The breakdown of the six-month FX forward gives us an equivalent loan in USD for USD10 million and an equivalent deposit in JPY for JPY1200 million (that is, the USD nominal of 10 million multiplied by the reference spot rate of 120). We then have:

$$10\,000\,000 \cdot 0.01\,\% \cdot 180/360 = 500$$

$$1\,200\,000\,000 \cdot 0.01\,\% \cdot 180/360 = 60\,000$$

The equivalent loan in USD has a VBP of $-$USD500 (with fall in rates in play), and the equivalent deposit in JPY a VBP of $+$JPY60 000 (with rise in rates in play). For the FRA, we have:

$$100\,000\,000 \cdot 0.01\,\% \cdot (180 - 90)/360 = 2\,500$$

Table 9.8   FX forward

Product	P/S	Currency	Nom.	P/S	Currency	Nom.	Spot	Forward
Six-month future	P	USD	10 million	S	JPY	1170 million	120	117

Table 9.9   FRA

Product	P/S	Currency	Nominal	Price
FRA 3–6	S	DKK	100 million	3.3 %

Table 9.10   Total VBP per currency

Product/currency	USD	JPY	DKK
Loan	−500		
Deposit		+60 000	
FRA			−2 500
Total	−500	+60 000	−2 500

The VBP for the FRA totals −DKK2 500 (with fall in rates in play). The total VBP per currency (Table 9.10) is equal to the sum of the VBP for each asset making up the portfolio in this currency.

The total VBP of the portfolio is equal to the sum of the VBPs for each currency taken as an absolute value, for the least favourable correlations are taken as a matter of caution. This gives us Table 9.11.

Using the data in the previous example, that is, a portfolio cash equivalent of EUR1 000 000 and a VBP that cannot exceed EUR2 000 per million euros invested, in the event of maximum exposure according to the VBP criterion, a variation of 1 % (100 basis point) in interest rates in the unfavourable direction will be needed to reach the stop loss, as the stop loss is fixed at 20 % of the portfolio cash equivalent at the most.

In fact, 20 % of EUR1 million totals a maximum loss of EUR200 000, a sum that will be reached if for a VBP of EUR2000 a variation of 100 basis points in the unfavourable direction occurs (2 000 × 100 is equal to 200 000).

Table 9.12 sets out the limits and outstanding for the VBP.

Table 9.11   Total VBP of portfolio

Currency/VBP	VBP	ABS (VBP) in EUR
USD	500	454.55
JPY	60 000	454.55
DKK	2500	336.33
Total	–	1 245.43

Table 9.12   VBP outstanding

Maximum VBP (EUR)	Pf. VBP (EUR)	Use of limit
2 000	1 245.43	62.27 %

9.2.2.4   *Maximum VaR for portfolio*

As we saw in detail in Chapter 6, *VaR* is a number that represents for the portfolio the estimate of the maximum loss for a 24-hour horizon, with a probability of occurrence of 99 changes out of 100 that the effective loss on the portfolio will never exceed that estimate (and therefore only 1 chance in 100 of the effective loss on the portfolio exceeding that estimate).

The *VaR* on the portfolio is calculated daily, in historical simulation, independently of any (statistical) distributional hypothesis.

The *VaR* outstanding can never exceed the difference (limit) between

1. the stop loss for the portfolio; and
2. the potential overall loss on the portfolio taken as an absolute value on the date of calculation of the *VaR*.

In fact, if the forecast of the maximum loss exceeds the total that 'can' still be lost, that is, the difference between the maximum acceptable loss and what is already being lost, the tendency to move outside the limit on the maximum loss criterion becomes unreasonable.

Example

Assume the portfolio shown in the first example of this chapter, which shows a stop loss of EUR19 and a potential overall loss on the portfolio of −EUR10 (Table 9.13).

The said portfolio can lose a further EUR9 before becoming out of limits for the maximum acceptable loss criterion.

The *VaR*, that is the forecast of the maximum loss on the portfolio during the next 24 hours, can never exceed the difference between:

• the stop loss for the portfolio, namely EUR19; and
• the potential overall loss on the portfolio taken as an absolute value on the date of calculation of the *VaR*, that is, EUR10.

The total of EUR9 is the total that the portfolio still has left to lose.

Table 9.13 Stop loss

Stop loss	Potential loss	Use of limit
EUR19	−EUR10	52.63 %

10
Optimising the Global
Portfolio via *VaR*

As explained in Section 3.2, the modern portfolio theory (MPT) produced by Markowitz[1] is based on the idea that the risk[2] linked to a portfolio of assets (for a given return on the portfolio in question) can be minimised by combining risk and return so that unfavourable variations in assets are at best compensated by the favourable variations in one or more other assets. This is the principle of portfolio diversification.

Although it is admitted that the distribution of the 'return' random variable is characterised by the mean–variance pairing,[3] it is easy to formulate this problem mathematically. By considering the variance on the return as a risk measurement, the portfolio will be optimised by minimising the variance of its return for a fixed expected value of it.

Variance as a measurement of risk, however, still has the disadvantage of including both risk of loss and risk of gain; and it is here that the concept of *VaR* plays an important role. *VaR*, unlike variance, actually measures a risk of loss linked to the portfolio and minimisation of that loss will not therefore take account of the favourable variations in relation to the expected yield average.

Unfortunately, *VaR* cannot easily be modelled mathematically and the methods of calculating it are numerical simulation methods (historical simulation method, Monte Carlo method). As such, they are accompanied by relatively restrictive hypotheses (estimated variance–covariance matrix method). In fact, the only case in which there is a simple mathematical representation of *VaR* is where the hypothesis of normality has been validated.

In this case, as has been seen in Section 6.2.2, *VaR* will be expressed as a function of the q-quantile of the law of distribution of variations in the value Δp_t:

$$VaR_q = z_q \sigma(\Delta p_t) - E(\Delta p_t)$$

We are therefore interested in asset portfolio optimisation methods that satisfy the normal law hypothesis; this is especially the case for equities.[4] In particular, we will be adapting two recognised portfolio optimisation methods, i.e. Sharpe's simple index method (see Section 3.2.4) and the EGP method (see Section 3.2.6), to suit *VaR* and will see the ways in which it improves the optimisation process.

It must be remembered in this regard that the two methods chosen deal with the issue of optimisation in totally different ways. Sharpe's method tends to construct an efficiency limit, which is a parametric solution to the problem of optimisation,[5] while the EGP

---

[1] Markowitz H., Portfolio selection, *Journal of Finance*, Vol. 7, No. 1, 1952, pp. 77–91. Markowitz H., *Portfolio Selection: Efficient Diversification of Investments*, John Wiley & Sons, Ltd, 1991. Markowitz H., *Mean Variance Analysis in Portfolio Choice and Capital Markets*, Basil Blackwell, 1987.

[2] The market risk.

[3] This is the case, for example, with normal distribution.

[4] The statistical distribution of a share is in fact leptokurtic but becomes normal for a sufficiently long period of measurement.

[5] There will be one solution for each portfolio return value envisaged.

method searches for the portfolio that will optimise the risk premium, that is, the single solution that will maximise the relation

$$\Psi_P = \frac{E_P - R_F}{\sigma_P}$$

in which R_F represents the yield reckoned to be free of market risk.

10.1   TAKING ACCOUNT OF *VaR* IN SHARPE'S SIMPLE INDEX METHOD

10.1.1   The problem of minimisation

The aim of the portfolio optimisation method perfected by Markowitz is to construct the efficiency frontier (see Chapter 3). The optimal portfolio will therefore be a function of the usefulness of the investor's risk.[6] From a mathematical point of view, each expected return value has an associated Lagrangian function:

$$L(X_1, \ldots, X_N, m) = \sigma_P^2 - \lambda E_P + m \left(\sum_{j=1}^{N} X_j - 1 \right)$$

From this, the optimisation equations can be obtained:

$$\begin{cases} L'_{X_i} = 0 \; i = 1, \ldots N \\ L'_m = 0 \end{cases}$$

The first series of equations expresses the minimisation[7] of the portfolio variance. The second is the constraint relative to the composition of the portfolio.

In this context, the Sharpe index expresses the assets on the basis of which the optimal portfolio needs to be built, according to an index common to all the assets in question[8] ($R_i = a_i + b_i R_I + \varepsilon_i$) and provides a quasi-diagonal form[9] for the variance optimisation equations by the introduction of an additional constraint:[10]

$$\sum_{i=1}^{N} b_i X_i = Y$$

Taking account of *VaR* in Sharpe's method will therefore consist of replacing the variance with the *VaR* in the expression of the Lagrangian function

$$L(X_1, \ldots, X_N, Y, m_1, m_2) = z_q \sigma_P - E_P - \lambda E_P + m_1 \left(\sum_{j=1}^{N} X_j - 1 \right) + m_2 \left(\sum_{j=1}^{N} X_j b_j - Y \right)$$

referring to the expression of *VaR* in the normality hypotheses.

---

[6] On this subject, the Lagrangian parameter *l* plays an important role in the matter of portfolio choice (Broquet C., Cobbaut R., Gillet R. and Vandenberg A., *Gestion de Portefeuille*, De Boeck, 1997, pp. 304–13).

[7] In fact, these equations express the optimisation of the variance, which corresponds to a minimisation because of the convex form of the variance.

[8] Methods that involve several groups of assets each dependent on one index are known as 'multi-index methods'. Sharpe's is a simple index method.

[9] The coefficients matrix for the equation system is diagonal.

[10] Refer to Section 3.2.4 for notations.

This form of Lagrangian function is very different from the classical form, as it involves the standard deviation and not the portfolio variance. We will see that this leads to a number of complications with regard to the implementation of the critical line algorithm.

10.1.2   Adapting the critical line algorithm to *VaR*

We have based our workings on the philosophy of the efficiency frontier construction methods in order to build up a *VaR* minimisation method for a portfolio for a given return on that portfolio. This has led us to adapt the Lagrangian function using Sharpe's method. We will now adapt the critical line algorithm, used most notably in Sharpe's method, to *VaR*.

The optimisation equations are written as:

$$
\begin{cases}
z_q (\sigma_P)'_{X_i} - a_i - \lambda a_i + m_1 b_i + m_2 = 0 & i = 1, \ldots, N \\
z_q (\sigma_P)'_Y - E_I - \lambda E_I - m_2 = 0 \\
\displaystyle\sum_{j=1}^{N} X_j b_j = Y \\
\displaystyle\sum_{j=1}^{N} X_j = 1
\end{cases}
$$

The terms

$$
\begin{cases}
(\sigma_P)'_{X_i} & i = 1, \ldots, N \\
(\sigma_P)'_Y
\end{cases}
$$

being expressed as depending on the various assets involved:

$$
\begin{cases}
(\sigma_P)'_{X_i} = \left(\sqrt{\displaystyle\sum_{j=1}^{N} X_j^2 \sigma_{\varepsilon_j}^2 + Y^2 \sigma_I^2} \right)'_{X_i} = \dfrac{X_i \sigma_{\varepsilon_i}^2}{\sigma_P} & i = 1, \ldots, N \\
(\sigma_P)'_Y = \left(\sqrt{\displaystyle\sum_{j=1}^{N} X_j^2 \sigma_{\varepsilon_j}^2 + Y^2 \sigma_I^2} \right)'_Y = \dfrac{Y \sigma_I^2}{\sigma_P}
\end{cases}
$$

The system of equations becomes:

$$
\begin{cases}
z_q \dfrac{X_i \sigma_{\varepsilon_i}^2}{\sigma_P} - a_i - \lambda a_i + m_1 b_i + m_2 = 0 & i = 1, \ldots, N \\
z_q \dfrac{Y \sigma_I^2}{\sigma_P} - E_I - \lambda E_I - m_2 = 0 \\
\displaystyle\sum_{j=1}^{N} X_j b_j = Y \\
\displaystyle\sum_{j=1}^{N} X_j = 1
\end{cases}
$$

The optimisation equations then assume an implicit and non-linear form as S_P is itself a function of X_I. This problem can be resolved if we use an iterative method for resolving the nonlinear equations on the basis of Picard's iteration,[11] as:

- it shows the financial conditions that imply the presence of a solution;
- it supplies a start point close to that solution (that is, the corner portfolios), thus allowing rapid convergence.[12]

The resolution algorithm will therefore be the one described in Figure 10.1.

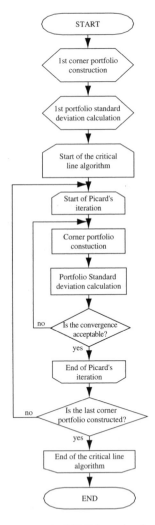

Figure 10.1   Algorithm for taking account of *VaR* in a simple index model

---

[11] See for example Burden R. L. and Faires D. J., *Numerical Analysis*, Prindle, Weber & Schmidt, 1981; Litt F. X., *Analyse numérique, première partie*, ULG, 1999, pp. 143–50; Nougier J. P., *Méthodes de calcul numérique*, Masson, 1993.

[12] Global convergence methods, such as the bisector method, converge in all cases but relatively slowly.

10.1.3   Comparison of the two methods

We have compared Sharpe's simple index method with the *VaR* minimisation method described above.[13] To this end, we have chosen to construct the efficiency frontier relative to the equity portfolio for the Spanish market index, IBEX35, using the two methods. The comparison of the portfolios obtained is based on *VaR* at 99 %, 95 % and 90 %. The range of portfolios compared has been constructed[14] so as to correspond to a range of given values for the expected returns.

The convergence towards an optimal portfolio is of one significant figure of *VaR* by iteration. The results obtained from the two methods are identical to three significant figures, which implies that at least four iterations are needed to produce a difference between the methods. Moreover, each iteration requires calculation of the standard deviation for the portfolio. In consequence, the number of calculations required to construct the efficiency frontier will be very high indeed.[15]

In addition, as Sharpe's method fixes the return value in its minimisation problem, the minimisation of *VaR* will eventually minimise the variance, thus removing much of the interest in the method.

Taking account of *VaR* in efficiency frontier construction methods does not therefore interest us greatly, although it does provide something positive for risky portfolios.

10.2   TAKING ACCOUNT OF *VaR* IN THE EGP[16] METHOD

10.2.1   Maximising the risk premium

Unlike Sharpe's simple index method, the EGP method does not look to construct an efficiency frontier. Instead, it looks for the portfolio that will maximise the risk premium

$$\Psi_P = \frac{E_P - R_F}{\sigma_P}$$

In addition, the philosophy of the EGP method is not limited merely to solving an optimisation equation. Instead, it aims to apply a criterion of choice of securities through comparison of the risk premiums[17] of the security and of the portfolio.

Finally, remember that this method is based on the same hypotheses as Sharpe's method, namely that the return on each security can be expressed as a function of the market return (or of a representative index), and that the CAPM is valid.

Using the condition of optimisation of the risk premium $(\Psi_P)'_{X_i} = 0$ as a basis, we look to obtain a relation of the type[18] $Z_i = \frac{b_i}{\sigma_{\varepsilon_i}^2}(\theta_i - \phi_K)$, where θ_i is a measurement of the risk premium on the asset (i) and ϕ_K is a measurement of the risk premium[19] of the portfolio if it included the asset (i).

---

[13] Explicit calculations are to be found on the CD-ROM, file 'Ch 10'.

[14] The basis used is the fact that a linear combination of corner portfolios is in itself optimal (Broquet C., Cobbaut R., Gillet R. and Vandenberg A., *Gestion de Portefeuille*, De Boeck, 1997).

[15] In our case, the total number of operations needed for the *VaR* minimisation method will be about five times the total in Sharpe's simple index method.

[16] Elton, Gruber and Padberg (see Section 3.2.6).

[17] In fact, we are not comparing the risk premiums but the expressions of those premiums.

[18] It can be shown (Vauthey P., *Une approche empirique de l'optimisation de portefeuille*, eds., Universitaires Fribourg Suisse, 1990) that the formula is valid, with or without a bear sale.

[19] Also known as 'acceptability threshold'.

From that relation, the assets to be introduced into the portfolio, and from that, the composition of the portfolio, will be deduced.[20] The merits of the method will therefore also depends on the proper definition of the terms θ_i and ϕ_K.

10.2.2 Adapting the EGP method algorithm to VaR

The basic idea of taking account of *VaR* in portfolio optimisation methods is to replace variance (or the standard deviation) with *VaR* in the measurement of the risk.

As the EGP method is based on the concept of risk premium, it is at that level that we introduce the *VaR*:

$$\Psi_P = \frac{E_P - R_F}{z_q \sigma_P - E_P}$$

The expression of the condition of optimisation of the *VaR* premium, according to the return on the assets, produces:

$$(\Psi_P)'_{X_i} = \left(\frac{\displaystyle\sum_{j=1}^{N} X_j (E_j - R_F)}{z_q \sigma_P - E_P} \right)'_{X_i} = 0$$

In other words:

$$\frac{E_i - R_F}{z_q \sigma_P - E_P} - \frac{E_P - R_F}{(z_q \sigma_P - E_P)^2} (z_q \sigma_P - E_P)'_{X_i} = 0$$

If it is assumed that $z_q \sigma_P - E_P \neq 0$,[21] and taking account of the expression of the *VaR* premium, $E_i - R_F - \Psi_P (z_q \sigma_P - E_P)'_{X_i} = 0$ can be written:

$$E_i - R_F - \Psi_P \left[\frac{z_q}{\sigma_P} \left(b_i \sigma_I^2 \sum_{j=1}^{N} b_j X_j + X_i \sigma_{\varepsilon_i}^2 \right) - E_i \right] = 0$$

By suggesting

$$Z_i = \frac{z_q \Psi_P}{\sigma_P} X_i.$$

the equality becomes

$$E_i (1 + \Psi_P) - R_F - b_i \sigma_I^2 \sum_{j=1}^{N} b_j Z_j - Z_i \sigma_{\varepsilon_i}^2 = 0.$$

or alternatively:

$$Z_i = \frac{1}{\sigma_{\varepsilon_i}^2} \left[E_i (1 + \Psi_P) - R_F - b_i \sigma_I^2 \sum_{j=1}^{N} b_j Z_j \right].$$

---

[20] It can be shown that the assets to be retained in the portfolio, if the portfolio is free of bear sales, are those for which the term $\theta_i - \phi_K$ (a measure of the additional risk premium provided for each asset considered) is positive.

[21] This will always be the case if the *VaR* premium is bounded, a necessary hypothesis for calculating a maximum on this variable.

By multiplying the two members of the equation by b_I and summarising, we arrive at:

$$\sum_{i=1}^{N} Z_i b_i = \sum_{i=1}^{N} \frac{b_i}{\sigma_{\varepsilon_i}^2} \left[E_i(1 + \Psi_P) - R_F - b_i \sigma_I^2 \sum_{j=1}^{N} b_j Z_j \right]$$

$$\left(1 + \sigma_I^2 \sum_{i=1}^{N} \frac{b_i^2}{\sigma_{\varepsilon_i}^2}\right) \cdot \sum_{i=1}^{N} Z_i b_i = \sum_{i=1}^{N} \frac{b_i}{\sigma_{\varepsilon_i}^2} [E_i(1 + \Psi_P) - R_F]$$

By introducing the expression of $\sum_{i=1}^{N} Z_i b_i$ into that of Z_i, we finally arrive at:

$$Z_i = \frac{b_i}{\sigma_{\varepsilon_i}^2} \left[\frac{E_i(1 + \Psi_P) - R_F}{b_i} - \frac{\sigma_I^2 \sum_{j=1}^{N} \frac{b_j}{\sigma_{\varepsilon_j}^2} [E_j(1 + \Psi_P) - R_F]}{1 + \sigma_I^2 \sum_{j=1}^{N} \frac{b_j^2}{\sigma_{\varepsilon_j}^2}} \right]$$

or:

$$Z_i = \frac{b_i}{\sigma_{\varepsilon_i}^2} (\theta_i - \phi)$$

This is similar to the relation used in the classical EGP method for determining the assets to be included in the portfolio when short sales are authorised.

If short sales are forbidden, we proceed as explained in Section 3.2.6, and calculate $Z_i = \frac{b_i}{\sigma_{\varepsilon_i}^2}(\theta_i - \phi_K)$, where ϕ_k is the maximum value for

$$\phi_k = \frac{\sigma_I^2 \sum_{j=1}^{k} \frac{b_j}{\sigma_{\varepsilon_j}^2} [E_j(1 + \Psi_P) - R_F]}{1 + \sigma_I^2 \sum_{j=1}^{k} \frac{b_j^2}{\sigma_{\varepsilon_j}^2}}$$

after the securities have been sorted according to their decreasing θ_i values.

Note that the terms E_j and Ψ_P are implicit functions of the X_i values.[22] Given that Ψ_P is nonlinear in X_i, the algorithm of the EGP method must incorporate a Picard process, for the same reasons as in Section 10.1.2 (see Figure 10.2).

10.2.3   Comparison of the two methods

We will now compare the classical EGP method with the 'EGP–*VaR*' method that we have just covered. For this purpose, we will be using a numerical example.

Example

We have chosen to determine the portfolio with optimal *VaR* premium relative to the equities on the Spanish market index (IBEX35) using the two methods.

---

[22] X_i represents the weighting of the security (i) in the portfolio. This is the unknown aspect of the problem.

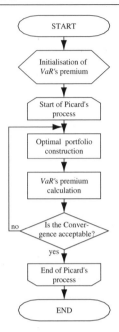

Figure 10.2   Algorithm for taking account of *VaR* in the EGP method

The comparison of the portfolios obtained is based on the *VaR* premium for a *VaR* at 99 %, 95 % and 90 %. The historical period for the rates retained runs from 11 April 1995 to 11 April 2000. We have chosen as the risk-free rate the interbank rate 'Euribor 1 week' for 11 April 2000, which was 3.676 %.[23] See Tables 10.1–10.6.

10.2.4   Conclusion

It will be noted first of all that the two methods used propose portfolios higher than the market index, regardless of the starting hypotheses applied.

Table 10.1   Composition of portfolio (*VaR* at 99 %)

	EGP	EGP–*VaR*
Indra Systems	0.094135885	0.092850684
Tele Pizza	0.154240348	0.152162629
Amadeus Global Travel	0.110170100	0.108288303
NH Hotels (Ex-Cofir)	0.131113608	0.130958267
Altadis	0.123080404	0.123684551
Union Fenosa	0.161211661	0.160615701
Terra Networks	0.041129011	0.039914293
Active de Constr. Y Serv.	0.063707852	0.064207223
Corp. Fin. Alba	0.084216091	0.086193217
Acciona	0.015113720	0.015959957
Aguas Barcelona	0.021991319	0.026165174

[23] Data obtained from the 'Bank of Finland' site.

Table 10.2   Performance of portfolio (*VaR* at 99%)

	IBEX35	EGP	EGP–*VaR*
Weekly return on portfolio	0.004742222	0.011161026	0.011069952
Standard deviation for portfolio	0.028795127	0.033061249	0.032773963
VaR of portfolio at 99% (weekly horizon)	0.062243883	0.065749358	0.065172119
Portfolio risk premium	0.140570337	0.316580440	0.316576644
Portfolio *VaR* premium	0.065030338	0.159188547	0.159201074

Table 10.3   Composition of portfolio (*VaR* at 99%)

	EGP	EGP–*VaR*
Indra Systems	0.094135885	0.092329323
Tele Pizza	0.154240348	0.151319771
Amadeus Global Travel	0.110170100	0.107524924
NH Hotels (Ex-Cofir)	0.131113608	0.130895251
Altadis	0.123080404	0.123929632
Union Fenosa	0.161211661	0.160373940
Terra Networks	0.041129011	0.064409801
Active de Constr. Y Serv.	0.063707852	0.064409801
Corp. Fin. Alba	0.084216091	0.086995268
Acciona	0.015113720	0.016347870
Aguas Barcelona	0.021991319	0.026452697

Table 10.4   Performance of portfolio (*VaR* at 95%)

	IBEX35	EGP	EGP–*VaR*
Weekly return on portfolio	0.004742222	0.011161026	0.011033007
Standard deviation for portfolio	0.028795127	0.033061249	0.032657976
VaR of portfolio at 99% (weekly horizon)	0.062243883	0.065749358	0.042751414
Portfolio risk premium	0.140570337	0.316580440	0.316569713
Portfolio *VaR* premium	0.065030338	0.159188547	0.241828870

Table 10.5   Composition of portfolio (*VaR* at 90%)

	EGP	EGP–*VaR*
Indra Systems	0.094135885	0.091788929
Tele Pizza	0.154240348	0.150446144
Amadeus Global Travel	0.110170100	0.106733677
NH Hotels (Ex-Cofir)	0.131113608	0.130829934
Altadis	0.123080404	0.124183660
Union Fenosa	0.161211661	0.160123355
Terra Networks	0.041129011	0.038910766
Active de Constr. Y Serv.	0.063707852	0.064619774
Corp. Fin. Alba	0.084216091	0.087826598
Acciona	0.015113720	0.016749943
Aguas Barcelona	0.021991319	0.027787219

Table 10.6   Performance of portfolio (*VaR* at 90 %)

	IBEX35	EGP	EGP–*VaR*
Weekly return on portfolio	0.004742222	0.011161026	0.010994713
Standard deviation for portfolio	0.028795127	0.033061249	0.032538097
VaR of portfolio at 99 % (weekly horizon)	0.062243883	0.065749358	0.030045589
Portfolio risk premium	0.140570337	0.316580440	0.316559138
Portfolio *VaR* premium	0.065030338	0.159188547	0.342820104

A comparison of the performances of the optimised portfolios shows that the results obtained by EGP–*VaR* in terms of '*VaR* premium' are higher than the classical EGP method at all *VaR* confidence levels.[24]

Contrarily, however, it is evident that the EGP method provides a risk premium – in terms of variance – higher than that of EGP–*VaR*. This result clearly shows that optimising the risk in terms of variance is not consistent with optimising the risk in terms of financial loss.

Next, it will be noted that the iterations in the Picard process, essential in the EGP–*VaR* method, do not really interfere with the algorithm as the convergence of the process is of five significant figures per iteration.

Finally, it must be stressed that the superiority of EGP–*VaR* over EGP becomes more marked as the level of confidence falls. This can be explained by the fact that with a lower level of confidence in the calculation of the *VaR*, one is more optimistic about its value and therefore about the *VaR* premium as well. This reduces interest in the method to some extent, as the method is only really useful if the level of confidence that can be shown in the portfolio is sufficiently high.

In order to assess the additional benefit of the EGP–*VaR* method, we place ourselves in the least favourable but most realistic case, in which we wish to optimise the *VaR* premium for a 99 % level of confidence. In the example presented, the *VaR* premium ratio is

$$\frac{\Psi_P^{EGP-VaR}}{\Psi_P^{EGP}} \approx 1.00008$$

This implies that with an equal *VaR*, the ratio of weekly yields will also be 1.00008 and the ratio of annual yields will be 1.00416. As the weekly yields are in the region of 1.1 %, the annual yield will be in the region of 77 %. If we start with two portfolios of USD1 000 000 with identical *VaR* values, the portfolio proposed by the EGP–*VaR* method will propose an expected annual yield of USD3200 more than the portfolio with the classical EGP method.

In conclusion, taking account of *VaR* in the EGP method supplies *VaR* premium portfolios greater than the usual method (equal *VaR*) for a very small additional amount of calculation. In addition, it is evident that the increase in value brings a significant increase in annual yield.

10.3   OPTIMISING A GLOBAL PORTFOLIO VIA *VaR*

At present, a portfolio manager's work consists as much of choosing the keys for partitioning the various categories of assets ('asset allocation') as of choosing the specific assets that

---

[24] Calculation of *VaR* with 90 %, 95 % or 99 % probability.

will make up the portfolio ('stock picking'). In consequence, most of the portfolios will not consist exclusively of equities. In this context, generalisation of methods for optimising equity portfolios in moving to global portfolios shows its true importance.

The current practice followed by portfolio managers consists of optimising different asset portfolios separately and combining them subsequently. In many cases, the discretionary clients are managed on the basis of a very restricted number of benchmarks (for example, equity benchmarks, bond benchmarks, monetary fund benchmarks and shareholder fund benchmarks). These are combined with each other linearly in order to offer enough model portfolios for the clients needs; this is referred to as pooling. In our example, we could combine the four portfolios two by two in sections of 10%, which would lead to $\binom{4}{2} \cdot 11 = 66$ model portfolios that represent the client portfolio management methods.

Here we offer an alternative solution that allows a global optimal portfolio to be constructed by generalising the method shown in the preceding paragraph. In this case, the optimisation process will involve correlations between assets of different natures estimated for different maturity dates. The estimated variance–covariance matrix method will help us to estimate *VaR* within our method.

10.3.1 Generalisation of the asset model

The generalisation proposed involves the inclusion of assets other than equities in the portfolio. The first stage will therefore involve generalisation of the asset model used in the EGP method, namely $R_i = a_i + b_i R_I + \varepsilon_i$.

To start, we note that the introduction of the estimated variance–covariance matrix method into our method involves more restrictive hypotheses than those used for equities:

- the hypothesis of stationarity of returns;
- the hypothesis of normality in asset returns;
- the hypothesis of linear dependency
  — of prices on assets with respect to risk factor prices; and
  — of returns on assets in relation to risk factor prices.[25]

These hypotheses will allow us to carry out the following developments.

A very general way of representing an asset according to its risk factors is to apply the Taylor[26] development to the asset according to the risk factors:

$$R_i(X_1^r, \ldots, X_n^r, t) = R_i(0) + \sum_{k=1}^{n}(R_i)'_{X_k^r} X_k^r + (R_i)'_t t + \sum_{k=1}^{n}\sum_{l=1}^{n}(R_i)''_{X_k^r, X_l^r} \frac{X_k^r X_l^r}{2}$$

$$+ \sum_{k=1}^{n}(R_i)''_{X_k^r, t} \frac{X_k^r t}{2} + (R_i)''_{t,t} \frac{t^2}{2} + \ldots + \varepsilon_i$$

Here, ε_i represents the error in the development and X_k^r is the kth risk factor.

---

[25] This is especially the case with shares (CAPM).
[26] The specific case in which the development is made in the area close to the reference point 0 is called the MacLaurin development.

In the case of assets that are linear according to their risk factors and independent of time, all the terms of order higher than 1 will disappear and it is possible to write:

$$R_i(X_1^r, \ldots, X_n^r, t) = R_i(0) + \sum_{k=1}^{n} (R_i)'_{X_k^r} X_k^r$$

In the case of nonlinear assets independent of time such as bonds, the time-dependent terms will disappear but the Taylor development will not stop at the first order:

$$R_i(X_1^r, \ldots, X_n^r, t) = R_i(0) + \sum_{k=1}^{n} (R_i)'_{X_k^r} X_k^r + \sum_{k=1}^{n} \sum_{l=1}^{n} (R_i)''_{X_k^r, X_l^r} \frac{X_k^r X_l^r}{2} + \cdots + \varepsilon_i$$

However, when the risk factors are small[27] ($X_k^r \ll 1$), the higher-order terms will be low in relation to the first-order term and they can be ignored. This therefore brings us to the expression obtained for the purely linear assets:[28]

$$R_i(X_1^r, \ldots, X_n^r, t) = R_i(0) + \sum_{k=1}^{n} (R_i)'_{X_k^r} X_k^r + \varepsilon_i$$

In addition, some future linear assets, such as FRAs, can be linked to one or more risk factors by construction or mapping.[29] This is also the case for bonds when they are expressed according to their coupons rather than the market rate. In this case, the asset does not have its own risk, as this risk is always a function of the factor taken into account, in which case we have once again:

$$R_i(X_1^r, \ldots, X_n^r, t) = R_i(0) + \sum_{k=1}^{n} (R_i)'_{X_k^r} X_k^r$$

Finally, this model will not be valid for time-dependent nonlinear assets, such as options, as in this case the time-connected terms cannot be ignored in relation to the terms linked to other risk factors and we cannot therefore reach an expression of the kind:

$$R_i = a_i + b_i R_I + \varepsilon_i$$

To sum up, if we propose

$$\begin{cases} b_{ik} = (R_i)'_{X_k^r} & k = 1, \ldots, n \\ a_i = R_i(0) \end{cases}$$

---

[27] In reality, this will be valid when the risk factor value is close to the reference point around which the development is made. In our case (MacLaurin development) this reference point is 0 and the relative return on the risk factor must be close to 0.

[28] Bonds are nonlinear when expressed according to interest rates. They are linear when expressed according to the corresponding zero coupon.

[29] This is the case when the estimated variance and covariance matrix method is used for calculating VaR.

We will obtain the generalised form for all the linear assets and assets that can be made linear[30] from the following equation:

$$R_i = a_i + \sum_{k=1}^{n} b_{ik} X_k^r + \varepsilon_i$$

Here, ε_I will be zero in the case of assets that are linear by construction.

10.3.2 Construction of an optimal global portfolio

We will now adapt the EGP–*VaR* method developed in Section 10.2 to the general expression of a linear asset or asset that can be made linear according to its risk factors. This in fact corresponds to a multiple linear regression on the risk factors with the relations:[31]

$$\begin{cases} \text{cov}(\varepsilon_i, \varepsilon_j) = \delta_{ij} \sigma_{\varepsilon_i}^2 \\ E(\varepsilon_i) = 0 \\ a_i = \text{constant} \end{cases}$$

The expression of the variance and covariances according to those of the n risk factors then becomes

$$\sigma_{ij} = \sum_{k=1}^{n} \sum_{l=1}^{n} b_{ik} b_{jl} \sigma_{kl}^r + \delta_{ij} \sigma_{\varepsilon_i}^2$$

Here, σ_{kl}^r represents the covariance between the risk factors X_k^r and X_l^r.

From the preceding equation, we deduce the expression of the variance for a portfolio consisting of N assets:[32]

$$\sigma_P^2 = \sum_{i=1}^{N} \sum_{j=1}^{N} X_i X_j \sigma_{ij} = \sum_{i=1}^{N} \sum_{j=1}^{N} X_i X_j \sum_{k=1}^{n} \sum_{l=1}^{n} b_{ik} b_{jl} \sigma_{kl}^r + \sum_{i=1}^{N} X_i^2 \sigma_{\varepsilon_i}^2$$

Developments similar to those made in Section 10.2.2 lead to the equation:

$$E_i(1 + \Psi_P) - R_F - \sum_{k=1}^{n} \sum_{l=1}^{n} b_{ik} \sigma_{kl} \sum_{j=1}^{N} b_{lj} Z_j - Z_i \sigma_{\varepsilon_i}^2 = 0$$

As stated above, some assets do not have their own expression of risk: $\sigma_{\varepsilon_i}^2 = 0$.

As z_i depends on $\dfrac{1}{\sigma_{\varepsilon_i}^2}$, the equations will therefore have to be adapted.

If we proceed as before, in an iterative way, we will with the same definition of K arrive at:

$$E_i(1 + \psi_P) - R_F - \sum_{j=1}^{K} Z_j \sum_{k=1}^{n} \sum_{l=1}^{n} b_{ik} \sigma_{kl} b_{lj} - Z_i \sigma_{\varepsilon_i}^2 = 0$$

By suggesting

$$v_{ij} = \sum_{k=1}^{n} \sum_{l=1}^{n} b_{ik} \sigma_{kl} b_{lj}$$

---

[30] The case of nonlinear time-independent assets.

[31] The quantity that is worth 1 if $i = j$ and 0 if $i \neq j$ is termed δ_{ij}.

[32] The X_j proportions of the securities in the portfolio should not be confused with the risk factors X_k^r.

We arrive successively at:

$$E_i(1 + \Psi_P) - R_F - \sum_{j=1}^{K} v_{ij} Z_j - Z_i \sigma_{\varepsilon_i}^2 = 0$$

$$E_i(1 + \Psi_P) - R_F - \sum_{j=1}^{K-1} v_{ij} Z_j - v_{ii} Z_i - Z_i \sigma_{\varepsilon_i}^2 = 0$$

$$\frac{E_i(1 + \Psi_P) - R_F}{v_{ii} + \sigma_{\varepsilon_i}^2} - \frac{\sum_{j=1}^{K-1} v_{ij} Z_j}{v_{ii} + \sigma_{\varepsilon_i}^2} = Z_i$$

That is:

$$\theta_i - \phi_K = Z_i$$

This equation is equivalent to the relation in Section 10.2 that gives the composition of the portfolio.

The process will therefore be equivalent to the case of the equities:

- Classification of equities according to decreasing θ_I values.
- Iterative calculation of Z_I rates according to the above equation in the order of classification of the equities.
- Stopping at first asset for which $Z_I < 0$ (K of them will thus be selected).
- Deduction of the portfolio composition by $X_i = \dfrac{Z_i}{\sum_{j=1}^{K} Z_j}$.
- Calculation of the *VaR* premium.
- Subsequent iteration of the Picard process.

10.3.3 Method of optimisation of global portfolio

The main difficulty of moving from a portfolio of equities to a global portfolio comes from the fact that the global portfolio introduces a range of financial products that are very different in terms of their behaviour when faced with risk factors and of their characteristic future structure.

The first effect of this is that we are not envisaging a case in which all the financial instruments included contain optional products. The second is that it is now necessary to choose a global risk calculation method, in our case that of *VaR*.

The *VaR* calculation method used here is that of the estimated variance–covariance matrix. This choice is based on the fact that this method is 'the most complete *VaR* calculation technique from the operational point of view',[33] but predominantly because it is the only method that allows *VaR* to be expressed explicitly according to the composition of the equities. In this regard, it is the one best adapted to our method.

In practice, the estimated variance–covariance matrix method expresses a position in terms of cashflows and maps these flows for the full range of risk factors available.

---

[33] Esch L., Kieffer R. and Lopez T., *Value at Risk – Vers un risk management moderne*, De Boeck, 1997, p. 111.

We then obtain the expression of the discounted price of the asset according to the risk factors:[34]

$$p_i = \sum_{k=1}^{n} A_{ik} X_k^r$$

This will lead to the expression in terms of the equivalent returns:

$$R_i = \sum_{k=1}^{n} b_{ik} R_k^r$$

Where:

$$\begin{cases} R_i = \dfrac{p_{i,t} - p_{i,t-1}}{p_{i,t-1}} \\[2ex] R_k^r = \dfrac{X_{k,t}^r - X_{k,t-1}^r}{X_{k,t-1}^r} \\[2ex] b_{ik} \approx \dfrac{A_{ik} X_k^r}{\displaystyle\sum_{j=1}^{n} A_{ij} X_j^r} \end{cases}$$

It must be stressed that in our case, if mapping can be avoided (either because it is possible to apply linear regression to the risk factor as is the case for equities, or because it is possible to express the return on the asset directly as a function of the risk-factor return), we will skip this stage.

In the specific case of non-optional derivative products, for which the discounted price (or current value) is initially zero, the return on them cannot be deduced. In this case, the derived product will be separated into two terms with a non-zero price. For example, a FRA 6–9 long will be split into a nine-month loan and a six-month deposit. The expression of the expected return on the equity according to the risk factor returns will follow as:

$$E_i = \sum_{k=1}^{n} b_{ik} E_k^r$$

Note

The expression above supposes that the terms A_{ik} are constant. In addition, the equities do not require mapping over a full range of products as they are expressed according to spot positions on market indices and we will therefore retain, in this case:

$$R_i = a_i + b_i R_I + \varepsilon_i$$

We will now summarise the stages of this method.

1. The first stage consists of choosing the characteristics of the population of assets from which we will choose those that will optimise the portfolio. It will be particularly important to choose the maturity dates, due dates etc. from the assets in question as these will condition the value of the *VaR* and therefore the optimisation of the portfolio.

---

[34] Note that this mapping can be applied to prices, to each term or directly to yields. In this situation, calculation of the z_j values will suffice.

2. The second stage of the optimisation process involves a search for all the coefficients involved in the equations:

$$E_i = \sum_{k=1}^{n} b_{ik} E_k^r$$

$$\sigma_{ij} = \sum_{k=1}^{n} \sum_{l=1}^{n} b_{ik} b_{jl} \sigma_{kl}^r + \delta_{ij} \sigma_{\varepsilon_i}^2$$

This will be supplied by the historical periods of the assets and the estimated vari-ance–covariance matrix method. This stage will also condition the temporal horizon for optimising the *VaR* premium. In addition, these positions do not require any map-ping, which means that the equities may be understood in the classical way through linear regression on the corresponding market index.

3. The third stage consists of optimising the *VaR* premium in the true sense, the premium being arrived at according to the scheme described in Section 10.3.2.

In its general outlay, the algorithm is similar to that described in Section 10.2.2 and specifically involves the Picard iteration. The flow chart shown in Figure 10.3 sets out the main lines to be followed.

Example

In order not to complicate the exposition unnecessarily, we will deal with the case of a basket of assets containing (see Tables 10.7–10.11):

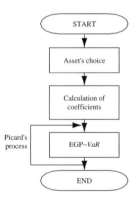

Figure 10.3   Algorithm for optimising a global portfolio using *VaR*

Table 10.7   Daily volatility and yield of assets

	Variance	Return
Equity 1	0.001779239	0.006871935
Equity 2	0.000710298	0.003602820
Equity 3	0.000595885	0.003357344
Equity 4	0.002085924	0.004637212
Equity 5	0.000383731	0.003891459
Bond 1	7.11199E-05	0.000114949
Bond 2	4.01909E-05	0.000125582

Table 10.8 Expression of assets in terms of risk factors

Assets	Market index	Rate, 1 year	Rate, 2 years	Rate, 3 years	Rate, 4 years	Rate, 5 years	Rate, 7 years	Rate, 9 years	Rate, 10 years
Equity 1	0.907016781	0	0	0	0	0	0	0	0
Equity 2	0.573084264	0	0	0	0	0	0	0	0
Equity 3	−0.524903478	0	0	0	0	0	0	0	0
Equity 4	0.982081231	0	0	0	0	0	0	0	0
Equity 5	0.421222706	0	0	0	0	0	0	0	0
Bond 1	0	0.047260003	0.045412546	0.043420969	0.041501147	0.822405334	0	0	0
Bond 2	0	0.044719088	0.042970958	0.041086458	0.039269854	0.058192226	0.0793941	0.046557894	0.647809442

- One five-year bond in euros, coupon 5 % repayment at par.
- One 10-year bond in euros, coupon 6 % reimbursement at par.
- Five equities based on the same market index.

The *VaR* is calculated at 99 % probability and with a horizon of one day. The risk-free rate is 3.75 %.

The data relative to these shares and the associated risk factors are purely fictitious.[35]

We can see first of all that the composite portfolio beats each of the assets in isolation, thus clearly showing the diversification effect sought.

In addition, it is best to stress that when applied to a portfolio of bonds, this method offers real optimisation of the yield/*VaR* ratio, unlike the known portfolio immunisation methods. In the case of bonds, the method proposed is therefore not an alternative, but an addition to the immunisation methods.

Table 10.9   Classification of assets

Classification	
Equity 5	1.238051233
Equity 2	1.180947722
Equity 3	0.921654797
Equity 1	0.764163854
Equity 4	0.620600304
Bond 2	0.614979773
Bond 1	0.19802287

Table 10.10   Composition of portfolio

Classification	
Equity 1	0.070416113
Equity 2	0.114350746
Equity 3	0.068504735
Equity 4	0.036360401
Equity 5	0.146993068
Bond 1	0.041847479
Bond 2	0.521527457

Table 10.11   *VaR* premiums on the various assets

Classification	*VaR* premium
Equity 1	0.031922988
Equity 2	0.028453485
Equity 3	0.024136102
Equity 4	0.023352806
Equity 5	0.030366115
Bond 1	0.000722099
Bond 2	0.001690335
Portfolio	0.0576611529

---

[35] See the CD-ROM attached to this book, 'Global optimisation of *VaR* premium.xls'.

Finally, the major advantage of this method is that it allows a portfolio to be optimised in terms of asset allocation as well as stock picking, which is not the case with the pooling methods. In pooling, the combinations of benchmarks do not take account of the correlation between these and still less take account of the correlation between each asset making up the benchmarks. This is the great advantage of the method, as asset allocation accounts for the greater part of a portfolio manager's work.

11

Institutional Management: APT Applied to Investment Funds

The APT[1] model described in Section 3.3.2 allows the behaviour of investment funds to be analysed in seven points.

11.1 ABSOLUTE GLOBAL RISK

Normal volatility (the 'standard deviation' of statisticians) is a measurement of the impact of all market conditions observed during a year on the behaviour of an asset. It summarises recent history. If other market conditions had prevailed, the same calculation would have given another volatility. As risk has to be calculated *a priori*, the probable average volatility for the period ahead must be determined in advance.

Absolute risk, calculated within the APT framework, is the most reliable forecast of the probable average volatility of an asset. The APT system calculates the global risk for the fund, which it breaks down into:

- systematic risk and APT factor-sensitivity profile;
- residual or specific risk.

The systematic profile consists of a series of 'rods', each of which represents the sensitivity of the fund to the corresponding systematic risk factors. Systematic risk is the quadratic mean of all the sensitivities to the various systematic factors. The observation of the profile suggests a genetic similarity; systematic risk is thus the product of a genetic code, a kind of 'DNA' of the risk of each instrument. This will allow portfolio adjustments to be measured with respect to its objective and the risk of performance divergence to be ascertained:

- Two very different systematic risk profiles will lead to a significant probability of divergence (Figure 11.1).
- In contrast, two very similar systematic risk profiles will have a correspondingly significant probability of similar behaviour (Figure 11.2).

11.2 RELATIVE GLOBAL RISK/TRACKING ERROR

The relative risk of a portfolio with respect to a target calculated using APT is a very reliable *a priori* risk estimator.

When the global risk for a portfolio has been calculated with respect to a target (*ex ante* tracking error), a series of risk tranches can be traced. These ranges are a very reliable

---

[1] Interested readers should read Ross S. A., The arbitrage theory of capital asset pricing, *Journal of Economic Theory*, 1976, pp. 343–62. Dhrymes P. J., Friend I. and Gultekin N. B., A critical re-examination of the empirical evidence on the arbitrage pricing theory, *Journal of Finance*, No. 39, 1984, pp. 323–46. Chen N. F., Roll R. and Ross S. A., Economic Forces of the Stock Market, *Journal of Business*, No. 59, 1986, pp. 383–403.

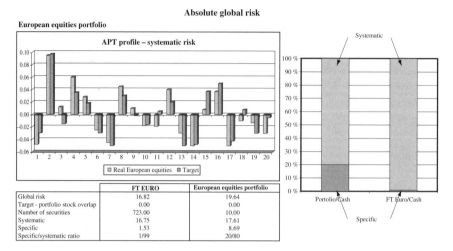

Figure 11.1   Stock picking fund

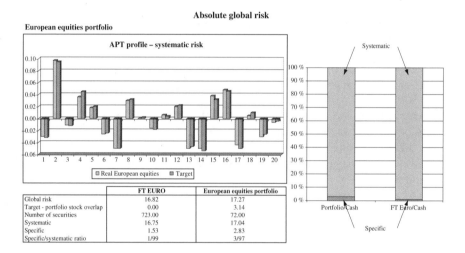

Figure 11.2   Index fund

indicator of the *a priori* risk, and can be used as an indicator of overperformance or underperformance.

When the portfolio reaches the upper range, 96 % (Figure 11.3), the probability of rising above the range will have dropped to 2 %. Conversely, the probability of arbitrage of the strategy by the market, in accordance with the theory of APT, is close to certainty (98 %).

The opposite to this is underperformance, which pulls the relative performance of the portfolio down towards the lower range. It should lead the manager, after analysis of his portfolio and validation of his initial strategy, to wait for his portfolio to rebound; the brief period of underperformance should in principle be arbitrated by the market.

Thus, by taking care to track the relative performance of the portfolio regularly with respect to its target within the risk ranges, we will have a very reliable indicator of when

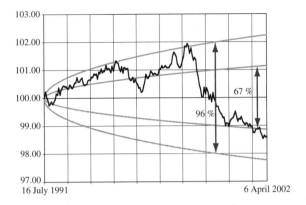

Figure 11.3 *Ex ante* tracking error

to revise the portfolio in cases of overperformance or to maintain the strategy in cases of underperformance.

The 98 %-*VaR* is the maximum loss with 98 % probability for a portfolio in relation to a risk-free asset, on a clearly defined horizon.

If the *ex ante* tracking error is calculated in relation to the risk-free asset, 98 %-*VaR* will be represented according to time by the second lower envelope.

11.3   RELATIVE FUND RISK VS. BENCHMARK ABACUS

The 'best' (minimum risk) curve gives the minimum tracking error for a number of securities (*x*-axis) held in the portfolio – the deviation of the fund with respect to the benchmark (*y*-axis), as shown in Figure 11.4.

For each portfolio studied one can, with knowledge of its number of securities, locate one's relative risk on the graph and note the vertical distance that separates it from the minimum risk curve.

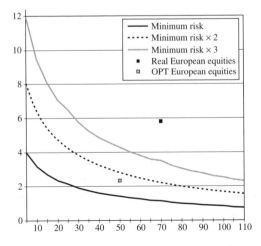

Figure 11.4   The best

For any structured portfolio, the optimum weightings for the securities held can be identified in order to minimise the relative global risk.

In Figure 11.4, the black square shows the relative global risk of the initial portfolio and the grey square that of the optimised portfolio (securities the same as the initial portfolio, but weightings altered and possibly down to zero). For a given preselection of securities, the grey square indicates the minimum relative global risk that can be reached with this choice of securities.

11.4 ALLOCATION OF SYSTEMATIC RISK

The allocation of systematic risk allows the distribution of the risk to be displayed according to key variables: sector, country, economic variables, financial variables etc. The allocation can be made taking account of statistical dependencies (joint allocation) or otherwise (independent allocation). For example, in a European portfolio, the 'financial sector' variable can be linked to MSCI Europe Finance index, and the 'long-term France interest rate' variable can be linked to the 10-year Matif index.

11.4.1 Independent allocation

As the portfolio's systematic risk is represented by its APT factor-sensitivity vector, it is possible to calculate the portfolio's sensitivity to each of the independent variables taken individually.

The portfolio's sensitivity to each of the variables is calculated by projecting the portfolio's systematic risk vector onto the vector that represents the systematic risk of the variable. The length of the projection shows the sensitivity of the portfolio to the variable.

Figure 11.5 shows that the portfolio has hardly any sensitivity to the performance of variable D as the length of the projection of its systematic risk onto that of variable D is close to zero.

The various sensitivities thus calculated with respect to several different variables allow the individual contribution made by each variable to the portfolio's systematic behaviour to be measured. They can be compared to each other but not added together.

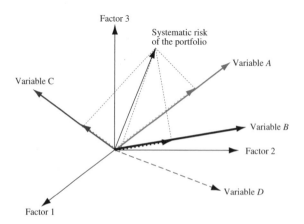

Figure 11.5   Independent allocation

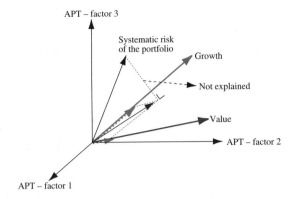

Figure 11.6   Joint allocation

11.4.2   Joint allocation: 'value' and 'growth' example

As the systematic risk of the portfolio is expressed by its APT factor-sensitivity vector, it can be broken down into the explicative variables 'growth' and 'value', representing the S&P Value and the S&P Growth (Figure 11.6).

One cannot, however, be content with projecting the portfolio risk vector onto each of the variables. In fact, the 'growth' and 'value' variables are not necessarily independent statistically. They cannot therefore be represented by geometrically orthogonal variables.

It is in fact essential to project the portfolio risk vector perpendicularly onto the space of the vectors of the variables. In the present example, it is a matter of projection onto the 'growth' and 'value' variables plan.

Once this projection is calculated, the trace thus produced needs to be again projected onto the two axes to find out the contribution made by each variable to the systematic risk of the portfolio.

It is clear from this example that the two variables retained only explain part of the systematic risk of the portfolio. The component of the portfolio's systematic risk not explained by the explicative variables chosen is represented by the perpendicular vector. This perpendicular component allows allocation of the systematic risk to be completed. This component is not a residual.

Whatever the extent of the explicative variables retained, it is essential to calculate this additional component very accurately. If it is not calculated, its contribution will appear as a residual, neutral by definition in statistical terms, while it is in fact systematic.

This is the exact problem encountered by all the models constructed on the basis of regression on extents of prespecified variables. These variables do not explain the systematic component, as it is orthogonal to them (that is, statistically independent).

11.5   ALLOCATION OF PERFORMANCE LEVEL

In the same way as the APT model allows a portfolio's risk to be broken down *ex ante* over the range of independent variables, it also allows the portfolio's performance to be broken down *ex post* over the same independent variables for variable periods between 1991 and the present.

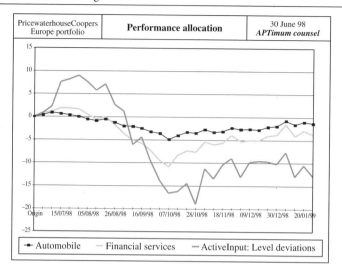

Figure 11.7 Allocation of performance level

The technique used is termed 'factor-mimicking portfolios'; each risk factor can be mimicked by an arbitrage portfolio. For example, it is possible to construct a portfolio that presents a unitary sensitivity to factor 8 and zero sensitivity to the other factors. This is called a factor-8 mimicking portfolio.

Being aware of the composition of 20 portfolios that mimic 20 statistical factors, we can also find out the profitability of the securities making up the portfolios and therefore find out the factors. Being aware of the various sensitivities of the funds to the various factors and their yields, we can allocate the performance levels.

In Figure 11.7, the performance level is explained by the contributions made by all the variables from the automobile and financial sectors.

11.6 GROSS PERFORMANCE LEVEL AND RISK WITHDRAWAL

The adjusted APT performance for the risk is equal to the historical performance over a given period divided by the APT beta for the fund, compared to a reference strategy that can be the average for the fund within a category or an index.

The APT beta measures the overall sensitivity of the fund to this reference strategy. The APT beta is not identical to the traditional beta in the financial assets equilibrium model, which only measures the sensitivity of the funds to certain market measurements such as an index. Graphically, it is the orthogonal projection of the systematic risk vector for the fund onto the vector for the average in the category (Figure 11.8).

However, like the traditional beta, it is a number for which the average for a given homogeneous group, like European equities, is 1. A number in excess of 1 indicates that the fund is more sensitive to the systematic risk factors that its pairs. A number less than 1 indicates that the fund is less sensitive.

Let us consider a fund A invested in European equities with a gross performance level that over one year has reached 16.58 %. On the basis of this gross performance level, this

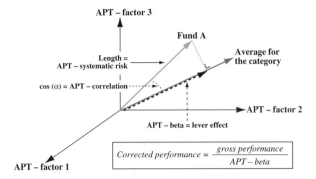

Figure 11.8 Gross performance level and risk withdrawal

fund A will be classified 63rd out of the 314 in its category. Let us take as a reference within this category the virtual fund equal to the average for the funds.

The vector that represents the systematic risk for fund A differs from the systematic risk for the average virtual fund, taken as a reference in length and in position within the area. This difference between the two vectors indicates the probability that the behaviour patterns will diverge. Fund A follows a strategy identical to that of the reference fund for a proportion equal to its projection onto the reference fund. This is the beta APT.

The beta APT measures the proportion of the fund's performance covered by the reference strategy. As the beta APT is less than 1 (0.867), this indicates that fund A is less 'invested' than the reference fund within the reference strategy. If Fund A had been as much 'invested' as the reference fund in the reference strategy, its performance level would have reached 16.58/0.867 = 19.12, that is, its gross performance multiplied by its withdrawal coefficient of $1/\beta$. This performance level is the withdrawal performance of fund A within the average strategy. If the withdrawal coefficient $1/\beta$ is very different from 1 (for example 0.8 or 1.2), this indicates that the strategy of A is very different compared to the reference for the category. This may be caused by:

- either the angle between vector **A** (absolute systematic risk) and the average vector for the category, which is very open;
- or by vector **A** being too long or too short.

11.7 ANALYSIS OF STYLE

The APT model calculates an absolute systematic risk vector for each fund. As these calculations are carried out for a very wide range of funds, it will be noticed that the vectors for all the funds dealt with group together naturally in clearly demarcated cones. Each cone represents a group of funds, such as, for example, 'European equity funds'.

Once the map graph (Figure 11.9) has been completed, it will allow:

- the actual homogeneous management categories to be delimited;
- all funds to be located within one of these categories;
- its level of typicality to be measured;
- its withdrawal performance to be calculated in relation to the average strategy for the category.

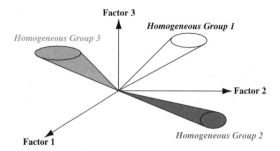

Figure 11.9   Map graph

In practice, it will be noted that the angle of opening of each cone is less than 24°. In general, only funds with E values between 0.8 and 12 will be included.

Part V
From Risk Management to Asset and Liability Management

Introduction

In addition to the traditional functions allocated to risk management, such as management of credit risks and market risks in certain banking products, the discipline has also expanded into the study of operational risks and random insurance risks.

The aim of asset and liability management, or ALM, is to arrive at an understanding of the problems of risk (rates, exchange etc.) across the whole balance sheet.

Techniques for Measuring Structural Risks in Balance Sheets

The aim of the developments that follow is to make the analytical tools used in ALM easily understandable.

Understanding of the concepts must not be treated separately from understanding of the accounting, banking and financial data needed to use the concepts.

Naturally, ALM is normally managed through management software packages. The interface between computer processes and software applications allows essential elements such as the type of product and its characteristics in terms of flows and currency type to be captured.

First, we will introduce the traditional ALM tools and models, together with the possible uses for *VaR* in ALM.

On the other hand, the interface between ALM software and the bank's computer network cannot be achieved effectively without addressing the contractual hazards particular to certain products. In fact, how can liquidity risk and therefore interest rate risk be known on contracts that do not have a contractual maturity, such as a current account? How can a floating-rate contract be modelled? These two elements present real practical problems for the use of analytical tools in traditional risks such as liquidity or interest rate gaps or even in calculating a duration for the balance sheet.

Next, we will propose techniques for modelling floating-rate products and calculate maturity and the liquidity risk profiles for products that have no maturity dates.

12.1 TOOLS FOR STRUCTURAL RISK ANALYSIS IN ASSET AND LIABILITY MANAGEMENT

Let us take the balance sheet of a bank in order to illustrate the asset and liability management tools (Table 12.1).

The equity portfolio consists of a negotiable treasury bond with a nominal rate of 4.5 % and five-year maturity. The variable-risk equity portfolio is held long term (15 years). It is not a trading portfolio.

The property loan book has a 20-year term at rates that are adjusted every six months based on Euribor six-month (3.1 % at t_0) and a 10-year maturity. Interest is paid on 15 June and 15 December in each year. The principal is reimbursed on maturity.

The bonds are issued at a fixed rate of 5.5 % over five years, with a single bullet payment on maturity.

The demand deposits are held in a replicating portfolio, a concept that we will explain in more detail later. Of the current account balances 20 % vary over the month and are refinanced through the interbank market at one month. Of the deposits 30 % have a maturity date of two years and 50 % have five years.

Interbank: the *nostri* and *lori* have a reporting period of one day and maturity of 50 % one month and 50 % three months.

Table 12.1 Simplified balance sheet

Assets		Liabilities	
Tangible fixed assets	10	Equity fund	15
Bond portfolio	30	Bonds issued	20
Share portfolio	10	Non-interest-bearing current accounts	25
Property Loans	20	Interbank	10
Total	70	Total	70

Table 12.2 Rate curve

[1 day–3 months]	2.5 %
[3 months–1 year]	3.0 %
[1 year–3 years]	3.5 %
[3 years–6 years]	4.0 %
[6 years–10 years]	4.5 %

Market conditions: Euribor six-month rate 3.1 %; rate curve noted at actuarial rate (see Table 12.2).

12.1.1 Gap or liquidity risk

Liquidity risk appears in a bank when the withdrawal of funds exceeds the incoming deposits over a defined period. The liquidity mismatch measures the foreseeable differences on various future dates between the full totals of liabilities and assets.

The projections represent the provisional needs for liquidity and refinancing and are a basic management tool. Gaps may be calculated in terms of cashflows or in stocks.

Mismatches in cashflow terms are the differences between the variation in assets and the variation in liabilities (funds coming in and funds going out) during a given period. They determine the need for new finance during the period through calculations of future flow maturities (Table 12.3).

Gaps in positions are the differences between the liability totals in assets and in liabilities on a given date. They determine the total cumulative liquidity need at a given date. The gaps in cashflow represent the variations in gaps for positions from one period to another. The stocks gap must be identical in terms of absolute value to the cumulative cashflow mismatches from the very beginning (see Table 12.4).

Table 12.3 Liquidity gaps (in flows)

Mismatches in cashflow	1 day– 1 month	1 month– 3 months	3 months– 1 year	1 year– 3 years	3 years– 6 years	6 years– 10 years	Over 10 years
Falls in assets	0				30	20	5
Falls in liabilities	−10	−5		−7.5	−32.5		
Gap	−10	−5	0	−7.5	−2.5	20	5
Cumulative gap		−15	−15	−22.5	−25	−5	0

Table 12.4 Liquidity gaps (in stocks)

Position gaps: liability and asset movements	1 day– 1 month	1 month– 3 months	3 months– 1 year	1 year– 3 years	3 years– 6 years	6 years– 10 years	Over 10 years
Tangible fixed assets							10
Portfolio converted into fixed assets					30		
Variable risk share portfolio							10
Credits on fixed assets						20	
Total assets							
Equity funds							15
Issue of bonds					20		
Current account deposits not paid	5			7.5	12.5		
Interbank	5	5					
Total liabilities							
Gap	−10	−15	−15	−22.5	−25	−5	0

Position gaps are negative as the assets depreciate more slowly than the liabilities, leading to a treasury deficit over the period as a whole (a positive gap represents an excess of resources).

12.1.2 Rate mismatches

The rate mismatch is linked to the liquidity gap, as all forms of liquidity necessitate financing. The interest rate gap is the difference between floating rate assets and liabilities over a certain period. Interest rate gaps can be calculated in stocks or in flows, on a balance sheet in a state of equilibrium.

To construct a gap analysis, we begin by compiling the balance sheet for operations in progress, specifying their maturity date and rate. Each future maturity date gives rise to a cashflow. This flow will be positive for the assets as it corresponds to the repayment of a loan or payment of a supplier. The flows are shown in the repayment schedule on the date corresponding to their maturity. The difference between the cumulative flow of assets and the cumulative flow of liabilities represents the capital invested at an unknown rate. The gap schedule summarises the simple information that shows the cashflow manager the future development in his rate position; that is, his exposure to the rate risk. This information, however, does not give him any information on the price that will be payable if he decides to rebalance his balance sheet in terms of totals or duration. Neither does the cashflow manager know the sensitivity of the repayment schedule to fluctuations in rates. The fineness of the breakdown of repayment schedules varies greatly from one institution to another and is a function of the number and total value of the positions in play. The short term must be less than one year, in accordance with the budgetary and accounting horizon, which is annual (Table 12.5).

Table 12.5   Gap report

Gap: liability and asset movements	1 day–1 month	1 month–3 months	3 months–1 year	1 year–3 years	3 years–6 years	6 years–10 years	Over 10 years
Tangible fixed assets							10
Portfolio converted into fixed assets					30		
Variable risk share portfolio							10
Credits on fixed assets			20				
Assets	0	0	20	0	30	0	20
Equity fund							15
Issue of bonds					20		
Current account deposits not paid							
Interbank	10						
Liabilities	10	0	0	0	20	0	15
Rate mismatches (margins or flow)	−10	0	20	0	10	0	5
Cumulative rate or asset mismatches	−10	−10	10	10	20	0	5

The bank's interest rate margin will benefit from a rise in rates in three months. After three months, the position is long as there are more assets sensitive to variations in rates than liabilities. Contrarily, up to three months the bank will have a short position in rates. Naturally, this gap report will be used as a basis for the simulations that we will show later.

A reading of the gap profiles gives an overall idea of the finance needs for the period. The creation of liquidity and rate gap reports is a common method as the procedure is easy to understand, calculate and display. In addition, it allows the impact of a change in rates on the interest margin to be estimated. The method does, however, have a number of drawbacks:

- The aggregation into periods masks the risks inherent within the method.
- It is not possible to calculate a single indicator.

12.1.3   Net present value (NPV) of equity funds and sensitivity

In ALM, return and risk are generally determined using two key indicators:

- The net interest income (or interest rate margin).
- NPV (or market value).

In the interest rate gap, we saw the concept of interest margin, which represents the budgetary point of view and was short term in nature. Now, we will look at the market value or NPV, which will represent the point of view of supply and will be long term in nature. The NPV for the equity fund is obtained by the difference between the assets and liabilities as evaluated under market conditions using a mark-to-market approach. The NPV must be calculated on the basis of flows in capital and interest, while the gap schedule is only compiled in relation to the liabilities on elements of assets and liabilities. The NPV for the equity fund is an approach to the bank's value. In this case, it is considered that the market value of the bank depends on the value of the asset portfolio and the cost of the debt. This approach also suggests that all the entries in the balance sheet are negotiable. Unfortunately, however, measuring the NPV is not sufficient as it is static, hence the interest in a study of sensitivity, the concept presented before together with duration (see Section 4.2). It does not take account of the potential rate fluctuation risks. On the other hand, the interest and capital flows are often actualized on the basis of a single rate curve without taking account of the spread in credit risk inherent in certain assets (retail credits).

12.1.4 Duration of equity funds

The *NPV* of equity funds is static and sensitive to changes in interest rates. To measure this sensitivity, the duration of equity funds can be calculated. We have shown before that the market value of an asset is a function of its duration. By definition:

- MVA = market value of the asset.
- MVL = market value of the liability.
- D_{ef} = equity funds duration.
- D_a = duration of the asset.
- D_l = duration of the liability.

$$\frac{\Delta NPV}{\Delta r} = -D_{ef} \cdot \frac{NPV}{1+r}$$

The duration of the equity fund is the algebraic sum of the durations of the elements making up the portfolio

$$
\begin{aligned}
D_{ef} &= -\frac{\Delta NPV}{\Delta r} \cdot \frac{1+r}{NPV} \\
&= -\frac{\Delta(MVA - MVL)}{\Delta r} \cdot \frac{1+r}{NPV} \\
&= -\left(\frac{-D_a \cdot MVA}{1+r} + \frac{D_l \cdot MVL}{1+r} \right) \cdot \frac{1+r}{NPV} \\
&= \frac{D_a \cdot MVA - D_l \cdot MVL}{NPV}
\end{aligned}
$$

We have demonstrated the conditions for which the market value of the equity fund is immunised. The *NPV* of the equity fund is not sensitive to variations in interest rates when $D_a \cdot MVA = D_l \cdot MVA$, which corresponds to a zero equity fund duration. D_{ef} can assume any value. High values correspond to high sensitivity of economic equity fund value to rate changes in one direction or the other.

12.2 SIMULATIONS

The aim of simulations is to explore the future configurations of rate curves and their impact on interest margins or value-measuring instruments (current value of equity fund or economic reserve, which is the difference between the NPV and the accounting value of the asset).

There are four main analytical categories of simulation, from the simplest to the most complex.

- The first category of simulation relates to the rate curves with balance sheet volumes for each ALM product renewed in the same way on transactional bases. The effect of rate changes will be felt in existing contracts and in new production, according to the transactional rollover hypothesis. A contract with accounting value of 100 maturing within two months will be renewed in the same way every two months for the same accounting value.
- The second category of simulation relates to the rate curves with balance sheet volumes for each ALM product renewed in the same way according to the initial terms of each contract. The effect of rate changes will be felt in existing contracts and in new production, according to the contractual rollover hypothesis. A contract with accounting value of 100 maturing within two months will be renewed in the same way within two months for the same accounting value, with a term renewed as before (for example, one year).
- The third category of simulation relates both to rates and to balance sheet volumes of ALM products. This simulation is both more complex and more realistic, as volumes can be sensitive to changes in interest rates. In this case a contract with 100 maturing within two months will be renewed on a contractual basis with a total of $100 + a\%$ or $100 - a\%$.
- The fourth category of simulation also uses the previous simulation by introducing the commercial and balance sheet development strategy. In this case a contract with 100 maturing within two months will be renewed on new or identical contractual bases with a total of $100 + a\%$ or $100 - a\%$.

The aim of the simulations is to optimise the liquidity and rate covers. It is easily understandable that this optimisation process will become more complex when the sensitivities of the balance sheet volumes to rates are used and the effects of commercial policies and development strategies are included in the balance sheet.

For each type of simulation, one or more rate scenarios can be used. When the banking institutions use a single scenario rate, the most frequently used method is a parallel shift of rates per currency per 100 basis points. This single scenario is in fact a stress scenario. It can be usefully added to by truly macroeconomic bank forecasts of rate curves, produced using the forward rates based on market forecasts and on the theory of anticipation, or through a series of scenarios that makes use of stochastic rate generators (Hull White, Vasicek, etc). Naturally, these scenarios are closer to a true margin forecast and to short-term and medium-term value indicators.

Once the rate scenario has been drawn up, the methods for changing the rate conditions on existing contracts and/or on new production will depend on the type of rate. There are three types of interest rate:

- Variable rates, with recurring revision periods. These contracts are altered according to market parameters (floating rate) or other indicators (such as bank resource costs). In this case, the ALM information system must allow the revision periods for each old or new contract to be identified and the methods of revision to be known.

- The variable or floating-rate contracts, with non-recurring revision periods, depend on indicators that are not a contractual function of market indicators. In this case, the rates will be revised on the bank's initiative. For floating rates, the model must allow the probable period of revision to be known for each rate scenario. This revision is applied to all the outstanding amounts on old or new contracts. Floating-rate contracts can be integrated into ALM by using a theoretical model founded on *NPV* or by using a behavioural approach founded on canonical correlations and logistic regression. These methods will be introduced later.
- Fixed rates require knowledge of the historical correlations between the market rates and the contract rates. These correlations, based on the market reference rate, will apply to new productions.

12.3   USING *VaR* IN ALM

VaR is used in a very specific ways in asset and liability management. This market risk-measuring instrument was initially used for dealing-room or treasury activities. Of course the time horizon used is that of one day in order to assess the market risk for that day and to satisfy the control requirements of the middle office. ALM is not concerned with this very short-term trading logic. If *VaR* is used, the *VaR* will be calculated on a longer period, generally one month. *VaR* assesses the market risk for the bank's balance sheet as a whole and not just for market activities in the narrow sense. The month is also linked to the organisational process adopted for ALM, as the asset and liability management committee usually meets on a monthly basis.

This instrument is a useful addition to the instruments introduced earlier as being based essentially on interest rate risk. Finally, for practical reasons, the method used is generally J. P. Morgan's, as the variance–covariance matrix data for the interest rates and exchanges required are available free of charge on the Internet.

12.4   REPRICING SCHEDULES (MODELLING OF CONTRACTS WITH FLOATING RATES)

We now introduce two concepts that are essential for optimising ALM tools. Their aim is to define the maturity dates for products without specified dates and to arrive at an understanding of the non-contractual methods of revising rates for products with floating rates. The maturity date definition models, or replicating portfolios, and the repricing models, are essential for calculating a J. P. Morgan type of *VaR* for the whole of the balance sheet, and for calculating a gap in liquidity or interest rates, a duration for non-maturity date products and a net present value.

12.4.1   The conventions method

In the absence of research reports, a large number of banks use an arbitrary convention for integrating floating-rate products into interest rate risk analytics tools. Some banks with floating-rate contracts admit as the next rate revision the average historical interval for which the floating rates have remained stable. This calculation must obviously be made for each type of floating-rate product, as the behaviour of the revision process is not the same from one product to another.

Like every convention, this approach is far from perfect as we will clearly see that the rate revision periods are irregular.

12.4.2   The theoretical approach to the interest rate risk on floating rate products, through the net current value

The problem of floating rates is a complex one, as we are often looking at demand products or products without maturity dates, on which banking clients carry out arbitrage between different investment products. In addition, the floating rates may be regulated and conditioned by business strategy objectives.

There are very few academic works on the interest rate risk for floating-rate products. Where these works exist, they remain targeted towards demand savings products. The academic approach has limited itself to integrating the interest rate risks for floating-rate contracts by calculating the net current value on the basis of volume and market rate simulations. This *NPV* approach is difficult to reconcile with an interest-rate risk analysis built on the basis of a 'gap'. The *NPV* analysis gives interesting theoretical information on the alteration to the value of the balance sheet items, as well as accounting and market values. However, the NPV does not give any information on the variation in the bank's margin following a change in rates. The interest-rate risk on 'retail' products is often a margin variation risk. The *NPV* analysis is therefore of limited interest for the 'retail' section of the balance sheet (deposits and credits), in which most of the floating-rate products are found. Ausubel[1] was the first to calculate the net current value of floating-demand deposits by using a determinist process for volumes and rates.

More recently, Selvaggio[2] and Hutchinson and Pennachi[3] have used a specific model of the reference monetary rate by taking a stochastic process based on the square root with a recurrence function towards the average. Other stochastic models have also been used, such as those of Heath, Jarrow and Morton[4] and of Hull and White[5] in the works by Sanyal.[6]

The hypotheses necessary for this methodology are in fact postulates:

- This approach considers that demand products consist of short-term flows. This has serious consequences as the updating coefficients used for the *NPV* are essentially short-term market rates. This has the effect of denying the existence of 'replicating portfolios'[7] of long maturity in demand products. In a replicating portfolio, stable long-term demand contracts cannot be updated with a short-term rate.
- The construction methods for the models suggest three stages. First, an econometric link must be established between the historical volume of the product and the monetary

---

[1] Ausubel L., The failure of competition in the credit card market, *American Economic Review*, 1991, pp. 50–81.

[2] Selvaggio R., Using the OAS methodology to value and hedge commercial bank retail demand deposit premiums, *The Handbook of Asset/Liability Management*, Edited by F. J. Fabozzi and A. Konishi, 1996.

[3] Hutchinson D. and Pennachi G., Measuring rents and interest rate risk in imperfect financial markets: the case of retail bank deposit, *Journal of Financial and Quantitative Analysis*, 1996, pp. 399–417.

[4] Heath D., Jarrow R. and Morton A, Bond pricing and the term structure of interest rates: a new methodology for contingent claims valuation, *Econometrica*, 1992, pp. 77–105.

[5] Hull J. and White A., Pricing interest rate derivative securities, *Review of Financial Studies*, 1990, pp. 573–92.

[6] Sanyal A., *A continuous time Monte Carlo implementation of the Hull and White one-factor model and the pricing of core deposit*, unpublished manuscript, December 1997.

[7] The 'replicating portfolio' suggests breaking down a stock (for example, total demand deposits at moment t) in flow, each with a specific maturity date and nominal value. This concept is the subject of the next development.

reference rate. Next, a Monte Carlo simulation will specify the monetary rates. This stage uses the Hull and White discrete model. The total of these possible rates will allow the future volumes to be defined and updated using the same rate. The mathematical anticipation of the current values obtained represents the *NPV*, for which the expression is as follows:

$$\text{NPV}_0 = \sum_{t=1}^{T} E_0 \left[\frac{D_t(r_t - s_t)}{(1 + r_0 \cdot \ldots \cdot (1 + r_t)} \right]$$

Here:

E_0 is the mathematical expectation operator at time 0.
D_t is the nominal total of deposits at time t.
$r_0, \ldots, r_t$ are the short-term rates for times $0, \ldots, t$.
s_t is the rate at which the product pays at time t.
$r_t - s_t$ is the definition of the spread.

This spread is a difference between a market reference rate and the contract rate. The concept of spread is an interesting one; it is an average margin, generally positive, for creditor rates in relation to market rates. The postulate for the approach, however, is to consider that the spread is unique and one-dimensional as it is equal by definition to the difference between the monetary market rate and the contract rate. Here again we find the postulate that considers that the demand product flows are short-term flows. A spread calculated only on the short-term flows would have the effect of denying the existence of the long-term 'replicating portfolio' on the products without maturity dates.

In the absence of a precise definition of reference rates, and with the aim of generalising for products that are not necessarily demand products, the spread should be calculated for the whole of the zero-coupon curve range. Our approach uses the static and dynamic spread.

12.4.3 The behavioural study of rate revisions

12.4.3.1 Static and dynamic spread

It must be remarked that there is no true theory of floating rates. The revision of rates is actually a complex decision that clearly depends on the evolution of one or more market interest rates. These market and contractual rates allow a spread or margin, which should be profitable to the bank, to be calculated. The difference will depend on the segmentation of clients into private individuals, professionals and businesses and on the commercial objectives particular to each product. When the margin falls, the duration of the fall in the spread prior to the adjustment or revision of rates may be longer or shorter. Following this kind of drop in margin, certain product rates will be adjusted more quickly than others because of the increased sensitivity of the volumes to variations in rates and depending on the competition environment. This dynamic, specific to each product or to each bank, is difficult to model. It can, however, be affirmed that there are three types of explanatory variable.

- the time variable between two periods of revision, for respecting the diachronic dynamic.

- the static margins or *static spreads* calculated at regular intervals. We are taking a two-month period to calculate this static spread.

$$SS = r_t - s_t$$

- a selective reduction of a static margin will not allow it alone to bring about a revision in rates. The revision of rates will be effective only if the fall in the static spread is confirmed and intensifies. This *dynamic spread* or DS[8] can be obtained by calculating the surface area between the floating rate and the zero-coupon rate between two revision periods. This surface area allows the sensitivity of the bank's products to rates, as well as the bank's business policy, to be taken into account. In our analysis, the volume is an endogenous variable.

$$DS = \int_{T=1}^{n} (r_t - s_t)\, dt$$

After analysing the correlations between the zero-coupon rates, we have calculated the static and dynamic spreads bimonthly, on a historical period running from 1991 to 1999 (see the example on investment credits on the CD-ROM).

12.4.3.2 Data analysis method

The scheme shown in Figure 12.1 allows the problem to be displayed. On the x-axis we have the bimonthly time scale, which here begins on 1 January 1991. The y-axis shows the rates of interest expressed as basis points and the various changes in the zero-coupon rates. More specifically, the rates used are 3 months, 2 years, 5 years and 10 years, split into periods of 15 days.

The stepped curve corresponds to the historical rates for the floating-rate product presented – the investment credits granted to the liberal professions by a bank. The aim

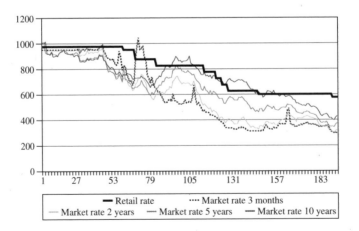

Figure 12.1   History of floating rates on investment credits and a few market rates

---

[8] Or cumulative static margins between two revision periods.

of the method is to disassociate the bimonthly periods of equilibrium from the periods of non-equilibrium, which are in fact the periods situated immediately prior to the rate revisions. The method consists of three stages:

- Analysis of the correlations on the rate curve.
- Analysis of the canonical correlations on the explanatory variables.
- The logistic regression on the variables selected.

A. Analysis of correlations on zero-coupon rates

The first stage is a simple analysis of the correlations between the various maturity dates of the zero-coupon rates.[9] Thanks to the matrix of correlations, rates that are closely correlated are excluded from the analysis. The other rates, when retained, are used to calculate the static and dynamic spreads. These spreads are defined in two different ways.

The static margins are first of all calculated by making the difference between the annual floating contract rate and the annual zero-coupon rate for a maturity date (example: static margin 'A' 3 months, 6 months etc.) but also by transforming the margin obtained into a proportional two-weekly rate (static margin 'B' 3 months, 6 months etc.). The space between analyses, or the period, is 15 days in the study.

Dynamic margins, meanwhile, are obtained by adding the simple two-weekly interest period by period since the last change of rate (dynamic margin 'A') and by calculating the compound interest on the two-weekly margin at moment t since the last moment of revision (dynamic margin 'B').

The static and dynamic margins are calculated on the basis of the zero-coupon rates. The information on the coupon curves can easily be found on Bloomberg (pages: State bond rate curves). It is not a good idea to use the Strips curves (for State bonds separated to create a structured zero-coupon product). These curves are difficult to use as they suffer, among other things, from liquidity problems.

To calculate the zero-coupon curves, we have divided the State bond curves into coupons using the classic 'step-by-step' method. Up to one year, we have taken the *bank offered rate* or BOR.

Description of the step-by-step method

The following bullet rates apply after interpolation (linear and otherwise):

- 1 year $\times$ 1 $= 10\%$
- 2 years $\times$ 2 $= 10.10\%$
- 3 years $\times$ 3 $= 10.20\%$
- 4 years $\times$ 4 $= 10.30\%$

The zero-coupon rate at one year is 10%, that is ZCB 1 year.

The zero-coupon rate at two years is 10.105%. When the actuarial rates are used, we have in fact the following equality for a main bond with maturity:

$$100 = 10.10/1 + \text{ZCB 1 year} + 100 + 10.10/(1 + \text{ZCB 2 years})^2$$

---

[9] A matrix of correlations is obtained: correlation between 3-month and 6-month rates, 3-month and 1-year rates, 3-month and 2-year rates, etc.

Hence:

$$ZCB \; 2 \; \text{years} = \sqrt{\frac{110.1}{100 - \dfrac{10.1}{1.1}}} - 1$$

$$= 10.105\,\%$$

Method of calculating static and dynamic margins

In the Excel sheets on the CD-ROM, the retail and zero-coupon rates are expressed in basis points. As we have no precise theoretical indications on the definition of the margins, we have calculated the two types of margin using two different methods of calculation. The following example will allow a better understanding of how the Excel sheets are calculated, that is:

- At t_0, ZCB = 950 and the rate = 800 basis points.
- At t_1, ZCB = 975 and the rate = 800 basis points.
- t is a two-monthly period.

For the static margins:

- First method: the difference in basis points between the repricing rate and the zero-coupon rate is calculated, hence $950 - 800 = 150$ at t_0, $975 - 800 = 175$ at t_1.
- Second method: 0.015 is the differential of the annual rate converted into a twice-monthly proportional rate (26 periods).

$$\left[\left(1 + \frac{0.0150}{26} \right) \cdot 100 - 100 \right] \cdot 100 = 5.769 \text{ at } t_0$$

$$\left[\left(1 + \frac{0.0175}{26} \right) \cdot 100 - 100 \right] \cdot 100 = 6.73 \text{ at } t_1$$

This second method allows the dynamic margin to be calculated on another scale of values, as the data are not centred reduced (average 0; standard deviation 1).

We are converting the spread or the rate differential into a twice-monthly proportional rate (52 weeks/2 = 26). This is the 'gain' in basis points for the bank over a twice-monthly period.

There are two methods of calculation for dynamic margins.

- First method

$$\left[\left(1 + \frac{0.0150}{26} \right) \cdot 100 - 100 \right] \cdot 100 = 5.769 \text{ at } t_0$$

The 'gain' for the bank over a two-monthly period.

$$\left[\left(1 + \frac{0.0175}{26} \right)^2 \cdot 100 - 100 \right] \cdot 100 = 13.46 \text{ at } t_1$$

The 'gain' capitalised by the bank over two periods from the rate differential noted in second period.

- Second method

$$\left[\left(1 + \frac{0.0150}{26}\right) \cdot 100 - 100 \right] \cdot 100 = 5.769 \text{ at } t_0$$

The 'gain' for the bank over a two-monthly period.

$$\left[\left(1 + \frac{0.0150}{26}\right) \cdot 100 - 100 \right] \cdot 100 + \left[\left(1 + \frac{0.0175}{26}\right) \cdot 100 - 100 \right] \cdot 100 = 12.499 \text{ at } t_1$$

The 'gain' for the bank over two periods from the rate differential noted for first and second period.

Analysis of correlations between changes in zero-coupon rates

The static and dynamic margins are only calculated on the least correlated points within the zero-coupon curve. In fact, the calculation of the margins on closely correlated points contributes nothing in terms of information, as the margins obtained will be similar.

The process is a simple one. The currency curves are found on Excel, and SAS (the statistical software) accepts the data through simple copying and pasting. For the analysis of the correlations between curves, the SAS algorithm must be programmed, with a3m being the market rate at 3 months, b6m the rate at 6 months, c1a the rate at 1 year etc., as can be found on the CD-ROM.

The static and dynamic margins for products in BEF/LUF have been calculated on the basis of the least correlated points, that is: 3 months, 2 years, 4 years, 6 years and 10 years.

The classical statistical procedure uses correlation tests to exclude the correlated variables from the analysis (example: non-parametric Spearman test). Here, the procedure is different as the rates are all correlated globally.

The act of taking the rates least correlated to each other allows the calculation of the margins and procedures to be reduced in size.

B. Canonical correlation analysis

The second stage uses the little-known concept of canonical correlation analysis for making an optimal selection of static and dynamic margins.

Canonical correlation analysis is carried out on the basis of canonical analysis, which is now an old concept, having first been introduced in 1936 by Hotelling.[10]

The method is very productive in terms of theory as it takes most forms of data analysis as a specific case. The method is currently available as an algorithm (SAS software) but is not frequently used because of problems with interpreting and using the results.

Canonical analysis can be used when a variable is linked linearly to another variable. In our study, we have the static margins linked linearly to margins or dynamic spreads. When there are two types of variables linked linearly by canonical analysis, some variables may be excluded if there is an opposite sign between the standardised canonical coefficient and the sign of the correlation between the variable and the canonical factor. The excluded variables are known as 'suppresser variables'.

---

[10] Hotelling H., Relation between two sets of variables, *Biometrica*, 321–77, 1936.

When there is a linear link between the two series of variables to be selected, tests[11] have shown that the canonical correlation method is more suitable than a simple selection built on the basis of statistical correlations. The canonical correlations are shown in Appendix 5.

Examples of investment credits (CD-ROM)

For investment credits, the static margins have been calculated on the 3-month, 2-year, 5-year and 10-year rates. Analysis of the canonical correlations on the static and dynamic differences gives us the following linear combination for the highest proper value in a two-monthly study from 1991 to 1999.

Table 12.6 shows the results for the static margins.

For the next stage in the method, we will select the static spreads: Margin A 3 months, Margin B 3 months, Margin A 10 years.

Table 12.7 shows the results for the dynamic margins:

For the next stage in the method, therefore, we will not select the dynamic spreads: margin A 2 years, margin B 2 years, margin A 5 years.

The canonical correlation to the square for ξ^1, η^1 is good as it totals 0.85353. This value is significant at the 1 % threshold according to statistic F. On the other hand, the

Table 12.6 Canonical correlations (static margins)

Static spreads	ξ^1 first canonical factor	Correlation between margin and canonical variable	Suppresser variables
Margin A, 3 months	−0.3474	−0.7814	
Margin B, 3 months	−1.0656	−0.7861	
Margin A, 2 years	0.9069	−0.1222	Yes
Margin B, 2 years	0.0794	−0.1178	Yes
Margin A, 5 years	−0.0960	0.5411	Yes
Margin B, 5 years	−0.0875	0.5238	Yes
Margin A, 10 years	0.1520	0.7160	
Margin B, 10 years	−0.0001	0.7208	Yes

Table 12.7 Canonical correlations (dynamic margins)

Static spreads	η^1 first canonical factor	Correlation between margin and canonical variable	Suppresser variables
Dynamic margin A, 3 months	−2.1657	−0.5231	
Dynamic margin B, 3 months	−0.4786	−0.4433	
Dynamic margin A, 2 years	2.0689	−0.1327	Yes
Dynamic margin B, 2 years	0.3585	−0.2473	Yes
Dynamic margin A, 5 years	−0.4387	0.2556	Yes
Dynamic margin B, 5 years	0.1665	0.1360	
Dynamic margin A, 10 years	0.1505	0.5547	
Dynamic margin B, 10 years	0.0472	0.5149	

---

[11] In this regard, we will mention the applicative works by: Cooley W. W. and Lohnes P. R., *Multivariate Data Analysis*, John Wiley & Sons, Ltd, 1971. Tatsuoka M. M. *Multivariate Analysis*, John Wiley & Sons, Ltd, 1971. Mardia K. V., Kent J. T. and Bibby J. M., *Multivariate Analysis*, Academic Press, 1979 or Damel P., "*La modélisation des contrats bancaires à taux révisable: une approche utilisant les corrélations canoniques*", Banque et Marchés, mars avril, 1999.

hypothesis H_0 of the absence of correlation between λ_1 (the first proper value) and λ_2 (the second proper value) is verified with a probability of 0.9999 on the basis of the Wilks lambda test. The canonical factors ξ^1 and η^1 are therefore of good quality.

Tables 12.6 and 12.7 identify the 'suppresser variables', that is, the variables excluded from the analysis, as we have a contrary and contradictory sign between the coefficient of the canonical axis and the sign of the correlation.

This method allows the variables, belonging to two analytical groups between which a linear relation can be established, to be chosen in the optimal way.

The following stage is the use of the logistic regression as an explanatory model for the differentiation between the periods of equilibrium (absence of revision) and periods of interruption (period with change of rate). The logistic model is constructed on the basis of static and dynamic spreads and of time. The model is also particular to each product and to each bank, for reasons stated above.

C. Logistic regression

Logistic regression is a binomial model of conditional probability, known and in frequent use (see Appendix 6). The variable to be explained takes the value 0 in a period of equilibrium and 1 in a period of non-equilibrium (the two-month period before the change in rate). The model is optimised using the Newson–Raphson nonlinear iterative method.

Our example contains nine changes of rate (value 1) and 188 periods of equilibrium. The model is adjusted in the classical way by excluding the variables that do not differ significantly from 0 (χ^2 test). We use the concept of pairs to illustrate the convergence between the observed reality (periods 0 and 1) and the periods 0 and 1 given by the logistic model equation. The pair (observation 0 of equilibrium and observation 1 of interruption) will be concordant if the probability of a change in rate at the first observation is less than the probability of the second by more than 0.02. Otherwise, the pair will not concord. A pair will be uncertain when the difference between the two probabilities is small and they are less than 0.02 apart. The rates of concordance, uncertainty and discordance for the pairs are calculated on the basis of the total number of possible pairs combining an observation of equilibrium (value 0) with an interruption value (value 1).

Repricing model on professional investment credits

Optimisation of logistic regression

Regression is optimised in the classical way by excluding the variables that do not differ significantly from zero ($Pr > \chi^2$) step by step. The exclusion of variables is conditioned in all cases by the degree of adjustment of the model. The rate of concordance between the model and the observed reality must be maximised. The SAS output will be *association of predicted probabilities and observed responses – concordant: 97.9%.*

In the following example (Table 12.8), the variable Mc10yr has a probability of 76.59% of being statistically zero. Excluding it will lead to deterioration in the rate of concordance between the observations (repricing–non-repricing) and the forecasts for the model (repricing–non-repricing). This variable must remain in the model.

There are other criteria for measuring the performance of a logistic regression, such as the logarithm of likelihood. The closer the log of likelihood is to zero, the better the adjustment of the model to the observed reality ($-2\log L$ in SAS output). The log of likelihood can also be approximated by the MacFadden R^2: $R^2 = 1$ ($-2\log L$ intercept only/$-2\log L$ intercept and covariates).

Table 12.8 Logistic regression

Variables	DF	Parameter estimate	Standard error	Wald chi-square	Proba over chi-square	Odds ratio[12]
Constant	1	35.468	12.1283	8.5522	0.0035	
Time	1	−0.2669	0.2500	1.1404	0.2856	0.766
M3m	1	0.3231	0.1549	4.3512	0.0370	1.381
Ma3m	1	−5.9101	3.4407	2.9504	0.0859	0.003
Ma10y	1	0.9997	0.7190	1.9333	0.1644	2.718
Mc3m	1	0.0335	0.0709	0.2236	0.6363	1.034
Mac3m	1	−0.0731	0.0447	2.6772	0.1018	0.929
Mac5y	1	0.1029	0.1041	0.9766	0.323	1.108
Mc10y	1	0.0227	0.0762	0.0887	0.7659	1.023
Mac10y	1	−0.1146	0.102	1.2618	0.2613	0.892

Association of predicted probabilities and observed responses

Concordant = 97.9 %
Discordant = 2.1 %
Tried   = 0 % (1692 pairs)

In the model, the probability of a change in rate increases with:

- time;
- the fall in the static spread A at 3 months;
- the rise in the static spread B at 3 months;
- the fall in the static spread A 10 years;
- the slowing of the rise in the dynamic spreads A 3 months, B 5 months and A 10 years;
- the rise in the dynamic margins B 3 months and B 10 years.

Displaying the model

For each model, the linear combination on the historical data must be programmed. This will allow the critical value of the model needed for dissociating the repricing periods from the periods of equilibrium to be determined. As the dissociation is not 100 %, there is no objective value. The critical value chosen conditions the statistical error of the first and second area. In the example, the value 1.11 allows almost all the repricing to be obtained without much anticipation of the model for the actual repricing periods (see model CD-ROM and critical value).

The method presented was applied to all the floating-rate products for a bank every two months for nine years maximum in the period 1991 to 1999, depending on the historical data available and the creation date of the products. The results are encouraging as the rates of convergence between the models and the observed reality, with just a few exceptions, are all over 90 %.

The classic method, based on the choice of dynamic and static spreads through simple statistical correlation, has been tested. This method shows results very far removed from those obtained using the method proposed, as the rate of concordance of pairs was less than 80 %.

---

[12] The odds ratio is equal to the exponential of the parameter estimated: e^b. A variation in a unit within the variable (here time and the spreads) makes the probability of 'repricing' alter by $1 - e^b$.

12.4.3.3   Use of the models in rate risk management

This behavioural study allows the arbitrary rate-change conventions to be replaced to good advantage. Remember that the conventions in the interest-rate gaps often take the form of a simple calculation of an average for the periods during which rates are not changed. Working on the hypothesis that the bank's behaviour is stable, we can use each model as a prospective by calculating the static and dynamic spreads on the basis of the sliding forward rates, for example over one year. This floating-rate integration method gives us two cases:

• The rate change occurs between today's date and one year from now. In this case, the contract revision date will be precisely on that date.
• The rate change is not probable over a one-year horizon. In this case, the date of revision may be put back to the most distant prospective date (in our example, in one year).

Naturally, using an interest-rate gap suggests in the first instance that the rate-change dates are known for each contract, but also that the magnitude of the change can be anticipated in order to assess the change in the interest margin. Our method satisfies the first condition but does not directly give us the magnitude of the change. In fact, between two repricing periods we see a large number of situations of equilibrium. In practice, the ALM manager can put this free space to good use to optimise the magnitude of the change and profit from a long or short balance-sheet position. This optimisation process is made easier by the model. In fact, a change with too low a magnitude will necessitate a further change, while a change with too high a magnitude may be incompatible with the historical values of the model (see the statistics for magnitude of changes).

Modelling the repricing improves knowledge of the rate risk and optimises the simulations on the interest margin forecasts and the knowledge of the market risk through *VaR*.

12.4.3.4   Remarks and criticisms

Our behavioural approach does, however, have a few weak points. The model specifies the revision dates without indicating the total change in terms of basis points. It is not a margin optimisation model. Another criticism that can be levelled relates to the homogeneity of the period studied. A major change in one or more of the parameters set out previously could disrupt or invalidate the model estimated. Finally, this empirical method cannot be applied to new floating-rate products.

Despite these limitations, the behavioural approach to static and dynamic spreads, based on the analysis of canonical correlations, gives good results and is sufficiently flexible to explain changes in rates on very different products. In fact, in our bank's balance sheet, we have both liability and asset products each with their own specific client segmentation.

The behavioural method allows complex parameters to be integrated, such as the business policy of banks, the sensitivity of adjustment of volumes to market interest rates, and competition environment.

12.5   REPLICATING PORTFOLIOS

In asset and liability management, a measurement of the monthly *VaR* for all the assets as a whole is information of first importance on the market risk (rate and change). It is a measurement that allows the economic forecasts associated with the risk to be assessed.

ALM software packages most frequently use J. P. Morgan's interest and exchange rate variance-covariance matrix, as the information on duration necessary for making the calculation is already available. It is well known that products without a maturity date are a real stumbling block for this type of *VaR* and for ALM.

There is relatively little academic work on the studies that involve attributing maturity dates to demand credit or debit products. The aim of 'replicating portfolios' is to attribute a maturity date to balance-sheet products that do not have one. These portfolios combine all the statistical or conventional techniques that allow the position of a product without a maturity date to be converted into an interwoven whole of contracts that are homogeneous in terms of liquidity and duration.

'Replicating portfolios' can be constructed in different ways. If the technical environment allows, it is possible to construct them contract by contract, defining development profiles and therefore implicit maturity dates for 'stable' contracts. Where necessary, on the basis of volumes per type of product, the optimal value method may be used. Other banks provide too arbitrary definitions of replicating portfolios.

12.5.1 Presentation of replicating portfolios

Many products do not have a certain maturity date, including, among others, the following cases:

- American options that can be exercised at any time outside the scope of the balance sheet.
- Demand advances and overcharges on assets.
- Current liability accounts.

The banks construct replicating portfolios in order to deal with this problem. This kind of portfolio uses statistical techniques or conventions. The assigned aim of all the methods is to transform an accounting balance of demand products into a number of contracts with differing characteristics (maturity, origin, depreciation profile, internal transfer rate etc.). At the time of the analysis, the accounting balance of the whole contract portfolio is equal to the accounting balance of the demand product. Figures 12.2–12.4 offers a better understanding of replicating portfolio construction.

The replicating portfolio presented consists of three different contracts that explain the accounting balances at t_{-1}, t_0 and t_1. The aim of the replicating portfolio is to represent the structure of the flows that make up the accounting balance.

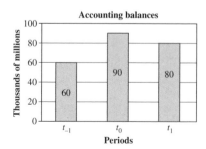

Figure 12.2 Accounting balances on current accounts

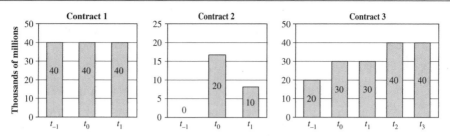

Figure 12.3 Contracts making up the replicating portfolio

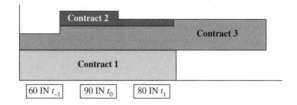

Figure 12.4 Replicating portfolio constructed on the basis of the three contracts

12.5.2   Replicating portfolios constructed according to convention

To present the various methods, we are taking the example of current accounts. There are two types of convention for constructing a replicating portfolio. The first type can be described as simplistic; they are used especially for demand deposits with an apparently stable monthly balance. On the basis of this observation, some banks construct the replicating portfolio by applying linear depreciation to the accounting balance at moment t over several months. As the depreciation is linear over several months or even several years, the banking institutions consider that the structure of the flows making up the accounting balance is stable overall in the short term. In fact, only 1/12 of the balance is depreciated at the end of one month (1/6 in the second month, etc.) in a replicating portfolio constructed over 12 months.

This arbitrary technique, which has no statistical basis, is unsatisfactory as many current accounts are partially or totally depreciated over one month because of the monthly nature of the income.

The second class of conventions covers the conventions that are considered as more sophisticated and these do call in part on statistical studies. Because of the very restrictive hypotheses retained, construction of the replicating portfolio remains within the scope of convention. For example: we calculate two well-known statistical indicators to assess a volatile item like the arithmetical mean and the monthly standard deviation for the daily balances of all the deposits. The operation is repeated every two months, every quarter etc. in order to obtain the statistical volatility indicators (average, standard deviation) on a temporal horizon that increases from month to month. The interest, of course, is in making the calculation over several years in order to refine support for stable resources for long-term functions such as credit facilities.

Thanks to these indicators it is possible, using probability theory, to calculate the monthly portion of the deposits that will be depreciated month by month. For example:

to define the unstable portion of deposits for one month, we calculate first the probability that the current account will be in debit balance compared to the monthly average and the standard deviation for the totals observed over the month. The probability obtained is equal to the unstable proportion for one month. We can also write in the general case that the probability associated with the percentage of deposits depreciated equals $\Pr[x < 0]$ with σ as the standard deviation over a period (one or two months etc.) for the daily totals of deposits and μ as the arithmetical mean for the deposits over the same period.

With this method, part of the deposits is depreciated or deducted each month until depreciation is complete. In other words, the balance sheet is deflated. For example: the demand deposit entry in the balance sheet represents EUR 10 000 million, and this sum will be broken down into monthly due dates that generally cover several years. Naturally, this convention for constructing a replicating portfolio is more satisfying than a simple arbitrary convention. Some serious weaknesses have, however, been noted.

In fact, if we have a product with a credit balance, the proportion depreciated during the first month will be the probability of the balance becoming a debit balance in view of the monthly arithmetical mean and standard deviation calculated and observed. Under this approach, the instability amounts to the probability of having a debit balance (for a product in liabilities) or a credit balance (for a product in assets). It is considered that the credit positions capable of being debited to a considerable extent are probably stable! This shows the limits of the approach built on the global basis balance or the practice of producing the total accounting position day by day.

12.5.3   The contract-by-contract replicating portfolio

The other methods consist of producing more accurate projections for demand products on the basis of statistical analyses. The first prerequisite for a statistical analysis to be consistent is to identify correctly each component that explains the overall development. In other words, the statistical analysis builds up the replicating portfolio account by account and day by day. The portfolio is not built on the daily accounting balance that brings together the behaviour of all the accounts. The banks allocate one account per type of product and per client. The account-by-account analysis is more refined as it allows the behaviour of the flows to be identified per type of client.

The account-by-account daily analysis includes technical problems of database constitution, including those in the large system or 'mainframe' environment, because of the volume created by the large number of current accounts or cheques and the need for historical entries.

After the completion of this first stage, considerable thought was applied to define the concept of stability in theoretical terms. To carry out this work, we used two concepts:

- The first was the method of the account-by-account replicating portfolio. We considered that the balance observed at moment t is the product of a whole set of interwoven accounts with different profiles and cashflow behaviour and nonsimultaneous creation dates.
- The second concept is the stability test, adopted for defining a stable account statistically. The test used is the standardised range or SR. This is a practical test used to judge the normality of a statistical distribution, as it is easy to interpret and calculate. SR is a measurement of the extent of the extreme values in the observations for a sample

dispersion unit (the standard deviation[13]). It is expressed as follows:

$$SR = \frac{\max(X_i) - \min(X_i)}{\sigma_X}$$

This test allows three types of statistical distribution to be identified: a normal or Gaussian distribution, a flat distribution with higher statistical dispersion than that of a normal law, and a distribution with a statistical dispersion lower than that of a normal law.

It can be considered that a demand current account is stable within the third typology.

The difference between the extreme values, $\max(X_i) - \min(X_i)$, is low because of the standard different. The SR statistical test can be carried out with several intervals of confidence, and the test can be programmed with differentiated intervals of confidence.

It is preferable to use a wide interval of confidence to judge the daily stability of the account in order to avoid the problem of making monthly income payments. In addition, the second condition for daily account stability is the absence of debit balances in the monthly historical period values. In a monthly historical period, it is preferable to take a wider interval of confidence when the history of the deposits shows at least one debit balance, and a narrower interval otherwise.

After the stable accounts have been identified, we can reasonably create repayment schedules by extending the trends or historical tendencies. On the statistically stable accounts, two major trend types exist. In the upward trend, the deposits are stable over a long term and the total observed at moment t will therefore be depreciated once over a long period; this may be the date of the historical basis. In the downward trend, it is possible by prolonging the trend to find out the future date of complete depreciation of the account. Therefore, the balance of the account at moment t is depreciated linearly until the maturity date obtained by prolonging the trend.

In order to provide an explanation, we have synthesised the conditions of stability in Table 12.9. We have identified four cases. 'SR max' corresponds to a wide interval of confidence, while 'SR min' corresponds to a narrower interval of confidence.

Table 12.9 Stability typologies on current account deposits

Type of case	Daily stability	Monthly stability	Historical monthly balances	Type of trend	Maturity date
1	Yes (SR max)	Yes (SR min)	Always in credit	Upward & horizontal	Duration of history of data
2	Yes (SR max)	Yes (SR min)	Always in credit	Downward	Duration of trend prolongation
3	Yes (SR max)	Yes (SR max)	At least one debit balance	Generally upward	Duration of history of data
4	Yes (SR max)	No (SR min)	Always in credit	No trend	Duration of history of data (for historical min. total)

---

[13] There are of course other statistical tests for measuring the normality of a statistical distribution, such as the χ^2 test, the Kolmogorov–Smirnov test for samples with over 2000 contracts, and the Wilk–Shapiro test where needed.

The fourth case requires further explanation. These accounts are always in a credit balance on the daily and monthly histories, but are not stable on a monthly basis.

On the other hand, there is a historical minimum credit balance that can be considered to be stable. Economists name this liquidity as 'liquidity preference'. In this case, the minimum historical total will be found in the long-term repayment schedule (the database date). The unstable contracts, or the unstable part of a contract, will have a short-term maturity date (1 day to 1 month).

This method will allow better integration of products into the liquidity management tools and rate risk without maturity dates. Based on the SR test and the account-by-account replicating portfolio, it is simple in design and easy to carry out technically.

Specifically, an accounting position of 120 will be broken down as follows. The unstable part will have a maturity date of one day or one month, and the stable part will be broken down two months from the date of the historical period. If the history and therefore the synthetic maturity dates are judged insufficient, especially on savings products without maturity dates, it is possible under certain hypotheses to extrapolate the stability level and define a long maturity period over smaller totals. The historical period is 12 months. A volume of 100 out of the 130 observed is defined as stable. The maturity period is therefore one year. It is also known that the volatility of a financial variable calculated over a year can be used as a basis for extrapolating the volatility calculated over two years by multiplying the standard deviation by the time root: $\sigma_{2 \text{ years}} = \sigma_{1 \text{ year}} \cdot \sqrt{2}$.

It can be considered that the stable part diminishes symmetrically in proportion to time. The stable part at five years can thus be defined: $100 \cdot 1/\sqrt{5} = 100 \cdot 0.447 = 44.7\%$. We therefore have 30 at one day, 55.27 at one year and 44.73 at five years.

The stability obtained on the basis of a monthly and daily history therefore takes overall account of the explanatory variables of instability (arbitrage behaviour, monthly payment of income, liquidity preference, anticipation of rates, seasonality etc.).

In this method, the interest rate is an exogenous variable. The link between changes in stability and interest rates therefore depends on the frequency of the stability analysis. It allows specific implicit maturity dates to be found while remaining a powerful tool for allocating resources on a product without a maturity date located among the assets. For a liability bank, a good knowledge of flows will allow resources to be replaced over the long term instead of the interbank system and therefore provide an additional margin if the rate curve is positive. For an asset bank, this procedure will allow better management of the liquidity risk and the rate risk.

Contrarily, this historical and behavioural approach to the replicating portfolios poses problems when rate simulations are carried out in ALM. In the absence of an endogenous rate variable, knowledge of the link between rate and replicating portfolio will be limited to history. This last point justifies the replicating portfolio searches that include interest rates in the modelling process.

12.5.4 Replicating portfolios with the optimal value method

12.5.4.1 Presentation of the method

This method was developed by Smithson[14] in 1990 according to the 'building approach' or 'Lego approach'. The method proposes a definition of optimal replicating portfolios

---

[14] Smithson C., A Lego approach to financial engineering. In The *Handbook of Currency and Interest Rate Risk Management*, edited by R. Schwarz and C. W. Smith Jr., New York Institute of Finance, 1990 or Damel P., "*L'apport de replicating portfolio ou portefeuille répliqué en ALM: méthode contrat par contrat ou par la valeur optimale*", Banque et Marchés, mars avril, 2001.

by integrating market interest rates and the anticipated repayment risk, and considers the interest rate(s) to be endogenous variables. This perspective is much more limited than the previous one when the bank carries out stochastic or other rate simulations on the ALM indicators (*VaR, NPV* for equity funds, interest margins etc.).

In this method, it is considered that the stable part of a product without a maturity date is a function of simple rate contracts with known maturity dates. In this problem, the definition of stability is not provided contract by contract but on the basis of daily or monthly accounting volumes. An equation allows optimal representation of the chronological series of the accounting positions. This first point defines a stable part and a volatile part that is the statistical residue of the stability equation.

The volatile part is represented by a short-term bond with a short-term monetary reference rate (such as one month).

The stable part consists of a number of interwoven zero-coupon bonds with reference rates and maturity dates from 3 months to 15 years. The weave defines a refinancing strategy based on the monetary market and the primary bond market.

The stable part consists of rate products. The advantage of this approach is therefore that the early repayment rate is taken into account together with any 'repricing' of the product and the volume is therefore linked to the reference interest rates. The model contains two principal equations.

- $Volum_t$ represents the accounting position at moment t.
- $Stab_t$ represents the stable part of the volume at moment t.
- rr_t is the rate for the product at moment t and taux1m, taux2m etc. represent the market reference rates for maturity rates 1 month, 2 months etc.
- ε_t represents the statistical residual or volatile part of the accounting positions.
- br_{it} represents an interest for a zero-coupon bond position with maturity date i and market reference rate i at time t
- α_i represents the stable part replicated by the br_{it} position.
- $\Sigma\alpha_i$ equals 1 ($i = 3$ months to 15 years).
- mr_t represents the portion of the demand product rate that is not a function of the market rate. mr_t is also equal to the difference between the average weighted rate obtained from the interwoven bonds and the floating or fixed retail rate. This last point also includes the repricing strategy and the spread, which will be negative on liability products and positive on asset products.

Wilson[15] was the first to use this approach specifically for optimal value. His equations can be presented as follows:

$$Volum_t = Stab_t + \varepsilon_t \tag{a}$$

$$Volum_t \cdot rr_t = \varepsilon_t \cdot r_{1\ month,t} + \sum_{i=3\ months}^{15\ years} \alpha_i br_{it} + mr_t + \delta_t \tag{b}$$

with the constraint: $\sum_{i=3\ months}^{15\ years} \alpha_i = 1$.

---

[15] Wilson T., Optimal value: portfolio theory, *Balance Sheet*, Vol. 3, No. 3, Autumn 1994.

Example of replicated zero-coupon position

br_{6m} is a bond with a six-month maturity date and a market reference rate of six months. It will be considered that the stable part in t_1 is invested in a six-month bond at a six-month market rate. At t_2, t_3, t_4, t_5 and t_6 the new deposits (difference between $Stab_{t-1}$ and $Stab_t$) are also placed in a six-month bond with a six-month reference market rate for t_2, t_3, t_4, t_5 and t_6. At t_7 the stable part invested at t_1 has matured. This stable party and the new deposits will be replaced at six months at the six-month market rate prevailing at $t = 7$. br_{it} functions with all the reference rates from three months to 15 years.

After econometric adjustment of this two-equation model, α_i readily gives us the duration of this demand product. The addition properties of the duration are used. If $\alpha_{1y} = 0.5$ and $\alpha_{2y} = 0.5$, the duration of this product without a maturity date will be 18 months.

12.5.4.2 Econometric adjustment of equations

A. The stability or definition equation

There are many different forecasting models for the chronological series. For upward accounting volumes, the equation will be different from that obtained from decreasing or sine wave accounting values. The equation to be adopted will be the one that minimises the term of error ε.

Here follows a list (not comprehensive) of the various techniques for forecasting a chronological series:

- regression;
- trend extrapolations;
- exponential smoothing;
- autoregressive moving average (ARMA).

Wilson uses exponential smoothing. The stability of the volumes is an exponential function of time,

$$Stab_t = b_0 \cdot e^{b_1 t} + \varepsilon_t$$

or

$$\log Stab_t = \log b_0 + b_1 \cdot t + \delta_t$$

Instead of this arbitrary formula, we propose to define the volumes on the basis of classical methods or recent research into chance market models specialised in during the temporal series study. These models are much better adapted for estimating temporal series. The ARMA model is a classical model; it considers that the volumes observed are produced by a random stable process, that is, the statistical properties do not change over the course of time.

The variables in the process (that is, mathematical anticipation, valuation–valuation) are independent of time and follow a Gaussian distribution. The variation must also be finished. Volumes will be observed at equidistant moments (case of process in discrete time). We will take as an example the floating-demand savings accounts in LUF/BEF from 1996 to 1999, observed monthly (data on CD-ROM). The form given in the model is that of the recurrence system,

$$Volum_t = a_0 + \sum_{i=1}^{p} a_i Volum_{t-i} + \varepsilon_t$$

where $a_0 + a_1 Volum_{t-1} + \ldots + a_p Volum_{t-p}$ represents the autoregressive model that is ideal or perfectly adjusted to the chronological series, thus being devoid of uncertainty, and ε_t is a mobile average process.

$$\varepsilon_t = \sum_{i=0}^{q} b_i u_{t-i}$$

The u_{t-l} values constitute 'white noise' (following the non-autocorrelated and centred normal random variables with average 0 and standard deviation equal to 1). ε_t is therefore a centred random variable with constant variance. This type of model is an ARMA type model (p, q).

Optimisation of ARMA model (p, q)

The first stage consists of constructing the model on the observed data without transformation ($Volum_t$).

The first solution is to test several ARMA models $(p, 1)$ and to select the model that maximises the usual adjustment criteria:

- The function of log of likelihood. Box and Jenkins propose the lowest square estimators (R-square in the example or adjusted), identical to the maximum likelihood estimators if it is considered that the random variables are distributed normally. This last point is consistent with the ARMA approach.
- AIC (Akaike's information criterion).
- Schwartz criteria.
- There are other criteria, not referenced in the example (FPE: final prediction error; BIC: Bayesian information criterion; Parsen CAT: criterion of autoregressive transfer function).

The other process consists of constructing the model on the basis of the graphic autocorrelation test. This stage of identification takes account of the autocorrelation test with all the possible intervals $(t - n)$. This autocorrelation function must be downward or depreciated oscillating. In the example, the graph shows on the basis of the bilateral Student test ($t = 1.96$) that the one- and two-period intervals have an autocorrelation significantly different from 0 at the confidence threshold of 5 %. The ARMA model will have an AR component equal to two (AR(2)).

This stage may be completed in a similar way by partial autocorrelation, which takes account of the effects of the intermediate values between $Volum_t$ and $Volum_{t+r}$ in the autocorrelation. The model to be tested is ARMA (2, 0). The random disturbances in the model must not be autocorrelated. Where applicable, the autocorrelations ·have not been included in the AR part. There are different tests, including the Durbin–Watson

Table 12.10   ARMA (2, 2) model

R-square = 0.7251		Adjusted R-square = 0.6773
Akaike Information Criteria − AIC(K) = 43.539		
Schwartz Criteria − SC(K) = 43.777		
Parameter estimates	STD error	T-STAT
AR(1) 0.35356	0.1951	1.812
AR(2) 0.40966	0.2127	1.926
MA(1) 0.2135E-3	0.1078	0.0019
MA(2) − 0.91454	0.05865	−15.59
Constant 0.90774E + 10	0.7884E + 10	1.151
Residuals		
Skewness 1.44		
Kurtosis 7.51		
Studentised range 5.33		

non-autocorrelation error test. In the example of the savings accounts, the optimal ARMA model with a distribution normal and noncorrelated residue is the ARMA (2, 2) model with an acceptable R^2 of 0.67. This model is therefore stationary, as the AR total is less than 1.

The ARMA (2, 2) model (Table 12.10) obtained is as follows. The monthly accounting data, the zero-coupon rates for 1 month, 6 months, 1 year, 2 years, 4 years, 7 years and 10 years can be found on the CD-ROM. The model presented has been calculated on the basis of data from end November 1996 to end February 1999.

If the model is nonstationary (nonstationary variance and/or mean), it can be converted into a stationary model by using the integration of order r after the logarithmic transformation : if y is the transformed variable, apply the technique to $\Delta(\Delta(\ldots \Delta(y_t))) - r$ times− instead of $y_t(\Delta(y_t)) = y_t - y_{t-1})$. We therefore use an ARIMA(p, r, q) procedure.[16] If this procedure fails because of nonconstant volatility in the error term, it will be necessary to use the ARCH-GARCH or EGARCH models (Appendix 7).

B. The equation on the replicated positions

This equation may be estimated by a statistical model (such as SAS/OR procedure PROC NPL), using multiple regression with the constraints

$$\sum_{i=3 \text{ months}}^{15 \text{ years}} \alpha_i = 1 \quad \text{and} \quad \alpha_i \geq 0$$

It is also possible to estimate the replicated positions (b) with the single constraint (by using the SAS/STAT procedure)

$$\sum_{i=3 \text{ months}}^{15 \text{ years}} \alpha_i = 1$$

In both cases, the duration of the demand product is a weighted average of the durations. In the second case, it is possible to obtain negative α_i values. We therefore have a synthetic investment loan position on which the duration is calculated.

---

[16] Autoregressive integrated moving average.

Table 12.11 Multiple regression model obtained on BEF/LUF savings accounts on the basis of a SAS/STAT procedure (adjusted R-square 0.9431)

Variables	Parameter estimate	Standard error	Prob $> (T)$
Intercept (global margin)	−92 843 024	224 898 959	0.6839
F1M (stable part)	0.086084	0.00583247	0.0001
F6M (stable rollover)	−0.015703	0.05014466	0.7573
F1Y (stable rollover)	0.036787	0.07878570	0.6454
F2Y (stable rollover)	0.127688	0.14488236	0.3881
F4Y (stable rollover)	3.490592	1.46300205	0.0265
F7Y (stable rollover)	−4.524331	2.94918687	0.1399
F10Y (stable rollover)	1.884966	1.63778119	0.2627

If $\alpha_{1y} = 2.6$ and $\alpha_{6m} = -1.6$ for a liability product, duration $= 1(1.6/2.6)0.5 = 0.69$ of a year.

The bond weaves on the stable part have been calculated on the basis of the zero-coupon rates (1 month, 6 months, 1 year, 2 years, 4 years, 7 years, 10 years). See Table 12.11.

The equation (b) is very well adjusted, as R^2 is 94.31 %. The interest margin is of course negative, as the cost of the resources on liabilities is lower than the market conditions. Like Wilson, we consider that the margin between the average rate for the interwoven bonds and the product rate is constant over the period. Possibly it should also be considered that the margin is not constant, as the floating rate is not instantaneously re-updated according to changes in market rates. On the other hand, the quality of the clients and therefore the spread of credit are not necessarily constant over the period. The sum of coefficients associated with the interwoven bond positions is 1.

This multiple linear regression allows us to calculate the duration of this product without a maturity date on the basis of the synthetic bond positions obtained. In the example, the duration obtained from the unstable and stable positions equals 1.42 years.

Appendices

Appendix 1

Mathematical Concepts[1]

1.1 FUNCTIONS OF ONE VARIABLE

1.1.1 Derivatives

1.1.1.1 Definition

The derivative[2] of function f at point x_0 is defined as $f'(x_0) = \lim_{h \to 0} \dfrac{f(x_0 + h) - f(x_0)}{h}$,

if this limit exists and is finite.

If the function f is derivable at every point within an open interval $]a; b[$, it will constitute a new function defined within that interval: the derivative function, termed f'.

1.1.1.2 Geometric interpretations

For a small value of h, the numerator in the definition represents the increase (or decrease) in the value of the function when the variable x passes from value x_0 to the neighbouring value $(x_0 + h)$, that is, the length of AB (see Figure A1.1).

The denominator in the same expression, h, is in turn equal to the length of AC. The ratio is therefore equal to the slope of the straight line BC. When h tends towards 0, this straight line BC moves towards the tangent on the function graph, at point C.

The geometric interpretation of the derivative is therefore as follows: $f'(x_0)$ represents the slope of the tangent on the graph for f at point x_0. In particular, the sign of the derivative characterises the type of variation of the function: a positive (resp. negative) derivative has a corresponding *increasing* (resp. *decreasing*) function. The derivative therefore measures the speed at which the function increases (resp. decreases) in the neighbourhood of a point.

The derivative of the derivative, termed the second derivative and written f'', will therefore be positive when the function f' is increasing, that is, when the slope of the tangent on the graph for f increases when the variable x increases: the function is said to be *convex*. Conversely, a function with a negative second derivative is said to be *concave* (see Figure A1.2).

1.1.1.3 Calculations

Finally, remember the elementary rules for calculating derivatives. Those relative to operations between functions first of all:

$$(f + g)' = f' + g'$$
$$(\lambda f)' = \lambda f'$$

---

[1] Readers wishing to find out more about these concepts should read: Bair J., *Mathématiques générales*, De Boeck, 1990. Esch L., *Mathématique pour économistes et gestionnaires*, De Boeck, 1992. Guerrien B., *Algèbre linéaire pour économistes*, Economica, 1992. Ortega M., *Matrix Theory*, Plenum, 1987. Weber J. E., *Mathematical Analysis (Business and Economic Applications)*, Harper and Row, 1982.

[2] Also referred to as *first derivative*.

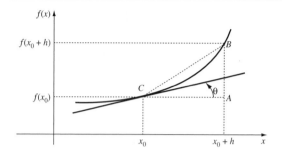

Figure A1.1   Geometric interpretation of derivative

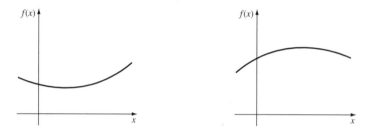

Figure A1.2   Convex and concave functions

$$(fg)' = f'g + fg'$$

$$\left(\frac{f}{g}\right)' = \frac{f'g - fg'}{g^2}$$

Next, those relating to compound functions:

$$[g(f)]' = g'(f) \cdot f'$$

Finally, the formulae that give the derivatives for a few elementary functions:

$$(x^m)' = mx^{m-1}$$

$$(e^x)' = e^x$$

$$(a^x)' = a^x \ln a$$

$$(\ln x)' = \frac{1}{x}$$

$$(\log_a x)' = \frac{1}{x \ln a}$$

1.1.1.4   Extrema

The point x_0 is a *local maximum* (resp. *minimum*) of the function f if

$$f(x_0) \geq f(x) \qquad (\text{resp. } f(x_0) \leq f(x))$$

for any x close to x_0.

The extrema within an open interval for a derivable function can be determined thanks to two conditions.

- The first-order (necessary) condition states that if x_0 is an *extremum* of f, then $f'(x_0) = 0$. At this point, called the *stationary point*, the tangent at the graph of f is therefore horizontal.
- The second-order (sufficient) condition allows the stationary points to be 'sorted' according to their nature. If x_0 is a stationary point of f and $f''(x_0) > 0$, we then have a minimum; in the opposite situation, if $f''(x_0) < 0$, we have a maximum.

1.1.2 Taylor's formula

Consider a function f that one wishes to study in the neighbourhood of x_0 (let us say, at $x_0 + h$). One method will be to replace this function by a polynomial – a function that is easily handled – of the variable h:

$$f(x_0 + h) = a_0 + a_1 h + a_2 h^2 + \cdots$$

For the function f to be represented through the polynomial, both must:

- take the same value at $h = 0$;
- have the same slope (that is, the same first derivative) at $h = 0$;
- have the same convexity or concavity (that is, the same second derivative) at $h = 0$;
- and so on.

Also, the number of conditions to be imposed must correspond to the number of coefficients to be determined within the polynomial. It will be evident that these conditions lead to:

$$a_0 = f(x_0) = \frac{f(x_0)}{0!}$$

$$a_1 = f'(x_0) = \frac{f'(x_0)}{1!}$$

$$a_2 = \frac{f''(x_0)}{2} = \frac{f''(x_0)}{2!}$$

$$\cdots$$

$$a_k = \frac{f^{(k)}(x_0)}{k!}$$

$$\cdots$$

Generally, therefore, we can write:

$$f(x_0 + h) = \frac{f(x_0)}{0!} + \frac{f'(x_0)}{1!}h + \frac{f''(x_0)}{2!}h^2 + \cdots + \frac{f^{(n)}(x_0)}{n!}h^n + R_n$$

Here R_n, known as the expansion remainder, is the difference between the function f to be studied and the approximation polynomial. This remainder will be negligible under certain conditions of regularity as when h tends towards 0, it will tend towards 0 more quickly than h^n.

The use of Taylor's formula in this book does not need a high-degree polynomial, and we will therefore write more simply:

$$f(x_0 + h) \approx f(x_0) + \frac{f'(x_0)}{1!}h + \frac{f''(x_0)}{2!}h^2 + \frac{f'''(x_0)}{3!}h^3 + \cdots$$

For some elementary functions, Taylor's expansion takes a specific form that is worth remembering:

$$e^x \approx 1 + \frac{x}{1!} + \frac{x^2}{2!} + \frac{x^3}{3!} + \cdots$$

$$(1 + x)^m \approx 1 + \frac{m}{1!}x + \frac{m(m-1)}{2!}x^2 + \frac{m(m-1)(m-2)}{3!}x^3 + \cdots$$

$$\ln(1 + x) \approx x - \frac{x^2}{2} + \frac{x^3}{3} - \cdots$$

A specific case of power function expansion is the *Newton binomial formula*:

$$(a + b)^n = \sum_{k=0}^{n} \binom{n}{k} a^k b^{n-k}$$

1.1.3 Geometric series

If within the Taylor formula for $(1 + x)^m$, x is replaced by $(-x)$ and m by (-1), we will obtain:

$$\frac{1}{1 - x} \approx 1 + x + x^2 + x^3 + \cdots$$

It is easy to demonstrate that when $|x| < 1$, the sequence

$$1$$
$$1 + x$$
$$1 + x + x^2$$
$$\cdots$$
$$1 + x + x^2 + \cdots + x^n$$
$$\cdots$$

will converge towards the number $1/(1 - x)$.

The limit of this sequence is therefore a sum comprising an infinite number of terms and termed a *series*. What we are concerned with here is the geometric series:

$$1 + x + x^2 + \cdots + x^n + \cdots = \sum_{n=0}^{\infty} x^n = \frac{1}{1 - x}$$

A relation linked to this geometric series is the one that gives the sum of the terms in a *geometric progression*: the sequence t_1, t_2, t_3 etc. is characterised by the relation

$$t_k = t_{k-1} \cdot q \quad (k = 2, 3, \ldots)$$

the sum of $t_1 + t_2 + t_3 + \cdots + t_n$ is given by the relation:

$$\sum_{k=1}^{n} t_k = \frac{t_1 - t_{n+1}}{1-q} = t_1 \frac{1-q^n}{1-q}$$

1.2   FUNCTIONS OF SEVERAL VARIABLES

1.2.1   Partial derivatives

1.2.1.1   Definition and graphical interpretation

For a function f of n variables $x_1, x_2, \ldots, x_n$, the concept of derivative is defined in a similar way, although the increase h can relate to any of the variables. We will therefore have n concepts of derivatives, relative to each of the n variables, and they will be termed partial derivatives. The partial derivative of $f(x_1, x_2, \ldots, x_n)$ with respect to x_k at point $(x_1^{(0)}, x_2^{(0)}, \ldots, x_n^{(0)})$ will be defined as:

$$f'_{x_k}(x_1^{(0)}, x_2^{(0)}, \ldots, x_n^{(0)})$$

$$= \lim_{h \to 0} \frac{f(x_1^{(0)}, x_2^{(0)}, \ldots, x_k^{(0)} + h, \ldots, x_n^{(0)}) - f(x_1^{(0)}, x_2^{(0)}, \ldots, x_k^{(0)}, \ldots, x_n^{(0)})}{h}$$

The geometric interpretation of the partial derivatives can only be envisaged for the functions of two variables as the graph for such a function will enter the field of three dimensions (one dimension for each of the two variables and the third, the ordinate, for the values of the function). We will thus be examining the partial derivatives:

$$f'_x(x_0, y_0) = \lim_{h \to 0} \frac{f(x_0 + h, y_0) - f(x_0, y_0)}{h}$$

$$f'_y(x_0, y_0) = \lim_{h \to 0} \frac{f(x_0, y_0 + h) - f(x_0, y_0)}{h}$$

Let us now look at the graph for this function $f(x, y)$. It is a three-dimensional space (see Figure A1.3).

Let us also consider the vertical plane that passes through the point (x_0, y_0) and parallel to the Ox axis. Its intersection with the graph for f is the curve C_x. The same reasoning as that adopted for the functions of one variable shows that the partial derivative $f'_x(x_0, y_0)$ is equal to the slope of the tangent to that curve C_x at the axis point (x_0, y_0) (that is, the slope of the graph for f in the direction of x). In the same way, $f'_y(x_0, y_0)$ represents the slope of the tangent to C_y at the axis point (x_0, y_0).

1.2.1.2   Extrema without constraint

The point $(x_1^{(0)}, \ldots, x_n^{(0)})$ is a *local maximum* (resp. *minimum*) of the function f if

$$f(x_1^{(0)}, \ldots, x_n^{(0)}) \geq f(x_1, \ldots, x_n) \quad [\text{resp. } f(x_1^{(0)}, \ldots, x_n^{(0)}) \leq f(x_1, \ldots, x_n)]$$

for any $(x_1, \ldots, x_n)$ close to $(x_1^{(0)}, \ldots, x_n^{(0)})$.

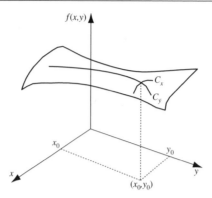

Figure A1.3   Geometric interpretation of partial derivatives

As for the functions of a single variable, the extrema of a derivable function can be determined thanks to two conditions.

- The first-order (necessary) condition states that if $x^{(0)}$ is an *extremum* of f, then all the partial derivatives of f will be zero in $x^{(0)}$:

$$f'_{x_i}(x^{(0)}) = 0 \qquad (i = 1, \ldots, n)$$

When referring to the geometric interpretation of the partial derivatives of a function of two variables, at this type of point (x_0, y_0), called the *stationary point*, the tangents to the curves C_x and C_y are therefore horizontal.

- The second-order (sufficient) condition allows the stationary points to be 'sorted' according to their nature, but first and foremost requires definition of the *Hessian matrix* of the function f at point x, made up of second partial derivatives of f:

$$H(f(x_1, \ldots, x_n)) = \begin{pmatrix} f''_{x_1 x_1}(x) & f''_{x_1 x_2}(x) & \cdots & f''_{x_1 x_n}(x) \\ f''_{x_2 x_1}(x) & f''_{x_2 x_2}(x) & \cdots & f''_{x_2 x_n}(x) \\ \vdots & \vdots & & \vdots \\ f''_{x_n x_1}(x) & f''_{x_n x_2}(x) & \cdots & f''_{x_n x_n}(x) \end{pmatrix}$$

If $x^{(0)}$ is a stationary point of f and $H(f(x))$ is p.d. at $x^{(0)}$ or s.p. in a neighbourhood of $x^{(0)}$, we have a minimum. In the opposite situation, if $H(f(x))$ is n.d. at $x^{(0)}$ or s.n. in a neighbourhood of $x^{(0)}$, we have a maximum.[3]

1.2.1.3   Extrema under constraint(s)

This is a similar concept, but one in which the analysis of the problem of extrema is restricted to those x values that obey one or more constraints.

---

[3] These notions are explained in Section 1.3.2.1 in this Appendix.

The point $(x_1^{(0)}, \ldots, x_n^{(0)})$ is a *local maximum* (resp. *minimum*) of the function f under the constraints

$$\begin{cases} g_1(x) = 0 \\ \cdots \\ g_r(x) = 0 \end{cases}$$

If $x^{(0)}$ verifies the constraints itself and

$$f(x_1^{(0)}, \ldots, x_n^{(0)}) \geq f(x_1, \ldots, x_n) \qquad [\text{resp. } f(x_1^{(0)}, \ldots, x_n^{(0)}) \leq f(x_1, \ldots, x_n)]$$

for any $(x_1, \ldots, x_n)$

$$\begin{cases} \text{in a neighbourhood of } (x_1^{(0)}, \cdots, x_n^{(0)}) \\ \text{satisfying the } r \text{ constraints} \end{cases}$$

Solving this problem involves considering the *Lagrangian function* of the problem. We are looking at a function of the $(n+r)$ variables $(x_1, \ldots, x_n; m_1, \ldots, m_r)$, the latest r values – known as *Lagrangian multipliers* – each correspond to a constraint:

$$L(x_1, \ldots, x_n; m_1, \ldots, m_r) = f(x) + m_1 \cdot g_1(x) + \cdots + m_r \cdot g_r(x)$$

We will not go into the technical details of solving this problem. We will, however, point out an essential result: if the point $(x^{(0)}; m^{(0)})$ is such that $x^{(0)}$ verifies the constraints and $(x^{(0)}; m^{(0)})$ is a extremum (without constraint) of the Lagrangian function, then $x^{(0)}$ is an extremum for the problem of extrema under constraints.

1.2.2   Taylor's formula

Taylor's formula is also generalised for the n-variable functions, but the degree 1 term, which reveals the first derivative, is replaced by n terms with the n partial derivatives:

$$f'_{x_i}(x_1^{(0)}, x_2^{(0)}, \ldots, x_n^{(0)}) \qquad i = 1, 2, \ldots, n$$

In the same way, the degree 2 term, the coefficient of which constitutes the second derivative, here becomes a set of n^2 terms in which the various second partial derivatives are involved:

$$f''_{x_i x_j}(x_1^{(0)}, x_2^{(0)}, \ldots, x_n^{(0)}) \qquad i, j = 1, 2, \ldots, n$$

Thus, by limiting the writing to the degree 2 terms, Taylor's formula is written as follows:

$$f(x_1^{(0)} + h_1, x_2^{(0)} + h_2, \ldots, x_n^{(0)} + h_n) \approx f(x^{(0)}) + \frac{1}{1!} \sum_{i=1}^{n} f'_{x_i}(x^{(0)}) h_i$$

$$+ \frac{1}{2!} \sum_{i=1}^{n} \sum_{j=1}^{n} f''_{x_i x_j}(x^{(0)}) h_i h_j + \cdots$$

1.3 MATRIX CALCULUS

1.3.1 Definitions

1.3.1.1 Matrices and vectors

The term *n-order matrix* is given to a set of n^2 real numbers making up a square table consisting of n rows and n columns.[4] A matrix is generally represented by a capital letter (such as A), and its elements by the corresponding lower-case letter (a) with two allocated indices representing the row and column to which the element belongs: a_{ij} is the element of matrix A located at the intersection of row i and column j within A. Matrix A can therefore be written generally as follows:

$$A = \begin{pmatrix} a_{11} & a_{12} & \cdots & a_{1j} & \cdots & a_{1n} \\ a_{21} & a_{22} & \cdots & a_{2j} & \cdots & a_{2n} \\ \vdots & \vdots & & \vdots & & \vdots \\ a_{i1} & a_{i2} & \cdots & a_{ij} & \cdots & a_{in} \\ \vdots & \vdots & & \vdots & & \vdots \\ a_{n1} & a_{n2} & \cdots & a_{nj} & \cdots & a_{nn} \end{pmatrix}$$

In the same way, a vector of n dimension is a set of n real numbers forming a columnar table. The elements in a vector are its components and are referred to by a single index.

$$\vec{X} = \begin{pmatrix} x_1 \\ x_2 \\ \vdots \\ x_i \\ \vdots \\ x_n \end{pmatrix}$$

1.3.1.2 Specific matrices

The diagonal elements in a matrix are the elements a_{11}, a_{22}, ..., a_{nn}. They are located on the diagonal of the table that starts from the upper left-hand corner; this is known as the principal diagonal.

A matrix is defined as *symmetrical* if the elements symmetrical with respect to the principal diagonal are equal: $a_{ij} = a_{ji}$. Here is an example:

$$A = \begin{pmatrix} 2 & -3 & 0 \\ -3 & 1 & \sqrt{2} \\ 0 & \sqrt{2} & 0 \end{pmatrix}$$

---

[4] More generally, a matrix is a rectangular table with the format (m, n); m rows and n columns. We will, however, only be looking at square matrices here.

An upper triangular matrix is a matrix in which the elements located underneath the principal diagonal are zero: $a_{ij} = 0$ when $i < j$. For example:

$$A = \begin{pmatrix} 0 & 2 & -1 \\ 0 & 3 & 0 \\ 0 & 0 & 5 \end{pmatrix}$$

The concept of a lower triangular matrix is of course defined in a similar way.

Finally, a *diagonal matrix* is one that is both upper triangular and lower triangular. Its only non-zero elements are the diagonal elements: $a_{ji} = 0$ when i and j are different. Generally, this type of matrix will be represented by:

$$A = \begin{pmatrix} a_1 & 0 & \cdots & 0 \\ 0 & a_2 & \cdots & 0 \\ \vdots & \vdots & \ddots & \vdots \\ 0 & 0 & \cdots & a_n \end{pmatrix} = \text{diag}\,(a_1, a_2, \ldots, a_n)$$

1.3.1.3   Operations

The sum of two matrices, as well as the multiplication of a matrix by a scalar, are completely natural operations: the operation in question is carried out for each of the elements. Thus:

$$(A + B)_{ij} = a_{ij} + b_{ij}$$

$$(\lambda A)_{ij} = \lambda a_{ij}$$

These definitions are also valid for the vectors:

$$(\vec{X} + \vec{Y})_i = x_i + y_i$$

$$(\lambda \vec{X})_i = \lambda x_i$$

The product of two matrices A and B is a matrix of the same order as A and B, in which the element (i, j) is obtained by calculating the sum of the products of the elements in line i of A with the corresponding elements in column j in B:

$$(AB)_{ij} = a_{i1}b_{1j} + a_{i2}b_{2j} + \cdots + a_{in}b_{nj} = \sum_{k=1}^{n} a_{ik}b_{kj}$$

We will have, for example:

$$\begin{pmatrix} 2 & 0 & -1 \\ 3 & -2 & 1 \\ -3 & 2 & 0 \end{pmatrix} \cdot \begin{pmatrix} 0 & 5 & -2 \\ 3 & -1 & 0 \\ 2 & 0 & -1 \end{pmatrix} = \begin{pmatrix} -2 & 10 & -3 \\ -4 & 17 & -7 \\ 6 & -17 & 6 \end{pmatrix}$$

Despite the apparently complex definition, the matrix product has a number of classical properties; it is associative and distributive with respect to addition. However, it needs to be handled with care as it lacks one of the classical properties: it is not commutative. AB does not equal BA!

The product of a matrix by a vector is defined using the same "lines by columns" procedure:

$$(A\vec{X})_i = \sum_{k=1}^{n} a_{ik} x_k$$

The transposition of a matrix A is the matrix A^t, obtained by permuting the symmetrical elements with respect to the principal diagonal, or, which amounts to the same thing, by permuting the role of the lines and columns in matrix A:

$$(A^t)_{ij} = a_{ji}$$

A matrix is thus symmetrical if, and only if, it is equal to its transposition. In addition this operation, applied to a vector, gives the corresponding line vector as its result.

The inverse of matrix A is matrix A^{-1}, if it exists, so that: $AA^{-1} = A^{-1}A = \mathrm{diag}(1, \ldots, 1) = I$.

For example, it is easy to verify that:

$$\begin{pmatrix} 1 & 0 & 1 \\ -2 & 1 & -3 \\ 0 & 1 & 0 \end{pmatrix}^{-1} = \begin{pmatrix} 3 & 1 & -1 \\ 0 & 0 & 1 \\ -2 & -1 & 1 \end{pmatrix}$$

Finally, let us define the trace of a matrix. The trace is the sum of the matrix's diagonal elements:

$$\mathrm{tr}(A) = a_{11} + a_{22} + \cdots + a_{nn} = \sum_{i=1}^{n} a_{ii}$$

1.3.2 Quadratic forms

1.3.2.1 Quadratic form and class of symmetrical matrix

A *quadratic form* is a polynomial function with n variables containing only second-degree terms:

$$Q(x_1, x_2, \ldots, x_n) = \sum_{i=1}^{n} \sum_{j=1}^{n} a_{ij} x_i x_j$$

If we construct a matrix A from coefficients a_{ij} ($i, j = 1, \ldots, n$) and the vector X of the variables x_i ($i = 1, \ldots, n$), we can give a matrix expression to the quadratic form:

$$Q(\vec{X}) = \vec{X}^t A \vec{X}.$$

In fact, by developing the straight-line member, we produce:

$$\vec{X}^t A \vec{X} = \sum_{i=1}^{n} x_i (A\vec{X})_i$$

$$= \sum_{i=1}^{n} x_i \sum_{j=1}^{n} a_{ij} x_j$$

$$= \sum_{i=1}^{n} \sum_{j=1}^{n} a_{ij} x_i x_j$$

A quadratic form can always be associated with a matrix A, and vice versa. The matrix, however, is not unique. In fact, the quadratic form $Q(x_1, x_2) = 3x_1^2 - 4x_1x_2$ can be associated with matrices $A = \begin{pmatrix} 3 & -2 \\ -2 & 0 \end{pmatrix}$ $B = \begin{pmatrix} 3 & 0 \\ -4 & 0 \end{pmatrix}$ $C = \begin{pmatrix} 3 & -6 \\ 2 & 0 \end{pmatrix}$, as well as infinite number of others. Amongst all these matrices, only one is symmetrical (A in the example given). There is therefore *bijection* between all the quadratic forms and all the symmetrical matrices.

The *class* of a symmetrical matrix is defined on the basis of the sign of the associated quadratic form. Thus, the non-zero matrix A is said to be positive definite (p.d.) if $\vec{X}^t A \vec{X} > 0$ for any $\vec{X}$ not equal to 0, and semi-positive (s.p.) when:

$$\begin{cases} \vec{X}^t A \vec{X} \geq 0 \text{ for any } \vec{X} \neq 0 \\ \text{there is one } \vec{Y} \neq 0 \text{ so that } \vec{Y}^t A \vec{Y} = 0 \end{cases}$$

A matrix is negative definite (n.d.) and semi-negative (s.n.) by the inverse inequalities, and the term non-definite is given to a symmetrical matrix for which there are some $\vec{X}$ and $\vec{Y} \neq 0$ so that $\vec{X}^t A \vec{X} > 0$ and $\vec{Y}^t A \vec{Y} < 0$.

The symmetrical matrix $A = \begin{pmatrix} 5 & -3 & -4 \\ -3 & 10 & 2 \\ -4 & 2 & 8 \end{pmatrix}$ is thus p.d., as the associated quadratic form can be written as:

$$Q(x, y, z) = 5x^2 + 10y^2 + 8z^2 - 6xy - 8xz + 4yz$$
$$= (x - 3y)^2 + (2x - 2z)^2 + (y + 2z)^2$$

This form will never be negative, and simply cancels out when:

$$x - 3y = 0$$
$$2x - 2z = 0$$
$$y + 2z = 0$$

That is, when $x = y = z = 0$.

1.3.2.2   Linear equation system

A system of n linear equations with n unknowns is a set of relations of the following type:

$$\begin{cases} a_{11}x_1 + a_{12}x_2 + \cdots + a_{1n}x_n = b_1 \\ a_{21}x_1 + a_{22}x_2 + \cdots + a_{2n}x_n = b_2 \\ \cdots \\ a_{n1}x_1 + a_{n2}x_2 + \cdots + a_{nn}x_n = b_n \end{cases}$$

In it, the a_{ij}, x_j and b_i are respectively the coefficients, the unknowns and the second members. They are written naturally in both matrix and vectorial form: A, X and B. Using this notation, the system is written in an equivalent but more condensed way:

$$AX = B$$

For example, the system of equations

$$\begin{cases} 2x + 3y = 4 \\ 4x - y = -2 \end{cases}$$

can also be written as:

$$\begin{pmatrix} 2 & 3 \\ 4 & -1 \end{pmatrix} \begin{pmatrix} x \\ y \end{pmatrix} = \begin{pmatrix} 4 \\ -2 \end{pmatrix}$$

If the inverse of matrix A exists, it can easily be seen that the system admits one and just one solution, given as $X = A^{-1}X$.

1.3.2.3 Case of variance–covariance matrix[5]

The matrix $V = \begin{pmatrix} \sigma_1^2 & \sigma_{12} & \cdots & \sigma_{1n} \\ \sigma_{21} & \sigma_2^2 & \cdots & \sigma_{2n} \\ \vdots & \vdots & \ddots & \vdots \\ \sigma_{n1} & \sigma_{n2} & \cdots & \sigma_n^2 \end{pmatrix}$, for the variances and covariances of a number

of random variables $X_1, X_2, \ldots, X_n$ is a matrix that is either p.d. or s.p.

In effect, regardless of what the numbers $\lambda_1, \lambda_2, \ldots, \lambda_n$ are, not all zero and making up the vector $\vec{\Lambda}$, we have:

$$\vec{\Lambda}^t V \vec{\Lambda} = \sum_{i=1}^{n} \sum_{j=1}^{n} \lambda_i \lambda_j \sigma_{ij} = \mathrm{var} \left(\sum_{i=1}^{n} \lambda_i X_i \right) \geq 0$$

It can even be said, according to this result, that the variance–covariance matrix V is p.d. except when there are coefficients $\lambda_1, \lambda_2, \ldots, \lambda_n$ that are not all zero, so that the random variable $\lambda_1 X_1 + \cdots + \lambda_n X_n = \sum_{i=1}^{n} \lambda_i X_i$ is degenerate, in which case V will be s.p. This degeneration may occur, for example, when:

- one of the variables is degenerate;
- some variables are perfectly correlated;
- the matrix V is obtained on the basis of observations of a number strictly lower than the number of variables.

It will then be evident that the variance–covariance matrix can be expressed as a matrix, through the relation:

$$V = E[(\vec{X} - \vec{\mu})(\vec{X} - \vec{\mu})^t]$$

1.3.2.4 Choleski factorisation

Consider a symmetrical matrix A positive definite. It can be demonstrated that there exists a lower triangular matrix L with strictly positive diagonal elements so that $A = LL^t$.

---

[5] The concepts necessary for an understanding of this example are shown in Appendix 2.

This factorisation process is known as a Choleski factorisation. We will not be demonstrating this property, but will show, using the previous example, how the matrix L is found:

$$LL^t = \begin{pmatrix} a & 0 & 0 \\ b & c & 0 \\ d & f & g \end{pmatrix} \begin{pmatrix} a & b & d \\ 0 & c & f \\ 0 & 0 & g \end{pmatrix} = \begin{pmatrix} a^2 & ab & ad \\ ab & b^2+c^2 & bd+cf \\ ad & bd+cf & d^2+f^2+g^2 \end{pmatrix}$$

$$= A = \begin{pmatrix} 5 & -3 & -4 \\ -3 & 10 & 2 \\ -4 & 2 & 8 \end{pmatrix}$$

It is then sufficient to work the last equality in order to find a, b, c, d, f and g in succession, which will give the following for matrix L.

$$L = \begin{pmatrix} \sqrt{5} & 0 & 0 \\ -\dfrac{3\sqrt{5}}{5} & \dfrac{\sqrt{205}}{5} & 0 \\ -\dfrac{4\sqrt{5}}{5} & -\dfrac{2\sqrt{205}}{205} & \dfrac{14\sqrt{41}}{41} \end{pmatrix}$$

Appendix 2

Probabilistic Concepts[1]

2.1 RANDOM VARIABLES

2.1.1 Random variables and probability law

2.1.1.1 Definitions

Let us consider a fortuitous phenomenon, that is, a phenomenon that under given initial conditions corresponds to several possible outcomes. A numerical magnitude that depends on the observed result is known as a *random variable* or r.v.

In addition, probabilities are associated with various possible results or events defined in the context of the fortuitous phenomenon. It is therefore interesting to find out the probabilities of the various events defined on the basis of the r.v. What we are looking at here is the concept of *law of probability* of the r.v. Thus, if the r.v. is termed X, the law of probability of X is defined by the range of the following probabilities: $\Pr[X \in A]$, for every subset A of $\mathbf{R}$.

The aim of the concept of probability law is a bold one: the subsets A of $\mathbf{R}$ are too numerous for all the probabilities to be known. For this reason, we are content to work with just the $]-\infty; t]$ sets. This therefore defines a function of the variable t, the cumulative distribution function or simplier distribution function (d.f.) of the random variable $F(t) = \Pr[X \leq t]$.

It can be demonstrated that this function, defined in $\mathbf{R}$, is increasing, that it is between 0 and 1, that it admits the ordinates 0 and 1 as horizontal asymptotics $\lim_{t \to \pm\infty} F(t) = \begin{cases} 1 \\ 0 \end{cases}$, and that it is right-continuous: $\lim_{s \to t+} F(s) = F(t)$.

These properties are summarised in Figure A2.1.

In addition, despite its simplicity, the d.f. allows almost the whole of the probability law for X to be found, thus:

$$\Pr[s < X \leq t] = F(t) - F(s)$$

$$\Pr[X = t] = F(t) - F(t-)$$

2.1.1.2 Quantile

Sometimes there is a need to solve the opposite problem: being aware of a probability level u and determining the value of t so that $F(t) = \Pr[X \leq t] = u$.

This value is known as the quantile of the r.v. X at point u and its definition are shown in Figure A2.2.

---

[1] Readers wishing to find out more about these concepts should read: Baxter M. and Rennie A., *Financial Calculus*, Cambridge University Press, 1996. Feller W., *An Introduction to Probability Theory and its Applications* (2 volumes), John Wiley and Sons, Inc., 1968. Grimmett G. and Stirzaker D., *Probability and Random Processes*, Oxford University Press, 1992. Roger P., *Les outils de la modélisation financière*, Presses Universitaires de France, 1991. Ross S. M., *Initiation aux probabilités*, Press Polytechniques et Universitaires Romandes, 1994.

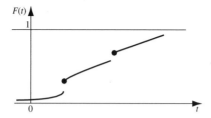

Figure A2.1   Distribution function

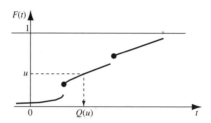

Figure A2.2   Quantile

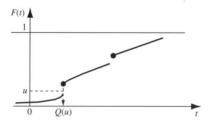

Figure A2.3   Quantile in jump scenario

In two cases, however, the definition that we have just given is unsuitable and needs to be adapted. First of all, if the d.f. of X shows a jump that covers the ordinate u, none of the abscissas will correspond to it and the abscissa of the jump, naturally, will be chosen (see Figure A2.3).

Next, if the ordinate u corresponds to a plateau on the d.f. graph, there is an infinite number of abscissas on the abscissa to choose from (see Figure A2.4).

In this case, an abscissa defined by the relation $Q(u) = um + (1 - u)M$ can be chosen. The quantile function thus defined generalises the concept of the reciprocal function of the d.f.

2.1.1.3 Discrete random variable

A discrete random variable corresponds to a situation in which the set of possible values for the variable is finite or infinite countable. In this case, if the various possible values

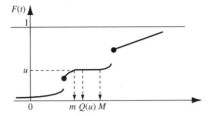

Figure A2.4   Quantile in plateau scenario

and corresponding probabilities are known

$$\begin{pmatrix} x_1 & x_2 & \cdots & x_n & \cdots \\ p_1 & p_2 & \cdots & p_n & \cdots \end{pmatrix}$$

$$\Pr[X = x_i] = p_i \qquad i = 1, 2, \ldots, n, \ldots$$

$$\sum_i p_i = 1$$

The law of probability of X can be easily determined:

$$\Pr[X \in A] = \sum_{\{i : x_i \in A\}} p_i$$

The d.f. of a discrete r.v. is a stepped function, as the abscissas of jumps correspond to the various possible values of X and the heights of the jumps are equal to the associated probabilities (see Figure A2.5).

In particular, a r.v. is defined as *degenerate* if it can only take on one value x (also referred to as a certain variable): $\Pr[X = x] = 1$.

The d.f. for a degenerate variable will be 0 to the left of x and 1 from x onwards.

2.1.1.4   Continuous random variable

In contrast to the discrete r.v., the set of possible values for a r.v. could be continuous (an interval, for example) with no individual value having a strictly positive probability:

$$\Pr[X = x] = 0 \qquad \forall x$$

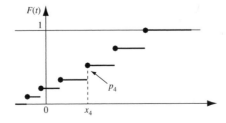

Figure A2.5   Distribution function for a discrete random variable

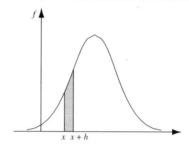

Figure A2.6   Probability density

In this case, the distribution of probabilities over the set of possible values is expressed using a density function f: for a sufficiently small h, we will have $\Pr[x < X \le x + h] \approx hf(x)$.

This definition is shown in Figure A2.6.

The law of probability is obtained from the density through the following relation:

$$\Pr[X \in A] = \int_A f(x)\,dx$$

And as a particular case:

$$F(t) = \int_{-\infty}^{t} f(x)\,dx$$

2.1.1.5   Multivariate random variables

Often there is a need to consider several r.v.s simultaneously $X_1, X_2, \ldots, X_m$, associated with the same fortuitous phenomenon.[2] Here, we will simply show the theory for a bivariate random variable, that is, a pair of r.v.s (X, Y); the general process for a multivariate random variable can easily be deduced from this.

The law of probability for a bivariate random variable is defined as the set of the following probabilities: $\Pr[(X, Y) \in A]$, for every subset A of $\mathbf{R}^2$. The *joint distribution function* is defined $F(s, t) = \Pr([X \le s] \cap [Y \le t])$ and the discrete and continuous bivariate random variables are defined respectively by:

$$p_{ij} = \Pr([X = x_i] \cap [Y = y_j])$$

$$\Pr[(X, Y) \in A] = \iint_A f(x, y)\,dx\,dy$$

Two r.v.s are defined as *independent* when they are not influenced either from the point of view of possible values or through the probability of the events that they define. More formally, X and Y are independent when:

$$\Pr([X \in A] \cap [Y \in B]) = \Pr[X \in A] \cdot \Pr[Y \in B]$$

for every A and B in $\mathbf{R}$.

---

[2] For example, the return on various financial assets.

It can be shown that two r.v.s are independent if, and only if, their joint d.f. is equal to the product of the d.f.s of each of the r.v.s: $F(s, t) = F_X(s) \cdot F_Y(t)$. And that this condition, for discrete or continuous random variables, shows as:

$$p_{ij} = \Pr[X = x_i] \cdot \Pr[Y = y_j]$$

$$f(x, y) = f_X(x) \cdot f_Y(y)$$

2.1.2 Typical values of random variables

The aim of the typical values of a r.v. is to summarise the information contained in its probability law in a number of representative parameters: parameters of location, dispersion, skewness and kurtosis. We will be looking at one from each group.

2.1.2.1 Mean

The mean is a central value that locates a r.v. by dividing the d.f. into two parts with the same area (see Figure A2.7).

The mean μ of the r.v. X is therefore such that:

$$\int_{-\infty}^{\mu} F(t)\, dt = \int_{\mu}^{+\infty} [1 - F(t)]\, dt$$

The mean of a r.v. can be calculated on the basis of the d.f.:

$$\mu = \int_{0}^{+\infty} [1 - F(t)]\, dt - \int_{-\infty}^{0} F(t)\, dt$$

the formula reducing for a positive r.v. as follows:

$$\mu = \int_{0}^{+\infty} [1 - F(t)]\, dt$$

It is possible to demonstrate that for a discrete r.v. and a continuous r.v., we have the formulae:

$$\mu = \sum_{i} x_i\, p_i$$

$$\mu = \int_{-\infty}^{+\infty} x f(x)\, dx$$

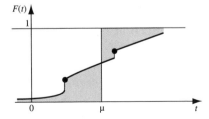

Figure A2.7 Mean of a random variable

The structure of these two formulae shows that μ integrates the various possible values for the r.v. X by weighting them through the probabilities associated with these values. It can be shown[3] that these formulae generalised into an abstract integral of $X(\omega)$ with respect to the measure of probability Pr in the set Ω of the possible outcomes ω of the fortuitous phenomenon. This integral is known as the *expectation* of the r.v. X:

$$E(X) = \int_\Omega X(\omega)\,d\Pr(\omega)$$

According to the foregoing, there is equivalence between the concepts of expectation and mean $(E(X) = \mu)$ and we will interchange both these terms from now on.

The properties of the integral show that the expectation is a linear operator:

$$E(aX + bY + c) = aE(X) + bE(Y) + c$$

And that if X and Y are independent, them $E(XY) = E(X) \cdot E(Y)$.

In addition, for a discrete r.v. or a continuous r.v., the expectation of a function of a r.v. variable is given by:

$$E(g(X)) = \sum_i g(x_i) p_i$$

$$E(g(X)) = \int_{-\infty}^{+\infty} g(x) f(x)\,dx$$

Let us remember finally the *law of large numbers*,[4] which for a sequence of independent r.v.s $X_1, X_2, \ldots, X_n$ with identical distribution and a mean μ, expresses that regardless of what $\varepsilon > 0$ may be

$$\lim_{n \to \infty} \Pr\left[\left| \frac{X_1 + X_2 + \cdots + X_n}{n} - \mu \right| \le \varepsilon \right] = 1$$

This law justifies taking the average of a sample to estimate the mean of the population and in particular estimating the probability of an event through the frequency of that event's occurrence when a large number of realisations of the fortuitous phenomenon occur.

2.1.2.2 Variance and standard deviation

One of the most commonly used dispersion indices (that is, a measurement of the spread of the r.v.s values around its mean) is the variance σ^2, defined as:

$$\sigma^2 = \text{var}(X) = E[(X - \mu)^2]$$

---

[3] This development is part of measure theory, which is outside the scope of this work. Readers are referred to Loeve M., *Probability Theory* (2 volumes), Springer-Verlag, 1977.
[4] We are showing this law in its weak form here.

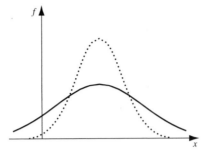

Figure A2.8   Variance of a random variable

By developing the right member, we can therefore arrive at the variance

$$\sigma^2 = E(X^2) - \mu^2$$

For a discrete r.v. and a continuous r.v., this will give:

$$\sigma^2 = \sum_i (x_i - \mu)^2 p_i = \sum_i x_i^2 p_i - \mu^2$$

$$\sigma^2 = \int_{-\infty}^{+\infty} (x - \mu)^2 f(x)\,dx = \int_{-\infty}^{+\infty} x^2 f(x)\,dx - \mu^2$$

An example of the interpretation of this parameter is found in Figure A2.8.

It can be demonstrated that $\mathrm{var}(aX + b) = a^2\,\mathrm{var}(X)$. And that if X and Y are independent, then $\mathrm{var}(X + Y) = \mathrm{var}(X) + \mathrm{var}(Y)$.

Alongside the variance, the dimension of which is the square of the dimension of X, we can also use the standard deviation, which is simply the square root:

$$\sigma = \sqrt{\mathrm{var}(X)}$$

2.1.2.3   Fisher's skewness and kurtosis coefficients

Fisher's skewness coefficient is defined by:

$$\gamma_1 = \frac{E[(X - \mu)^3]}{\sigma^3}$$

It is interpreted essentially on the basis of its sign: if $\gamma_1 > 0$ (resp. <0), the distribution of X will be concentrated to the left (resp. the right) and spread out to the right (resp. the left). For a symmetrical distribution, $\gamma_1 = 0$. This interpretation is shown in Figure A2.9.

Fisher's kurtosis coefficient is given by:

$$\gamma_2 = \frac{E[(X - \mu)^4]}{\sigma^4} - 3$$

It is interpreted by comparison with the normal distribution (see Section A.2.2.1). This distribution has a kurtosis coefficient of 0. Distributions with higher kurtosis than the normal law (also termed *leptokurtic*) are more pointed in the neighbourhood of their

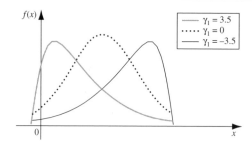

Figure A2.9   Skewness coefficient of a random variable

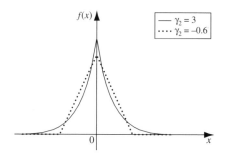

Figure A2.10   Kurtosis coefficient of a random variable

mean and present fatter tails (and are therefore less important for intermediate values) than normal distribution; they are characterised by a positive γ_2 parameter. Of course, the distributions with lower kurtosis have a negative kurtosis coefficient (see Figure A2.10).

For discrete or continuous r.v.s, the formulae that allows $E(g(X))$ to be calculated are used as usual.

2.1.2.4 Covariance and correlation

We now come to the parameters relative to the bivariate random variables. Covariance between two r.v.s, X and Y, is defined by: $\sigma_{XY} = \text{cov}(X, Y) = E[(X - \mu_X)(Y - \mu_Y)]$ and can also be calculated by $\text{cov}(X, Y) = E(XY) - \mu_X\mu_Y$.

For discrete r.v.s and continuous r.v.s, the covariance is calculated by:

$$\text{cov}(X, Y) = \sum_i \sum_j (x_i - \mu_X)(y_j - \mu_Y)p_{ij}$$

$$= \sum_i \sum_j x_i y_j p_{ij} - \mu_X\mu_Y$$

$$\text{cov}(X, Y) = \int_{-\infty}^{+\infty} \int_{-\infty}^{+\infty} (x - \mu_X)(y - \mu_Y)f(x, y)\,dx\,dy$$

$$= \int_{-\infty}^{+\infty} \int_{-\infty}^{+\infty} xyf(x, y)\,dx\,dy - \mu_X\mu_Y$$

The covariance is interpreted as follows: we are looking at the degree of linear connection that exists between the two r.v.s. A positive covariance thus corresponds to values of the product $(X - \mu_X)(Y - \mu_Y)$ that will be mostly positive and the two factors will be mostly of the same sign. High values for X (greater than μ_X) will correspond to high values for Y (greater than μ_Y) and low values for X will correspond to low values for Y. The same type of reasoning also applies to negative covariance.

It can be demonstrated that:

$$\text{cov}(aX + bY + c, Z) = a\ \text{cov}(X, Z) + b\ \text{cov}(Y, Z)$$

$$\text{cov}(X, X) = \text{var}(X)$$

$$E(XY) = E(X) \cdot E(Y) + \text{cov}(X, Y)$$

$$\text{var}(X + Y) = \text{var}(X) + \text{var}(Y) + 2\text{cov}(X, Y)$$

and that if X and Y are independent, their covariance is zero. In this case, in fact:

$$\text{cov}(X, Y) = E[(X - \mu_X)(Y - \mu_Y)]$$
$$= E(X - \mu_X)E(Y - \mu_Y)$$
$$= (E(X) - \mu_X)(E(Y) - \mu_Y)$$
$$= 0$$

Another parameter, which measures the degree of linear connection between the two r.v.s is the correlation coefficient:

$$\rho_{XY} = \text{corr}(X, Y) = \frac{\sigma_{XY}}{\sigma_X \cdot \sigma_Y}$$

The interest in the correlation coefficient in comparison to covariance is that we are looking at a number without dimension, while the covariance measurement unit is equal to the product of the units of the two r.v.s. Also, the correlation coefficient can only assume values between -1 and 1 and these two extreme values correspond to the existence of a perfect linear relation (increasing or decreasing depending on whether $\rho = 1$ or $\rho = -1$) between the two r.v.s.

Two r.v.s whose correlation coefficient (or covariance) is zero are termed *non-correlated*. It has been said earlier that independent r.v.s are noncorrelated, but the inverse is not true! The independence of two r.v.s in fact excludes the existence of any relation between the variables, while noncorrelation simply excludes the existence of a linear relation.

2.2   THEORETICAL DISTRIBUTIONS

2.2.1   Normal distribution and associated ones

2.2.1.1   Normal distribution

Remember that a *normal* random variable with parameters $(\mu; \sigma)$ is defined by its density:

$f(x) = \dfrac{1}{\sqrt{2\pi}\sigma} \exp\left[-\dfrac{1}{2}\left(\dfrac{x - \mu}{\sigma}\right)^2\right]$, which is shown graphically in Figure A2.11.

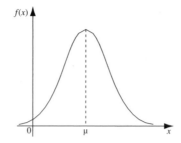

Figure A2.11   Normal density

The normal density graph is symmetrical with respect to the vertical straight line of abscissa μ and shows two points of inflexion, at $(\mu - \sigma)$ and $(\mu + \sigma)$.

The typical values for this distribution are given by:

$$E(X) = \mu$$
$$\text{var } (X) = \sigma^2$$
$$\gamma_1(X) = 0$$
$$\gamma_2(X) = 0$$

If the r.v. X is distributed following a normal law with parameters $(\mu; \sigma)$, it can be demonstrated that the r.v. $(aX + b)$ is also distributed according to a normal law. In particular, the r.v. $\dfrac{X - \mu}{\sigma}$ follows a normal law with parameters $(0; 1)$. This is known as a *standard normal* law.

The preceding result can be generalised: if the r.v.s X_1, X_2, ..., X_n are independent and normally distributed with $E(X_k) = \mu_k$, $\text{var}(X_k) = \sigma_k^2$, $k = 1, \ldots, m$, then the r.v. $\sum_{k=1}^{m} a_k X_k + b$ will follow a normal law with parameters

$$\left(\sum_{k=1}^{m} a_k \mu_k + b, \sqrt{\sum_{k=1}^{m} a_k^2 \sigma_k^2} \right)$$

2.2.1.2   Central limit theorem

The importance of this normal law in probability theory and statistics stems from the well-known *central limit theorem*, which states that if the r.v.s X_1, X_2, ..., X_n ....:

- are independent;
- have finite mean μ_k and standard deviation σ_k $(k = 1, \ldots, n, \ldots)$;
- and do not have any weighting variance with respect to the whole set $\lim_{n \to \infty}$ $\dfrac{\sigma_k^2}{\sigma_1^2 + \cdots + \sigma_n^2} = 0 \; \forall k,$

then the distribution of the r.v., $\dfrac{(X_1 + \cdots + X_n) - (\mu_1 + \cdots + \mu_n)}{\sqrt{\sigma_1^2 + \cdots + \sigma_n^2}}$, tends towards a standard normal law when n tends towards infinity.

Much more intuitively, the central limit theorem states that the sum of a large number of independent effects, none of which has a significant variability with respect to the set, is distributed according to the normal law without any hypothesis on the distribution of the various terms in the sum.

2.2.1.3 Multi-normal distribution

An m-variate random variable $(X_1, X_2, \ldots, X_m)$, is said to be distributed according to a multi-normal law with parameters $(\mu; V)$ if it allows multi-variate density given by $f(x_1, \ldots, x_m) = \dfrac{1}{\sqrt{(2\pi)^m \, \mathrm{dtm}(V)}} \exp\left[-\dfrac{1}{2}(\vec{x} - \vec{\mu})^t V^{-1}(\vec{x} - \vec{\mu})\right]$, in which $\vec{\mu}$ and V represent respectively the vector of means and the variance–covariance matrix of the r.v.s X_k ($k = 1, \ldots, m$).

The property of the linear combination of normal independent r.v.s can be generalised as follows: for a multi-normal random variable $\vec{X}$ with parameters $(\vec{\mu}; V)$, and a matrix A that allows an inverse, the m-variate random variable $A\vec{X} + \vec{b}$ is itself distributed according to a multi-normal parameter law $(A\vec{\mu} + \vec{b}; AVA^t)$.

For the specific case $m = 2$, the multi-normal density is termed binormal and written as

$$f(x_1, x_2) = \frac{1}{2\pi \sigma_1 \sigma_2 \sqrt{1 - \rho^2}} \exp\left\{ \frac{-1}{2(1 - \rho^2)} \left[\left(\frac{x_1 - \mu_1}{\sigma_1}\right)^2 \right.\right.$$
$$\left.\left. -2\rho \left(\frac{x_1 - \mu_1}{\sigma_1}\right) \left(\frac{x_2 - \mu_2}{\sigma_2}\right) + \left(\frac{x_2 - \mu_2}{\sigma_2}\right)^2 \right]\right\}$$

2.2.1.4 Log-normal distribution

Let us now return to a one-dimensional distribution linked to the normal law. A r.v. X is said to be distributed according to a *log-normal law* with parameter $(\mu; \sigma)$ when $\ln X$ is normally distributed with the parameters $(\mu; \sigma)$. It can be easily demonstrated that this r.v. will only take positive values and that it is defined by the density

$$f(x) = \frac{1}{\sqrt{2\pi}\sigma x} \exp\left[-\frac{1}{2}\left(\frac{\ln x - \mu}{\sigma}\right)^2\right] \qquad (x > 0)$$

The graph for this density is shown in Figure A2.12 and its typical values are given by:

$$E(X) = e^{\mu + \frac{\sigma^2}{2}}$$
$$\mathrm{var}(X) = e^{2\mu + \sigma^2}(e^{\sigma^2} - 1)$$
$$\gamma_1(X) = (e^{\sigma^2} + 2)\sqrt{e^{\sigma^2} - 1}$$
$$\gamma_2(X) = (e^{3\sigma^2} + 3e^{2\sigma^2} + 6e^{\sigma^2} + 6)(e^{\sigma^2} - 1)$$

This confirms the skewness with concentration to the left and the spreading to the right, observed on the graph.

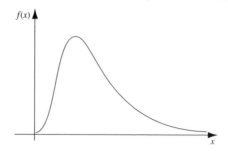

Figure A2.12   Log-normal distribution

We would point out finally that a result of the same type as the central limit theorem also leads to the log-normal law: this is the case in which the effects represented by the various r.v.s accumulate through a multiplication model rather than through an addition model, because of the fundamental property of the logarithms: $\ln(x_1 \cdot x_2) = \ln x_1 + \ln x_2$.

2.2.2   Other theoretical distributions

2.2.2.1   Poisson distribution

The Poisson r.v., with parameter μ, is a discrete X r.v. that takes all the complete positive integer values 0, 1, 2 etc. with the associated probabilities of:

$$\Pr[X = k] = e^{-\mu}\frac{\mu^k}{k!} \qquad k \in \mathbf{N}$$

The typical values for this distribution are given by:

$$E(X) = \mu$$

$$\mathrm{var}(X) = \mu$$

2.2.2.2   Binomial distribution

The Bernoulli scheme is a probability model applied to a very wide range of situations. It is characterised by

- a finite number of independent trials;
- during each trial, two results only – success and failure – are possible;
- also during each trial, the probability of a success occurring is the same.

If n is the number of trials and p the probability of each success succeeding, the term used is Bernoulli scheme with parameters $(n; p)$ and the number of successes out of the

n tests is a binomial parameter r.v., termed $B(n, p)$. This discrete random variable takes the values 0, 1, 2, $\ldots$, n with the following associated probabilities:[5]

$$\Pr[B(n; p) = k] = \binom{n}{k} p^k (1 - p)^{n-k} \qquad k \in \{0, 1, \ldots, n\}$$

The sum of these probabilities equals 1, in accordance with Newton's binomial formula. In addition, the typical values for this distribution are given by:

$$E(B(n; p)) = np$$

$$\mathrm{var}(B(n; p)) = np(1 - p)$$

The binomial distribution allows two interesting approximations when the n parameter is large. Thus, for a very small p, we have the approximation through Poisson's law with np parameter:

$$\Pr[B(n; p) = k] \approx e^{-np} \frac{(np)^k}{k!}$$

For a p that is not to close to 0 or 1, the binomial r.v. tends towards a normal law with parameters $(np; \sqrt{np(1 - p)})$, and more specifically:

$$\Pr[B(n; p) = k] \approx \Phi\left(\frac{k - \mu + \frac{1}{2}}{\sigma}\right) - \Phi\left(\frac{k - \mu - \frac{1}{2}}{\sigma}\right)$$

2.2.2.3 Student distribution

The Student distribution, with n degrees of freedom, is defined by the density

$$f(x) = \frac{\Gamma(\frac{\nu+1}{2})}{\Gamma(\frac{\nu}{2})\sqrt{\nu\pi}} \left(1 + \frac{x^2}{\nu}\right)^{-(\nu+1)/2}$$

In this expression, the gamma function is defined by $\Gamma(n) = \int_0^{+\infty} e^{-x} x^{n-1} \, dx$.

This generalises the factorial function as $\Gamma(n) = (n - 1) \cdot \Gamma(n - 1)$ and for integer n, we have: $\Gamma(n) = (n - 1)!$

This is, however, defined for n values that are not integer: all the positive real values of n and, for example:

$$\Gamma(\tfrac{1}{2}) = \sqrt{\pi}$$

We are not representing the graph for this density here, as it is symmetrical with respect to the vertical axis and bears a strong resemblance to the standard normal density graph, although for $\nu > 4$ the kurtosis coefficient value is strictly positive:

$$E(X) = 0$$

$$\mathrm{var}(X) = \frac{\nu}{\nu - 2}$$

$$\gamma_1(X) = 0$$

$$\gamma_2(X) = \frac{6}{\nu - 4}$$

----

[5] Remember that $\binom{n}{k} = \dfrac{p!}{p!(n - p)!}$

Finally, it can be stated that when the number of degrees of freedom tends towards infinity, the Student distribution tends towards the standard normal distribution, this asymptotic property being verified in practice as soon as ν reaches the value of 30.

2.2.2.4 Uniform distribution

A r.v. is said to be *uniform* in the interval $[a; b]$ when the probability of its taking a value between t and $t + h$[6] depends only on these two boundaries through h. It is easy to establish, on that basis, that we are looking at a r.v. that only takes a value within the interval $[a; b]$ and that its density is necessarily constant:

$$f(x) = 1/(b - a) \quad (a < x < b)$$

Its graph is shown in Figure A2.13.

The principal typical values for the uniform r.v. are given by:

$$E(X) = \frac{a + b}{2}$$

$$\mathrm{var}(X) = \frac{(a - b)^2}{12}$$

$$\gamma_1(X) = 0$$

$$\gamma_2(X) = -\frac{6}{5}$$

This uniform distribution is the origin of some simulation methods, in which the generation of random numbers distributed uniformly in the interval $[0; 1]$ allows distributed random numbers to be obtained according to a given law of probability (Figure A2.14). The way in which this transformation occurs is explained in Section 7.3.1. Let us examine here how the (pseudo-) random numbers uniformly distributed in $[0; 1]$ can be obtained.

The sequence $x_1, x_2, \ldots, x_n$ is constructed according to residue classes. On the basis of an initial value of ρ_0 (equal to 1, for example), we can construct for $i = 1, 2, \ldots, n$ etc.:

$$\begin{cases} x_i = \text{decimal part of } (c_1 \rho_{i-1}) \\ \rho_i = c_2 x_i \end{cases}$$

Here, the constants c_1 and c_2 are suitably chosen, Thus, for $c_1 = 13.3669$ and $c_2 = 94.3795$, we find successively as shown in Table A2.1:

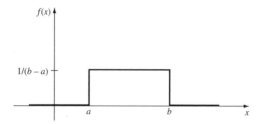

Figure A2.13   Uniform distribution

---

[6] These two values are assumed to belong to the interval $[a; b]$.

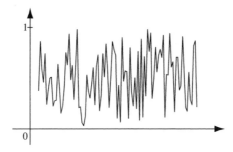

Figure A2.14   Random numbers uniformly distributed in [0; 1]

Table A2.1 x_I and ρ_I

i	x_i	ρ_i
0		
1	0.366900	34.627839
2	0.866885	81.813352
3	0.580898	55.768652
4	0.453995	42.847849
5	0.742910	70.115509
6	0.226992	21.423384
7	0.364227	34.375527
8	0.494233	46.645452
9	0.505097	47.670759
10	0.210265	19.844676

2.2.2.5   Generalised error distribution

The generalised distribution of errors for parameter v is defined by the density

$$f(x) = \frac{\sqrt{3v}}{2\left(\Gamma\left(\frac{1}{v}\right)\right)^{3/2}} \exp\left[-\left(\frac{|x|}{\sqrt{\frac{v}{3}}\Gamma\left(\frac{1}{v}\right)}\right)^{v}\right].$$

The graph for this density is shown in Figure A2.15.

This is a distribution symmetrical with respect to 0, which corresponds to a normal distribution for $n = 2$ and gives rise to a leptokurtic distribution (resp. negative kurtosis distribution) for $n < 2$ ($n > 2$).

2.3   STOCHASTIC PROCESSES

2.3.1   General considerations

The term *stochastic process* is applied to a random variable that is a function of the time variable: $\{X_t : t \in T\}$.

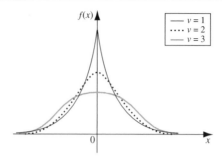

Figure A2.15   Generalised error distribution

If the set T of times is discrete, the stochastic process is simply a sequence of random variables. However, in a number of financial applications such as Black and Scholes' model, it will be necessary to consider stochastic processes in continuous time.

For each possible result $\omega \in \Omega$, the function of $X_t(\omega)$ of the variable t is known as the *path* of the stochastic process.

A stochastic process is said to have independent increments when, regardless of the times $t_1 < t_2 < \ldots < t_n$, the r.v.s

$$X_{t_1}, X_{t_2} - X_{t_1}, X_{t_3} - X_{t_2}, \ldots$$

are independent. In the same way, a stochastic process is said to have stationary increments when for every t and h the r.v.s $X_{t+h} - X_t$ and X_h are identically distributed.

2.3.2   Particular stochastic processes

2.3.2.1   The Poisson process

We consider a process of random occurrences of an event in time, corresponding to the set $[0; +\infty[$. Here, the principal interest does not correspond directly to the occurrence times, but to the number of occurrences within given intervals. The r.v. that represents the number of occurrences within the interval $[t_1, t_2]$ is termed $n(t_1, t_2)$.

This process is called a Poisson process if it obeys the following hypotheses:

- the numbers of occurrences in separate intervals of time are independent;
- the distribution of the number of occurrences within an interval of time only depends on that interval through its duration: $\Pr[n(t_1, t_2) = k]$ is a function of $(t_2 - t_1)$, which is henceforth termed $p_k(t_2 - t_1)$;
- there is no multiple occurrence: if h is low, $\Pr[n(0; h) \geq 2] = o(h)$;
- there is a rate of occurrence α so that $\Pr[n(0; h) = 1] = \alpha h + o(h)$.

It can be demonstrated that under these hypotheses, the r.v. 'number of occurrences within an interval of duration t' is distributed according to a Poisson law for parameter αt:

$$p_k(t) = e^{-\alpha t} \frac{(\alpha t)^k}{k!} \qquad k = 0, 1, 2, \ldots$$

To simplify, we note $X_t = n(0; t)$. This is a stochastic process that counts the number of occurrences over time. The path for such a process is therefore a stepped function, with the abscissas for the jumps corresponding to the occurrence times and the heights of the jumps being equal to 1. It can be demonstrated that the process has independent and stationary increments and that $E(X_t) = \text{var}(X_t) = \alpha t$.

This process can be generalised as follows. We consider:

- A Poisson process X_t as defined above; with the time of the kth occurrence expressed as T_k, we have: $X_t = \#\{k : T_k \leq t\}$.
- A sequence $Y_1, Y_2, \ldots$ of independent and identically distributed r.v.s, independent of the Poisson process.

The process $Z_t = \sum_{\{k:T_k \leq t\}} Y_k$ is known as a *compound Poisson process*.

The paths of such a process are therefore stepped functions, with the abscissas for the jumps corresponding to the occurrence times for the subjacent Poisson process and the heights of the jumps being the realised values of the r.v.s Y_k. In addition, we have:

$$E(Z_t) = \alpha t \cdot \mu_Y$$

$$\text{var}(Z_t) = \alpha t \cdot (\sigma^2{}_Y + \mu^2{}_Y)$$

2.3.2.2   Standard Brownian motion

Consider a sequence of r.v.s X_k, independent and identically distributed, with values $(-\Delta X)$ and ΔX with respective probabilities 1/2 and 1/2, and define the sequence of r.v.s as Y_n through $Y_n = X_1 + X_2 + \cdots + X_n$. This is known as a symmetrical *random walk*. As $E(X_k) = 0$ $\text{var}(X_k) = (\Delta X)^2$, we have $E(Y_n) = 0$ $\text{var}(Y_n) = n(\Delta X)^2$.

For our modelling requirements, we separate the interval of time $[0; t]$ in n subintervals of the same duration $\Delta t = t/n$ and define $Z_t = Z_t^{(n)} = Y_n$. We have:

$$E(Z_t) = 0 \qquad \text{var}(Y_n) = n(\Delta X)^2 = \frac{(\Delta X)^2}{\Delta t} t.$$

This variable Z_t allows the discrete development of a magnitude to be modelled. If we then wish to move to continuous modelling while retaining the same variability per unit of time, that is, with: $\dfrac{(\Delta X)^2}{\Delta t} = 1$, for example, we obtain the stochastic process $w_t = \lim_{n \to \infty} Z_t^{(n)}$.

This is a *standard Brownian motion* (also known as a *Wiener process*). It is clear that this stochastic process w_t, defined on $\mathbf{R}^+$, is such that $w_0 = 0$, that w_t has independent and stationary increments, and that in view of the central limit theorem w_t is distributed according to a normal law with parameters $(0; \sqrt{t})$. It can be shown that the paths of a Wiener process are continuous everywhere, but cannot generally be differentiated. In fact

$$\frac{\Delta w_t}{\Delta t} = \frac{\varepsilon \sqrt{\Delta t}}{\Delta t} = \frac{\varepsilon}{\sqrt{\Delta t}}$$

where, ε is a standard normal r.v.

2.3.2.3 *Itô process*

If a more developed model is required, w_t can be multiplied by a constant in order to produce variability per time unit $(\Delta X)^2/\Delta t$ different from 1 or to add a constant to it in order to obtain a non-zero mean:

$$X_t = X_0 + b \cdot w_t$$

This type of model is not greatly effective because of the great variability of the development in the short term, the standard deviation of X_t being equal[7] to $b\sqrt{t}$.

For this reason, this type of construction is applied more to variations relating to a short interval of time:

$$dX_t = a \cdot dt + b \cdot dw_t$$

It is possible to generalise by replacing the constants a and b by functions of t and X_t:

$$dX_t = a_t(X_t) \cdot dt + b_t(X_t) \cdot dw_t$$

This type of process is known as the Itô process. In financial modelling, several specific cases of Itô process are used, and a *geometric Brownian motion* is therefore obtained when:

$$a_t(X_t) = a \cdot X_t \qquad b_t(X_t) = b \cdot X_t$$

An Ornstein–Uhlenbeck process corresponds to:

$$a_t(X_t) = a \cdot (c - X_t) \qquad b_t(X_t) = b$$

and the square root process is such that:

$$a_t(X_t) = a \cdot (c - X_t) \qquad b_t(X_t) = b\sqrt{X_t}$$

2.3.3 Stochastic differential equations

Expressions of the type $dX_t = a_t(X_t) \cdot dt + b_t(X_t) \cdot dw_t$ cannot simply be handled in the same way as the corresponding determinist expressions, because w_t cannot be derived. It is, however, possible to extend the definition to a concept of stochastic differential, through the theory of stochastic integral calculus.[8]

As the stochastic process z_t is defined within the interval $[a; b]$, the *stochastic integral* of z_t is defined within $[a; b]$ with respect to the standard Brownian motion w_t by:

$$\int_a^b z_t \, dw_t = \lim_{\substack{n \to \infty \\ \delta \to 0}} \sum_{k=0}^{n-1} z_{t_k} (w_{t_{k+1}} - w_{t_k})$$

---

[7] The root function presents a vertical tangent at the origin.
[8] The full development of this theory is outside the scope of this work.

where, we have:

$$a = t_0 < t_1 < \ldots < t_n = b$$

$$\delta = \max_{k=1,\ldots,n} (t_k - t_{k-1})$$

Let us now consider a stochastic process Z_t (for which we wish to define the stochastic differential) and a standard Brownian motion w_t. If there is a stochastic process z_t such that $Z_t = Z_0 + \int_0^t z_s \, dw_s$, then it is said that Z_t admits the *stochastic differential* $dZ_t = z_t \, dw_t$.

This differential is interpreted as follows: the stochastic differential dZ_t represents the variation (for a very short period of time dt) of Z_t, triggered by a random variation dw_t weighted by z_t, which represents the volatility of Z_t at the moment t.

More generally, the definition of $dX_t = a_t(X_t) \cdot d_t + b_t(X_t) \cdot dw_t$ is given by

$$X_{t_2} - X_{t_1} = \int_{t_1}^{t_2} a_t(X_t) \, dt + \int_{t_1}^{t_2} b_t(X_t) \, dw_t$$

The stochastic differential has some of the properties of ordinary differentials, such as linearity. Not all of them, however, remain true. For example,[9] the stochastic differential of a product of two stochastic processes for which the stochastic differential of the factors is known,

$$dX_t^{(i)} = a_t^{(i)} \, dt + b_t^{(i)} \, dw_t \qquad i = 1, 2$$

is given by:

$$d(X_t^{(1)} X_t^{(2)}) = X_t^{(1)} \, dX_t^{(2)} + X_t^{(2)} \, dX_t^{(1)} + b_t^{(1)} b_t^{(2)} \, dt$$

Another property, which corresponds to the derivation formula for a compound function, is the well-known *Itô formula*.[10] This formula gives the differential for a two-variable function: a stochastic process for which the stochastic differential is known, and time. If the process X_t has the stochastic differential $dX_t = a_t dt + b_t dw_t$ and if $f(x, t)$ is a C_2-class function, the process $f(X, t)$ will admit the following stochastic differential:

$$df(X_t, t) = \left[f_t'(X_t, t) + f_x'(X_t, t)a_t + \frac{1}{2} f_{xx}''(X_t, t)b_t^2 \right] \cdot dt + f_x'(X_t, t)b_t \cdot dw_t$$

---

[9] We will from now on leave out the argument X in the expression of s functions a and b.
[10] Also known as the Itô's lemma.

Appendix 3

Statistical Concepts[1]

3.1 INFERENTIAL STATISTICS

3.1.1 Sampling

3.1.1.1 Principles

In inferential statistics, we are usually interested in a population and the variables measured on the individual members of that population. Unfortunately, the population as a whole is often far too large, and sometimes not sufficiently well known, to be handled directly. For cases of observed information, therefore, we must confine ourselves to a subset of the population, known as a *sample*. Then, on the basis of observations made in relation to that sample, we attempt to deduce (infer) conclusions in relation to the population.

The operation that consists of extracting the sample from the population is known as *sampling*. It is here that probability theory becomes involved, constituting the link between the population and the sample. It is defined as simply random when the individual members are extracted independently from the population and all have the same probability of being chosen. In practice, this is not necessarily the case and the procedures set up for carrying out the sampling process must imitate the chance as closely as possible.

3.1.1.2 Sampling distribution

Suppose that we are interested in a parameter θ of the population. If we extract a sample $x_1, x_2, \ldots, x_n$ from the population, we can calculate the parameter θ for this sample $\theta(x_1, x_2, \ldots, x_n)$.

As the sampling is at the origin of the fortuitous aspect of this procedure, for another sample $x_1', x_2', \ldots, x_n'$, we would have obtained another parameter value $\theta(x_1', x_2', \ldots, x_n')$.

We are therefore constructing a r.v. Θ, in which the various possible values are the results of the calculation of θ for all the possible samples. The law of probability for this r.v. Θ is known as the *sampling distribution*.

In order to illustrate this concept, let us consider the sampling distribution for the mean of the population and suppose that the variable considered has a mean and variance μ and σ^2 respectively. On the basis of the various samples, it is possible to calculate an average on each occasion:

$$\overline{x} = \frac{1}{n} \sum_{i=1}^{n} x_i \qquad \overline{x}' = \frac{1}{n} \sum_{i=1}^{n} x_i' \qquad \cdots$$

[1] Readers interested in finding out more about the concepts developed below should read: Ansion G., *Econométrie pour l'enterprise*, Eyrolles, 1988. Dagnelie P., *Théorie et méthodes statistique*, (2 volumes), Presses Agronomiques de Gembloux, 1975. Johnston J., *Econometric Methods*, McGraw-Hill, 1972. Justens D., *Statistique pour décideurs*, De Boeck, 1988. Kendall M. and Stuart A., *The Advanced Theory of Statistics* (3 volumes), Griffin, 1977.

We thus define a r.v. $\overline{X}$ for which it can be demonstrated that:

$$E(\overline{X}) = \mu$$

$$\mathrm{var}(\overline{X}) = \frac{\sigma^2}{n}$$

The first of these two relations justifies the choice of the average of the sample as an *estimator* for the mean of the population. It is referred to as an *unbiased* estimator.

Note

If we examine in a similar way the sampling distribution for the variance, calculated on the basis of a sample using $s^2 = \frac{1}{n}\sum_{i=1}^{n}(x_i - \overline{x})^2$, the associated r.v. S^2 will be such that $E(S^2) = \frac{n-1}{n}\sigma^2$.

We are no longer looking at an unbiased estimator, but an asymptotically unbiased estimator (for n tending towards infinity). For this reason, we frequently choose the following expression as an estimator for the variance: $\frac{1}{n-1}\sum_{i=1}^{n}(x_i - \overline{x})^2$.

3.1.2 Two problems of inferential statistics

3.1.2.1 Estimation

If the problem is therefore one of estimating a parameter θ of the population, we must construct an estimator Θ that is a function of the values observed through the sampling procedure. It is therefore important for this estimator Θ to be of good quality for evaluating the parameter θ. We thus often require an *unbiased estimator*: $E(\Theta) = \theta$.

Nevertheless, of all the unbiased estimators, we want the estimator adopted to have other properties, and most notably its dispersion around the central value θ to be as small as possible. Its variance $\mathrm{var}(\Theta) = E((\Theta - \theta)^2)$ must be minimal.[2]

Alongside this selective estimation (there is only one estimation for a sample), a precision is generally calculated for the estimation by determining an interval $[\Theta_1; \Theta_2]$ centred on the value Θ that contains the true value of the parameter θ to be estimated with a given probability:

$$\Pr[\Theta_1 \leq \theta \leq \Theta_2] = 1 - \alpha$$

with $\alpha = 0.05$, for example. This interval is termed the *confidence interval* for θ and the number $(1 - \alpha)$ is the *confidence coefficient*.

This estimation by confidence interval is only possible if one knows the sampling distribution for θ, for example because the population obeys this or that known distribution or if certain asymptotic results, such as central limit theorem, can be applied to it.

Let us examine, by way of an example, the estimate of the mean of a normal population through confidence interval. It is already known that the 'best' estimator is the average of sampling, which is distributed following a normal law with parameters $\left(\mu; \dfrac{\sigma}{\sqrt{n}}\right)$ and

---

[2] For example, the sample average is the unbiased estimator for the minimal variance for the average of the population.

the r.v. $\dfrac{\overline{X} - \mu}{\sigma/\sqrt{n}}$ is thus standard normal. If the quantile for this last distribution is termed $Q(u)$, we have:

$$\Pr\left[Q\left(\frac{\alpha}{2}\right) \leq \frac{\overline{X} - \mu}{\sigma/\sqrt{n}} \leq Q\left(1 - \frac{\alpha}{2}\right)\right] = 1 - \alpha$$

$$\Pr\left[\overline{X} - \frac{\sigma}{\sqrt{n}}Q\left(1 - \frac{\alpha}{2}\right) \leq \mu \leq \overline{X} - \frac{\sigma}{\sqrt{n}}Q\left(\frac{\alpha}{2}\right)\right] = 1 - \alpha$$

$$\Pr\left[\overline{X} - \frac{\sigma}{\sqrt{n}}Q\left(1 - \frac{\alpha}{2}\right) \leq \mu \leq \overline{X} + \frac{\sigma}{\sqrt{n}}Q\left(1 - \frac{\alpha}{2}\right)\right] = 1 - \alpha$$

This last equality makes up the confidence interval formula for the mean; it can also be written more concisely as:

$$\text{I.C.}(\mu) : \overline{X} \pm \frac{\sigma}{\sqrt{n}}Q\left(1 - \frac{\alpha}{2}\right) \quad \text{(s.p.}\alpha)$$

We indicate that in this last formula, the standard deviation for the population σ is generally not known. If it is replaced by its estimator calculated on the basis of the sample, the quantile for the distribution must be replaced by the quantile relative to the Student distribution at $(n - 1)$ degrees of freedom.

3.1.2.2 Hypothesis test

The aim of a hypothesis test is to confirm or refute a hypothesis formulated by a population, on the basis of a sample. In this way, we will know:

- The *goodness-of-fit tests:* verifying whether the population from which the sample is taken is distributed according to a given law of probability.
- The *independence tests* between certain classification criteria defined on the population (these are also used for testing independence between r.v.s).
- The *compliance tests:* verifying whether a population parameter is equal to a given value.
- The *homogeneity tests:* verifying whether the values for a parameter measured on more than one population are the same (this requires one sample to be extracted per population).

The procedure for carrying out a hypothesis test can be shown as follows. After defining the hypothesis to be tested H_0, also known as the null hypothesis, and the alternative hypotheses H_1, we determine under H_0 the sampling distribution for the parameter to be studied. With the fixed confidence coefficient $(1 - \alpha)$, the sample is allocated to the region of acceptance (AH_0) or to the region of rejection (RH_0) within H_0.

Four situations may therefore arise depending on the reality on one hand and the decision taken on the other hand (see Table A3.1).

Zones (a) and (d) in Table A3.1 correspond to correct conclusions of the test. In zone (b) the hypothesis is rejected although it is true; this is a first-type error for which the probability is the complementary α of the confidence coefficient fixed beforehand. In zone

Table A3.1 Hypothesis test conclusions

reality	Decision	
	AH$_0$	RH$_0$
H$_0$	a	b
H$_1$	c	d

(c), the hypothesis is accepted although it is false; this is a second-type error for which the probability β is unknown. A good test will therefore have a small parameter β; the complementary $(1 - \beta)$ of this probability is called the *power* of the test.

By way of an example, we present the compliance test for the mean of a normal population. The hypothesis under test is, for example, H$_0$: $\mu = 1$.

The rival hypothesis is written as: H$_1$: $\mu \neq 1$.

Under H$_0$, the r.v. $\dfrac{\overline{X} - 1}{\sigma/\sqrt{n}}$ follows a normal law and the hypothesis being tested will therefore be rejected when:

$$\frac{|\overline{X} - 1|}{\sigma/\sqrt{n}} > Q\left(1 - \frac{\alpha}{2}\right) \quad \text{(s.p.}\alpha\text{)}.$$

Again, the normal distribution quantile is replaced by the quantile for the Student distribution with $(n - 1)$ degrees of freedom if the standard deviation for the population is replaced by the standard deviation for the sample.

3.2   REGRESSIONS

3.2.1   Simple regression

Let us assume that a variable Y depends on another variable X through a linear relation $Y = aX + b$ and that a series of observations is available for this pair of variables (X, Y): (x_t, y_t) $t = 1, \ldots, n$.

3.2.1.1   Estimation of model

If the observation pairs are represented on the (X, Y) plane, it will be noticed that there are differences between them and a straight line (see Figure A3.1). These differences

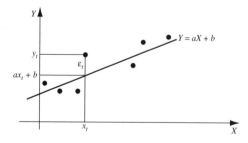

Figure A3.1   Simple regression

may arise, especially in the field of economics, through failure to take account of certain explanatory factors of variable Y.

It is therefore necessary to find the straight line that passes as closely as possible to the point cloud, that is, the straight line for which $\varepsilon_t = y_t - (ax_t + b)$ are as small as possible overall. The criterion most frequently used is that of minimising the sum of the squares of these differences (referred to as the *least square method*). The problem is therefore one of searching for the parameters a and b for which the expression

$$\sum_{t=1}^{n} \varepsilon_t^2 = \sum_{t=1}^{n} \left[y_t - (ax_t + b) \right]^2$$

is minimal. It can be easily shown that these parameters total:

$$\hat{a} = \frac{S_{xy}}{s_x^2} = \frac{\displaystyle\sum_{t=1}^{n}(x_t - \overline{x})(y_t - \overline{y})}{\displaystyle\sum_{t=1}^{n}(x_t - \overline{x})^2}$$

$$\hat{b} = \overline{y} - \hat{a}\overline{x}$$

These are unbiased estimators of the real unknown parameters a and b. In addition, of all the unbiased estimators expressed linearly as a function of y_t, they are the ones with the smallest variance.[3] The straight line obtained using the procedure is known as the *regression line*.

3.2.1.2   *Validation of model*

The significantly explanatory character of the variable X in this model can be proved by testing the hypothesis H_0: $a = 0$.

If we are led to reject the hypothesis, it is because X significantly explains Y through the model, that is therefore validated. Because under certain probability hypotheses on the residuals ε_t the estimator for a is distributed according to a Student law with $(n - 2)$ degrees of freedom, the hypothesis will be rejected (and the model therefore accepted) if

$$\frac{|\hat{a}|}{s_a} > t_{1-\alpha/2}^{(n-2)} \quad \text{(s.p.}\alpha)$$

where s_a is the standard deviation for the estimator for a, measured on the observations.

3.2.2   **Multiple regression**

The regression model that we have just presented can be generalised when several explanatory variables are involved at once:

$$Y = \alpha_0 + \alpha_1 X_1 + \cdots + \alpha_k X_k.$$

---

[3] They are referred to as BLUE (Best Linear Unbiased Estimators).

In this case, if the observations x and y and the parameters α are presented as matrices

$$X = \begin{pmatrix} 1 & x_{11} & \cdots & x_{1k} \\ 1 & x_{21} & \cdots & x_{2k} \\ \vdots & \vdots & \ddots & \vdots \\ 1 & x_{n1} & \cdots & x_{nk} \end{pmatrix} \qquad \vec{Y} = \begin{pmatrix} y_1 \\ y_2 \\ \vdots \\ y_n \end{pmatrix} \qquad \vec{\alpha} = \begin{pmatrix} \alpha_1 \\ \alpha_2 \\ \vdots \\ \alpha_n \end{pmatrix},$$

it can be shown that the vector for the parameter estimations is given by $\hat{\vec{\alpha}} = (X^t X)^{-1}(X^t \vec{Y})$.

In addition, the Student validation test shown for the simple regression also applies here. It is used to test the significantly explanatory nature of a variable within the multiple model, the only alteration being the number of degrees of freedom, which passes from $(n-2)$ to $(n-k-1)$. We should mention that there are other tests for the overall validity of the multiple regression model.

3.2.3 Nonlinear regression

It therefore turns out that the relation allowing Y to be explained by $X_1, X_2, \ldots, X_k$ is not linear: $Y = f(X_1, X_2, \ldots, X_k)$.

In this case, sometimes, the relation can be made linear by a simple analytical conversion. For example, $Y = aX^b$ is converted by a logarithmic transformation:

$$\ln Y = \ln a + b \ln X$$

$$Y^* = a^* + bX^*$$

We are thus brought round to a linear regression model.

Other models cannot be transformed quite so simply. Thus, $Y = a + X^b$ is not equivalent to the linear model. In this case, much better developed techniques, generally of an iterative nature, must be used to estimate the parameters for this type of model.

Appendix 4

Extreme Value Theory

4.1 EXACT RESULT

Let us consider a sequence of r.v.s $X_1, X_2, \ldots, X_n$, independent and identically distributed with a common distribution function F_X. Let us also consider the sequence of r.v.s Z_1, $Z_2, \ldots, Z_n$, defined by:

$$Z_k = \max(X_1, \ldots, X_k). \quad k = 1, \ldots, n$$

The d.f. for Z_n is given by:

$$
\begin{aligned}
F^{(n)}(z) &= \Pr[\max(X_1, \ldots, X_n) \leq z] \\
&= \Pr([X_1 \leq z] \cap \cdots \cap [X_n \leq z]) \\
&= \Pr[X_1 \leq z] \cdot \cdots \cdot \Pr[X_n \leq z] \\
&= F_X^n(z)
\end{aligned}
$$

Note

When one wishes to study the distribution of an extreme Z_n for a large number n of r.v.s, the precise formula established by us is not greatly useful. In fact, we need to have a result that does not depend essentially on the d.f., as F_x is not necessarily known with any great accuracy. In addition, when n tends towards the infinite, the r.v. Z_n tends towards a degenerate r.v., as:

$$
\lim_{n \to \infty} F^{(n)}(z) = \begin{cases} 0 & \text{si } F_X(z) < 1 \\ 1 & \text{si } F_X(z) = 1 \end{cases}
$$

It was for this reason that asymptotic extreme value theory was developed.

4.2 ASYMPTOTIC RESULTS

Asymptotic extreme value theory originates in the work of R. A. Fisher,[1] and the problem was fully solved by B. Gnedenko.[2]

4.2.1 Extreme value theorem

The *extreme value theorem* states that under the hypothesis of independence and equal distribution of r.v.s $X_1, X_2, \ldots, X_n$, if there are also two sequences of coefficients $\alpha_n > 0$

---

[1] Fisher R. A. and Tippett L. H. C., Limiting forms of the frequency distribution of the largest or smallest member of a sample, *Proceedings of the Cambridge Philosophical Society*, Vol. 24, 1978, pp. 180–90.
[2] Gnedenko B. V., On the distribution limit of the maximum term of a random series, *Annals of Mathematics*, Vol. 44, 1943, pp. 423–53.

and β_n ($n = 1, 2, \ldots$) so that the limit (for $n \to \infty$) of the random variable

$$Y_n = \frac{\max(X_1, \ldots, X_n) - \beta_n}{\alpha_n}$$

is not degenerate, it will admit a law of probability defined by a distribution function that must be one of the following three forms:

$$\Lambda(z) = \exp[-e^{-z}]$$

$$\Phi(z) = \begin{cases} 0 & z \leq 0 \\ \exp[-z^{-k}] & z > 0 \end{cases}$$

$$\Psi(z) = \begin{cases} \exp[-(-z)^k] & z < 0 \\ 1 & z \geq 0 \end{cases}$$

Here, k is a positive constant. These three laws are known respectively as *Gumbel's law* for Λ, *Fréchet's law* for Φ and *Weibull's law* for Ψ.

The parameter α_n is a parameter for measuring the dispersion of the law of probability. The parameter β_n, meanwhile, is a location parameter that when n tends towards infinity tends towards the limit distribution mode.[3]

We should point out that although the hypotheses of independence and equal distribution of the initial r.v.s are demanding, the extreme value theorem allows for extensions if these hypotheses are partly taken by default.

4.2.2 Attraction domains

There is the question of knowing for what type of initial d.f. F_X the distribution of extremes tends towards Gumbel's, Fréchet's or Weibull's law. Gnedenko has also provided an answer to this question. These sets of d.f.s F_X are the attraction domains for each of the three laws.

The attraction domain for Gumbel's law Λ is characterised by the presence of a number x_0 for which $F_X(x_0) = 1$ and $F_X(x) < 1$ when $x < x_0$, so that there exists a continuous function g verifying:

$$\begin{cases} \lim_{x \to x_0-} g(x) = 0 \\ \lim_{x \to x_0-} \dfrac{1 - F_X[x(1 + yg(x))]}{1 - F_X(x)} = e^{-y} \quad \forall y \end{cases}$$

It will be seen that the initial F_X laws that verify this condition are laws for which the density has a tail with at least exponential decrease, such as the normal law, the exponential law or the chi-square law.

The attraction domain for Fréchet's law Φ is characterised by the presence of a positive parameter k, so that

$$\lim_{x \to \infty} \frac{1 - F_X(x)}{1 - F_X(ux)} = u^k \quad \forall u > 0$$

---

[3] That is, the value that corresponds to the maximum of the probability density.

The laws covered by this description are the laws for which the tails decrease less rapidly than the exponential, such as Student's law, Cauchy's law and stable Pareto's law.

Finally, the attraction domain of Weibull's law Ψ is characterised by the presence of a number x_0 for which $F_X(x_0) = 1$ and $F_X(x) < 1$ when $x < x_0$, and the presence of a positive parameter k, so that

$$\lim_{x \to 0-} \frac{1 - F_X(x_0 + ux)}{1 - F_X(x_0 + x)} = u^k \qquad \forall u > 0$$

This category contains the bounded support distributions, such as the uniform law.

4.2.3 Generalisation

A. F. Jenkinson has been able to provide Gnedenko's result with a unified form.

In fact, if for Fréchet's law Φ it is suggested that $z = 1 - \tau y$ and $k = -1/\tau$, we will find, when $\tau < 0$ and we obtain

$$\exp[-z^{-k}] = \exp[-(1 - \tau y)^{1/\tau}]$$

a valid relation for $z > 0$, that is, $y > 1/\tau$ (for the other values of y, the r.v. takes the value 0).

In the same way, for Weibull's law Ψ, it is suggested that $z = \tau y - 1$ and $k = 1/\tau$. We then find, when $\tau > 0$ and we obtain

$$\exp[-(-z)^k] = \exp[-(1 - \tau y)^{1/\tau}]$$

a valid relation for $z < 0$, that is, $y < 1/\tau$ (for the other values of y, the r.v. takes the value 1).

We therefore have the same analytical expression in both cases. We will also see that the same applies to Gumbel's law Λ. By passage to the limit, we can easily find:

$$\lim_{\tau \to 0\pm} \exp[-(1 - \tau y)^{1/\tau}] = \exp\left[- \lim_{n \to \pm\infty} \left(1 - \frac{y}{n}\right)^n\right] = \exp[-e^{-y}]$$

which is the expression set out in Gumbel's law.
To sum up: by paring $a(y) = \exp[-(1 - \tau y)^{1/\tau}]$, the d.f. F_Y of the extreme limit distribution is written as follows:

$$\text{If } t < 0,\ F_Y(y) = \begin{cases} 0 & \text{si } y \le 1/\tau \\ a(y) & \text{si } y > 1/\tau \end{cases} \qquad \text{(Fréchet's law)}.$$

$$\text{If } t = 0,\ F_Y(y) = a(y) \qquad \forall y \text{ (Gumbel's Law)}.$$

$$\text{If } t > 0,\ F_Y(y) = \begin{cases} a(y) & \text{si } y < 1/\tau \\ 1 & \text{si } y \ge 1/\tau \end{cases} \qquad \text{(Weibull's law)}.$$

This, of course, is the result shown in Section 7.4.2.

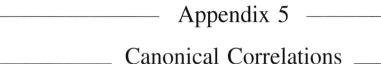

Appendix 5

Canonical Correlations

5.1 GEOMETRIC PRESENTATION OF THE METHOD

The aim of *canonical analysis*[1] is to study the linear relations that exist between the static spreads and dynamic spreads observed on the same sample. We are looking for a linear combination of static spreads and a linear combination of dynamic spreads that are as well correlated as possible.

We therefore have two sets of characters: $x_1, x_2, \ldots, x_p$ on one hand and $y_1, y_2, \ldots, y_q$ on the other hand. In addition, it is assumed that the characters are centred, standardized and observed for in the same number n of individuals.

Both sets of characters generate the respective associated vectorial subspaces, V_1 and V_2 of **R**. We also introduce the matrices **X** and **Y** with respective formats (n, p) and (n, q), in which the various columns are observations relative to the different characters.

As the characters are centred, the same will apply to the vectorial subspaces. Geometrically, therefore, the problem of canonical analysis can be presented as follows: we need to find $\xi \in \varepsilon V_1$ and $\eta \in V_2$, so that $\cos^2(\xi, \eta) = r^2(\xi, \eta)$ is maximised.

5.2 SEARCH FOR CANONICAL CHARACTERS

Let us assume that the characters ξ^1 and η^1 are solutions to the problem – see Figure A5.1.

The angle between ξ^1 and η^1 does not depend on their norm (length). In fact, V_1 and V_2 are invariable when the base vectors are multiplied by a scalar and therefore $\cos^2(\xi^1, \eta^1)$ does not depend on the base vector norms. It is then assumed that $\|\xi^1\| = \|\eta^1\| = 1$.

The character η^1 must be co-linear with the orthogonal projection of ξ^1 over V_2, which is the vector of V_2 that makes a minimum angle with ξ^1. This condition is written as

$$A_2\xi^1 = r_1\eta^1$$

where $r^2_1 = \cos^2(\xi^1, \eta^1)$ and A_2 is the operator of the orthogonal projection on V_2. In the same way, we have $A_1\eta^1 = r_1\xi^1$. These two relations produce the system

$$\begin{cases} A_1 A_2 \xi^1 = \lambda_1 \xi^1 \\ A_2 A_1 \eta^1 = \lambda_1 \eta^1 \end{cases}$$

where $\lambda_1 = r^2_1 = \cos^2(\xi^1, \eta^1)$.

It is therefore deduced that ξ^1 and η^1 are respectively the eigenvectors of operators $A_1 A_2$ and $A_2 A_1$ associated with the same highest eigenvalue λ_1, this value being equal

---

[1] A detailed description of this method and other multivariate statistical methods, is found in Chatfield C. and Collins A. J., *Introduction to Multivariate Analysis*, Chapman & Hall, 1980. Saporta G., *Probabilities, Data Analysis and Statistics*, Technip, 1990.

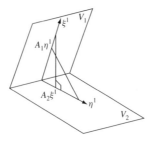

Figure A5.1   Canonical correlations

to their squared cosine or their squared correlation. The characters ξ^1 and η^1 are deduced from each other by a simple linear application:

$$\eta^1 = \frac{1}{\sqrt{\lambda_1}} A_2 \xi^1 \quad \text{and} \quad \xi^1 = \frac{1}{\sqrt{\lambda_1}} A_1 \eta^1.$$

The following canonical characters are the eigenvectors of $A_1 A_2$, associated with the eigenvalue λ_1 sorted in decreasing order. If the first canonical characters of order i are written

$$\xi^i = a_1 x_1 + \cdots + a_p x_p \quad \text{and} \quad \eta^i = b_1 y_1 + \cdots + b_q y_q$$

(in other words, in terms of matrix, $\xi^i = Xa$ and $\eta^i = Yb$) and if the diagonal matrix of the weights is expressed as D, it can be shown that:

$$\begin{cases} b = \dfrac{1}{\sqrt{\lambda_i}} (Y^t DY)^{-1} (X^t DY)^t a \\[2mm] a = \dfrac{1}{\sqrt{\lambda_i}} (X^t DX)^{-1} (X^t DY) b \end{cases}$$

Algebraic Presentation of Logistic Regression

Let Y be the binary qualitative variable (0 for periods of equilibrium, 1 for breaks in equilibrium) that we wish to explain by the explanatory quantitative variables $X_{1,p,}$. The model looks to evaluate the following probabilities:

$$p_i = \Pr\left([Y=1]\,\big|\,[X_1 = x_{i1}; \ldots; X_p = x_{ip}]\right)$$

The logistic regression model[1] is a nonlinear regression model. Here, the specification for the model is based on the use of a logistic function:

$$G(p) = \ln\left(\frac{p}{1-p}\right)$$

In this type of model, it is considered that there is linear dependency between $G(p_i)$ and the explanatory variables:

$$G(p_i) = \beta_0 + \beta_1 x_{i1} + \cdots + \beta_p x_{ip}$$

where, $\beta_0, \beta_1, \ldots, \beta_p$ are the unknown parameters to be estimated. By introducing the vector $\boldsymbol{\beta}$ for these coefficients, so that

$$z_i = \begin{pmatrix} 1 \\ x_{i1} \\ \vdots \\ x_{ip} \end{pmatrix}$$

the binomial probability can be expressed in the form

$$p_i = \frac{e^{\beta z_i}}{1 + e^{\beta z_i}}$$

The method for estimating the parameters is that of maximising the probability function through successive iterations. This probability function is the product of the statistical density relative to each individual member:

$$L(\beta) = \prod_{\{i:y_i=1\}} e^{\beta z_i} \cdot \prod_{\{i:y_i=0\}} \frac{1}{1 + e^{\beta z_i}}$$

---

[1] A detailed description of this method and other multivariate statistical methods, is found in Chatfield C. and Collins A. J., *Introduction to Multivariate Analysis*, Chapman & Hall, 1980. Saporta G., *Probabilities, Data Analysis and Statistics*, Technip, 1990.

7.1 ARCH-GARCH MODELS

The ARCH-GARCH (auto-regressive conditional heteroscedasticity or generalised auto-regressive conditional heteroscedasticity) models were developed by Engel[1] in 1982 in the context of studies of macroeconomic data. The ARCH model allows specific modelling of variance in terms of error. Heteroscedasticity can be integrated by introducing an exogenous variable x, which provides for variance in the term of error. This modelling can take one of the following forms:

$$y_t = e_t \cdot x_{t-1} \quad \text{or} \quad y_t = e_t \cdot y_{t-1}$$

Here, e_t is a white noise (sequence of r.v.s not correlated, with zero mean and the same variance).

In order to prevent the variance in this geometric series from being infinite or zero, it is preferable to take the following formulations:

$$y_t = a_0 + \sum_{i=1}^{p} a_i y_{t-i} + \varepsilon_t$$

with:

$$
\begin{cases}
E(\varepsilon_t) = 0 \\
\text{var}(\varepsilon_t) = \gamma + \sum_{i=1}^{q} \alpha_i \varepsilon_{t-i}^2
\end{cases}
$$

This type of model is generally expressed as $AR(p) - ARCH(q)$ or $ARCH(p, q)$.

7.2 EGARCH MODELS

These models, unlike the ARCH-GARCH model, allow the conditional variance to respond to a fall or rise in the series in different ways. This configuration is of particular interest in generally increasing financial series. An example of this type of model is Nelson's:[2]

$$
\begin{cases}
x_t = \mu + \sqrt{h_t} \chi_t \\
\ln h_t = \alpha + \beta \ln h_{t-1} + \delta \left(|\chi_t| - \sqrt{2/\pi} \right) + \gamma \chi_{t-1}
\end{cases}
$$

Here, χ_t / I_{t-1} follows a standard normal law (I_{t-1} representing the information available at the moment $t - 1$).

---

[1] Engel R. F., Auto-regressive conditional heteroscedasticity with estimate of the variance of United Kingdom inflation, *Econometrica* No. 50, 1982, pp. 987–1003. A detailed presentation of the chronological series models will also be found in Droebske J. J, Fichet B. and Tassi P., *Modélisation ARCH, théorie statistique et applications dans le domaine de la finance*, Éditions ULB, 1994; and in Gourjeroux C., *Modèles ARCH et applications financières*, Economica, 1992.

[2] Nelson D. B., Conditional heteroscedasticity in asset returns: a new approach, *Econometrica* No. 39, 1991, pp. 347–70.

Appendix 8
Numerical Methods for Solving Nonlinear Equations[1]

An equation is said to be nonlinear when it involves terms of degree higher than 1 in the unknown quantity. These terms may be polynomial or capable of being broken down into Taylor series of degrees higher than 1.

Nonlinear equations cannot in general be solved analytically. In this case, therefore, the solutions of the equations must be approached using iterative methods. The principle of these methods of solving consists in starting from an arbitrary point – the closest possible point to the solution sought – and involves arriving at the solution gradually through successive tests.

The two criteria to take into account when choosing a method for solving nonlinear equations are:

- Method convergence (conditions of convergence, speed of convergence etc.).
- The cost of calculating of the method.

8.1 GENERAL PRINCIPLES FOR ITERATIVE METHODS

8.1.1 Convergence

Any nonlinear equation $f(x) = 0$ can be expressed as $x = g(x)$.

If x_0 constitutes the arbitrary starting point for the method, it will be seen that the solution x^* for this equation, $x^* = g(x^*)$, can be reached by the numerical sequence:

$$x_{n+1} = g(x_n) \quad n = 0, 1, 2, \ldots$$

This iteration is termed a Picard process and x^*, the limit of the sequence, is termed the fixed iterative point.

In order for the sequence set out below to tend towards the solution of the equation, it has to be guaranteed that this sequence will converge. A sufficient condition for convergence is supplied by the following theorem: if $x = g(x)$ has a solution a within the interval $I = [a - b; a + b] = \{x : |x - a| \leq b\}$ and if $g(x)$ satisfies Lipschitz's condition:

$$\exists L \in [0; 1[: \forall x \in I, \quad |g(x) - g(a)| \leq L|x - a|$$

Then, for every $x_0 \in I$:

- all the iterated values x_n will belong to I;
- the iterated values x_n will converge towards a;
- the solution a will be unique within interval I.

---

[1] This appendix is mostly based on Litt F. X., *Analyse numérique, première partie*, ULG, 1999. Interested readers should also read: Burden R. L. and Faires D. J., *Numerical Analysis*, Prindle, Weber & Schmidt, 1981; and Nougier J. P., *Méthodes de calcul numérique*, Masson, 1993.

We should also show a case in which Lipschitz's condition is satisfied: it is sufficient that for every $x \in I$, $g'(x)$ exists and is such that $|g'(x)| \leq m$ with $m < 1$.

8.1.2 Order of convergence

It is important to choose the most suitable of the methods that converge. At this level, one of the most important criteria to take into account is the speed or order of convergence.

Thus the sequence x_n, defined above, and the error $e_n = x_n - a$. If there is a number p and a constant $C > 0$ so that

$$\lim_{n \to \infty} \frac{|e_{n+1}|}{|e_n|^p} = C$$

p will then be termed the order of convergence for the sequence and C is the asymptotic error constant.

When the speed of convergence is unsatisfactory, it can be improved by the Aitken extrapolation,[2] which is a convergence acceleration process. The speed of convergence of this extrapolation is governed by the following result:

- If Picard's iterative method is of the order p, the Aitken extrapolation will be of the order $2p - 1$.
- If Picard's iterative method is of the first order, Aitken's extrapolation will be of the second order in the case of a simple solution and of the first order in the case of a multiple solution. In this last case, the asymptotic error constant is equal to $1 - 1/m$ where m is the multiplicity of the solution.

8.1.3 Stop criteria

As stated above, the iterative methods for solving nonlinear equations supply an approached solution to the solution of the equation. It is therefore essential to be able to estimate the error in the solution.

Working on the mean theorem:

$$f(x_n) = (x_n - a)f'(\xi), \text{ with } \xi \in [x_n; a]$$

we can deduce the following estimation for the error:

$$|x_n - a| \leq \frac{|f(x_n)|}{M}, \quad |f'(x_n)| \geq M, \quad x \in [x_n; a]$$

In addition, the rounding error inherent in every numerical method limits the accuracy of the iterative methods to:

$$\varepsilon_a = \frac{\delta}{f'(a)}$$

---

[2] We refer to Litt F. X., *Analyse numérique, première partie*, ULG 1999, for further details.

in which δ represents an upper boundary for the rounding error in iteration n:

$$\delta \geq |\delta_n| = \overline{f}(x_n) - f(x_n)$$

$\overline{f}(x_n)$ represents the calculated value for the function.

Let us now assume that we wish to determine a solution a with a degree of precision ε. We could stop the iterative process on the basis of the error estimation formula.

These formulae, however, require a certain level of information on the derivative $f'(x)$, information that is not easy to obtain. On the other hand, the limit specification ε_a will not generally be known beforehand.[3] Consequently, we are running the risk of ε, the accuracy level sought, never being reached, as it is better than the limit precision $\varepsilon_a (\varepsilon < \varepsilon_a)$. In this case, the iterative process will carry on indefinitely.

This leads us to accept the following stop criterion:

$$\begin{cases} |x_n - x_{n-1}| < \varepsilon \\ |x_{n+1} - x_n| \geq |x_n - x_{n-1}| \end{cases}$$

This means that the iteration process will be stopped when the iteration n produces a variation in value less than that of the iteration $n + 1$. The value of ε will be chosen in a way that prevents the iteration from stopping too soon.

8.2 PRINCIPAL METHODS

Defining an iterative method is based ultimately on defining the function $h(x)$ of the equation $x = g(x) \equiv x - h(x)f(x)$.

The choice of this function will determine the order of the method.

8.2.1 First order methods

The simplest choice consists of taking $h(x) = m = $ constant $\neq 0$.

8.2.1.1 Chord method

This defines the *chord method* (Figure A8.1), for which the iteration is $x_{n+1} = x_n - mf(x_n)$.

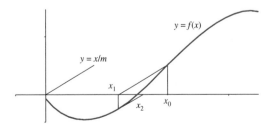

Figure A8.1   Chord method

---

[3] This will in effect require knowledge of $f'(a)$, when a is exactly what is being sought.

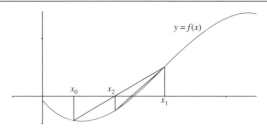

Figure A8.2   Classic chord method

The sufficient convergence condition (see Section A8.1.1) for this method is $0 < mf'(x) < 2$, in the neighbourhood of the solution. In addition, it can be shown that
$\lim_{n\to\infty} \dfrac{|e_{n+1}|}{|e_n|} = |g'(a)| \neq 0$.

The chord method is therefore clearly a first-order method (see Section A8.1.2).

8.2.1.2 Classic chord method

It is possible to improve the order of convergence by making m change at each iteration:

$$x_{n+1} = x_n - m_n f(x_n)$$

The *classic chord method* (Figure A8.2) takes as the value for m_n the inverse of the slope for the straight line defined by the points $(x_{n-1}; f(x_{n-1}))$ and $(x_n; f(x_n))$:

$$x_{n+1} = x_n - \frac{x_n - x_{n-1}}{f(x_n) - f(x_{n-1})} f(x_n)$$

This method will converge if $f'(a) \neq 0$ and $f''(x)$ is continuous in the neighbourhood of a. In addition, it can be shown that

$$\lim_{n\to\infty} \frac{|e_{n+1}|}{|e_n|^p} = \left(\frac{f''(a)}{2f'(a)} \right)^{1/p} \neq 0$$

for $p = \frac{1}{2}(1 + \sqrt{5}) = 1.618\ldots > 1$, which greatly improves the order of convergence for the method.

8.2.1.3 Regula falsi method

The *regula falsi* method (Figure A8.3) takes as the value for m_n the inverse of the slope for the straight line defined by the points $(x_{n'}; f(x_{n'}))$ and $(x_n; f(x_n))$ where n' is the highest index for which $f(x_{n'}).f(x_n) < 0$:

$$x_{n+1} = x_n - \frac{x_n - x_{n'}}{f(x_n) - f(x_{n'})} f(x_n)$$

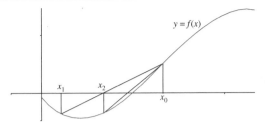

Figure A8.3   *Regula falsi* method

This method always converges when $f(x)$ is continuous. On the other hand, the convergence of this method is linear and therefore less effective than the convergence of the classic chord method.

8.2.2   Newton–Raphson method

If, in the classic chord method, we choose m_n so that $g'(x_n) = 0$, that is, $f'(x_n) = 1/m_n$, we will obtain a second-order iteration.

The method thus defined,

$$x_{n+1} = x_n - \frac{f(x_n)}{f'(x_n)}$$

is known as the Newton-Raphson method (Figure A8.4).

It is clearly a second-order method, as

$$\lim_{n \to \infty} \frac{|e_{n+1}|}{|e_n|^2} = \frac{1}{2}\left|\frac{f''(a)}{f'(a)}\right| \neq 0$$

The Newton–Raphson method is therefore rapid insofar as the initial iterated value is not too far from the solution sought, as global convergence is not assured at all.

A convergence criterion is therefore given for the following theorem. Assume that $f'(x) \neq 0$ and that $f''(x)$ does not change its sign within the interval $[a; b]$ and $f(a).f(b) < 0$.

If, furthermore,

$$\left|\frac{f(a)}{f'(a)}\right| < b - a \quad \text{and} \quad \left|\frac{f(b)}{f'(b)}\right| < b - a$$

the Newton–Raphson method will converge at every initial arbitrary point x_0 that belongs to $[a; b]$.

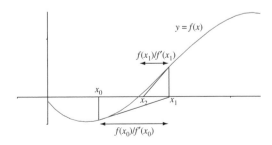

Figure 8.4   Newton–Raphson method

The classic chord method, unlike the Newton–Raphson method, requires two initial approximations but only involves one new function evaluation at each subsequent stage. The choice between the classic chord method and the Newton–Raphson method will therefore depend on the effort of calculation required for evaluation $f'(x)$.

Let us assume that the effort of calculation required for evaluation of $f'(x)$ is θ times the prior effort of calculation for $f(x)$.

Given what has been said above, we can establish that the effort of calculation will be the same for the two methods if:

$$\frac{1+\theta}{\log 2} = \frac{1}{\log p} \quad \text{in which} \quad p = \frac{1+\sqrt{5}}{2}$$

is the order of convergence in the classic chord method.

In consequence:

- If $\theta > (\log 2/\log p) - 1 \sim 0.44 \rightarrow$ the classic chord method will be used.
- If $\theta \leq (\log 2/\log p) - 1 \sim 0.44 \rightarrow$ the Newton–Raphson method will be used.

8.2.3   Bisection method

The *bisection method* is a linear convergence method and is therefore slow. Use of the method is, however, justified by the fact that it converges overall, unlike the usual methods (especially the Newton–Raphson and classic chord methods). This method will therefore be used to bring the initial iterated value of the Newton–Raphson or classic chord method to a point sufficiently close to the solution to ensure that the methods in question converge.

Let us assume therefore that $f(x)$ is continuous in the interval $[a_0; b_0]$ and such that[4] $f(a_0).f(b_0) < 0$. The principle of the method consists of putting together a converging sequence of bracketed intervals, $[a_1; b_1] \supset [a_2; b_2] \supset [a_3; b_3] \supset \ldots$, all of which contain a solution of the equation $f(x) = 0$.

If it is assumed that[5] $f(a_0) < 0$ and $f(b_0) > 0$, the intervals $I_k = [a_k; b_k]$ will be put together by recurrence on the basis of I_{k-1}.

$$[a_k; b_k] = \begin{cases} [m_k; b_{k-1}] & \text{if} \quad f(m_k) < 0 \\ [a_{k-1}; m_k] & \text{if} \quad f(m_k) > 0 \end{cases}$$

Here, $m_k = (a_{k-1} + b_{k-1})/2$. One is thus assured that $f(a_k) < 0$ and $f(b_k) > 0$, which guarantees convergence.

The bisection method is not a Picard iteration, but the order of convergence can be determined, as $\lim_{n\to\infty} \dfrac{|e_{n+1}|}{|e_n|} = \dfrac{1}{2}$. The bisection method is therefore a first-order method.

8.3   NONLINEAR EQUATION SYSTEMS

We have a system of n nonlinear equations of n unknowns: $f_i(x_1, x_2, \ldots, x_n) = 0$ $i = 1, 2, \ldots, n$. Here, in vectorial notation, $f(x) = 0$. The solution to the system is an n-dimensional vector a.

---

[4] This implies that $f(x)$ has a root within this interval.
[5] This is not restrictive in any way, as it corresponds to $f(x) = 0$ or $-f(x) = 0$, $x \in [a_0; b_0]$, depending on the case.

8.3.1   General theory of n-dimensional iteration

n-dimensional iteration general theory is similar to the one-dimensional theory. The above equation can thus be expressed in the form:

$$x = g(x) \equiv x - A(x) f(x)$$

where A is a square matrix of nth order.
  Picard's iteration is always defined as

$$x_{k+1} = g(x_k) \quad k = 0, 1, 2 \text{ etc.}$$

and the convergence theorem for Picard's iteration remains valid in n dimensions.
  In addition, if the Jacobian matrix $J(x)$, defined by $[J(x)]_{ij} = \left(g_j(x)\right)'_{x_i}$ is such that for every $x \in I$, $\|J(x)\| \leq m$ for a norm compatible with $m < 1$, Lipschitz's condition is satisfied.
  The order of convergence is defined by

$$\lim_{k \to \infty} \frac{\|e_{k+1}\|}{\|e_k\|^p} = C$$

where C is the constant for the asymptotic error.

8.3.2   Principal methods

If one chooses a constant matrix A as the value for $A(x)$, the iterative process is the generalisation in n dimensions of the chord method.
  If the inverse of the Jacobian matrix of f is chosen as the value of $A(x)$, we will obtain the generalisation in n dimensions of the Newton–Raphson method.
Another approach to solving the equation $f(x) = 0$ involves using the ith equation to determine the $(i + 1)^{\text{th}}$ component. Therefore, for $i = 1, 2, \ldots, n$, the following equations will be solved in succession:

$$f_i(x_1^{(k+1)}, \ldots, x_{i-1}^{(k+1)}, x_i, x_{i+1}^{(k)}, \ldots, x_n^{(k)}) = 0$$

with respect to x_i. This is known as the *nonlinear Gauss–Seidel method*.

Bibliography

CHAPTER 1

The Bank for International Settlements, Basle Committee for Banking Controls, *Sound Practices for the Management and Supervision of Operational Risk*, Basle, February 2003.

The Bank for International Settlements, Basle Committee for Banking Controls, *The New Basle Capital Accord*, Basle, January 2001.

The Bank for International Settlements, Basle Committee for Banking Controls, *The New Basle Capital Accord: An Explanatory Note*, Basle, January 2001.

The Bank for International Settlements, Basle Committee for Banking Controls, *Vue d'ensemble du Nouvel accord de Bâle sur les fonds propres*, Basle, January 2001.

Cruz M. G., *Modelling, Measuring and Hedging Operational Risk*, John Wiley & Sons, Ltd, 2002.

Hoffman D. G., *Managing Operational Risk: 20 Firm-Wide Best Practice Strategies*, John Wiley & Sons, Inc, 2002.

Jorion P., *Financial Risk Manager Handbook (Second Edition)*, John Wiley & Sons, Inc, 2003.

Marshall C., *Measuring and Managing Operational Risks in Financial Institutions*, John Wiley & Sons, Inc, 2001.

CHAPTER 2

The Bank for International Settlements, BIS Quarterly Review, *Collateral in Wholesale Financial Markets*, Basle, September 2001.

The Bank for International Settlements, Basle Committee for Banking Controls, *Internal Audit in Banks and the Supervisor's Relationship with Auditors*, Basle, August 2001.

The Bank for International Settlements, Basle Committee for Banking Controls, *Sound Practices for Managing Liquidity in Banking Organisations*, Basle, February 2000.

The Bank for International Settlements, Committee on the Global Financial System, *Collateral in Wholesale Financial Markets: Recent Trends, Risk Management and Market Dynamics*, Basle, March 2001.

Moody's, *Moody's Analytical Framework for Operational Risk Management of Banks*, Moody's, January 2003.

CHAPTER 3

Bachelier L., *Théorie de la spéculation*, Gauthier-Villars, 1900.

Bechu T. and Bertrand E., *L'Analyse Technique*, Economica, 1998.

Binmore K., *Jeux et théorie des jeux*, De Boeck & Larcier, 1999.

Brealey R. A. and Myers S. C., *Principles of Corporate Finance*, McGraw-Hill, 1991.

Broquet C., Cobbaut R., Gillet R., and Vandenberg A., *Gestion de Portefeuille*, De Boeck, 1997.

Chen N. F., Roll R., and Ross S. A., Economic forces of the stock market, *Journal of Business*, No. 59, 1986, pp. 383–403.

Copeland T. E. and Weston J. F., *Financial Theory and Corporate Policy*, Addison-Wesley, 1988.

Devolder P., *Finance stochastique*, Éditions ULB, 1993.

Dhrymes P. J., Friend I., and Gultekin N. B., A critical re-examination of the empirical evidence on the arbitrage pricing theory, *Journal of Finance*, No. 39, 1984, pp. 323–46.

Eeckhoudt L. and Gollier C., *Risk*, Harvester Wheatsheaf, 1995.

Elton E. and Gruber M., *Modern Portfolio Theory and Investment Analysis*, John Wiley & Sons, Inc, 1991.

Elton E., Gruber M., and Padberg M., Optimal portfolios from single ranking devices, *Journal of Portfolio Management*, Vol. 4, No. 3, 1978, pp. 15–19.

Elton E., Gruber M., and Padberg M., Simple criteria for optimal portfolio selection, *Journal of Finance*, Vol. XI, No. 5, 1976, pp. 1341–57.

Elton E., Gruber M., and Padberg M., Simple criteria for optimal portfolio selection: tracing out the efficient frontier, *Journal of Finance*, Vol. XIII, No. 1, 1978, pp. 296–302.

Elton E., Gruber M., and Padberg M., Simple criteria for optimal portfolio selection with upper bounds, *Operation Research*, 1978.

Fama E. and Macbeth J., Risk, return and equilibrium: empirical tests, *Journal of Political Economy*, Vol. 71, No. 1., 1974, pp. 607–36.

Fama E. F., Behaviour of stock market prices, *Journal of Business*, Vol. 38, 1965, pp. 34–105.

Fama E. F., Efficient capital markets: a review of theory and empirical work, *Journal of Finance*, Vol. 25, 1970.

Fama E. F., Random walks in stock market prices, *Financial Analysis Journal*, 1965.

Gillet P., L'efficience des marchés financiers, *Economica*, 1999.

Gordon M. and Shapiro E., Capital equipment analysis: the required rate profit, *Management Science*, Vol. 3, October 1956.

Grinold C. and Kahn N., *Active Portfolio Management*, McGraw-Hill, 1998.

Lintner J., The valuation of risky assets and the selection of risky investments, *Review of Economics and Statistics*, Vol. 47, 1965, pp. 13–37.

Markowitz H., *Mean-Variance Analysis in Portfolio Choice and Capital Markets*, Blackwell Publishers, 1987.

Markowitz H., Portfolio selection, *Journal of Finance*, Vol. 7, No. 1, 1952, pp. 419–33.

Mehta M. L., *Random Matrices*, Academic Press, 1996.

Miller M. H. and Modigliani F., Dividend policy, growth and the valuation of shares, *Journal of Business*, 1961.

Morrison D., *Multivariate Statistical Methods*, McGraw-Hill, 1976.

Roger P., *L'évaluation des Actifs Financiers*, de Boeck, 1996.

Ross S. A., The arbitrage theory of capital asset pricing, *Journal of Economic Theory*, 1976, pp. 343–62.

Samuelson P., Mathematics on Speculative Price, *SIAM Review*, Vol. 15, No. 1, 1973.

Saporta G., *Probabilités, Analyse des Données et Statistique*, Technip, 1990.

Sharpe W., A simplified model for portfolio analysis, *Management Science*, Vol. 9, No. 1, 1963, pp. 277–93.

Sharpe W., Capital asset prices, *Journal of Finance*, Vol. 19, 1964, pp. 425–42.

Von Neumann J. and Morgenstern O., *Theory of Games and Economic Behaviour*, Princeton University Press, 1947.

CHAPTER 4

Bierwag G., Kaufmann G., and Toevs A (Eds.), *Innovations in Bond Portfolio Management: Duration Analysis and Immunisation*, JAI Press, 1983.

Bisière C., *La Structure par Terme des Taux d'intérêt*, Presses Universitaires de France, 1997.

Brennan M. and Schwartz E., A continuous time approach to the pricing of bonds, *Journal of Banking and Finance*, Vol. 3, No. 2, 1979, pp. 133–55.

Colmant B., Delfosse V., and Esch L., *Obligations, les notions financières essentielles*, Larcier, 2002.

Cox J., Ingersoll J., and Ross J., A theory of the term structure of interest rates, *Econometrica*, Vol. 53, No. 2, 1985, pp. 385–406.

Fabozzi J. F., *Bond Markets, Analysis and Strategies*, Prentice-Hall, 2000.

Heath D., Jarrow R., and Morton A., *Bond Pricing and the Term Structure of Interest Rates: a New Methodology*, Cornell University, 1987.

Heath D., Jarrow R., and Morton A., Bond pricing and the term structure of interest rates: discrete time approximation, *Journal of Financial and Quantitative Analysis*, Vol. 25, 1990, pp. 419–40.

Ho T. and Lee S., Term structure movement and pricing interest rate contingent claims, *Journal of Finance*, Vol. 41, No. 5, 1986, pp. 1011–29.

Macauley F., *Some Theoretical Problems Suggested by the Movements of Interest Rates, Bond Yields and Stock Prices in the United States since 1856*, New York, National Bureau of Economic Research, 1938, pp. 44–53.

Merton R., Theory of rational option pricing, *Bell Journal of Economics and Management Science*, Vol. 4, No. 1, 1973, pp. 141–83.

Ramaswamy K. and Sundaresan M., The valuation of floating-rates instruments: theory and evidence, *Journal of Financial Economics*, Vol. 17, No. 2, 1986, pp. 251–72.

Richard S., An arbitrage model of the term structure of interest rates, *Journal of Financial Economics*, Vol. 6, No. 1, 1978, pp. 33–57.

Schaefer S. and Schwartz E., A two-factor model of the term structure: an approximate analytical solution, *Journal of Financial and Quantitative Analysis*, Vol. 19, No. 4, 1984, pp. 413–24.

Vasicek O., An equilibrium characterisation of the term structure, *Journal of Financial Economics*, Vol. 5, No. 2, 1977, pp. 177–88.

CHAPTER 5

Black F. and Scholes M., The pricing of options and corporate liabilities, *Journal of Political Economy*, Vol. 81, 1973, pp. 637–59.

Colmant B. and Kleynen G., *Gestion du risque de taux d'intérêt et instruments financiers dérivés*, Kluwer 1995.

Copeland T. E. and Wreston J. F., *Financial Theory and Corporate Policy*, Addison-Wesley, 1988.

Courtadon G., The pricing of options on default-free bonds, *Journal of Financial and Quantitative Analysis*, Vol. 17, 1982, pp. 75–100.

Cox J., Ross S., and Rubinstein M., Option pricing: a simplified approach, *Journal of Financial Economics*, No. 7, 1979, pp. 229–63.

Devolder P., *Finance stochastique*, Éditions ULB, 1993.

Garman M. and Kohlhagen S., Foreign currency option values, *Journal of International Money and Finance*, No. 2, 1983, pp. 231–7.

Hicks A., *Foreign Exchange Options*, Woodhead, 1993.

Hull J. C., *Options, Futures and Others Derivatives*, Prentice Hall, 1997.

Krasnov M., Kisselev A., Makarenko G., and Chikin E., *Mathèmatiques supérieures pour ingénieurs et polytechniciens*, De Boeck, 1993.

Reilly F. K. and Brown K. C., *Investment Analysis and Portfolio Management*, South-Western, 2000.

Rubinstein M., Options for the undecided, in *From Black–Scholes to Black Holes, Risk Magazine*, 1992.

Sokolnikoff I. S. and Redheffer R. M., *Mathematics of Physics and Modern Engineering*, McGraw-Hill, 1966.

CHAPTER 6

Blattberg R. and Gonedes N., A comparison of stable and Student descriptions as statistical models for stock prices, *Journal of Business*, Vol. 47, 1974, pp. 244–80.

Fama E., Behaviour of stock market prices, *Journal of Business*, Vol. 38, 1965, pp. 34–105.

Johnson N. L. and Kotz S., *Continuous Univariate Distribution*, John Wiley & Sons, Inc, 1970.

Jorion P., *Value at Risk*, McGraw-Hill, 2001.

Pearson E. S. and Hartley H. O., *Biometrika Tables for Students*, Biometrika Trust, 1976.

CHAPTER 7

Abramowitz M. and Stegun A., *Handbook of Mathematical Functions*, Dover, 1972.

Chase Manhattan Bank NA, *The Management of Financial Price Risk*, Chase Manhattan Bank NA, 1995.

Chase Manhattan Bank NA, *Value at Risk, its Measurement and Uses*, Chase Manhattan Bank NA, undated.

Chase Manhattan Bank NA, *Value at Risk*, Chase Manhattan Bank NA, 1996.

Danielsson J. and De Vries C., *Beyond the Sample: Extreme Quantile and Probability Estimation*, Mimeo, Iceland University and Tinbergen Institute Rotterdam, 1997.

Danielsson J. and De Vries C., Tail index and quantile estimation with very high frequency data, *Journal of Empirical Finance*, No. 4, 1997, pp. 241–57.

Danielsson J. and De Vries C., *Value at Risk and Extreme Returns*, LSE Financial Markets Group Discussion Paper 273, London School of Economics, 1997.

Embrechts P. Klüppelberg C., and Mikosch T., *Modelling External Events for Insurance and Finance*, Springer Verlag, 1999.

Galambos J., *Advanced Probability Theory*, M. Dekker, 1988, Section 6.5.

Gilchrist W. G., *Statistical Modelling with Quantile Functions*, Chapman & Hall/CRC, 2000.

Gnedenko B. V., On the limit distribution of the maximum term in a random series, *Annals of Mathematics*, Vol. 44, 1943, pp. 423–53.

Gourieroux C., Modèles ARCH et applications financières, *Economica*, 1992.

Gumbel E. J., *Statistics of Extremes*, Columbia University Press, 1958.

Hendricks D., Evaluation of Value at Risk Models using Historical Data, *FRBNY Policy Review*, 1996, pp. 39–69.

Hill B. M., A simple general approach to inference about the tail of a distribution, *Annals of Statistics*, Vol. 46, 1975, pp. 1163–73.

Hill I. D., Hill R., and Holder R. L, Fitting Johnson curves by moments (Algorithm AS 99), *Applied Statistics*, Vol. 25, No. 2, 1976, pp. 180–9.

Jenkinson A. F., The frequency distribution of the annual maximum (or minimum) values of meteorological elements, *Quarterly Journal of the Royal Meteorological Society*, Vol. 87, 1955, pp. 145–58.

Johnson N. L., Systems of frequency curves generated by methods of translation, *Biometrika*, Vol. 36, 1949, pp. 1498–575.

Longin F. M., From value at risk to stress testing: the extreme value approach, *Journal of Banking and Finance*, No. 24, 2000, pp. 1097–130.

Longin F. M., Extreme Value Theory: Introduction and First Applications in Finance, *Journal de la Société Statistique de Paris*, Vol. 136, 1995, pp. 77–97.

Longin F. M., The asymptotic distribution of extreme stock market returns, *Journal of Business*, No. 69, 1996, pp. 383–408.

McNeil A. J., *Estimating the Tails of Loss Severity Distributions using Extreme Value Theory*, Mimeo, ETH Zentrum Zurich, 1996.

McNeil A. J., Extreme value theory for risk managers, in *Internal Modelling and CAD II*, Risk Publications, 1999, pp. 93–113.

Mina J. and Yi Xiao J., *Return to RiskMetrics: The Evolution of a Standard*, RiskMetrics, 2001.

Morgan J. P., *RiskMetrics™: Technical Document, 4th Ed.*, Morgan Guaranty Trust Company, 1996.

Pickands J., Statistical inference using extreme order statistics, *Annals of Statistics*, Vol. 45, 1975, pp. 119–31.

Reiss R. D. and Thomas M., *Statistical Analysis of Extreme Values*, Birkhauser Verlag, 2001.

Rouvinez C., Going Greek with VAR, *Risk Magazine*, February 1997, pp. 57–65.

Schaller P., *On Cash Flow Mapping in VAR Estimation*, Creditanstalt-Bankverein, CA RISC-199602237, 1996.

Stambaugh V., *Value at Risk*, not published, 1996.

Vose D., *Quantitative Risk Analysis*, John Wiley & Sons, Ltd, 1996.

CHAPTER 9

Lopez T., Délimiter le risque de portefeuille, *Banque Magazine*, No. 605, July–August 1999, pp. 44–6.

CHAPTER 10

Broquet C., Cobbaut R., Gillet R., and Vandenberg A., *Gestion de Portefeuille*, De Boeck, 1997.

Burden R. L. and Faires D. J., *Numerical Analysis*, Prindle, Weber & Schmidt, 1981.

Esch L., Kieffer R., and Lopez T., *Value at Risk – Vers un risk management moderne*, De Boeck, 1997.

Litt F. X., *Analyse numérique, première partie*, ULG, 1999.

Markowitz H., *Mean-Variance Analysis in Portfolio Choice and Capital Markets*, Basil Blackwell, 1987.

Markowitz H., *Portfolio Selection: Efficient Diversification of Investments*, Blackwell Publishers, 1991.

Markowitz H., Portfolio selection, *Journal of Finance*, Vol. 7, No. 1, 1952, pp. 77–91.

Nougier J-P., *Méthodes de calcul numérique*, Masson, 1993.

Vauthey P., *Une approche empirique de l'optimisation de portefeuille*, Eds. Universitaires Fribourg Suisse, 1990.

CHAPTER 11

Chen N. F., Roll R., and Ross S. A., Economic forces of the stock market, *Journal of Business*, No. 59, 1986, pp. 383–403.

Dhrymes P. J., Friends I., and Gultekin N. B., A critical re-examination of the empirical evidence on the arbitrage pricing theory, *Journal of Finance*, No. 39, 1984, pp. 323–46.

Ross S. A., The arbitrage theory of capital asset pricing, *Journal of Economic Theory*, 1976, pp. 343–62.

CHAPTER 12

Ausubel L., The failure of competition in the credit card market, *American Economic Review*, vol. 81, 1991, pp. 50–81.

Cooley W. W. and Lohnes P. R., *Multivariate Data Analysis*, John Wiley & Sons, Inc, 1971.

Damel P., *La modélisation des contrats bancaires à taux révisable: une approche utilisant les corrélations canoniques*, Banque et Marchés, mars avril, 1999.

Damel P., *L'apport de replicating portfolio ou portefeuille répliqué en ALM: méthode contrat par contrat ou par la valeur optimale*, Banque et Marchés, mars avril, 2001.

Heath D., Jarrow R., and Morton A., Bond pricing and the term structure of interest rates: a new methodology for contingent claims valuation, *Econometrica*, vol. 60, 1992, pp. 77–105.

Hotelling H., Relation between two sets of variables, *Biometrica*, vol. 28, 1936, pp. 321–77.

Hull J. and White A., Pricing interest rate derivative securities, *Review of Financial Studies*, vols 3 & 4, 1990, pp. 573–92.

Hutchinson D. and Pennachi G., Measuring rents and interest rate risk in imperfect financial markets: the case of retail bank deposit, *Journal of Financial and Quantitative Analysis*, vol. 31, 1996, pp. 399–417.

Mardia K. V., Kent J. T., and Bibby J. M., *Multivariate Analysis*, Academic Press, 1979.

Sanyal A., *A Continuous Time Monte Carlo Implementation of the Hull and White One Factor Model and the Pricing of Core Deposit*, unpublished manuscript, December 1997.

Selvaggio R., Using the OAS methodology to value and hedge commercial bank retail demand deposit premiums, *The Handbook of Asset/Liability Management*, Edited by F. J. Fabozzi & A. Konishi, McGraw-Hill, 1996.

Smithson C., A Lego approach to financial engineering in the *Handbook of Currency and Interest Rate Risk Management*, Edited by R. Schwartz & C. W. Smith Jr., New York Institute of Finance, 1990.

Tatsuoka M. M., *Multivariate Analysis*, John Wiley & Sons, Ltd, 1971.

Wilson T., Optimal value: portfolio theory, *Balance Sheet*, Vol. 3, No. 3, Autumn 1994.

APPENDIX 1

Bair J., *Mathématiques générales*, De Boeck, 1990.

Esch L., *Mathématique pour économistes et gestionnaires* (2nd Edition), De Boeck, 1999.

Guerrien B., *Algèbre linéaire pour économistes*, Economica, 1982.

Ortega J. M., *Matrix Theory*, Plenum, 1987.

Weber J. E., *Mathematical Analysis (Business and Economic Applications)*, Harper and Row, 1982.

APPENDIX 2

Baxter M. and Rennie A., *Financial Calculus*, Cambridge University Press, 1996.

Feller W., *An Introduction to Probability Theory and its Applications* (2 volumes), John Wiley & Sons, Inc, 1968.

Grimmett G. and Stirzaker D., *Probability and Random Processes*, Oxford University Press, 1992.

Kendall M. and Stuart A., *The Advanced Theory of Statistics* (3 volumes), Griffin, 1977.

Loeve M., *Probability Theory* (2 volumes), Springer-Verlag, 1977.

Roger P., *Les outils de la modélisation financière*, Presses Universitaires de France, 1991.

Ross S. M., *Initiation aux probabilitiés*, Presses Polytechniques et Universitaires Romandes, 1994.

APPENDIX 3

Ansion G., *Econométrie pour l'enterprise*, Eyrolles, 1988.

Dagnelie P., *Théorie et méthodes statistique* (2 volumes), Presses Agronomiques de Gembloux, 1975.

Johnston J., *Econometric Methods*, McGraw-Hill, 1972.

Justens D., *Statistique pour décideurs*, De Boeck, 1988.

Kendall M. and Stuart A., *The Advanced Theory of Statistics* (3 volumes), Griffin, 1977.

APPENDIX 4

Fisher R. A. and Tippett L. H. C., Limiting forms of the frequency distribution of the largest or smallest member of a sample, *Proceedings of the Cambridge Philosophical Society*, Vol. 24, 1928, pp. 180–90.

Gnedenko B. V., On the limit distribution for the maximum term of a random series, *Annals of Mathematics*, Vol. 44, 1943, pp. 423–53.

Jenkinson A. F., The frequency distribution of the annual maximum (or minimum) values of meteorological elements, *Quarterly Journal of the Royal Meteorological Society*, Vol. 87, 1955, pp. 145–58.

APPENDIX 5

Chatfield C. and Collins A. J., *Introduction to Multivariate Analysis*, Chapman & Hall, 1980.

Saporta G., *Probabilités, Analyse des Données et Statistique*, Technip, 1990.

APPENDIX 6

Chatfield C. and Collins A. J., *Introduction to Multivariate Analysis*, Chapman & Hall, 1980.

Saporta G., *Probabilités, Analyse des Données et Statistique*, Technip, 1990.

APPENDIX 7

Droesbeke J. J., Fichet B., and Tassi P, *Modélisation ARCH, thérine statistique et applications dans le domaine de la finance*, Éditions ULB, 1994.

Engel R. F., Auto-regressive conditional heteroscedasticity with estimate of the variance of United Kingdom inflation, *Econometrica*, No. 50, 1982, pp. 987–1003.

Gourieroux C., Modèles ARCH et applications financières, *Economica*, 1992.

Nelson D. B., Conditional heteroscedasticity in asset returns: a new approach, *Econometrica*, No. 39, 1991, pp. 347–70.

APPENDIX 8

Burden R. L. and Faires D. J., *Numerical Analysis*, Prindle, Weber & Schmidt, 1981.

Litt F. X., *Analyse numérique, première partie*, ULG, 1999.

Nougier J-P., *Méthods de calcul numérique*, Masson, 1993.

INTERNET SITES

http://www.aptltd.com

http://www.bis.org/index.htm

http://www.cga-canada.org/fr/magazine/nov-dec02/Cyberguide_f.htm

http://www.fasb.org

http://www.iasc.org.uk/cmt/0001.asp

http://www.ifac.org

http://www.prim.lu

Index

Index compiled by Annette Musker